Surendranath Banerjee

Surendranath Banerjee

Series Editor
M.A. Shewan

Editors
Saud Akhtar **R.K. Singh**

Himalaya Books Pvt. Ltd.

'Ramdoot', Dr. Bhalerao Marg, Girgaon, Mumbai - 400 004
Tel : (022) 23863863, Fax : (022) 23877178
Email : himpub@vsnl.com

First Edition : 2012

Published by : **H.B.P.L.**
"Pooja Apartments", 4-B, Murari Lal Street, Ansari Road,
Darya Ganj, New Delhi-110 002
Phones : 23270392, 23278631 Reliance : 30180392 to 396
Fax : 011-23256286 Email : hphdel@vsnl.com

Sole Distributers : HIMALAYA PUBLISHING HOUSE PVT. LTD.

Branch Offices

Mumbai : "Ramdoot", Dr. Bhalerao Marg, Girgaon, Mumbai-400 004.
Phones : 23860170/23863863 Fax : 022-23877178
Email : himpub@vsnl.com
Website : www.himpub.com

Nagpur : Kundanlal Chandak Industrial Estate, Ghat Road, **Nagpur - 440 018.**
Phone: 2738731, 3296733 Telefax : 0712-2721215

Bengaluru : No. 16/1 (Old 12/1), 1st Floor, Next to Hotel Highlands, Madhava Nagar, Race Course Road, **Bengaluru - 560 001.**
Phone : 22281541, 22385461, Telefax: 080-22286611

Hyderabad : No. 3-4-184, Lingampally, Besides Raghavendra Swamy Matham, Kachiguda, **Hyderabad - 500 027.** Phone: 040-27560041, 27550139, Mobile:- 09848130433 Telefax: 040-27560041

Chennai : No. 85/50, Bazullah Road, T. Nagar, **Chennai - 600 017.**
Phone: 044-28344020, 32463737, 42124860

Pune : No. 527, "Laksha" Apartment, First Floor, Mehunpura, Shaniwarpeth, (Near Prabhat Theatre), **Pune - 411 030.**
Phone: 020-24496323/24496333/32326733

Lucknow : Jai Baba Bhawan, Near Manas Complex, Church Road, Aliganj, **Lucknow - 226 024.** Phone: 0522-2339329, 9305302158, 9415349385

Ahmedabad : No. 114, "SHAIL", 1st Floor, Opp. Madhu Sudan House, C.G.Road, Navrang Pura, **Ahmedabad – 380 009.**
Phone: 079-26560126, Mobiles: 09327324149,09314679413

Ernakulam : No. 39/104 A, Lakshmi Apartment, Karikkamuri Cross Rd., Ernakulam, **Cochin – 682011**, Kerala. Phone: 0484-2378012, 2378016, Mob.: 09344199799

Bhubaneswar : 5 Station Square, **Bhubaneswar (Orissa) - 751 001.**
Mobile: 9861046007, E-mail:- orissa@himpub.com

Indore : Kesardeep Avenue Extension, 73, Narayan Bagh.Flat No. 302, IIIrd Floor, Near Humpty Dumpty School, Narayan Bagh, **Indore (M.P.) 452 007**
Mobile: 09301386468

Kolkata : 108/4, Beliaghata, Main Road, Near ID Hospital, Opp. SBI Bank **Kolkata - 700 010.** Mobile: 09910440956, E-mail:- nkmitra@himpub.com

Guwahati : House No. 15, Behind Prajjyotish College, Near Sharma Printing Press, P.O. Bharalumukh, Guwahati - 781009 (Assam
Mobile: 07439040301; 07439040302

Printed by : A to Z Printers, New Delhi

Preface

Biography, is now a form of literature, very much in vogue. In fact, biography is a description or account of someone's life and the times, which is usually published in the form of a book. A biography is more than a mention of personal facts (life, education, work, relationships and death), it also portrays the subject's experience of events. Technically speaking, a work is biographical, if it covers, all of a person's life. Biography writing has a long history. A biography is real. Ancient Greeks developed the biographical tradition, which we have inherited, although until the 5th century AD, when the word 'biographia' first appeared, in Damascius' "Life of Isodorus," biographical pieces were called simply "lives". It is quite likely that the Greeks were drawing on a pre-existing eastern tradition. Certainly Herodotus' "Histories" contains more detailed biographical information on Persian kings and subjects. The earliest surviving pieces, which we would identify as biographical are Isocrates' "Life of Evagoras" and Xenophon's "Life of Agesilaos," both from the fifth century BC. "Parallel Lives" by Plutarch, a Greek writing under the Roman empire, is a series of short biographies of eminent men.

The Golden Age of English biography emerged in late eighteenth century, the century in which the terms "biography" and "autobiography" entered English lexicon. The classic works of the period were Samuel Johnson's "Critical Lives of the Poets" and James Boswell's "Massive Life of Johnson". Generally American biography followed English model. By World War I, cheap hardcover reprints had become popular. The decade of the 1920s witnessed a biographical 'boom'. Later, biographical writings developed a lot and today biographies are written and compiled in the finest form of the genre. In India too, biography, as a form of literature has been evolved, cultivated and polished over the years. Here is an effort to promote this tradition further.

This series of biographies of great men, great women and celebrities in all walks of life is an adventurous academic endeavour, in its own right. A team of researchers and compilers has worked for a good period of time to accomplish the project. For this purpose, hundreds of books by eminent authors and editors have been consulted and referred to. We have benefited from various works, liberally, in order to illustrate and enrich this effort of ours. Present book is devoted to the great personality of Surendranath Banerjee.

Among the earliest of Indian politicians in the pre-independence era, Surendranath Banerjee, at a very young age, cleared the British instituted ICS examination, but was later dismissed, due to racial discrimination. He whipped up a strong protest against it. He was intensely swayed by liberal and progressive thinking. After graduating from the University of Calcutta, Surendranath travelled to England. During his stay in England, Banerjee acquainted himself with the works of Edmund Burke and other liberal philosophers. Upon returning to India, he started working as a professor of English at the Metropolitan Institution, the Free Church Institution and Ripon College. In the time to come, Banerjee went on to launch 'The Bengali' newspaper and the Indian National Association. He employed these forums to address political and social issues. He rebuked the racial discrimination through speeches, which made him very popular. After the Congress was set up, Banerjee merged Indian National Association with it. He served as Congress President also.

This is a compact and comprehensive account of the above mentioned great life, which is bound to attract the attention of scholars, researchers, students and the general readers, alike. Let's hope this humble effort would receive a warm welcome and due applause.

— ***Editors***

Contents

1

An Illustrious Life

Introduction

According to Bipin Chandra Pal "Surendranath was the only person who might justly claim an all-India leadership." Shri Surendranath Banerjee was another worthy son of India. He played a very significant role in the development of the liberal tradition in modern India. His life and activities form an integral part of the history of the Indian National Movement He did commendable service for the enlargement of the rights and liberties of the people.

Like Raja Ram Mohan Roy, Dadabhai Naoroji, Justice M.G. Ranade and Gokhale, he belonged to the liberal school of thought. He was also an admirer of the British rule in India. He had faith in the British fair play and justice. According to Surendranath Banerjee, India could get peace, prosperity and advancement only under the British Empire. Like other liberal thinkers, he also had faith in the constitutional methods. He was a good orator and writer. He was regarded by many as the life and soul of the national movement in India.

The Profile

Surendranath Banerjee was born on November 10, 1848 in the Jaltola region of Calcutta. The atmosphere in the Banerjee family was one of a tie between the old world forces and the new. Surendranath's grandfather was an orthodox Hindu and his father Durga Choran had deep faith in Western Culture and Civilization. He wrote in his autobiography, 'A Nation in Making', "Thus, in our home the two conflicting forces of those times met.." However, the peace of the family was not disturbed by this conflict. Brought up in such an atmosphere, Surendranath Banerjee represented a fine synthesis between the two extremes of Hindu conservatism and Western civilization. He inherited his father's revolutionary zeal and his grandfather's basic traditionalism.

Roots in the Village: Surendranath received his early education in a village Pathshala. Afterwards, he was admitted to the Dovetone college where he graduated in 1868. He had a distinguished educational career both in school and college. He was sent to England in 1868 where he joined the University College. He competed successfully for the civil service examination but was rejected on the ground of being overage. Surendranath appealed to the court of the Queen's Bench. The court asked the Civil Service Commissioner to show reasons for his rejection. The result was Surendranath was restored and sent to India.

Brief Career in Service: Later on, he was appointed as Assistant Magistrate at Sylhet. But after two year, he was dismissed from service on some charges. Then, he went to London to plead his case before the authorities at the Indian Office, but he could not achieve success. Surendranath Banerjee's dismissal from service created a nationwide resentment. In this connection, he wrote. "My case excited very strong feelings in the Indian community and the general belief among my country men was that if I were not an Indian I could not have been put to all this trouble and that the head and front of my offence was that I had entered the sacred premises of the Indian Civil Service, which so far had been jealously guarded against invasion by the children of the soil. Many years afterwards a Lieutenant Governor stated that it was a wicked proceeding." But his removal from the service proved a blessing in disguise so far as the country was concerned. As C.Y.

Chintamani remarks, "the loss of the government became the gain of the country."

A Distinguished Teacher: In 1876, Surendranath was appointed Professor of English in the Metropolitan Institution. In 1881, he joined the Free Church College as Professor of English literature. For 37 years, i.e., from 1875 to 1912, Surendranath Banerjee was fully engaged in active teaching work. He loved his students. He was a great educationist with a missionary zeal.

Surendranath attached more importance to education than politics. Thus, he wrote, "political work it more or less ephemeral, though nonetheless highly useful. Educational work has in it the element of permanent utility. The Empire of a teacher is an ever enduring Empire, which extends over the future The teachers are the masters of the future. I cannot think of a nobler calling than theirs."

Birth and Early Life

Surendranath Banerjee was born in Calcutta, in the province of Bengal to a Bengali Brahmin family. He was deeply influenced in liberal, progressive thinking by his father Durga Charan Banerjee, a doctor. Banerjee was educated at the Parental Academic Institution and at the Hindu College. After graduating from the University of Calcutta, he travelled to England in 1868, along with Romesh Chunder Dutt and Behari Lal Gupta to compete in the Indian Civil Service examinations. He cleared the competitive examination in 1869, but was barred owing to a dispute over his exact age. After clearing the matter in the courts, Banerjee cleared the exam again in 1871.

Beginning of the Career

After his selection for ICS, he was posted as assistant magistrate in Sylhet. However, Banerjee was dismissed soon from his job owing to racial discrimination. Banerjee went to England to protest this decision, but was unsuccessful. During his stay in England (1874–1875) he studied the works of Edmund Burke and other liberal philosophers.

Career in Education

Upon his return to India in June, 1875, Banerjee became an English professor at the Metropolitan Institution, the Free Church Institution and at the Ripon College, founded by him in 1882. He began delivering public speeches on nationalist and liberal political subjects, as well as Indian history.

Stint in Journalism

In 1879, he founded the newspaper, *The Bengali*. In 1883, when Banerjee was arrested for publishing remarks in his paper, in contempt of court, protests and hartals erupted across Bengal, and in Indian cities such as Agra, Faizabad, Amritsar, Lahore and Pune. The INA expanded considerably, and hundreds of delegates from across India came to attend its annual conference in Calcutta.

After the founding of the Indian National Congress in 1885 in Bombay, Banerjee merged his organisation with it owing to their common objectives and memberships. He was elected the Congress President in 1895 at Poona and in 1902 at Ahmedabad.

First Political Platform

His second great contribution was the foundation, on 26 July 1876, of the Indian Association which was intended to be the centre of an all India political movement. This was principally achieved by the all-India political tour undertaken by Surendranath on behalf of the Association.

Its nominal object was to organise a public protest against the reduction of the age-limit of the competitors for the Indian Civil Service Examination from 21 to 19, but the true aim and purpose of the tour was the awakening of a spirit of unity and solidarity among the people of the different parts of India, through the sense of a common grievance.

The Demise

Banerjee died on Aug. 6, 1925, at Barrackpore. He is remembered and widely respected today as a pioneer leader of Indian politics - first treading the path for Indian political empowerment. He published an important work, *A Nation in Making* which was widely acclaimed. The British respected him and referred to him during his later years as "Surrender Not" Banerjee.

But nationalist politics in India meant opposition, and increasingly there were others whose opposition was more vigorous and who came to centre stage. Banerjee could accept neither the extremist view of political action nor the non-cooperation of Gandhiji, then emerging as a major factor in the nationalist movement. Banerjee saw the Montagu-Chelmsford reforms of 1919 as substantially fulfilling Congress's demands, a position which further isolated him.

2

Many Faceted Personality

Great Man in the Making

Great thinker and political leader, Surendranath Banerjee was born in a reputed Brahmin family, settled in Calcutta. His father Durga Charan Banerjee was a medical practitioner and, as a student of the Hindu College, had imbibed modern liberal ideas. So, although the grandson of an orthodox Brahmin, Surendranath got his school education in the Parental Academic Institution, attended chiefly by Anglo-Indian boys. He graduated from the Calcutta University in 1868, and on 3 March, the same year proceeded to England along with Romesh Chunder Dutt and Bihari Lal Gupta to compete for the Indian Civil Service. He passed the competitive examination, held in 1869. There were some troubles over his exact age, and though he was declared disqualified, the question was settled in his favour after a reference to a law-court.

Being successful in the final examination in 1871, he returned to India and was posted at Sylhet as Assistant Magistrate. Sutherland, the District Magistrate, did not look upon his Indian subordinate with favour and took advantage of a technical error to make a formal complaint to the Government against Surendranath. A Commission appointed to enquire into the complaint found him guilty, and he was dismissed from service.

There is hardly any doubt that racial prejudice was at the bottom of the whole affair. Surendranath proceeded to England and appealed to the India Office. Not only was the grievous wrong not redressed, he was not permitted even to enrol himself as a Barrister.

New Career

On his return to India in June, 1875, Surendranath began his new career as a Professor of English, first in the Metropolitan Institution and then in the Free Church College, and lastly in the College founded by him and named Ripon College, now known as Surendranath College. He took full advantage of his teaching profession to make the Indian students inspired with a new sprit. For this purpose he delivered many public lectures in and outside Calcutta on suitable topics such as Indian Unity, Life and Teachings of Mazzini and the history of Shivaji, the Sikhs, etc.

Fighting against All Odds

The prospects before Surendranath were indeed very gloomy, but he did not lose heart. He believed that he suffered because he was an Indian and made a grim resolve to devote himself to the task of saving his helpless countrymen from similar predicament in future. During his stay in London from April, 1874 to May, 1875, he equipped himself for this task by intensive study of various subjects which included the writings of Burke, Mazzini and many other great liberal thinkers and patriots of the West.

Great Orator

In a speech delivered in 1878 he urged the young men of India to dedicate their lives and consecrate their energies to the good of their motherland. He was the most eloquent speaker that India has so far produced, and his inspiring address had marvellous effects on the young minds. The great nationalist leader, Bipin Chandra Pal, himself a great orator, writing of his student days remarks on the very first lecture of Surendranath: "It made a very powerful appeal to our infant patriotism and lent new strength and even bitterness to the anti-British feeling. The audience carried with them from this meeting a new patriotic fervour." Regarding

Surendranath's speech on Mazzini, he said; "The tyrannies of the Austrian army of occupation in Italy...made a profound impression on our sensitive minds....We saw or imagined a great similitude between the position of the Italians under Austrian domination and our own position under British rule."

Social and Religious Services

Thanks to the Brahmo Samaj and particularly the eloquent discourses of Keshab Chandra Sen, the English-educated young men of Bengal were hitherto attracted by the programme of social and religious reform. But the eloquence of Surendranath diverted their minds to nationalism, and as B. C. Pal, himself a Brahmo, admits, "Surendranatha's political propaganda gathered a much larger following than that of the social and religious revolt." This transference of Bengali youth's interest and energy to the political regeneration constitutes the first great contribution of Surendranath to the national cause of India.

Message Across the Country

Surendranath visited and addressed public meetings in a large number of important towns in North India as far as Lahore and also in the Presidencies of Bombay and Madras (1877-78). This propaganda tour of Surendranath constitutes a definite landmark in the history of India's political regeneration. For the first time there emerged the idea of India as a political unit, and its importance was not lost upon far-sighted Englishmen. Henry Cotton, a member of the I. C. S. wrote: "The Bengali Babus now rule public opinion from Peshawar to Chittagong. A quarter of a century ago there was no trace of this: the idea of any Bengali influence in the Punjab would have been a conception incredible to Lord Lawrence ... yet it is the case that during the past year the tour of a Bengali lecturer, lecturing in English in Upper India, assumed the character of a triumphal progress; and at the present moment the name of Surendranath Banerjee excites as much enthusiasm among the rising generation of Multan as in Dacca."

Far more significant was the public meetings of protest were held in Agra, Faizabad, Amritsar, Lahore, Poona and various other towns all over India. Even a Pandit of Kashmir, ignorant to English, burst into tears, crying, "Our Surendranath is in jail." Surendranath's successful tour had thus set the stage for a more practical demonstration of the newly awakened sense of political unity of I India in the shape of an all-India political conference sponsored by Indian Association. The first session of the National Conference held in Calcutta on 28, 29 and 30 December 1883, was attended by more than a hundred delegates from different parts of India. The second session, held in Calcutta on 25, 26, and 27 December 1885, was more representative than the first and the plan of holding annual session of the Conference in different parts of India was accepted.

Uncrowned King of Bengal

The strong leadership and personality which he displayed throughout that memorable campaign, particularly at the Barisal Conference, made him the 'uncrowned King of Bengal'. The reception accorded to him on his return from Barisal to Calcutta, and all along the way, was such as a King might envy. His carriage was drawn by his enthusiastic admirers who had ultimately the satisfaction of seeing that he did unsettle the Partition of Bengal which Lord Morley had declared to be a settled fact.

He had reached the climax of his political career in 1906, and then set in the decline. The cleavage between the Moderates and the Extremists led to the steady decline of the Moderate Party of which Surendranath was the strongest pillar. The Home Rule League and the emergence of Gandhiji made the people lose faith in the programme of the Moderate Party, and the publication of the Montagu Chelmsford Report was the signal of war between the Modrates and the rest. The Moderates went down, and when they walked out of the Congress in 1918, Surendranath along with them practically walked out of the history of India's struggle for freedom.

Foremost in Politics

Surendranath Banerjee began his political career sometimes in 1875. He founded the Indian Association in Calcutta on July 26, 1876. The main object of this association was to agitate for the introduction of representative government in India. The Indian

Association played a very significant role in the political life of the country. In 1876. Surendranath was elected a Member of Culcutta Corporation. Four times, he was elected a Member of Bengal Legislative Council in 1894, 1896, 1898 and 1900. In 1913 Surendranath was elected to the Imperial Council. For several years, he also edited the Bengali Journal.

Great Reformer

With the zeal of a new convert Surendranath steadily worked to make the Reforms a success. He accepted the Ministry and also the Knighthood, which closed the eventful career as a great national leader. His unpopularity was demonstrated by his crushing defeat at the General Election for the Bengal Legislative Council in 1923, and he retired from active politics and ploughed a lonely furrow till death relieved him on 6 August 1925.

Educationist and Journalist

Surendranath was an educationist. He was a great journalist and the Bengali, edited by him, occupied a very high place in Indian journalism and made a conspicuous contribution to the growth of nationalism in India. In 1909 he attended the Press Conference in London. He was a member of the Calcutta Corporation (1876-99) and resigned as a protest against Lord Curzon's policy of effectively destroying its popular character. But as a Minister he had the consolation of restoring its democratic character.

The Unsung Hero

It is great pity that Surendranath died, almost unwept, unmourned and unusing by the public excepting a very small class. Yet it should be remembered that Surendranath never abandoned the high ideals of his youth; only at the age of seventy he did not choose to follow the untrodden path which younger generations pursued in preference to the old one which, he believed, had brought the country within sight of the promised land the dream of his whole life. It is possible to argue that the path chosen by him would also have brought us freedom; and though there might have been delay it would have saved us from the partition of the country and the many other evils from which we have suffered during the last twenty-five years.

3

Political Journey

In Political Arena

Surendranath Banerjee founded the Indian National Association with Anandamohan Bose, the first Indian political organisation of its kind, on 26 July 1876. He used the organisation to tackle the issue of age-limit for Indian students appearing for ICS examinations. He condemned the racial discrimination perpetrated by British officials in India through speeches all over the country, which made him very popular.

Journey to Prison

The great popularity of Surendranath all over India was clearly demonstrated when he was sentenced to imprisonment on a charge of Contempt of Court for remarks made by him in his paper, the Bengali, against the Chief Justice of Calcutta High Court for ordering a Hindu to produce the image of his household deity in the Court. A wild outburst of indignation accompanied by 'hartal' all over Bengal such as was never before witnessed marked the political consciousness of the masses.

Surendranath was one of the most important public leaders who protested the partition of the Bengal province in 1905. Banerjee was in the forefront of the movement and organised protests, petitions and extensive public support across Bengal and India, which finally compelled the British to reverse the bifurcation in 1912. Banerjee became the patron of rising Indian leaders like Gopal Krishna Gokhale and Sarojini Naidu. Banerjee was also one of the senior-most leaders of the "moderate" Congress those who favoured accommodation and dialogue with the British - after the "extremists" - those who advocated revolution and political independence - led by Bal Gangadhar Tilak left the party in 1906.

Banerjee was an important figure in the Swadeshi movement — advocating goods manufactured in India against foreign products — and his popularity at its apex made him, in words of admirers, the "uncrowned King of Bengal." The declining popularity of moderate Indian politicians affected Banerjee's role in Indian politics. Banerjee supported the Morley-Minto reforms 1909 - which were resented and ridiculed as insufficient and meaningless by the vast majority of the Indian public and nationalist politicians. Banerjee was a critic of the proposed method of civil disobedience advocated by Mahatma Gandhi, then a rising popular leader of Indian nationalists and the Congress Party.

He was elected to the reformed Legislative Council of Bengal in 1921, knighted in the same year, and held office as minister for local self-government from 1921 to 1924.

Formation of Congress

For the first time in history a realistic picture of the political unity of India was held out before public eye, forestalling the Indian National Congress. The chief credits for this goes to Surendranath. Immediately after the conclusion of the second session of the National Conference in Calcutta, the first session of Indian National Congress was held at Bombay (28 December 1885).

The questions and problems discussed in this two all-India political conferences were practically identical and the National Conference was merged in the Indian National Congress. Surendranath was not invited to the first session of the Congress till at the very last moment when, preoccupied with the second session of the National Conference in Calcutta, he could not attend it.

It was apparent that the first session of the Congress was less successful from every point of view than the National Conference, and this perhaps explains why the authorities of the Congress were particularly anxious to enlist the sympathy and support of Surendranath for second session of the Indian National Congress to be held in Calcutta.

The Calcutta session of the Congress in 1886 marked a distinct advance in its tone and spirit and henceforth Surendranath played a leading part in the National Congress and twice became its President, in 1895 and 1902. It is undoubtedly due to the part of Surendranath and colleagues in Bengal that the Indian National Congress came to be looked upon, after the second session, as the handiwork of the Bengalis.

Such a view was expressed by Sir Syed Ahmed, Lord Dufferin and even the historian Malleson. It is not possible to discuss in detail in this short article the political activities of Surendranath as one of the most prominent leaders of Indian National Congress during the next twenty years. But reference must be made to the leading role he played in the unique agitation against the Partition of Bengal in 1905 and the Swadeshi and Boycott Movement which followed it.

President of Congress

Surendranath was one of the founders of the Indian National Congress and was its president at Poona in 1895 and again at Ahmedabad in 1902. He served the Indian National Congress till 1918. Afterwards, he along with other moderate leaders, organised a party, the liberal federation. Surendranath also gave evidence before the Joint Select Committee. In 1921, he became the minister for Local Self-government and Public Health in Bengal.

As Legislator

He was a member of the Indian Legislative Council for many years and did good work in that body. He had very liberal social and religious ideas. He advocated widow remarriage and raising the marriageable age of girls, and presided over the Provincial Social Conference.

Mission to England

Surendranath visited England several times; in 1890 as a member of a delegation sent by the Calcutta Corporation, in 1896, to give evidence before Welby Commission, and in 1910 to represent Indian in the Imperial Press Conference. He died on August 6, 1925 at the age of 77 years.

End of Political Career

Accepting the portfolio of minister in the Bengal government earned him the ire of nationalists and much of the public, and he lost the election to the Bengal Legislative Council in 1923 to Bidhan Chandra Roy, the candidate of the Swarajya Party - ending his political career for all practical purposes. He was knighted for his political support of the Empire. Banerjee made the Calcutta Municipal Corporation a more democratic body while serving as a minister in the Bengal government.

4

Political Thought

Banerjee's Works: The main elements of his political thought are to found in his autobiography, "A Nation in the Making." The views and thought of Surendranath Banerjee are available to us through his work "A Nation in the making." "He discussed in detail the political, social and economic problems of his times in this book. Surendranath was influenced by the self-sacrificing career of Joseph Mazzini. He imbibed the teachings of English liberal political thinkers, like Burke. J.S. Mill. Macaulay, etc. He was also inspired by the Indian liberals. His main political ideas are mentioned below:

Like Raja Ram Mohan Roy, Dadabhai Naoroji, Justice Ranade, etc., Surendranath Banerjee was an admirer of the British rule in India. For him the British rule was a blessing in disguise and was in the interest of the people India. He had deep faith in the British fair-play and justice. Thus, he said, "To England we look for inspiration and guidance.. We have been fed upon the strong food of English constitutional freedom. We have been taught to admire the eloquence and genius of the great masters of English Political Philosophy." He further wrote. "The noblest heritage which we can leave to our children and our children's children is the heritage of enlarged rights, safeguarded by the loyal devotion and the fervent enthusiasm of an emancipated people. Let us so work with confidence in each other, with unwavering loyalty to the British connection, that we accomplish this great object within a measurable distance of time."

Surendranath Banerjee regarded the British rule in India as providential, as one of the dispensations of the God of History. At the anniversary meeting of the Bhawanipur Students Association held on April 28. 1877, he referred that there were three main categories in England's mission to India: (i) To help towards the eradication of those evils which afflict Indian Society. (ii) To help in the formation of a manly, energetic, self-reliant Indian character. (iii) To introduce the art of self-government in India.

He thought that it was the British Empire which brought the dynamic political concepts of the West into contact with the old idealism of the East. In 1878, While addressing a meeting of the Students Association. Surendranath said, "It was England's mission in the fast to save, to regenerate, to emancipate from the chains of ignorance, error and superstition. 250 millions of human beings, to heal the wounds that have been inflicted on them by the rapacity of their former rulers, to develop in them a self-reliant, manly energetic character, to separate through the land, the great blessings of peace, contentment and happiness, but above all it is England's noble mission in the last to help towards the consummation of Indian Unity to reconcile the jarring conflicts of the diverse Indian nationalities, to bring them nearer together, to evoke in them a sentiment of brotherhood and make them feel that they have to make common cause for the redress of common grievances." Hence. Surendranath regarded the British rule in India beneficial for its peace, prosperity and progress.

Traditionalist View

Surendranath Banerjee had deep faith in India's past. According to him. India was the cradle of religions and the holy land of the cast. It produced great *saints* like Valmiki, Vyasa, Buddha, Sankara, Panini, Patanjali, etc. He wrote, "In the morning of the world on the banks of the Ganges and on the banks of the Jamuna the Vedic Rishis sang those hymns which represent the first yearning of infant humanity towards the Divine ideal.... we were the spiritual preceptors of mankind... our past takes us back to the dim twilight of history In those days, when the world was sunk into barbarism we were the guides and instructors of mankind." In his speech on The Study of Indian History, delivered on 24th June 1876 at Calcutta, he said. "Let us sit at the feet of our ancestors and hold communion with the master-minds of ancient India. Such communion is pleasing in these days of gubernatorial repression, in these days of political lifelessness and political stagnation, and when the future outlook is indeed so truly gloomy....in studying the past history of your country, you will find much that is antiquated, much that is obsolete, much perhaps, that will excite ridicule and laughter.

Hut let not nay such feeling overcome you. Approach reverentially the sacred records of your sires. Remember, that you are studying the sayings and doings of your revered ancestors, of those for whose sake alone you are now remembered, for whose sake alone the intellectual elite of Europe even now feel a deep and an ardent interest in your welfare. If you cannot attain the intellectual eminence of your ancestors, why not strive to emulate their moral grandeur. The road to moral greatness is not so steep or so slippery... upon the moral regeneration of your country depends its intellectual, its social and its political regeneration."

Ethical Politics

Like Gopal Krishna Gokhale, Surendranath Banerjee wanted to spiritualise politics. According to him politics and Morality should not be separated. They should go side by side. In his speech at Calcutta on 27th September 1888, on the Ram Mohan Roy Memorial Meeting he said. "Politics based upon religion or deep moral earnestness is the one thing that is needed for this country. Politics divorced from a high moral purpose becomes the paltry squabble for power in which humanity can feel no interest. Take the case of the Home Rule agitation. Withdraw from it the personality of Mr. Gladstone and his incense moral earnestness, withdraw from it the deep favour of the Irish Patriots, and it becomes a miserable struggle for political power in which the deeper interest of humanity are lost tight, of. Take again the case of the Pilgrim Fathers, the founders of American greatness.... They preferred exile to the miseries of a life where their conscientious convictions had to be sacrificed.. . They developed themselves into statesmen, and became the founders of the noblest government and the freest race that the world has ever seen." Like Cicero and Burke, he emphasised the need of moral foundations of political power. He did not accept the Machiavellian concept of state and politics. In his presidential address at the Poona Congress of 1895, Surendranath Banerjee said. "I desire to place the moral consideration in the forefront: that which is morally indefensible cannot be politically expedient. Politics divorced from morality is no politics at all. It is political jugglery of the worst description."

Faith in Human Nature

He believed in the goodness and nobility of human nature. At the meeting of the Students's Association, held on July 15, 1876, at Calcutta, he said, "their is a divinity in human nature which admidst our most precipitate flights downwards ever arrests us with the warning voice Thus, far shalt thou go and no further. The majesty of human nature will always vindicate for itself the position which rightly belongs to it. Human nature will allow itself to be tainted, to be polluted, to be infected but its divine image can never be effaced, can never be blotted out." In tins respect, he was very near to Rousseau.

Constitutional Methods

Like other Indian liberals. Surendranath was also an advocate of the constitutional agitation. He believed in peaceful and constitutional methods. He was deadly against the use of violence. Thus, he said, "Constitutional agitation will secure for us those rights and privileges, which in less favoured countries are obtained by sterner means. But peaceful are the means to he enforced, there is a stem duty to be performed by every Indian. And he who fails in that duty is a traitor before God and man." But he observed that this method was slow and needed great patience In his presidential address at Ahmedabad in 1902. Surendranath said. "Yet there are those who take a desponding view of the situation — who say that our methods are faulty, that we wasted our time and breath, or that at any rate the results achieved have not been commensurate with the sacrifices incurred or the efforts put-forth... The question is asked what is the good of persevering in methods and in sacrifices, when the out-turn of them all is so insignificant I ask — Has the time come for the final judgement? I ask — Are the results inadequate? Even if they were, what are twenty year in the lifetime of a nation? The triumphs of liberty are not won in a day. Liberty is a jealous goddess, exacting m her worship and claiming from her votaries prolonged and assiduous devotion. Read history, learn from it the inestimable lesson of patience and fortitude and the self-sacrificing devotion which a constitutional struggle for constitutional liberty involves."

Advocacy of Self-government

Surendranath Banerjee demanded self-government under the British Empire. In the legislature, he did commendable service for the enlargement of the rights and liberties of the Indian people. Thus, he observed that political rights were conductive to the material progress of the country. Throughout his life. Surendranath Banerjee had fought for the Indianisation of the services. He demanded that Indians should get more share in the administration. The Civil Service Examination should also be held simultaneously both in England and India. In support of self-government in India, he wrote. "Political inferiority involves moral degradation... A nation of slaves would never have produced a Patanjali, a Buddha, or a Valmiki. We want self-government in order that we might wipe off from us the badge of political inferiority and life our heads among the nations of the earth and fulfil the great destinies that are in store for us under the blessing of Divine Providence. We want self-government not only in our own interest but for the sake of humanity at large... It is our mission to become once again the spiritual guides of mankind, but we cannot fulfil that mission unless and until we ourselves are emancipated, we ourselves are free. That is the first indispensable equipment for the discharge of that great mission." To him self-government was the essential condition for national reconstruction.

Advocacy of Liberty

Babu Surendranath Banerjee was a staunch advocate of the concept of Liberty. He imbibed love for liberty from the writings of Burke. Macaulay. Mill. Fox, Pitt. Sheridan, etc. He realised that people could learn from the British constitutional history the idea of freedom and liberty. Surendranath demanded maximum rights and privileges for the Indian people. It was in the interest of the ruled and the rulers Thus, he said. "Every nation must be the arbiter of its own destinies — such as the omnipotent fact inscribed by nature with her own hands and in her own eternal book." According to Banerjee. "If power were vested in us to legislate, to control the finance and to carry on the administration through and by our own men, in accordance with principles laid down by our own representatives, we should have self-government in the truest sense, and possess the simplest facilities for developing our powers and faculties and taking our legitimate place among the nations of the earth."

Championing of National Unity

Surendranath Banerjee was a great lover of National Unity. According to him, national unity was the path to the promised land of freedom, hope and faith. He said, I have a strong conviction and an assured belief that there comes a time in the history of a nation's progress, when every man may verily be said to have a mission of his own to accomplish.

Such a time has now arrived for India.... the celestial mandate has been issued that every Indian must now do his duty, or stand condemned before God and man." Surendranath wanted all-India Unity on the political plane too.. He toured the whole of the country and got remarkable success He wrote, "For the first time under the British rule, India with its varied races and religions had been brought upon the same platform for a common and unified effort.

Thus, was it demonstrated ... that whatever might be our differences in respect of race and language or social and religious institutions, the people of India could combine and unite for the attainment of their common political ends...the ground was thus prepared for this great national and unifying movement" He also did positive efforts to promote friendly feelings between Hindus and Muslims. He believed that progress peace and prosperity could be attained only in United India.

Social Reforms

Surendranath Banerjee was not only a political thinker but was also interested in the social reform movement. He supported the cause of widow-remarriage, inter caste marriage, abolition of child marriage, removal of restrictions of foreign travel, etc. He raised a voice against all these social evils. According to Banerjee. India could advance politically only if all these evils were eradicated. He wanted that the process of social change should be slow and gradual. There should not be a sudden change. He believed that the Hindu society was changing and moving forward. He said, 'the question of sea-voyage, or child marriage, or even enforced widowhood is not today where it was in the later part of the nineteenth century". Fifty years ago I wan on out caste (being an England-returned Brahmin) in the village where I live. Today I am an honoured member of the community.

Crusade against Poverty

Like Dadabhai Naoroji and Justice M.G. Ranade. Surendranath Banerjee also discussed causes on the growing poverty of India. He was moved by the deplorable and miserable conditions of the Indian people. According to him, 'the economic condition of the people has an intimate bearing upon their political advancement'. In his presidential address at the Poona Congress in 1895, Surendranath outlined a five point scheme for the stoppage of the material retrogression of the country': (i) the revival of old Indian industries and the setting up of new ones; (ii) moderation in the assessment of land tax which would be fixed for a fairly long period so that the peasants could be free from economic harassments; (iii) the remission of those taxes, which adversely affect the poor people; (iv) the stoppage of the economic drain and bleeding of India by the adoption of suitable governmental regulations (v) the increasing employment of Indians in the public services in place of a costly foreign administrative agency.

Surendranath suggested the government to improve the economic conditions of the people He also preached the use of Swadeshi goods in place of Videshi goods. In this connection, he said:

"Swadeshism will save us from famine and pestilence and the nameless horrors which follow in the train of poverty. Take the Swadeshi vow and you will have laid broad and deep the foundations of your industrial and political emancipation. Be Swadeshi in ail things, in your thoughts and actions, in your ideals and aspirations. Bring back the ancient days of purity and self sacrifice. Restore the Aryavarta of olden times when the Rishis sang the praises of God and did good to men... Swadeshi does not exclude foreign ideals or foreign learning or foreign arts and industries, but insists that they shall be assimilated into the national systems, be moulded after the national pattern and be incorporated into the life of a nation. Such is my conception of Swadeshism."

In this respect, the Swadeshi movement was many-sided. It touched the three principal aspects of life, economic educational and political.

Negating Students' Participation in Politics

According to Surendranath Banerjee. "The students should certainly discuss politics and may even subject to proper control and guidance, take part in political work. But the students should not indulge in party politics which were against the principles of morality and righteousness". According to Banerjee true politics must be based on moral principles. It is said that once he refused to join the Calcutta University Institute because the students were excluded from discussing politics there. He was of the view that it was unwise to exclude students from politics. Ho also emphasised on the need of student discipline.

5

Speeches at Congress Sessions

Presidential Address at Poona Session

(The following is the full text of the Presidential Address to the Eleventh Indian National Congress held at Poona 1895:)

Presidential Duties and Responsibilities

Brother Delegates, Ladies and Gentlemen,—I thank you heartily for "electing me as President of this Congress. I can conceive of no higher honour—no loftier trust—no-more exalted dignity—than that to which you have summoned me by your united suffrages. The highest reward which in these days a public man may receive, next to the approbation of his own conscience, is the confidence of his fellow-countrymen. For him what higher mark of honour or what nobler incentive to duty could there be than his election as the President of an assembly like this which is the non-official Parliament of his nation? But great as the honour is, far higher is the responsibility which belongs to it. It is a part of the divine arrangement that where there is a privilege there is also a corresponding duty. Your President is not only your speaker; he is something more. It is his duty to maintain order, to regulate your proceedings and to facilitate the despatch of your business. Having regard to the magnitude of this assembly, this in itself would make a heavy demand upon the resources, physical and mental, of the strongest and the ablest among us. But your President has other duties imposed upon him. During the three days that the Congress is in session he is your spokesman, your organ, the right arm of your strength. He voices forth the spirit which animates you in your deliberations, the temper which guides you in the solemn and arduous task which lies before you.

One may well stagger at a responsibility so vast and so manysided; but your forbearance and generosity is the saving dement in the situation. The moment you induct any one into the chair—the moment you install him in his office—from that moment you accord him in an unstinted measure your sympathy and your support. You forgive him his faults—you overlook his mistakes—you help him in his task—and you send him forth to his work, with your prayers and your benedictions.

It has been truly remarked that the manner in which people conduct themselves at a public meeting is some evidence of their capacity for Self-Government. Judged by this test you are past-masters in the art. *(Cheers.)* For I know of no assembly more orderly in its conduct, more differential to constituted authority, more firm in its adherence to its programme and yet withal more moderate in the expression thereof than these yearly gatherings of the National Congress. *(Hear, hear.)* Nay more, weak as your President may be, he and the Congress are supported by an unseen force of immense potency. The good wishes of the educated community follow us. They are present in spirit, if not present in body! They are watching our deliberations with intense interest. They pour forth their heart's prayer for the success of our work. *(Loud cheers.)*

Congress Movement

I was not a little amused and interested to read in an English newspaper the other day a statement to the effect that the women of my province had idolised the Congress, and that it had duly found its place in the Hindu pantheon. The fact is laid hold of by the writer as evidence of the superstition and ignorance of the people and their incapacity for representative institutions. I was not aware that any responsible Congressman had over asked for representative institutions for our women or for the masses of our people. However, much we may love and respect our ladies, we do not think they are yet qualified for representative government. They are not even supposed to be qualified in England. Our demand is much more limited. We should be satisfied if we obtain representative institutions of a modified character for the educated community who by reason of their culture and enlightenment, their assimilation of English ideas and their familiarity with English methods of Government might be 'presumed to be qualified for such a boon. But it would be useless to traverse the statement or the inference which is sought to be deduced from it. It would be almost cruel to dissipate the little romance which has gathered round our great movement. But this I will say on your behalf, that God or no God, whether the Congress has found a place in the Hindu pantheon or not, it is enshrined in the hearts of the educated community of India—it excites their deepest reverence, stirs their most earnest enthusiasm—it is the God of their idolatry—it is indissolubly bound up with and forms part and parcel of the life of New India. *(Loud and prolonged cheers.)*

Local Controversies—a Crisis Averted

It would be mere affectation on my part were I to ignore these events which preceded the session of the Congress at Poona, and which for a time at least filled the public mind of India with alarm and anxiety. I am a stranger to your local politics and your local feeling. I have no right to judge. I have not the means to judge. Who am I that I should judge? But spectators sometimes see more of the game than the actual players. And this I will venture to say that those who were in favour of the Social Conference being held in the *Pandal* and those who were opposed to it were all animated by one common sentiment of devotion to the Congress movement. They differed in their methods. We "who stand outside your local controversies, while we sympathise with the deep-seated convictions of all parties and admire the noble sacrifice which the Secretary of the Conference has made to restore amity and concord, must ask you to exercise mutual charity, and forbearance to forget and to forgive, and to unite in one common effort to make this Congress worthy of the capital of Maharashtra, and an example to all future Congresses. In this connection I cannot help expressing my sense of admiration at the conciliatory attitude so strikingly displayed by Mr. Justice Kanade, Secretary of the Social Conference, at a, critical stage in the history of the controversy to which I have referred. It adverted a crisis which might have proved disastrous to the best interests of the Congress. The Congress owes a heavy debt of gratitude to Mr. Justice Ranado.

Cosmopolitan Character of the Congress

We cannot afford to have a schism in our camp. Already they tell us that it is a Hindu Congress, although the presence of our Mahomedan friends completely contradicts the statement. Let it not be said that this is the Congress of one social party rather than that of another. It is the Congress of United India, of Hindus and Mahomedans, of Christians, of Parsis and of Sikhs, of those who would reform their social customs and those who would not. Here we stand upon a common platform—here we have all Agreed to bury our social and religious differences, and recognise the one common fact that being subjects of the same Sovereign and living under the same Government and the same political institutions, we have common rights and common grievances. And 'we have called forth this Congress into existence with a view to safeguard and extend our rights and redress our grievances. What should we say of a Faculty of Doctors who fell out, because though in perfect accord as to the principles of their science, they could not agree as to the age at which they should marry their daughters, or whether they should remarry their widowed daughters or not.

Congress and Social Reforms

The Congress has now been in existence for eleven years. We have not as yet got a written Constitution, though I hope, we shall provide ourselves with one before we separate. But there has grown around us a body of usages, the unwritten customary law of the Congress, which govern our movement. If there is one principle more than another, which is uniformly accepted, and universally assented to, if is this—that, no matter what differences of opinion may exist among us as regards religious beliefs or social usages, they shall be no bar to our acting together in Congress—they shall not be permitted to interrupt the cordiality of our relations as Congressmen. Never was the truth of this remark more strikingly illustrated than in connection with the agitation on the Consent Bill. Congressmen and Congress leaders arrayed themselves on opposite sides. Sir Romesh Chander Mitter, whose ill-health we all deplore, and who if he were better would probably have occupied the chair which I so unworthily fill, strenuously opposed the Bill; our great leader, Mr. Allan' Hume, was as strenuously in favour of it. Our political opponents fanned the flames. They looked forward to an approaching schism. They were disappointed. We rapidly closed our ranks. This controversy took place in the early part of 1891; the Congress of 1891 held at Nagpur was as successful as any of the previous Congresses had been. Ours is a political and not a social movement; and it cannot be made a matter of complaint against us that we are not a social organisation any more than it can be urged against any of my lawyer friends that they are not doctors. Even in regard to political matters, such is our respect for the opinions of minorities, so far back as 1887 I think it was at the instance of Mr. Badruddin Tyabji who once was our President and whose elevation to the Bench of the Bombay High Court is a matter of national congratulation, a resolution was passed to the effect that where there is practical unanimity among a class, though in a minority in the Congress, that a question should not be discussed, it should forthwith be abandoned, "We who show such great respect for the opinions of others deserve at least an equal measure of consideration from all, be they friends or be they otherwise.

Dissension in the Congress Camp.

There is special danger to which an organisation, such as ours, is exposed and which must be guarded against. In the days of its infancy, when it is persecuted and reviled, the members stand fast together, their cohesion is great, and the compactness of the organisation is in proportion to the pressure of adverse circumstances brought to bear upon it. But when these days are past and gone, when the sun of prosperity begins to shine upon it, when the prestige of victory comes to be associated with its honoured name, when opposition has dwindled down to the proportions of an occasional and feeble protest, uttered by some journalist who is not abreast of the times and who has hot perhaps forgotten his old love for the movement, then we are confronted with the danger of there being developed from within the seeds of dissension and dispute. Believed from the pressure of adverse circumstances, the cohesion of the members is apt to grow less, their enthusiasm to cool and the consistency of the organisation to give way to the demoralising influence of success.

I am sure we have not yet arrived at the stage. We are still exposed to the taunts and jeers of our opponents —we are still regarded as a set of impracticable people whose knowledge of all things, specially of finance, leaves-much room for improvement; Our progress though satisfactory, considering our opportunities and the short time we have been in existence as an organisation, is insignificant when compared with what we have yet to achieve before we reach the goal of our aspirations, the promised land of equal freedom and of equal rights with British subjects, which has ever been the dream of Congress leaders, and which when realised will constitute, in the words of the late Sir Madhava Bow, " the soundest triumph of British administration and a crown of glory to British rule." Having regard to our achievements' in the past, the possibilities which unfold themselves in the future, and the trust we have assumed to safeguard and extend the sphere of our rights, we should be false to ourselves if we did not stand shoulder to shoulder, forgetful of all differences, in the one common endeavour to uphold the national interests as represented by the Congress.

Congress Constitution

This leads me to the question of the Constitution of the Congress. Having regard to recent events we must accord to it the forefront place—the place of honour—in our debates. I have referred to the usages, the unwritten law, of the Congress. It must be admitted that the time has come when we must clearly define these usages, and accord to them the deliberate and authoritative sanction of the Congress. The need of a Constitution was felt very early in the history of our movement. We are fighting a constitutional battle, and it was felt that we should place our organisation upon a constitutional basis! So far back as the year 1887 at the Third Session of the Congress held at Madras, the very first resolution that was passed was a resolution appointing a

Committee to draft a set of rules to be laid before the Congress on the last day of its sitting. I will read to you the Resolution:

> That a Committee be appointed consisting of the gentlemen marginally enumerated to consider what rules, if any, may now be usefully framed in regard to the institution and working of the Congress with inductions to report thereon on the 30th, instant,

In accordance with this Resolution the Committee reported on the 30th December, and a Resolution was passed to the effect that the rules be circulated to the Standing Congress Committees who were to work on them so far as practicable, and to report thereon to the next Congress. Let me reproduce the text of the Resolution:

> That the rules drafted by the Committee appointed under Resolution—stand over for consideration till next Congress, but that in the meantime copies be circulated to all Standing Congress Committees with the request that they will during the coming year act in accordance with these rules so far as they may seem to them possible and desirable, and report thereon ' to the next Congress with such further suggestions as to them may seem meet.

I regret to have to say that the matter was not reported to the next Congress which met at Allahabad and was not considered by them. It was not considered till 1894 at the Madras Congress of last year. In 1893, when the Congress met at Lahore, a strongly-felt wish was expressed in favour of providing the Congress with a Constitution without further loss of time. It was, I think, those good and self-sacrificing men connected with the Anglo-Vedic College who urged upon us the need of a Constitution. They pointed to their own great College as evidence of what might be done by organised effort proceeding upon a constitutional basis. Nothing however was done in 1893. It was too late to discuss the question. In 1894, at the last Session of the Congress held in Madras, the matter was again considered when the following Resolution was passed:

> That this congress is of opinion that the time has come when he Constitution of the Congress should be settled and rules and regulations laid down as to the number of delegates, their qualifications, the localities for assemblage and the like, and with this view the Congress requests the Standing Committee of Poona to draw up draft rules and circulate them among the different Standing Congress Committees for their report; these reports together with the draft rules and the report thereon to be laid before the next Congress for consideration.

The Poona Committee have, I understand, at the last moment drawn up a body of rules which they have circulated to the Congress Committee. The Standing Congress Committee have not considered these rules and the reports are not before us. I have not the smallest desire to excuse the Standing Congress Committees elsewhere at the expense of the Poona Committee. They might easily have moved in the matter and appealed to the Poona Committee; but they took no action—they slept over the matter. I think we must all share the responsibility of this tardy action on the part of the Poona Committee. We are never tired of reminding the Government of their broken promises.

The one charge which we urge against the Government—which we repeat *ad nauseam*—which we reiterate in season and out of season, is that they have made large promises which they have only inadequately redeemed, and that the measure of their performances fall short of the measure of their promises. Are we not in all conscience amenable to the same charge? We have more than once solemnly undertaken to provide the Congress with a Constitution. More than once have we broken this promise. Our declarations are a dead letter. We have not carried them out. But it is no use lamenting over the past. Let the dead past bury their dead. Let us retrieve the mistakes and omissions of the past. Let us, before we separate, have a few well-defined rules which will embody existing practice and obviate future difficulties. We may follow the precedent set by the Madras Congress of 1887; appoint a Committee to frame rules on the first day with instructions to report on or before the fast day of the Congress. We need not circulate these rules to the Standing Congress Committees. That is the old plea for inaction. We shall not have any rules at all if we are to repeat the hapless experiments of former years. Nor need our rules be like the laws of the Medes and the Persians, rigid and inflexible, admitting of no change, no modification. If we find any rule working badly, there is nothing to prevent our, changing it. I earnestly appeal to you, brother-delegates, as a fellow-worker and an old Congressman, to apply yourselves to this task.

It will be evidence of your practical wisdom, of your ready recognition of public opinion, and of your capacity to adapt yourselves to the environments of your situation. A Congress with a Constitution would be far more potent for good than a Congress without a Constitution. A representative body like the Congress, organised upon a constitutional basis, cannot long exist by the side of a bureaucratic Government without powerfully influencing it' for good. A Congress with a Constitution would be the living protest of the educated community against a form of administration, where the will of the few and not the voice of the many prevails.

Congress — its Growth and Development

From the consideration of the Constitution of the Congress we pass on to discuss the Constitution of the Government of this country; and as in our own case, so also here, much remains to be done.' At this stage, and standing upon the vantage-ground we happen, to occupy, we may pause for a moment to take a brief retrospect of the past, if only to derive from it the inspiration and guidance for the future. The illustrious men—I feel-the-less hesitation in bearing my humble testimony to their worth, as I was not one of them—who founded the Congress at Bombay—some of whom are dead and gone, whose memories we revere, and the memory of none do we cherish with a greater measure of reverence than that of the young, the versatile, the brilliant Kashinath Trimbak Telang—these illustrious men did not in their wildest dreams anticipate the great future which awaited their movement. In this connection I am reminded of the exquisite lines of Longfellow which occur in his " Spanish Student" describing the spirit which pervades the achievements of the man of genius. The man of genius, says he, finds around him all the moans of action; The shapeless masses,—the materials.

They lie everywhere around him. Footsore and weary with travel he comes, and with the uncouth charcoal he inscribes on the wall. And lo and behold ! transfigured by the magic of his touch:

> All its hidden virtues shine.
>
> It gleams a diamond.

The forces were there; the materials were there; they lay in shapeless masses. The hour had come; the men were there. They communicated to them the Promethean spark, the celestial fire which made them instinct with life, and under their controlling guidance, the Congress has 'developed into a movement fraught with unspeakable blessings to generations of my countrymen yet unborn. The birth of the Congress had, indeed, been foreseen by the great men who had been associated with the Anglo-Indian Government in the early stages of its progressive development, ' Macaulay, speaking from his place in Parliament on the occasion of the enactment of the Charter Act, used language which had about it the ring of prophetic-inspiration:

> It may be, said he, that the public mind of India may so expand under our system as to outgrow that system; that our subjects, being brought up under good Government, may develop a capacity for better Government, that being instructed in European knowledge they may crave for European institutions. I know not whether such a day will ever come, but when it does come, it will be the proudest day in the annals of England.

We have met to celebrate this day, the proudest in the annals of England and India. The National Congress is the outcome of those civilizing influences which Macaulay and his co-adjutors were instrumental in implanting in the Government of this country. It has a brilliant record. I will claim this for the Congress that it has not taken up a single question which it has not brought within the range of practical politics, or which it has not brought nearer to solution. You took up the question of the separation of judicial and executive functions. It has been declared to be a counsel of perfection by so high an authority as Lord Dufferin. You took up the Excise question. In my Province, in the more crowded districts, the outstills have been abolished. You agitated for the reform of the Police. In my province a Police Commission was appointed, and, though the Police remains very much what it was, I must say that a genuine effort is being made by the Government to give effect to the recommendations of the Commission. You insisted in season and out of season upon the wider employment of our countrymen in the higher offices of State.

The Public Service Commission was appointed; and, though I cannot congratulate the Government upon the manner in which it has dealt with the recommendations of the Commission as the outcome of their deliberations, the maximum limit of age for the Open Competitive Examination was raised. Last but not least is the crowning triumph of the Congress in the recognition by the Government of the representative element in the reconstitution of the enlarged Councils.

But the subjective triumph of the Congress—its moral victorious—are even more remarkable than its onward achievements. You have introduced a new spirit into the country. You have infused a new enthusiasm into your, countryman. You have brought together the scattered elements of a vast and diversified population—you have welded them into a compact and homogeneous mass—you have made them vibrato with the new-born sentiment of an awakened nationality—you have unified them for the common purposes of their political enfranchisement. Along "with the now-born impulse which you have thus communicated, and which draws its inspiration from the living examples of English greatness, you have placed before your countryman lofty ideals of public duty, which are slowly transforming the national character, imparting to the flexibility of the East, the stamina and the stability of the West. Above all, you have taught your countryman to glory in the British connection and to seek to perpetuate it not by submitting to invidious and irritating distinctions, but by claiming to participate in full in the rights of British citizenship.

Reform of Legislative Councils

Hitherto we had placed the reform of the Legislative Councils in the forefront among our topics of discussion. Then came the Councils Act of 1802 which reconstituted the Councils and enlarged their functions. What is our attitude with regard to this Act? Are we satisfied with it and with the manner in which it is being worked? I am afraid we must answer the question in the negative. We regard the measure in the light of a cautious experiment which is being tried by the Government. Caution is an element of statesmanship. But caution carried to an excess—caution which is but another name for timidity—is a mistake and may even amount to a blunder. We have no objection to the Government exercising due caution before it takes "a big jump into the unknown." Weighted with the sense of its great responsibility, the Government must look around before it makes an important departure from the lines of its ancient policy.

But what we complain of is, that the experiment might have been tried under conditions more favourable to its success, more consonant to the declarations which were made in Parliament by statesmen on both sides of the House at the time of the enactment of the measure. Mr. Gladstone looked forward to a living representation of the Indian people. Lord Salisbury was anxious that the machinery provided should give representation not to small sections of the people but to the living strength and the vital forces of the whole community. Have these anticipations been realised by the light of accomplished facts? In Bengal, seven elected members represent the living strength and the vital forces of a whole community of 70 millions of people. The Councils have been enlarged, but in no sense so as to provide even a tolerably moderate representation of the people. In the United Kingdom, a population of 40 millions is represented by 670 members. In Bengal, a population of 70 millions is represented by only seven elected members, or if you like, by 10 members if you take the nominated non-official members to represent the people, or by 20 members if you take the whole Council to represent the Province. "The result is, that the election taking place under a system of rotation, whole divisions are left unrepresented in the Council. Out of the 6 Divisions in Bengal at the present moment, the

Presidency Division which is the most important, and the Chota Nagpur and Orissa Divisions, are left out in the representation. I am aware that this is a faulty arrangement which might be rectified by lumping up the Divisions, as is done elsewhere, so as to enable the whole Province to take part in the elections. But is it possible under any conceivable arrangement, by any form of administrative manipulation,' to secure in the words of Mr. Gladstone, the living representation of the Indian people, or, in the words of Lord Salisbury, the representation of the whole community, and not of small sections of the people, without materially adding to the strength, of the elective element in the Councils? But we are confronted with a difficulty on the very threshold. Under Section 1 of the Indian Councils Act of 1892, the maximum number of additional members for the Governor-General's Council is fixed at 16, and the maximum number of additional members for the Legislative Councils of Madras and Bombay is fixed at 20; and as regards Bengal and the North-Western Provinces, the position seems to be still more unsatisfactory. The number of members for the Bengal Council is not to exceed 20, and that for the North-Western Provinces is not to exceed 15. Why in the Calcutta Municipality we have 75 members to represent a population of 700,000 inhabitants, and a much lesser number of rate-payers; in the District Boards in Bengal, the number varies from 10 to 40. In some of our more important Mofussil Municipalities, the number is more than 20;. in most Municipalities having an average income varying from Us. 10,000 to Rs. 20,000 a year, the number is fixed at 18. But hero, in the representation of great Province.", in their Legislative Councils, the number is never to exceed 25, and is often less. I am well aware of the difficulties of the Government. They must have a standing majority in the Councils. They will say:

> It is all very well for you to raise these objections. Your Counsel is a counsel of perfection, we admit. Bat there are practical difficulties in the way, which we, as practical administrators must take note of. We must have a standing majority in the Councils. If we add to the elective element, we must add to the number of nominated members. The requisite number of

officiate may not be available at the Presidency Towns, or if available, their appointment to the Councils may lead to serious administrative inconvenience and may involve additional expense—a matter which is not to be overlooked in these days it of poverty and impecauniosity.

We fully admit the force of these objections. But the difficulties are really not insuperable. They admit of easy solution. The Government need not appoint official members to the Council to secure a majority. There are plenty of people who, though non-officials, would in this respect serve them better than officials. The experience of public bodies, where officials and non-officials moot for the transaction of public business, entirety confirms this view of the matter. In the Calcutta Municipality, the proportion of elected members is two-thirds of the entire body, The Government is in a hopeless minority. The Chairman is an official and is appointed by the Government. He is the organ of the Government. Though, in a minority, I have never known a Chairman fail to carry through any Resolution upon which he has set his heart. Whenever he wants it, he has a majority. The experience of the District Boards in Bengal entirely bears out the same view. One-half of the members are elected, the other half are nominated. The nominated members are not necessarily officials. The Chairman is the Magistrate of the District. He holds the balance of power. He is the dictator of the situation. He rules the District Boards. In the Councils, the position of the Government will be still more favourable. The President will be the head of the Local Government, his prestige will be great, his personality will carry immense influence; and if the number of members be materially increased as we suggest, "though only one-half of them should be nominated and among the nominated members there should be non-officials, the Government will still have a standing majority.

Indian Councils Act

I say once again that if the Indian Councils Act is to be given effect to, in the spirit in which it was conceived by the distinguished statesmen who took part in its enactment, if it is to give to the people of India a living representation of the whole community and not of small sections of the people, the number of elected members must be sensibly increased; at any rate discretion should be given to the Government of India to increase the number, subject to such rules as the Government may think fit to make in that behalf. This can be easily done by a small modification of Section 1 of the Statute of 1892. Such a measure would strengthen the popular element in the Councils; but the Government would also share in the benefits which it would confer. A larger number of elected representatives in the Councils would place the Government in touch with the real opinion of the country. The voice that would be heard in the Councils would not be the voice of this party, or of that party, of this clique or of that, but the living voice of the Indian people.

I am well aware of the objections that will be urged against my proposal. It will be said: "You got the Councils Act amended only the other day. It is too-early to think of amending it again." To that I have an obvious reply to give: It is never too early to raise the cry for reform. We must cry betimes, cry late, cry incessantly, fill the air with our importunate clamour, and then only can we hope to move the Government to take any action. *Quieta non movere,* in the words of Sir Robert "Walpole, is the accepted creed of all Governments. They never move except under the irresistible pressure of a public opinion which will admit no delay or postponement. You have your own experience to guide you in the matter. You began the agitation for the reform of the Councils in 1885. In Bengal, we began it earlier, and the concession was made to us, though not in complete accordance with our anticipations or our wishes, only so recently as 1892. In making the present demand we are encouraged by the unquestionable success which has so far attended the experiment which is being tried. Sir Charles Elliott, speaking from his place as President of the Bengal Legislative Council, thus bore testimony to the distinct accession of strength to the Council which the addition of the elective element has secured:

> I am quite satisfied in my own mind that the extension of the Council has materially added to its strength, and to its popularity and to its power of doing good for the country. Of the Hon'ble Members present,

there are, I think, three whose term of office will come to an end before we meet next time and who may be re-elected or who may not. If they are re-elected, we shall welcome them back; if not, we hope we shall find in their successors, colleagues who are as generous and as zealous as they have been.

Interpellation in Legislative Councils

The Councils have been reconstituted, and their functions have been enlarged. The most important addition 'to the functions of the Councils consists in conferring upon members the right of interpellation. "We are truly grateful to the Government for this right. It is an inestimable boon. No Government which did not feel strong in the strength of conscious rectitude would venture to confer such a boon upon a foreign dependency. In " the dark days of the Second Empire' in France, when repression was the Order of the day, the Senate and the Chamber of Deputies were deprived of this right.

It was the feeling of conscious rectitude that in the main led the Executive Council of the Government of India to recommend that this right should be conferred upon Members of Council. Sir Charles Elliott has let us into the secrets of his " prison house." He told us the other day from his place as President of the Bengal Legislative Council, that Sir George Chesney argued in the Executive Council that the Government bad nothing to conceal. Lord Dufferin urged that it would often help the Government to dispel false reports and to clear up misconceptions which were embarrassing to the administration. Lord Dufferin never showed greater prescience. I will here only refer to two questions that were asked in the course of this year. A few months back it was reported in one of the Anglo-Indian papers of Calcutta— the *Indian Daily News,* I think it was—that the Government had it in contemplation to frame a new set of rules ' in connection with the Official Secrets Act with a view to render these rules more stringent in their operation. The report created a considerable stir. Articles appeared in the newspapers; the motives of Government were aspersed. A question was put in Council. The Chief Secretary replied that there was no truth in the report, and that the

Government did not mean to take any action in regard to these rules. The misconception was removed—the excitement disappeared. Take the other case. Some time ago there appeared a very sensational account of a murder case at Chittagong in one of the newspapers which, if true, implied a grave reflection upon the local officials. A question was put in Council. A very elaborate answer was given, and the conduct of the officials was placed in its proper light.

During the year now closing, ugly rumours were afloat to the effect that the Government intended to restrict the right. There went forth a unanimous protest against the proposed restriction from the Indian Press and from such organs of Anglo-Indian opinion as sympathised with the legitimate aspirations of the people. There was not, indeed, the shadow of a justification for the proposed restriction. Questions must always be more or less vexatious. To say that the questions were vexatious was to object to them, because they were questions. To say that the questions put were too many was to ignore the obvious circumstances of the situation. The Councils did not meet as often as might be expected—the opportunities for asking questions were limited, and they necessarily accumulated in the hands of members.

Right of Interpellation

It is, indeed, the unanimous testimony of officials and non-officials that the right has been exercised in a manner that is creditable to the members and conducive to the public interests. The writer on Indian affairs, in the Times, a discriminating judge in these matters, thus observes:

> The practical operation of the system indicates that the Viceregal forecast of its working, from Lord Ripon onwards, was the correct one. The questions asked in the Supremo and Provincial Legislatures during the past two years cover the whole area of Indian administration and of the economic interest of the people. With scarcely an exception, they have tended to a better understanding between the rulers and the ruled; and in important instances they have furnished a valuable opportunity of placing the actual facts before the public.

With regard to the exercise of the right in the Bengal Council, the same writer thus bears equally satisfactory testimony:

> In a forward Province like Bengal, with Calcutta as its capital, and a native Press extremely active if not always accurately informed, the practice of interpellation has proved even more useful. The Bengal Government has to deal with the chronic unrest arising out of the desire of the educated classes to enjoy an ever-increasing share of the higher posts of the Administration, The present Governor of Bengal has recognised the necessity of dealing with such aspirations in a spirit of fairness, and, indeed, of generosity. Sir Charles Elliott has opened up the higher offices of his Government to natives of India to an extent never dreamt of by his predecessors. ' It is only the confidence which Englishmen in India hate in the practical sagacity and Bound common sense of Sit Charles Elliott as an experienced administrator,' writes the leading Calcutta journal, ' that induces them to refrain from regarding with suspicion the liberal concessions which he has inaugurated, concessions which, as we have said, no other Government up to the present time has ventured to imitate. But a Section of the Bengal Press by a curious misapprehension demands that all offices for which the Public Service Commission declared natives to be eligible shall forthwith be filled by a native, irrespective of the fact that there may be many European officers better qualified for the individual post. It is, of course, unsuitable for a Government to enter into newspaper controversies, and a misconception of this character becomes a source of a widespread political disquiet in Bengal. Fortunately a distinguished Hindu member of the Bengal Council put a question which embodied the general misapprehension and enabled the Government to correct it.

From non-official let us pass on to official testimony and the testimony which I am going to quote is that of no-less exalted an official than Sir Charles Elliott. The late Lieutenant-Governor was a thoroughgoing official some would prefer to call him a typical bureaucrat. But at any rate he was no mean judge of the matter. This was what he said from his place as President of the Bengal Legislative Council:

> I think you will agree with me that the results have not altogether met the anticipations which we formed. Somehow or other—It is difficult to say how—a sort of idea has grown up in the public mind that an interpellation must necessarily be hostile, and that an Hon'ble Member who puts an interpellation may be presumed to have a desire to heckle the Government or to expose its shortcomings in some way or another. I think it is most unfortunate that such a feeling should have grown up. It has been due to criticisms which have been passed on the style of questions put not so much in this Council as in the Councils of other Provinces, and I think in many cases these criticisms, whether applied to other provinces or applied to this Province, have not been altogether reasonable or Sympathetic. X certainly feel that I have nothing very much to complain of as regards the spirit with which interpellations have been put here, but I think that we might put interpellations upon a better footing if it were thoroughly understood that the Government desire to deal with all the members of this Council as it trusted Councillors whom it wishes 'to associate with itself in its policy, and to whom it wishes to impart the information which it possesses.

"Having regard to the testimony of the high authorities I have quoted, might we not ask for the removal of those restrictions which seem to me to defeat the purposes of a beneficent legislation. In the House of Commons " sometimes when an answer has been given, further questions are addressed to the Minister on the same subject," apparently with a view to offer an explanation or remove a misconception. In the House of Lords greater latitude is allowed in putting questions (Erskine May, " Parliamentary Practice," page 329). In the House of Lords when a question is put, the member putting it may make a speech in explanation of the question and by way of preface to it. One of the objects which the Government had in view in conferring the right of interpellation was to afford opportunities for clearing up misconceptions with regard to the measures of Government and the conduct of officials. Looking at the matter from this standpoint, it seems to me that the object which the Government had in view would be best served by adopting the practice of the House of Commons—a practice which has been sanctioned by the wisdom of ages.

Poverty of India

The poverty of the masses of our countrymen has been the theme of endless discussion here and elsewhere. We know what the views of Mr. Dadabhai Naoroji are. He holds that the average income per head of the population in India is Rs. 20, against Lord Cromer's estimate of Rs. 27 a year. Whether it is Rs. 20 or Rs. 27 per head makes no difference. It is striking evidence of the deplorable poverty of the masses of our population. If you compare the economic condition of the masses of our people with that of more fortunately situated countries in Europe, this truth forces itself upon our attention with painful impressiveness. Lord Cromer is my authority. Lord Cromer, then Sir Evelyn Baring, gave some figures in 1882, which throw a lurid light upon the economic condition of our people. The average income of the population per head in Great Britain was estimated by him at £33 a year; in France it was £23; in Turkey, which is the poorest country in Europe, it was £4 Mulhal gives the income per head of the Russian population at £9.

Upon this income of .£33, the English taxpayer pays a tax of £ 2-12 per head; the Indian taxpayer upon his income of Rs. 20 or Rs. 27 a year, pays a tax of 2s. 6d. per head. The English taxpayer thus pays a tax of 7 per cent, upon his income of £33, while the Indian taxpayer pays a tax of 5 per cent, upon his income of Rs. 27. It will be readily admitted that five per cent, upon an income of Us. 27 is a much more serious matter—involves a much heavier sacrifice—than 7 per cent, upon an income of £33. I ask you to bear in mind one little consideration. The average calculation is made by dividing the whole income of the community, whatever it may be, among the heads of population.

But it is, after all, an average. There must be a large number whose income is below the average, as there must be a large number whose income is above it. I ask you for one moment to consider what must be the condition in life of that large number of people whose income is below Rs. 27 a year?

It is no wonder, then, that 40 millions of our people live upon one meal a day, as stated by Sir William Hunter, or that we have those periodical famines which decimate thousands and hundreds of thousands of our population. Cuvier has remarked that famines are impossible in this age. So they are in European countries, but not in this hapless land of ours, which a great orator in the last century described as " the garden of Asia, the granary of the East." We must all note with thankfulness that an influential journal like the *Pioneer,* supposed to be the exponent of official opinion, takes the popular view of the matter. That journal freely admits:

> That the passes in India are poor, very poor; that our administration is an expensive one; that money is often wasted in enterprises like the Chitral imbroglio, and that, in various directions without administrative injury, economy and retrenchment might be enforced.

Indian Poverty and the Salvation Army

I am glad to find that the Salvation Army have had their attention prominently called to the poverty-stricken condition of our masses. With an all-comprehensive philanthropy which does honour to their Christianity, they have not forgotten the Indian poor. Their scheme for the reclamation of the submerged tenth will include our submerged fifth. Their scheme for Indian peasant-settlements is well worth consideration; and, whatever we may think of its details, our sympathies must go forth on behalf of a project, so noble, so generous, so full of the spirit of true Christian charity.

Indian Industrial Development

Ours is a political organisation; but we cannot overlook considerations which affect the development of our industries and our manufactures. The economic condition of a people has an intimate bearing upon their political advancement. "Looking at the matter from this point of view, we feel that it is our duty to safeguard our industries. Their conservation is a matter of grave national importance. We have our cotton industry in Bombay, the jute industry in Bengal, the tea industry in Assam, and the coal and iron industries in Central and Southern India. Factory Acts which have hitherto been understood to be framed for the protection of operatives are now sought to be used for the avowed object of restricting and raising the cost of production.

> "Pressure," I understand, "is now to be put upon the Secretary of State to ignore the interests of the people of this country and to order a Factory Act for India, which will prevent our mills from competing with those in England."

Lancashire people engaged in cotton industry have attacked the cotton industry in India, insisting on a stricter Factory. Act and shorter working hours, quite oblivious of the hardships this would obviously entail on the people of India generally, and overlooking the fact that Japan is already a serious rival to India as well as England. Then the jute manufacturing industry has been threatened by the jute manufacturers in Dundee, on the plea that their trade is suffering from the competition of the Indian mills. They too seem to forget the important factor that there are many jute mills on the continent of Europe and go straight for the Indian mills, because they are under the British Government.

Parliamentary Committees of Enquiry into Indian Affairs

I now pass on to consider an important question which must soon engage a large share of public attention. You are aware that under the East India Company, Parliamentary Committees used to be appointed every 20 years on the eve of the renewal of the Charter of the Company. Some of the most beneficent chapters in Indian history are associated with the labours of these Committees. The investigations of the Parliamentary Committee of 1833 led to the enactment of the Charter Act of that year. One of the happy results of the labours of the Parliamentary Committee of 1853 was the throwing open to general competition of the appointments in the Indian Civil Service. Apart from these direct results, these periodical enquiries exercised a healthy influence over the course of Indian administration. Indian officials after all are men, and when they knew that after every 20 years there would be this examination, this scrutiny into Indian affairs, they naturally were careful as to the policy they pursued and as to the details of their administration. Ever since 1853—ever since India has passed under the Government of the Crown—there has not been a Parliamentary Committee of Enquiry into Indian affairs, with the exception of the abortive Committee that was appointed when Lord Randolph Churchill was Secretary of State. The Committee collapsed almost as soon as it was appointed, owing to the dissolution of Parliament.

British Congress Committee

It will be my duty later on to refer to the labours of the British Committee and of the Indian Parliamentary Committee. But, at this stage, I may be permitted to observe that the appointment of the Royal Commission was mainly due to their incessant and devoted efforts, and where all so richly deserve our thanks, it would be invidious to mention names. But if I am permitted to refer to any one who in a special degree is entitled to our acknowledgments, it is Sir William Wedderburn, the President of the British Committee. Sir William Wedderburn is well known in this Presidency, but his is a name which is held in universal honour throughout India as that of a fearless, self-sacrificing, and devoted champion of Indian interests. The one idea upon which he has been ceaselessly harping, ever since his retirement from official life made it possible for him to devote himself, according to the natural impulses of his generous heart, to the service of the land of his adoption, was the appointment of a Royal Commission to enquire into Indian expenditure. It formed the theme of his eloquent address from the Presidential chair of the Congress held at Bombay; and at last success has crowned his efforts and those of his colleagues.

Royal Commission

The Commission is now sitting. We regret the Commission has decided to carry on its deliberations with closed doors. We believe publicity would have materially helped the Commission in the important, work in which it is engaged. "Light, kindly light," is what we need amid " the encircling gloom " that surrounds us. None the less we expect great results from the labours of the Commission. We are confident the labours of the Commission will mark an epoch in the history of our financial relations with England. Sir Henry Fowler had indeed observed, when the Commission was appointed, that no question of policy would lie within the competence of the Commission. The terms, however, of the appointment do not seem to me to exclude the consideration of the policy which governs the administration of the Civil and Military expenditure of the Empire. The terms are wide enough to include such a consideration. The Commission is appointed to enquire into:

> (a) "the administration and management of the Military, and enquiry into Civil expenditure incurred under the authority of the Secretary of State for India in Council or of the Government of India;" and
> (b) "the apportionment of charges between the Governments of the United Kingdom and India for purposes in which both are interested."

Solemn Promises of the Sovereign

In asking for the wider employment of our countrymen in the public service, we not only take our stand upon the solemn promises of our Sovereign, which we cherish with the most affectionate ardour, but we rely upon high consideration of expediency. We are interested in the solvency of the Empire—in the financial stability of the Government; for with it are bound up the happiness and prosperity of our people. Therefore it is that we make this demand. The financial consideration runs through it all.

Tension between Hindus and Mohammedans

We all deplore the recent disturbances between. Hindus and Mohammedans. We would give worlds to avert' them. They throw back the cause of political advancement. But how rare is it that we find respectable people-mixed up in these disturbances. People who have anything to lose will not expose themselves to the risk. Those who have nothing to lose, with whom existence is one long incessant struggle, would dare all things and do all things. A people steeped in poverty represents a political danger, the magnitude of which it is difficult to exaggerate.

Too Many Questions before the Congress

It has, indeed, been Said that we should not take up too many questions, that we should content ourselves with a few, and press them upon the attention of Government, There is considerable force in this observation. By covering a wider ground, we lose in concentration, and we run the risk of losing in effect. The move important questions are apt to be lost sight of in the consideration of the less important ones. From the point of view of presentation to Government, this is a disadvantage! But the Congress being national, its interests embracing the whole field of national concerns, it is difficult to cm tail our programme, without leaving untouched a large number of questions which affect important interests. I think, however, we may adopt a middle course. I think we should give special prominence to a few questions only, such as Indian Finance, including the Home Charges and Military Expenditure, the separation of Judicial and Executive functions, the question of Simultaneous Examinations, the still further reform of the Legislative Councils and one or two other matters which might be mentioned.

Congress Work in England

From the consideration of our work hero we may pass on to discuss our work in England. Our voice would be that of one crying in the wilderness but for our organisation in London, the British Committee, our paper India, and our Parliamentary Committee. The money that we spend in England is worth its weight in gold. (Hear, hear.) It fructifies abundantly in the increasing interest which is being created in England in regard to Indian affairs. It is preparing the way for an abundant harvest of good in which, under the Providence of God, our children and our, children's children are destined to share. But how shall we fittingly describe the services of those good men and true, with Sir William Wedderburn at their head, who ungrudgingly devote their time and attention, often at considerably personal sacrifice, to work for us on the British Committee and the Parliamentary Committee I They say the word " gratitude," does not occur in our language. But the sentiment is there, deep-rooted in the hearts of our people; and in your name I desire to express our sense of profound gratitude to the members of the British Committee, and of the Indian Parliamentary Committee, for their disinterested services to India.

Never was there greater need than now for vigilance both here and in England: At the recent General Elections, our Parliamentary friends sustained a defeat all; along the line, Mr. Dadabhai Naoroji, Mr. Herbert Paul, Mr. W. S. Caine, *(cheers)* and other friends of' Indian reform, have all lost their seats, though we hope constituencies will soon be found for them which will return them to Parliament. My distinguished friend, Mr. W. C. Banerjee fought in the Liberal interest as bravely as man ever fought, *(loud cheers)* but he too was defeated. Mr. Bhownagree has been returned to Parliament in the Conservative interests. I hope and trust Mr. Bhowimggree will find time to read our programme and our proceedings; and if he does so, I am sure he will and that we are as warmly interested as we could be in the maintenance of Imperial unity and that we are advocates of reform and not of revolution, and of reform as a safeguard against revolution. He must know that reforms indefinitely postponed lead to violent changes—that reforms quietly, steadily, cautiously introduced, so that the new adapts itself to the old and the old becomes a part of the new, add to the stability and strength of Governments. I hope that as the result of his studies, he will see his way to sympathise with our programme. His conservatism in English politics need not stand in the way of his adoption of the very moderate programme of the Congress. Sir Richard Garth is a Conservative in politics. He is not able to accept the whole of our programme—he is not in favour of Simultaneous Examinations; but there is no stauncher friend of the Congress movement, whether among Liberals or Conservatives, and we Congressmen are deeply beholden to him for his defence of our cause, when it was assailed by the late Sir George Chesney.

Friends of India on the Liberal Side

We have endeavoured so far to steer clear of party politics. But the bulk of our friends belong to the Liberal side. With the exception of Mr. Pincott and Sir Richard Garth, I cannot at this moment think of any Conservative politician who sympathises with the Congress movement. From the Liberal ranks we have received the largest measure of sympathy. When the delegates- went to England in 1890, it was the Liberal Associations which organised their meetings in the Provincial centres. When the Liberals came into power, their sympathy with our popular aspirations was marked. It was a Liberal-Parliament that recorded the Resolution in favour of Simultaneous Examinations, though I regret to say that it was a Liberal Secretary of State who nullified that Resolution. It was a Liberal Government that practically ordered the withdrawal of the Jury Notification. It was the mandate of a Liberal Secretary of State, Lord Kimberley, that saved in Bengal the system of Local Self-Government menaced by the Municipal Bill of 1892. It was a Liberal Government, too, that reimposed the import duties on cotton goods in the interests of India.

Indian Questions as Part of Questions in England

Speaking for myself, I will say this, that until Indian questions are taken up as party questions, until they become factors in determining the issues of party contests, they cannot occupy a prominent place in English politics or engage a large measure of public attention in England. Before the English people can be expected to do justice to India, they must feel an interest in Indian topics, and, they will not, and cannot, feel any interest in them, so-long as Indian questions remain outside the pale of party politics. We have it on the authority of John Morley that " Indian affairs entered materially into the great battle of parties" in the last century, and the impeachment of Warren Hastings, which for its moral results was a great and far-reaching event, was mainly prompted by party considerations.

India's Loyalty to British Throne

What is our attitude with regard to the Government? I decline to discuss the charge of disloyalty which used to be brought against us in the early days of the Congress movement. Having regard to the official recognition which was extended to us by Lord Lansdowne's Government, this is no longer a question of practical politics. Are we then Her Majesty's constitutional Opposition in this country? I hardly think so. Our position is not analogous to that of a Parliamentary Opposition. A Parliamentary Opposition is bound to oppose all measures of the Government. It is its duty to oppose. It opposes for the more sake of opposition. Its opposition is actuated by considerations of' party spirit, under the influence of ' which the motives and the policy of the Government are liable to be needlessly aspersed. Our position is different. We are not bound to oppose the measures of Government. We are not expected to do so. Our countrymen would have a ground of complaint against us, if we did so, without sufficient cause. We do not oppose for the mere sake of opposition, and with a view to embarrass the Government, so that we may step into its place when the position is no longer tenable. We oppose bad measures. We support good measures. We may oppose the policy of the Government, but we impute no motives. Above all, our opposition is not dictated by any considerations of party-spirit, but by the solo and single-minded desire to serve our countrymen and to broaden and deepen the foundations of British rule upon the unchangeable basis of a nation's affections.

We should suffer a distinct loss of power were we to constitute ourselves into permanent opposition to the Government. If we oppose with discrimination and judgement, our protests will not fail to command sympathy and respect. But if we oppose in the spirit of captious, fault-finding, if we oppose for the more sake of opposition, if we oppose simply because somebody must oppose, we expose ourselves to the risk of being considered hostile critics even when our representations deserve a better fate.

Presidential Address at Ahmedabad Session

Brother-Delegates, Ladies and Gentlemen,

I thank you with all my heart for the great honour which you have done me by electing me as President of this Congress. An honour, such as this, is all the more gratifying to the recipient when he is reminded of the tenure by which he holds it, viz. the love, the esteem, the confidence of his fellow-countrymen. For us Indians the highest earthly honours, no matter by whom conferred, pale before a distinction which bears upon it the stamp of the approbation and the unstinted confidence of united India. Whether I deserve the honour or not, this I will say that the sanction by which I hold it is the highest, much higher than most sanctions by which authority is exercised here or elsewhere, viz. the choice of my fellow-countrymen. Here, if anywhere, there is the right divine for the exercise of authority.

This is the second time that you have summoned me to this great office. When I received your mandate, I obeyed it, but not without hesitation. For however partial I might be to my own merits—and who is not—I could not shut my eyes to the fact that there were many distinguished men who by their great public services and by their still nobler self-abnegation in the national cause have fully established their claims to the honour of the Presidential office. But the choice lay not with me. An expression of your wishes, firmly and authoritatively conveyed to me by those who are entitled to speak in your name and on your behalf, is and has always been to me a command, I overcome my scruples. I bowed to the national will. I appeal to the sympathies of my friends, and I invoked the blessing of Almighty Providence to sanctify our work. And here I am today, ready to cooperate with you and bring to a successful issue the labours of the Eighteenth National Congress.

This is the first time that Congress is held at Ahmedabad. We knew your, difficulties, and we admire the dauntless courage with which you faced them and the noble persistency with which you overcame them. Gujarat is but slowly emerging Worn the throes of one of the greatest calamities of the century. Since 1899 it was in the grip of a famine which, to use the words of the Viceroy, "has been the severest that India has ever known." The story is one of the darkest in Indian history, relieved only by the noble patience and fortitude of the sufferers and the strenuous efforts of the British Government to alleviate their distress. Your difficulties were realised by us, and now that you have overcome them and have held this session of the Congress, which bids fair to be one of the most successful, we applaud the public spirit which has been triumphant over obstacles so formidable and we hasten to offer you the felicitations of all India.

When the Congress was last invited to the Bombay Presidency, it was held at Poona. The capital of the Deccan, Poona is the intellectual centre of the Western Presidency. It is the focus and the starting-point of those forces which have shaped the aspirations and have determined the intellectual and political life of this Presidency. No longer the capital of the Peshwas, it aspires to a higher dominion— it seeks to assert its Empire over the hearts and convictions of men. Along with this Sovereignty is associated an honoured name held in universal esteem throughout the length and breadth of this wide—wide continent. Who can speak of Poona or think of it without being reminded of Poona's greatest son, whose loss we all deplore, whose memory we cherish with a pious and reverential affection? The foremost man of his generation; next to Ram Mohan Roy, the mightiest product of English education, the life, character and achievements of Mahadeo Govind Ranade constitute a national heritage, and if it be true, as indeed it is, that great men never die, he lives with us and amongst us with an immortality which is coextensive with the life of the race— the inspirer of our noble achievements, our comforter amid distress, he speaks trumpet-tongued from amid the deathlike silence of nothingness.

Special Features

The last Congress in the Bombay Presidency was held at Poona, a great intellectual centre. The Congress of this year is held at Ahmedabad, a great industrial centre. Having regard to the recent expansion of our programme, (I will not call it a departure) and to the interlinking in our minds of the industrial and the political movements, it seems to me that there is a special appropriateness in holding the present session of the Congress at Ahmedabad. It is an open declaration that we, the men of the Congress, regard the industrial and the political movements as indissolubly linked together—we hold that they are interdependent and that they act and react upon each other and by their mutual interaction swell the volume of both. If we cannot claim to be the originators of the industrial movement, this at any rate may fairly be laid to our credit that we have stimulated those forces and deepened those impulses which have brought it about. When the human mind is roused in one particular direction, the impulse is felt along the entire sphere of human activities. The industrial movement was bound to follow in the wake of the political movement. The industrial precedes or follows the political movement. In England it preceded it. The reform bill of 1832 was the outcome of the enormous expansion of manufacturing industries which was witnessed during the close of the 18th century. In India the order has been different, but here again the intimate relationship between the two movements is illustrated, and the political movement preceding the industrial, we claim that we have communicated the Prometheus spark which has vitalised the dying embers of Indian national life in all its spheres; we claim that we have fanned them forth into a living flame, full of warmth and brightness and radiance.

The industrial movement is flowing deep, fraught with national ideals. It partakes of the character of the parent movement. It follows in its footsteps with a truly filial piety. A widespread feeling has been roused in favour of the growth and expansion of indigenous arts and industries, and the distinguished men who organised the Industrial Exhibition in connection with the Calcutta Congress of last year have still further carried their high endeavours by opening a storehouse for Indian goods. Our infant industries need protection. But the Government, wedded to the traditions of free trade, will not grant them protection. If, however, protection by legislative enactment is impossible, may we not, by the fiat of the national will, afford them such protection as may lie in our power, if we resolve in our heart of hearts to avail ourselves, wherever practicable, of indigenous articles in preference to foreign goods. Has not the time come when the scattered national impulses may be focussed into an organic and organised whole for a supreme effort for the promotion of our industries? May we not obtain a complete and comprehensive list of Indian articles available for our varied requirements and seek to encourage their manufacture and stimulate their expansion? I quite agree that the process is expensive. But it is of the essence of protection to incur present pecuniary sacrifice in view of future gain, and our national industries, placed on a sound and satisfactory footing, under a moral protection, evoked by a lofty spirit of patriotism, will, in their own good time, bring in an abundant harvest of gold. All sacrifice, incurred for high national purposes and towards the attainment of great national ideals, is repaid with, compound interest. Such is the ordering of nature, the dispensation of Divine Providence; and the sacrifices we now make to restore our lost industries and to establish new ones will compensate us a hundred-fold by enabling us to supply our own wants and to check in part at least that depletion of the national wealth which more than anything else has contributed to the appalling poverty of our people. Our industrial helplessness is even more deplorable than our political impotency. And if the Congress can do aught to stimulate the forces which would improve our industrial condition, it would add one more to the many titles which it already possesses to the enduring gratitude of the people of India.

Nay more, it would fender a great service to the Government. It would relieve the Government, in part at least, of those serious administrative difficulties which have their roots in the deplorably straitened conditions of Indian life. It is therefore with all thankfulness I not that the Industrial Exhibition has come to be regarded as a necessary adjunct to the National Congress. Your Exhibition has been a magnificent success. It has been opened under distinguished auspices by a Prince, whose enlightenment and culture, whose broad and statesmanlike views and deep sympathy with all high endeavours for the public good have not only placed him in the forefront among the Sovereign Princes of India, but have won for him the unstinted homage and admiration of the educated community of India who are proud to reckon him as one of themselves.

It must be the heartfelt hope and prayer of every well-wisher of his country that the Industrial Exhibition which was opened by his Highness the Maharaja of Baroda may still further stimulate the industries of this great town and that this session of the Congress may for ever be associated in the minds of the people of Gujarat with a new epoch of industrial development tempered by deep and rational political convictions, prompted by unswerving loyalty, to the British connection. Let it never be forgotten that political rights minister to material progress and that an unenfranchised people can never work out their industrial salvation.

Delhi Durbar

The one feeling which is predominant in the breast of every true Congressman, which shapes and colours his political convictions and might be said to constitute the keynote of his political creed, is love and reverence for his Sovereign and his Country. He loves his Sovereign, because he loves his country and because, his Sovereign is the Head of the State and is the embodiment, of those constitutional principles which it is his aim and endeavour and the aspiration of his life to introduce into the government of his own country and which, when recognised as principles of Indian administration, he firmly believes, will conduce to the prosperity of his native land and the permanence of British rule in India.

Inspired by this feeling of love and reverence for the Head of the British constitution, our august Sovereign, we heard of His Majesty's illness with profound sorrow—we watched the progress of the disease with the utmost anxiety— and we rejoiced beyond measure on His Majesty's recovery, and from our temples and our mosques and our churches there went forth one great chorus of thanksgiving to the Great Giver of all good, for His abounding mercy in sparing to us our Sovereign, the embodiment of all our hopes and with whose reign are identified the fulfilment of our most cherished aspirations and the redemption of the solemn promises contained in the Queen's Proclamation.

The Coronation postponed by His Majesty's illness took place in August last. It was an event of imperial, of world-wide significance. The eyes of the civilized world were fixed upon it as upon an event which proclaimed to the nations of the earth the formal assumption of regal authority by the Sovereign of an Empire whose watchword is freedom and which has extended to the remotest corners of the world the blessing of constitutional liberty. To the people of India the Coronation was an event of unique importance. For the first time in the history of our relations with Britain, a King of England was crowned Emperor of Hindustan. For the first time in the history of our relations with Britain, Indian representatives were present at the 'Coronation of an English King, though If the truth is to be told, it must be said that the representation of the educated community was most inadequate. It is proposed to celebrate the Coronation by a great Durbar to be held at Delhi in the course of the next few days. The Durbar has been the subject of animated controversy both here and in

England. It has been fiercely Assailed by critics whose utterances are entitled to respectful attention. One of them has described it as "an act of uncalled-for extravagance," specially out of place at a time when the country is just emerging from the throes of a great famine, when despite the grateful rains which have done so much to improve the situation, there is still a large number of people who are in receipt of famine-relief and when it is proposed to saddle the Indian revenues with the charge of nearly a million sterling to meet the cost of the efficiency of the reformed British army in India. Of course there are others who have come forward to defend the Durbar.

The Tunes has lent to it its thunderous support and has recorded a vigorous protest against the Protestants. His Excellency the Viceroy has himself entered the arena; and in a speech conceived in his best style has defended the Durbar and the policy which it embodies. His Excellency has given us the assurance that the ceremonial "will be immeasurably less than the dimensions which a too tropical imagination has allowed it to assume and that a great State ceremonial will never have been conducted in India upon) more economical lines." I am not here concerned to defend the possessors of "a too tropical imagination" among whom, be it observed, are several Anglo-Indian Journalists of NOTO, one of whom at least has not lived in the tropics for many a long year. They are well able to defend themselves and have done 50. Despite their protests the Durbar will soon be an accomplished fact, and I do not know, that it will serve any useful purpose to refer at length to a controversy which has not altered the course of events and now possesses more or less an academic interest.

It is fast receding into the past and will soon vanish out of the domain of contemporary politics. But the rulers of India may learn a lesson and may take a warning from the statesmanship of the past History has condemned with unequivocal emphasis the Delhi Durbar of 1877 as an expensive pageant of doubtful utility. The time has passed by when a mere pageant, calculate to dazzle and to astonish, can leave an enduring impression upon the public mind of India. Thanks to the educational efforts of our rulers, to the wise, the sagacious and beneficent policy which they have followed, we have long since passed the stage of childhood and have entered upon a period of vigorous adolescence when we are able to discriminate the substance from the shadow. Let no one lay the flattering unction to his soul that the educational movement which has brought about this result is confined to a microscopic minority. The movement is becoming wider and deeper day by day, and while we are foolishly talking of a microscopic minority, the social forces, noiselessly but steadily working in the bosom of society, are developing results which promise to bring the entire community, the classes as well as the masses, within those educational influences which have leavened the upper ranks of the social system. The ideas of the educated few, says John Stuart Mill, are bound to filter downwards and become in the course of time, the ideas of the uneducated many. The process is in vigour operation in India, and let the rulers of the land take note of the fact. A mere pageant will not satisfy public opinion. It will emphasise the complaints that have been made. It is indeed an acceptable feature of the Durbar that there is to be an Industrial "Exhibition in connection with it where the products of indigenous arts and industries will be displayed. We are grateful to His Excellency for his interest in the development of our national arts and industries, and we may be permitted to express the hope that it may lead to abiding results. But that is not enough. The Durbar needs to be consecrated by the touch of a higher statesmanship.

It is to be a great historic event, as it is intended to be, it should form a landmark in our annals—it should be commemorated by some boon which would remind us and our children for all time to come of the occasion and of the principal actors therein. The pomp and glitter of the show, the fine dresses and equipages, even the Oriental magnificence of the scene, set off to the best advantage by the choicest rhetoric which the resources of the English language can supply, will not avail to rescue the Durbar from the corroding influence of time and oblivion. These things will be swept out of view amid the onward rush of events. They will be forgotten; the historic recollection will retain no trace of them; but the popular concession which enlarges the sphere of a people's rights and enhances their self-respect or which exalts the purity of the system under which justice is administered and improves its quality, or which once again commemorates the grand old precept that righteousness exalteth a nation will constitute an enduring monument of the ceremonial, worthy of the highest traditions of British statesmanship in India. Such a concession would be in entire accord with precedent and the recognised policy of the British Government on similar occasions. When Her Gracious Majesty the late Queen assumed the direct Government of India, a Durbar was held at Allahabad under the presidency of Lord Canning. A Proclamation was issued at that Durbar—it is the Proclamation of the 1st November 1858, the Magna Charta of our rights, which has been affirmed by successive Viceroys and has been accepted by Lord Curzon as the golden rule of his conduct.

It removed all racial disabilities and made merit the sole test of qualification for high office in India. It wiped out the badge of our political inferiority. It declared that whatever might have been the state of things in the days of the East India Company, a new regime had now dawned, and that under the direct Government of the Crown there were to be no inequalities, based upon distinctions of race or creed, and that all British subjects in India were to enjoy equal rights and possess equal facilities for serving the State. The next ceremonial associated with the Sovereign was the great Durbar of 1877 at which Her late Majesty assumed the title of Empress of India.

Lord Lytton presided at that ceremonial, and speaking as the representative of his Sovereign, he once again affirmed the principle of the Proclamation of the 1st November 1858. " But you—the Natives of India" said he, "whatever your race and whatever your creed have a recognised claim to share largely with your English fellow-subjects, according to your capacity for the task, in the administration of the country you inhabit. This claim is founded on the highest justice. It has repeatedly been affirmed by British and Indian statesmen and by the legislation of the Imperial Parliament. It is recognised by the Government of India as binding on its honour and consistent with all the aims of its policy." This authoritative declaration of imperial policy, this solemn reaffirmation of the principle of equal treatment was followed by the creation of the Statutory Civil Service which sought to render partial justice to the claims of the children of the soil for high and responsible office in the service of their own country.

Then came the Jubilee of Her late Majesty. It was celebrated by a great Durbar held in Calcutta in February 1887—just ten years after the Delhi Assemblage. Lord Dufferin presided at that celebration. Speaking as Viceroy and as the exponent of British policy in India, he foreshadowed the great boon which was soon to he bestowed and for which we hold his memory in grateful regard. He said in his Durbar speech:—"Glad and happy should I be, if during my sojourn among them (the people of India) circumstances permitted me to extend and to place upon a wider and more logical footing the political status which was so wisely given a generation ago by that great statesman, Lord Halifax, to such Indian gentlemen as by their influence, their acquirements and the confidence of their fellow-countrymen were marked out as useful adjuncts to our Legislative Councils." This was said in 1887, and in 1892 the Legislative Councils were enlarged and reconstituted, and for the first time in the history of India were placed upon a partially representative basis.

Thus, since the direct assumption of the Government by the Crown, every ceremonial held in connection with the Sovereign and commemorative of her grace has been signalised by a substantial concession to the people. This has been the uniform, the invariable, the traditional policy of the British Government in India for a period of nearly half a century. It is associated with great and illustrious names and has been consistently followed, irrespective of party considerations, whether the Viceroy was Liberal or Conservative. And if one party more than another was pledged to this policy, one might say that it was the Conservative party that was so pledged; for all these Durbars were held and all these boons were conferred while a Conservative Ministry was in power, as if the great repositories of Conservative traditions wanted to proclaim to the people of India their firm and unalterable conviction that a policy of cautious but continuous progress was essential for the highest purposes of Imperial conservation. Having regard to the traditional policy of the British Government, the people of India look forward with confidence to the bestowal of some boon, the concession of some popular rights, as commemorative of the occasion and of the affectionate interest which His Majesty feels in the welfare of his Indian subjects. To the people of India it would be a grievous disappointment if, on this the first and the greatest ceremonial occasion in connection with the new reign, the traditional policy of the British Government, consecrated by illustrious names and followed with unvarying consistency for nearly half a century, were to be departed from. The traditional policy of the British Government in this matter is in entire keeping with the immemorial usage of the East where royal celebrations, especially those which commemorate the assumption of Sovereign authority, are proclaimed to the people by beneficent gifts which evoke their gratitude, strengthen their loyalty and secure their attachment to the new Sovereign. It is therefore with all confidence that we would appeal to Lord Curzon to follow precedent and the immemorial usage of the East and convert what, it has been so confidently predicted, would be a mere pageant into a great historical event which will excite the love and reverence of the people, cement their loyalty, draw them closer to Britain and strengthen those ties of attachment between the two countries, upon which the greatness of the British Empire and the prosperity of India alike depend.

Speech at Bombay Session

Sir, it seems extraordinary that at this time of day nearly hundred and fifty years after the birth of British rule in India, and the daily increasing contact between the East and the West with the light and culture and knowledge pouring in a flood tide from all sides, with all the great Oriental nations vindicating the honour and the capacity of the Asiatic races on the battlefield, and the still higher regions of peaceful progress, it seems extraordinary that surrounded by these cheering prospects with these happy auguries of progress, we should be under the necessity — the painful necessity—of recording our protest, our national protest be it observed, for we are no longer a microscopic minority, against a policy which is calculated not only to put us back in the race of life, but is inconsistent with the great traditions of British rule in the East and with the honour of the English name in this country.

But, Sir, we have fallen upon evil times and upon evil tongues and we are by darkness and danger encompassed round. It may be, so strong are the forces of reaction that our voice may be like that of one crying in the wilderness, none heeding it and none responding to it, but all the same we have an obvious and plain duty to perform. We must cry out and cry loud and persistently until we make the air resound with our importunate voices, and until we have aroused the conscience of England to a sense of the great responsibility, which Englishmen owe to their vast dependency. (Hear, hear)

Sir, the Resolution declares that the new policy as laid down by the Resolution of the Government of India, of the 24th May, 1904, is inconsistent with the Proclamation and the Charter Act. Hitherto the provisions of the Charter Act and of the Proclamation and pledges and promises contained in them, and made by the Sovereign and the Parliament of Great Britain, had not been eluded; they are directly challenged and openly repudiated. (Hear, hear.) There is no such thing as standing still in the world of God's Providence. Moving is the universal law and the Government of India obeys that law. Lord Curzon tells us that the Government of India does not stand still for a day; we quite accept that statement. The Government moves and moves, but to our misfortune it is always moving in the wrong direction. (Laughters) It moves backward. (Renewed Laughter).

What Lord Curzon calls progress we call retrogression (hear, hear). Never was there a more striking illustration of this backward movement than what is afforded by the principles and policies laid down in the Resolution of the Government of India of the 24th May, 1904. What is the fundamental feature of that resolution? Mark the day of that Resolution. It was the 24th of May 1904. By a bitter irony of fate, the day which used to be the day of universal rejoicing throughout the length and breadth of this country and is now-a-days of pious memory of the birth day of our late Queen—(hear, hear) was selected to be a day for the reversal of her beneficent policy and the cancellation of her gracious Charter (Cries of 'Shame'). I will not dwell further upon this coincidence than to observe that the act appears to us—Hindus and Mahomedans—(hear, hear) in the light of an act of sacrilege and an act almost amounting to an outrage upon the revered memory of one— whom we cherish with the most pious reverence and affection. (Hear, hear.)

Well, Sir, what are the principle features of the new Resolution? They are two. In the first place, the Imperial Civil Service which old-fashioned people like myself prefer to call the Covenanted Civil Service) but in these days everything is imperial (Laughter). We have an Imperial party. Imperialistic Liberals—(laughter)—Imperialistic service and we have also Imperial Anglo-Indians (laughter). Well, Sir, in the first place, the Imperial Civil Service is to form the *Corps d' elite* which under the new policy is to be practically the monopoly of Europeans. In the second place, the appointments outside the ranks of the Imperial Civil Service may be filled up by the people of the country, subject, however, to very important modifications, viz., that the higher appointments in what are called the minor departments are to form practically the monopoly also of the Europeans and Eurasians because forsooth, they are alleged to possess a requisite degree of knowledge, resourcefulness and capacity for initiative which, it is alleged, constitute the heritage of the European races. (Laughter).

Sir, into the merits of this new policy I do not profess to enter at present I am more concerned just now with pointing out that it is in striking contrast with the Proclamation and the Charter Act. Under the new policy race is the test of qualification. Under the old policy, merit was the test of qualification. (hear, hear). Race is now the connotation of the qualities which formerly used to be associated with a high standard of education, duly tested. Sir, the Proclamation and the Charter Act were levelled against the assumption of racial superiority. The Charter Act removed all the racial disabilities in declaring the eligibility of Indians to the offices in the State. The Proclamation carried this beneficent policy a stage further. Not content with a mere passive boon, the Proclamation conferred a positive privilege (hear, hear.) The Charter Act had removed the badge of our racial inferiority. The Proclamation declared and affirmed that merit was the test of qualification, irrespectively of all racial considerations, whatsoever (Hear, hear). The Proclamation thus affirmed and established the beneficent intention of the framers of the Charter Act which could not be expressed within the cast-iron formulae of a legislative enactment (Hear, hear.) Clause 87 of the Charter Act enacts that "no natives nor any natural-born subject shall by reason of religion, birth, descent or colour or any of them be disqualified from holding any place under the said Company." What the Charter Act did was this—it removed the racial disabilities of the old Statute of George III. (cheers). It was the intention of the framers of the Charter Act that such a boon should be conferred. Lord Lansdowne said, from his place in the House of Lords, while commenting on the Charter Act that their Lordships would be remiss in the discharge of their duties to the people of Hindustan if they did not provide them with the amplest opportunities to develop their intellectual and moral faculties (Hear, hear.)

The Court of Directors in forwarding this despatch to their servants in India declared their policy in emphatic terms. Statesmen like Lord Lansdowne recognised the situation boldly declaring that "it is our further will that, so far as may be our subjects, of whatever race or creed, be freely, and impartially admitted to the offices in our service, the duties of which they are qualified by their education, their ability and their integrity duly to discharge." The Proclamation distinctly repeats the forward movements in that beneficent policy, which has found expression in the Charter Act, and which, I venture to hope, Sir, has done more than anything else to secure the gratitude and loyal attachment of the people of India to the British Rule (Cheers).

The Proclamation was issued on the first of November 1858, which is a Red-letter day in our history. I hope and trust that it may be a day of universal rejoicing and solemn celebration, if only we protest against that reactionary policy which seeks to tear up the Proclamation and scatter to the winds its beneficent provisions. The Proclamation was not an instrument of impulsive generosity. It was a solemn and a deliberate act of the State, which received the assent of a long line of illustrious Viceroys (Hear, hear.) It was recalled at the Delhi assemblage and ratified by our sovereign, the King-Emperor—while he assumed the administration of this great Empire (hear, hear) and it has been challenged by a high authority. It has been upheld by a higher authority. In the memorable words of Lord Ripon, the Proclamation is not a treaty and not a diplomatic instrument. It is obligatory upon those to whom it is addressed. But, Sir, it is now proposed to repudiate the Proclamation, not, I think, in so many words, but it is attempted to adopt a policy which is counter to the spirit of its beneficent intentions. Sir, I venture to say that there has been always a sinister and malignant influence in operation in the high councils of Government to interfere with the redemption of this gracious policy. I know that it is a very serious charge to bring against the Government of India, but, Sir, here we are in the temple of Truth and Honesty. (hear). I am prepared to prove the charge to the hilt.

Lord Lytton, speaking from his place as the Chancellor of the University of Calcutta, not only said that the promises and pledges of the Queen made to the people of this country remained inadequately redeemed but went much further than that and in a secret document—it is no longer a secret (laughter) —said: "We have broken to the heart the words of promise which we have uttered to the ear." The Duke of Argylle, from his place in the house of Lords, said in 1869: "I must say that we have not fulfilled the duty of the promises and engagements which we have made." But now for the first time, there is an open and avowed attempt made to repudiate the Proclamation by the substitution of this new policy. Lord Curzon has told us that the Proclamation is the golden rule of his conduct. Sir, I confess, that I find myself in a bewildering maze of difficulties. I try to reconcile his speech, I ask what becomes of this golden rule of his conduct in the light of the new policy to which I have just adverted? What is the justification for the new policy? Has the old policy been tried and found wanting? So far from this being the case, it is admitted on all hands that the great experiment inaugurated by the Proclamation, which has now been tried for a period of 50 years, has been attended with a marvellous measure of success. (Hear, hear.) Lord Curzon has appended certain figures to this Resolution, of May last showing that there has been a steady expansion of the policy with regard to the employment of our countrymen in the public service. Sir, if the figures justify that inference, what is the irresistible conclusion to which you are driven, except that day by day you are getting more and more qualified for the high appointments under the British Rule? If so, where is the justification for the reversal of this ancient policy? I venture to say that Lord

Curzon stands condemned out of his own mouth. But, gentlemen, we have another ground, and a stronger ground of complaint, and I am sure it is one you will endorse with cordiality and enthusiasm. Why are we precluded from high offices and why has this ban and ostracism been placed upon the whole community in respect of higher offices under the British rule? Is it because we are the representatives of an inferior race? Lord Curzon, from his place in the Imperial Council (I am quoting the substance of what he said) declared that by our environments, by our heritage and our upbringing we are unequal to the responsibility of high office under the British rule. I venture to say, Sir, that never was a deeper affront delivered to the people of India by the representative of the Sovereign. (Hear,hear). It is bad enough to repudiate the Proclamation, but it is adding insult to injury to cast a slur upon the people of this country. In your name and on your behalf, gentlemen, I desire to record my most emphatic protest against this assumption of our racial inferiority. (Cheers). Are Asiatics inferior to Europeans? Let Japan answer. (Cheers). Are Indians inferior to Europeans? Let Lord George Hamilton answer. (Loud Cheers). And Lord George Hamilton is not a friend of the people of this country. (Hear hear).

Gentlemen, are we the representatives of an inferior race, we, who are the descendant of those who, in the modern world, while all Europe was steeped in superstition and ignorance, held aloft the torch of civilization? Are we the representatives of an inferior race? From whose shores forsooth went forth those missionaries who have converted two-thirds of the human race into moral superiority. Sir, this charge of inferiority will not stand examination for a moment. We may possibly have fallen from the high ideals of the past, but even in modern times our representatives have been fully equal to the responsibilities of the imperial rule (Hear, hear.) Has the instinct of statesmanship and capacity for command disappeared in the midst of the environments of the present situation? (A Voice "No No"). If that was so, it would imply the greatest reflection upon the British rule. (Hear, hear). But happily we are spared that reflection and men like Sir Madhorao, Sir Dinker Rao, and Sir Salar Jang, Toder Mull, Abul Fazl and others have illustrated the annals of the modern Indian statesmanship. The truth is that it is not that we are wanting in character or capacity, but there is a deep-rooted suspicion in the minds of our rulers, that if the policy of the Proclamation were to be prosecuted and carried forward, later on a measure of political power would go into the hands of the Indians, which might imperil the interests of the Empire. (Cries of "Shame.") Of course, it is a great shame. (Cheers.) This great and mischievous policy of distrust and suspicion has engendered the modern spirit of Imperialism, which bodes no good either to India or to England. (Hear, hear). Sir, if I have not already tired your patience (Cries of "No, no.") I should like to refer to a number of figures which I have got here. I think my friend the Hon'ble Mr. Gokhale is looking at me through his spectacles (laughter)—perhaps he means to make use of the figures later on in the Viceregal Council—it is not my privilege to be there, but I am addressing a higher constituency—(Loud and prolonged cheers) a constituency of the representatives of my country (loud applause). I venture to make use of these figures with a view to refute the claims which have been urged by Lord Curzon. On the strength of these figures Lord Curzon explains that the British Government has treated the Indians with the unexampled liberality in the matter of employment of the people of this country in the public services. On the strength of these figures he says, " Is it possible to conceive that our administration has been too generous to the Europeans and too grudging to the native element?" He has thrown down the gauntlet, which I take up on your behalf and I will be able to point out from the examination of these figures that they entirely refute his proposition and support our contention that the British rule has been too exclusive in the matter of employment of our countrymen in the higher branches of the public service (hear, hear). These figures embrace a period of thirty-six years from 1867 to 1903.

According to the statement of the Government of India, in 1867, there were 13,431 appointments carrying salaries of Rs. 75 a month and upwards. The Hindus and Mahomedans occupied 72 p. c. of these appointments, while Europeans and Eurasians filled 28 p. c. In 1897, the total number of appointments came to 25,370, that is nearly double of what it had been in 1867 and our percentage was 56 (Cries of 'Shame') while the percentage of Europeans and Eurasians was 44 1 Mark, in 1867 our percentage was 72 and in 1897 it was 56! (Cries of "Shame.") That is to say, while the number of appointments had nearly doubled itself, our percentage had nearly gone down by one-half! (Loud cries of "Shame.") This is the illustration of the "unexampled liberality " of the British Government! (Loud cries of "Shame.") Our percentage ought to have been in 1897, if the percentage of 1867 had been kept up, 92 instead of 56. But let us proceed. Let us come down to the year 1903, when we find the total number of appointments to be 28,278, that is to say, nearly 3,000 more appoinments than were in 1897, and what have we for our percentage, for that is the crucial point? Our percentage was 56, that is to say, while in 1903 the number of appointments had increased by 3,000, our percentage remained the same, (shame) that is to say, as regards the entire number of appointments, our percentage had gone down I (Cries of "Shame.") We are, therefore, driven to the irresistible conclusion that, as the number of appointments increased from 1867 to 1897 and from 1897 to 1903, our percentage went down step by step as an illustration of the "unexampled liberality of the British Government"! (Ironical laughter.) I have not done yet (Renewed laughter.)

The higher you mount the lower becomes the percentage! Our percentage as regards the total number of appointments of Rs. 75 and upwards in 1903 was 56. Now take the appointments carrying salaries of Rs. 1000 and upwards. The percentage in 1893 was 14 out of the total number, while the percentage was 17 out of the total number of appointments carrying salaries of Rs. 500 and upwards! I have just now said that the higher you mount, the percentage becomes lower and lower. The it is that only 14 or 17 per cent, of the higher appointments fall to our lot, (shame), although the country is ours, the money is ours, and the bulk of the population is ours. (Hear, hear.)

Sir, this, of course, touches only the fringe of the whole question. (Hear, hear,) There are whole departments of the higher offices from which our countrymen are entirely excluded. (Shame.) I should like to know many Indians occupy responsible positions in the Political Departments? (A voice; "Not one.") I should like to know how many Indians there are who are occupying Commissioned ranks in the Army? (A voice: "Of course, none.") The native has, in these days, to be content with only a "Subadarship" or a "Resaldarship" (cries of "Shame,") and is subordinate to the youngest European Subaltern, who possibly was not born when the veteran won his spurs. (Loud applause.) Lord Curzon challenged comparison between the British Government and other Governments in respect of the matter of employment of their subjects in the higher offices of the State by searching through history from the time of the Romans. He said: "You will not find such examples." Well, Sir, I fear Lord Curzon has been indulging in a little romance. (Hear, hear and laughter.)

The Government of India is omnipotent and can do a great many things but it cannot convert facts into fictions. (Hear, hear.) Lord Curzon appeals to History and to some unearthed traditions, and he appeals to them with unhesitating confidence; but let History be our judge and our arbiter in this controversy. Gibbon in his "Decline and Fall of the Roman Empire" says that the grandsons of those who fought against Caesar became captains of the Roman legions—(Hear, hear)—and Governors of the Roman Provinces. (Hear, hear.) Markham in his " History of British India" says that the grandsons of those who fought against Baber at Paniput became Commanders, Governors and confidential advisers of their Sovereign. (Cheers.)

Raja Man Singh, who carried the Mogul standard from the Punjab on the East to Cabul on the West, became a Hindu Governor of a Mahomedan province in the heart of a fana-tical Mahomedan population ! (Hear, hear.) Where is the parallel of such a process in the British Indian History? Where is the Indian Governor of a British province? (Hear, hear.) Where is the Indian Commander of a British Division? Where is the Indian adviser of a British Viceroy and a member of his Executive Council? We have had Honorary Captains and Colonels at any rate—(Laughter)—Honorary Councillors and Captains, but they were Councillors and Captains who never counselled nor commanded. (Hear, hear and laughter.) It was an awkward diplomatic fiction in which Lord Curzon has deluded himself in indulging, in saying things which might look well in the medieval times. Look at the neighbouring nation which is more Asiatic than European and which is not known for the liberality of its administration. Rudyard Kipling was right when he said that Russia appears more to be the Western boundary of Asia than the Eastern boundary of Europe. There can be no comparison between the Russian and British rules. In spite of culture, freedom and higher ideals of the British Government, I am bound to say in justice to the Russian Government, that Government, in the matter of trusting its Asiatic subjects and associating them with the Government of the country, is distinctly more literal than the British Government. (Hear, hear.) You may be surprised at that statement, and if it rested upon my own authority I would not make it. (Laughter.) But it is what Sir Henry Lawrence said—the hero of Lucknow who died doing his duty in the siege of Lucknow in 1857.—"If Asiatics and Europeans can obtain honourable positions in the armies of Russia and France, surely Indians, after a tried service of a century under England's banner, are entitled to the same boon, nay justice." That state of things remains unaltered. Well, Sir, if we compare the administration of the Philippine Isles with the administration of India by the British Government, what becomes of Lord Curzon's boast? The Philippine Isles came under the American rule only the other day, and yet they have now obtained constitutional government ! There are a House of Commons and a House of Peers. The House of Commons is entirely elected, while as regards the House of Peers, three-eighths of it consists of the natives of the country ! (Hear, hear.)

You have in one of your resolutions a prayer to the effect that the natives of India may be appointed members of the Executive Council of the Viceroy. The American Government have already solved the question ! In the very first Council of the Philippine Islands there were three Philippine members of the Executive Council ! (Hear, hear.) Is it necessary to prolong this controversy any longer? We should rejoice if we could possibly re-echo the sentiments of Lord Curzon, but great as our loyalty is to the Throne, our allegiance to Truth is much greater, (hear, hear), and we are anxious, above all things, that there should be no delusion in the minds of the British Government as regards the administration of this country, and that we should not be led away by specious plausibilities of brilliant rhetoric. (Hear, hear) Sir, this is a very old question. It is associated with the illustrious names and with the high endeavours of some of our greatest men (Hear, hear.) Eleven years ago it seemed as if we were within a measurable distance of victory, for, then the House of Commons, under the leadership of Mr. Dadabhai Naoroji, (hear, hear), formed the principle of Simultaneous Examinations in regard to the Indian Civil Service, But we were doomed to a bitter disappointment. The then Secretary of State with the Imperialistic Liberals, which, I think, is only another name for a Tory in disguise (laughter) negatived this resolution by fortifying, himself with a body of local bureaucratic opinion, although in the archives of his office at that time there was a resolution of the Committee of his own Council, dated as far back as 1861, which declared that unless the Simultaneous Examinations were granted, the Queen's Proclamation must remain unredeemed. Sir, at the present moment, the hopes and visions of 1833 have been dispelled. We are passing through a terrible and acute crisis, one of the very worst in our annals. For, if Lord Curzon would not give us more, why should he take away that which we have? (Hear, hear,) True statesmanship places reliance upon the loyal attachment of the people to the British Crown. (Hear, hear.)

Gentlemen, we hear a great deal in these days about efficient administration. I yield to none in my appreciation of efficient administration. (Cheers.) But it has never occurred to the faddists, who speak of efficient administration, that the efficient administration cannot exist without the willing cooperation of the people concerned. (Hear, hear.) The Russian Government have made this discovery after a long and bitter humiliation, and the Czar has called into being a policy which, it is to be hoped, will liberalise the Russian institutions. (Hear, hear.) Sir, in this matter we take our stand upon the Proclamation which is our watchword and our battle-cry. (Cheers.) The gracious words of the Proclamation are inscribed on our banner (hear, hear) which we hold aloft. (Cheers.) It is the symbol of our unity. (Cheers.) It is the bond of our solemn league. (Cheers.) We desire to tell our rulers in all humility and with the utmost emphasis that we will not allow them to repudiate the Proclamation and to discard the gracious message which is given to us from the footsteps of the Throne and which is sanctified by the memory of one of the greatest Sovereigns of the modern times. (Hear hear.) We are resolved to use all the constitutional means at our disposal to safeguard the Proclamation. (Hear, hear.) We fully realise the gravity of the task which we have imposed upon ourselves. (Hear, hear.) We recognise the political situation and the political prospects, and we recognise the fact that the forces of reaction are now in the ascendant. But what is more, we are confident of success (hear, hear), and in this hopeful anticipation, Sir, we have been greatly encouraged by the proceedings of that Banquet which was given in your honour—(Hear, hear)—and in honour of our friend, Sir William Wedderburn, (Hear, hear.) Sir the fact of there being so many Englishmen and leaders of public opinion upon a common platform linked by the hand of sympathy towards the Indian people was an achievement memorable of its kind and augurs well for the success of our cause. (Hear, hear.) It augurs well for the success of the cause such as ours which is so moderate, so just and so patriot in its aims and aspirations. (Hear, hear.) The outlook may be gloomy and the clouds may frown upon us, but I venture to think that there will dawn a bright era—(Hear, hear)—when the provisions of the Queen's Proclamation will stand redeemed and upheld—(Cheers)—and when the policy of trust and confidence will supersede the policy of mistrust and suspicion (hear, hear), a policy in which Englishmen and Indians will combine together for the glory of England's great dependency in the East. (Hear, hear.) I venture to look forward to the advent of that day. (Cheers.) You and I may not witness that day. Our eyes are now growing dim with age, we may not witness that day, but let us each try an his own way according to his opportunities, according to his lights and according to the measure of his capacity to bring about this glorious consummation. (Hear, hear.) Let us be animated by great hope and great faith, and we shall be able to overcome all obstacles and to surmount all reactions (hear, hear), and great as pur cause is, God willing, it will triumph in the end. (Loud and ringing cheers).

Speech at Calcutta Session

Partition of Bengal

Mr. President, Your Highness, ladies and gentlemen,

The resolution has not yet been placed before you and I desire to do so with the permission of the President. In deference to the Bengali feeling, we have made a slight alteration in the resolution. My friend, Babu Matilal Ghose gave notice of an amendment in connection with this resolution. After consultation with our Bengali friends and having ascertained their opinions, we have accepted his amendment (cheers) and all reference to the commission of enquiry will be deleted (cheers and shouts of *Bande Mataram*). I will, therefore, now read the Resolution as amended:

> "That this Congress again records its emphatic protest against the Partition of Bengal and regrets that the present Government, while admitting that there were errors in the original plan and that it went wholly and decisively against the wishes of the majority of the people of Bengal, is disposed to look upon it as a settled fact, in spite of the earnest and persistent protest of the people and their manifest disinclination to accept it as final.
>
> "That this Congress, composed of representatives from all the provinces of this country, desires earnestly to impress upon the British Parliament and the present Liberal Government that it will be not only just but expedient to reverse or modify the Partition in such a manner, as to keep the entire Bengali-speaking community under one undivided administration and thus to restore contentment to so important a province as Bengal."

Sir, I think this Congress is to be congratulated upon the singular piece of good fortune in having obtained the adhesion of that illustrious representative of a great and princely family (cheers) in the capital of the new Province to this resolution (hear, hear). Henceforth, Nawab Athikulla,—(cheers) the worthy son of a worthy father, who surrendered his princely patrimony in obedience to fraternal feeling—henceforth this distinguished representative of a great and princely family will be recognised as our Captain-General in the campaign against the Partition.

Under his leadership, under his guidance, guided by his prestige and the greatness associated with his honoured name, we hope to triumph in this memorable campaign (cheers). Sir, it is our misfortune that it should be necessary for us from year to year, to appeal to your indulgence to accord to this question, a leading place in your deliberations. I know not how long this necessity will last. But this I do know, that, so long as the Partition is not reversed or modified, the Bengali-speaking community will never be satisfied (loud cheers) and that, no matter what concessions may be granted in other directions, they will not conciliate our people or allay their prevailing excitement (hear, hear).

Sir, we are told from time to time, that there is a lull in the agitation, a subsidence of the feeling which has prompted it. The other day, I was reading a letter which has appeared in the *Times* from a correspondent in India in which that correspondent observed that the agitation was on the wane. Sir, we are in the unfortunate position of a patient suffering from a painful disease in which there are periods of intermission but the patient knows no rest or peace so long as the root-cause of the mischief lies ingrained in his Constitution (hear, hear). Time blunts the edge of all sorrow. Time is our great healer. But time with its mollifying hands has not been able to soothe our wants. There it is festering in the depths of our hearts. There is no feeling deeper in the heart of the Bengali than that which is associated with the home and which gathers round the domestic circle.

The Bengali, be he a Hindu or a Mohammedan, feels the strongest repugnance to the breaking-up of his home; he relents with a fanaticism which is religious in its intensity. With equal pain and resentment does he view this separation from himself of his kith and kin, by the formation of a separate legislature and a separate Government. The Partition is in the nature of an outrage upon the deepest domestic associations (hear, hear). Call it a mere sentiment—an irrational sentiment, if you like; but there it is,—nobody can ignore it —moving the heart of our people with a power and intensity to which there is no parallel in the annals of our popular upheavals. That is not merely a sentimental consideration. There are deeper issues. They affect the whole of India. They concern what with us is the problem of problems, namely, the question of Self-government. If it were a question of territorial redistribution, all this excitement and irritation would be inexplicable. But the consideration is far more serious than that. The question is this:— Brother delegates, from the rest of India, I desire to draw your special attention to it.—The question is this: Whether the public opinion of a great province, expressed with singular unanimity and unequal emphasis, is to be flouted and treated with open and disguised contempt in a matter affecting the vital wellbeing of that Province ("Shame"). Thus, in another form, in another garb, we have the old, old question of the assertion of popular opinion and the vindication of the principle of Self-Government. It is in this form and in this sense that the question appeals with convincing force to the heart and conscience of the whole of India. Brother delegates, last year about this time, when we discussed this question, the Liberal Government had come into power, with Mr. Morley as Secretary of State for India. We had never known Mr. Morley in that capacity. We knew him more as an author than as a statesman. We knew him better—at any rate, I knew him better— as the biographer of Cobden and Burke, as the author of Compromise, than as the radical politician or the Chief Secretary for Ireland.

Many of us had, indeed, sat at his feet, in the sense that we had imbibed from his writings those lessons of political wisdom dominated by the higher considerations of expediency, which have their roots in the eternal moralities of things. We, therefore, hailed our political *Guru* as the controller of the destinies of our motherland; we hailed him, welcomed him to the place, to the seat of the great Akbar, in the full confidence that he would fill it with more than the wisdom, with scarcely less than the beneficence, of the greatest of the Mogul Emperors. If, perhaps, our expectations were pitched too high Mr. Morley is 'responsible for it. For, who can read his writings or rise from their perusal, without coming to the conclusion, that here is a master-figure in the world of thought and action, (cheers, hear, hear), and that his caution was but another name for that temper of mind, which gathers in the forces of action preliminary to a determined and vigorous effort. We realised the difficulties of his situation and were prepared to make large-allowances for that undiluted bureaucratic atmosphere, which he breathes every moment of his life, and in which he might be said to live and move and have his being.

For of all the bureaucracies, which govern or misgovern countries (hear, hear), the stiffest, the most reactionary, the slowest to move, the one, above all others, gifted with the fatal gift of a superabundance of confidence in its own infallibility, is the bureaucracy installed at the India Office. But all the same, people expected that a man of Mr. Morley's capacity and judgement, with his great influence over the country and the House, would rise superior to his environments, assert his personality and vindicate those lofty principles of Political Wisdom and Justice, which are inseparably associated with his honoured name.

Sir, we have been asked to wait, and that, by no other person than Sir William Wedderburn (cheers), one of the staunchest friends of the people of India and the same advice has been emphasised by another distinguished friend in India, whom I am looking out for, on the platform and whom I miss and whose sympathy for India and Indian aspirations is so well-known — I mean the Right Hon'ble Mr. Samuel Smith (cheers). We have been asked to wait. Wait we must; what else can we do? Waiting upon the will of our rulers has been our lot for the last three centuries. We shall certainly wait; but not in meek submission to the will of our rulers as the decree of an inexorable fate, but with the firm resolve to overcome that fate and work out our salvation (hear, hear).

Our rulers must recognise the new spirit born, it may be, of the huge blunder of the Partition, vibrating through our hearts, uplifting us to a higher plane of political effort. (cheers). We were, sirs, no longer Orientals, of the old type (hear, hear), content to grovel under the weight of an overmastering fate (hear hear) but we are Orientals, Your Highness, of the new school, enfranchised by English culture and English influences, revivified by the example of China, Japan (cheers) and last but not the least, of Persia, and as Orientals of the new school, we believe, that nations by themselves are made. (Cheers and shouts of *Bande Mataram*). Yes, we shall wait with patience, but it will not be the patience of inaction, but patience accompanied by vigorous, dauntless, self-sacrificing effort to undo that gigantic blunder and cruel wrong of the partition of Bengal. Mr. Morley declines to reopen the question on the ground that the Partition is a settled fact (cheers). We, in our turn, decline to accept it as a settled fact; we decline to accept a wrong —admitted to be wrong—an outrageous and deliberate insult upon the opinions of our people, as among the varieties of our life and our administration. Mr. President, you have, through a long course of distinguished services of self-dedication to the interests of your country, noted the triumphs of truth and justice in this world, even in connection with the attitude and the policy of reactionary Government A wrong is a lie and as such, it is opposed to the mandate of the Omnipotent and is in conflict with the moral order of the Universe. It cannot endure in this world of eternal varieties. We are bound to undo it. And if we persist, go on continuing this agitation, the Partition is doomed, foredoomed to withdrawal. Mr. Morley, let it be said to his credit, does not adduce any justification for the Partition. He makes two significant admissions—that it went wholly and decisively against the wishes of the majority of the people concerned and that there were errors in the original plan. With these admissions, it is difficult to see how Mr. Morley can long stand where he is. We have only to give him a push, a persistent push, from year to year and I think we will dislodge him from that position (laughter) ! A statesman is not bound to be logical and that is what Mr. Morley himself has said (laughter) ! Read his Life of Burke and you will find that it is so. He says that a statesman is not bound to be logical, but, I take it, that he is bound to be reasonable. If it were any other person I should have used the word rational, but I will not do so. He is bound to be reasonable, he is bound to be just, he cannot overcome the paramount claims of right-doing.

Righteousness exalteth a nation (hear, hear); righteousness is the very vital breath of Imperial statesmen. The most reactionary of Indian Viceroys has told us that the British Government is based upon the eternal moralities of things. The most reactionary of Indian Lawmakers—I do not know how it is, but the most reactionary of men in their practical politics, are the most liberal in their profession of politics—the most reactionary of Indian Lawmakers— do you know who that is?—some of us have had practical experience of him, the author of the Sedition Clause in the Penal Code—he has said from his place in the Imperial Legislative Council that a single act of conscious injustice done in India is more disastrous to the British rule than a great reverse sustained upon an Asiatic battlefield.

A wrong has been committed, and the Government itself has admitted it as such, and it is felt by the people as such. To perpetuate it and not to rectify it would be disastrous to the credit of the British rule. It will do more than anything else I can think of, to shake the popular confidence, the bulwark of States and Thrones in the justice and integrity of the Government. What is the Government for, if it will not rectify a wrong? That is the highest ambition, the noblest function of all Governments. It is their sacred duty to redress wrongs. Liberalism is wedded to progress. Progress involves the unsettling of the existing 'order of things. What has the Government been doing recently? Upsetting the educational policy of their predecessors, unsettling a settled fact. Mr. Morley admits that there are errors in the original plan. I take it, that if the Partition is to be a permanent institution and if there are errors in original plan, are they to find an abiding place in a permanent arrangement, fraught with the happiness and misery of millions of people?

The position is so irrational that even the *Pioneer* is constrained to say that, in the light of this admission, Mr. Morley himself has no option left to him but to reconsider the whole question. The *Pioneer* says that no question of temporary convenience can be made an excuse for perpetuating errors, and the right course would be to amend the Partition at once. But Mr. Morley's attitude is determined by the larger considerations of expediency. What those considerations are, he has not been pleased to tell us. He was challenged to state them by Mr. O'Donnell from his place in the House of Commons. But he did not accept the challenge. Are we then, to be driven to the conclusion that they are not such, as will bear the light of publicity and the test of scrutiny?

Brother delegates, differing, as I do, from Mr. Morley's views, I desire to meet him on his own ground and I hold that even upon considerations of political expediency, he is bound to undo or modify the Partition. Is not the contentment of the people, an asset of some importance to the Government? Sir, in the case of a foreign Government, such as ours, it is an asset of priceless value. Her Gracious Majesty the late Queen-Empress is my authority for it. For, in that gracious Proclamation of the 1st November 1858, which represents the high watermark of British statesmanship of the last generation, she said in the concluding words of Her Proclamation, that the strength of Her Empire lay in the contentment of Her people. The partition of Bengal strikes the root of that contentment. It has caused widespread dissatisfaction, it has alienated the people from the rulers (heat, hear). There could be no practical cooperation between them, when there is this yawning gulf. I will cite an illustration in point. I hope I have not tired your patience. (cries of "no, no").

The other day, a high official of the Indian Government visited Rajshahi in the new province with a view to found a Cooperative Credit Society. The help of the local leaders was invoked. But they refused point-blank to cooperate with him. The local correspondent of one of the newspapers of Calcutta wrote that the people had lost all confidence in the Government (hear hear). Lo and behold ! this is one of the fruits of the Partition. Mr. Morley wants new facts for him to reconsider the question. I present him with this. Here is fact No. 1. There are one or two more facts that I have to present to him.

A section of our people have lost all confidence in the utility of constitutional agitation, (hear, hear); they say that they decline to approach the Government with memorials and; petitions. They say what is the good of them all. Here, in the matter of Partition we have begged and prayed and protested, and entreated, the arts of sycophancy have been put into fullest requisition. But all in vain. They say, that self-respect demands that they should have nothing whatever to do with the Government (cries of *Bande Mataram).* I may say, gentlemen, that I am not in sympathy with that view at all. I think that the political agitation must be continued and I further think that petitions should be submitted. You may say 'no' to the end of your life; and you will not convince me that in this matter I am in the wrong. We are agreeing to differ there. Whatever that matter may be, there is the fact that a class has sprung up in our midst who do not believe in petitioning or praying to Government and who do not believe in constitutional agitation. This is the fruit No. 2 of Partition which may be laid before Mr. Morley (cheers). I have got another new fact to lay before Mr. Morley and that shall be the last.

In the new province, before Partition was carried out, Hindus and Mahomedans in most of the districts were living in the utmost cordiality and peace. In some districts—I am glad to be able to say, not in all—the relations have somewhat changed. I do not enter into the various causes that have brought them about. There is the fact, fruit No. 3, the difference between Hindus and Mahomedans caused by the Partition.

Gentlemen, this brings me to the question of the attitude of Mahomedans of India with regard to the Partition. Let me tell you that, before the Partition was carried out, with the solitary exception of Nawab Salimulla (cries of "shame"), everybody, Hindu and Mohammedan, was opposed to the Partition. (A cry, "so was Nawab Salimulla.)" That correction, I accept. He was opposed, I remember now, to the smaller scheme of Partition but since the large scheme was introduced and when he discovered he would be the premier nobleman of the new province, then there came a sudden change in him. That I think represents the true state of facts. The Mohammedan community were opposed to Partition and nothing has happened, since then, to bring about a change in the attitude of the Mahomedans in India, except that they have got a few more appointments in the ministerial subordinate police and executive service. Has the cause of Mohammedan education received an impetus? (Cries of" No"). Of course not Is sanitation better looked after? (Cries of "No"). Mahomedans have no reason to be satisfied with the Partition, and as a matter of fact, they do not support it. I will bring forward a few facts. There were no less than 259 anti-Partition demonstrations held in connection with the celebration of 16th October last. Out of this 259, at 135 meetings Hindus and Mahomedans joined for the purpose of protesting against the Partition (cheers). But that is not all. The foremost important anti-Partition meetings were those, held in Calcutta, Dacca, Faridpur and Mymensing. The Presidents of all these meetings were Mohammedan gentlemen of light and leading, most of whom I now see on the platform. My friend, Khan Bahadur Moulvi Mohammed Yusuf presided over the Calcutta meeting. Our friend, Nawab, Athikulla presided over the Dacca meeting. I know there were some pro-Partition meetings. But they were the work of one man, Nawab Salimulla, aided by his Anglo-Indian friends, official and non-official. (cries of shame). It is a great shame. That officials should support the pro-Partition agitation is a scandal of the gravest magnitude. The official support of public movements deprives them of all their significance. This fact was brought to the notice of Mr. Morley. And I hope that, the Government of the new Province has taken some action in this matter. I won't be long, I will finish in ten minutes.

Gentlemen, the volume of popular opinion is rising day by day. The enthronement of popular opinion is only question of time. 25 years ago, Lord Ripon said from his place as Chancellor of the University of Calcutta that time was fast approaching, when public opinion, even in India, was becoming the irresistible master of Government. There are those who would give the world to bring about the indefinite postponement of this blessed consummation and to see that they set Hindus against Mahomedans and Mahomedans against Hindus (cries of 'shame'). We ought to be on our guard against the machinations of the intriguers who are the enemies of Hindus and Mahomedans alike. The number of Mahomedans present at this meeting is not, as you said the other day, a hundred but the number is more than two hundred. You will be pleased to hear that we have hundred Mohammedan volunteers out of three hundreds. (cries of *Bande Mataram).* Speaking for myself as a member of the Hindu community, I desire to tell my Mohammedan fellow-countrymen that we notice with satisfaction the political ferment which we witness in the great Islamic community in India, We rejoice at the growing, aspirations of the Mohammedan community. From us Hindus, you will receive nothing but sympathy and cooperation, for, we recognise that you are brothers linked to us by an inseparable destiny. Hindus and Mahomedans, let us stand on a common platform — may it not be the platform of this Congress,— sanctified by public effort and devotion of our great men, may we Hindus and Mahomedans stand shoulder to shoulder on this sacred spot, this gathering of the people and nations of India, and by mutual effort, it may be by mutual forbearance and mutual charity, work out the great destinies that the God of nations has placed before us (cheers)!

Sir, I know not what the fate of this agitation will be. For the present, the signs are all against us. The future is enveloped in the deepest darkness and not the faintest streak of hope illumines the darkness of the situation. The heart of the stoutest many even quail, as he views the prospect before him. For eighteen long months have we carried on this agitation. Oh, God, for how much longer will it be our painful and laborious task to continue it ! From the depths of our heart cries out a voice, "Oh, continue it, so long as the wrong is not righted (cheers). Let the banner, which has been uplifted, float high in the breeze, the emblem of your Hope and Triumph, until success is yours; and if, perchance, the banner should drop from your sinking hands, the God of nations will raise up others in your places, who will carry it aloft, and aided by the irresistible forces of time, which make for justice and progress, they will carry it to an assured, if not, a speedy triumph." That is the voice that cries out from the innermost depths of our hearts and we bow to it.

Brother delegates, with us the partition is what the Home Rule is with the Irish. For 100 years, the Irish have fought for the Home Rule; for 100 years they have met with defeat and disappointment. For' 100 years, they have again and again come back to the charge. We mean to imitate the Irish along those constitutional lines, which will win for us the sympathy and support of civilized mankind, never yielding, but never despairing, possessing our souls in patience, with the firm confidence, that, as in the physical, so in the moral world, the darkest night is often but the precursor of the brightest day and holds concealed in its bosom the germs of those golden streaks which proclaim the advent of a new dawn.

Brother delegates, I have now one appeal to make to you. We want your help and your sympathy in this great struggle. Will it be extended to us? Say, yes or no. (The whole house shouted "yes" vociferously). I thank you for this demonstration of sympathy and I beg of you, when you go back to your homes, to record in your provincial meetings and your provincial associations, resolutions of protest against the cruel wrong which has been done to the people of Bengal. Let the Government know that when one province is injured, all the other provinces share the woe and the grief (cheers). The moral significance of such a demonstration, it would be impossible to exaggerate. It will constitute a bulwark of strength in our national struggle. It will invest the public opinion of a province with the potency of the national voice of all India. It will intensify the solidarity between province and province by making them the participators in their mutual sorrows and anxieties; and therefore, Brother delegates, with all confidence do I appeal to you, to stand by us in this, the greatest struggle, in which we are engaged, since we have come under British Rule; and to such an appeal made by afflicted Bengal to United India, there can be but one reply and it will be a reply which will voice forth the predominating sentiment of this great gathering, viz., that we are all brothers moved by mutual grievances, cemented by mutual hopes, animated by mutual aspirations and linked together by a common destiny, and that as brothers, we are resolved to fight for each other's rights and stand by one another in the hour of our darkest misfortune. *Bande Mataram* ! (shouts of *Bande Mataram).*

Speech at Madras Session

Welcome to Lord Curzon

Mr. President, Ladies and Gentlemen, I have the honour to move the following resolution:

That this Congress accords a respectful welcome to Lord Curzon, notes with gratitude his Lordship's words of sympathy for the people of India, and trusts the policy of progress and confidence in the people which has characterised the best traditions of British rule in this country will be followed during his Lordship's tenure of office in India, and authorises the President to wire the foregoing Resolution to His Lordship at Bombay.

Brother-Delegates, I wish this resolution had been a little more specific and had entered a little more into those outlines of policy which it is a matter of the first importance that we should at the earliest opportunity lay prominently before the coming Viceroy. With this reservation I will say that I cannot think of a resolution more appropriate, more suitable to the circumstances in which we find ourselves, or one more entirely in conformity with the temper and the genius of this great national gathering. We are the loyal representatives of a thoroughly loyal and law-abiding people, *(Hear, hear)* and as such, it is our duty and our privilege alike to accord a cordial greeting to the representative of our august Sovereign, *(cheers)* a Sovereign whose reign has been an era of unmixed beneficence and progress, whose domestic virtues and personal worth, the noblest adornments of exalted rank, have shed a lustre even upon the grandest throne in the world, *(cheers.)* Has our character for loyalty even been disputed or our right to approach the Sovereign impugned? A dark cloud of suspicion hung for some little time over a certain section of our countrymen in the Western Presidency in relation to certain recent events. So exalted a functionary as the Secretary of State from his place in Parliament had declared that an organised conspiracy had been formed among a certain section of the people of Poona *(shame)* with a view to subvert British rule. That suspicion, that dark cloud of suspicion has now been dispelled by the light, of accomplished events.

The Judge who tried Damodar Chapekar has distinctly declared from the Bench that the evidence has not disclosed the shadow of a shade of suspicion in support of the conspiracy theory, which must now disappear like the baseless fabric of a vision. (Hear, hear.) No, Sir, we are loyal, untenable loyal, loyal from sentiment, loyal from conviction, loyal from immemorial usage, loyal from deep-rooted anxiety for the wellbeing of future generations. (*Cheers*), The sentiment is there rooted in our heart of hearts, accentuated and intensified by the highest considerations of expediency; for we recognise the truth— recognise it with all the warmth and fervour of our ardent oriental temperaments— we recognise the truth that with the permanence of British rule in India are bound up the best prospects of our political advancement, our continued progress along those lines which are most conducive to our happiness, most conducive to the free and adequate development of those faculties which, in the fullness of time and under the ordering of Providence, will ensure to our people their destined place amongst the nationalities of the earth. *(Cheers).* No doubt, now and then there are deviations on the part of our rulers from the straight path of duty—temporary fluctuations — doubts and misgivings followed by the adoption of a reactionary policy. But these are passing aberrations like the eccentricities of the planets which soon resume their normal course in obedience to an inexorable law which secures to the universe its order, its beauty and its harmony. I am sorry I have to say it—but say I must—that at the present moment our rulers are passing through a temporary frenzy. (Mr. Wacha—influenza). My friend Mr. Wacha calls it influenza. I accept the emendation. But whatever it be—be it frenzy or be it influenza—no matter by what term we choose to call it—it will soon disappear in the pursuit of a beneficent policy. It is in this hope and in this confidence that we approach the representative of our Sovereign. I am not deterred—no, not even deterred for a moment—by the objection that was raised sometime ago by a high functionary, the highest in India—Lord Dufierin—that we are a microscopic minority. If that is a disability, we suffer from it in common with our rulers. They also are a microscopic minority, (Laughter)—a mere speck in the vast ocean of Indian interests—and if a microscopic minority may rule, a microscopic minority may also represent the bulk of their Countrymen, *(Cheers.)*

But whether a microscopic minority or not, we are the representatives of our countrymen, the elect of the people, chosen by a diviner mandate than that which belongs to any ruling authority; for those whom we seek to represent are the bone of our bone, the flesh of our flesh, people speaking the same language and breathing the same sentiments, worshipping the same God, nurtured amid the same traditions and aspirations *(Cheers)*. If we cannot represent them, then who else can? *(No, No)* We the much-despised educated community of India, are the natural leaders of the unenlightened masses, and therefore we have a right to approach the representative of our Sovereign.

Our cordial greeting to him has about it the elements of universality, for it embodies the judgement of the entire country, the Congress being the representative body which reflects the sentiments and feelings of the great Indian community. *(Checks)*. The resolution speaks of the words of sympathy which Lord Curzon has professed for the people of India. Sympathy is the keynote of the many utterances of his Lordship since he has been designated to his high office. At one of the great meetings held almost immediately after the announcement of his appointment, he made use of these words, "I love India, its people, its history, its Government, the complexities of its civilization and its life." At another meeting he said that the essential qualifications of a Viceroy of India were "courage and sympathy." And at a third meeting, (I am not giving you the dates which are not necessary, but the facts can be verified)—at a third meeting he spoke of the interests of India as being sacred to him. Now I ask, Brother-Delegates, how many of you regard those interests, the interests of your motherland as tiered, and how many of you that regard them in that light are prepared to treat them as such and to sanctify them by the touch of a higher reverence? *(Cries of All)* Yes, our country is sacred, To us it is the land of our sires consecrated by their ashes, endeared to us by a thousand tender associations—it is the land of our birth—it is the destined inheritance of our children and our children's children. It recalls to mind the past—the dim misty past, when India was peopled by the Vedic *Riskis* of old, who in the morning of the world sang those hymns which represent the first yearnings of infant humanity towards the divine ideal. It recalls the past; it places us in touch with the present; it embraces the future. The past, the present, the future blend together in one mighty majestic stream rolling onwards to the borders of eternity *(Cheers.* The procession of the ages pass before us in mute silence. The splendid achievements of the past, the dismal failures of the present, the brilliant possibilities of the future, all lie revealed to our astonished gaze. A Viceroy who is able to touch our imagination in this fashion, people it with images so consolatory and yet so suggestive, at once so soothing to our sense of national self-respect and so pregnant with ideals of reform, Mr. President, I venture to submit, is entitled to the lasting gratitude of our countrymen. *(Cheers),* Well, Sir, I think I speak the sense of this Congress, and I will venture to add, of the country at large, if I say that it is our earnest hope and prayer that when Lord Curzon retires from his high office after his administration, the regrets of a great community may follow him to his distant home and that his name may be inseparably linked in our minds with the names of the greatest of Anglo-Indian Statesmen and administrators whose memories excite and will continue to excite, to remotest ages, the gratitude of our people—the names of a Bentinck, a Canning and a Ripon. *(Cheers.)*

Sir, the Resolution expresses the hope that Lord Curzon during his Viceroyalty may adopt a policy of beneficence and progress, illustrative of the best traditions of the British Government. It is this policy which is the proudest monument of British rule. It is its strongest bulwark in times of Difficulty and danger. Well, Sir, when we express the hope that Lord Curzon may adopt a policy of progress and beneficence we make a suggestion. We suggest that a different policy is now being followed. We go further and we say the reverse of a policy of progress is now being pursued *(Laughter.)* Lord Curzon' is astute enough to read between the lines, and I only wish that we were astute enough to be a little more outspoken. *(Laughter.)* I do not see why you should, in praising the august representative of our Sovereign, omit representing to him the grievances we suffer from.

However, that may be, that which with us is a matter of frequent complaint, is the inadequate attention bestowed by those responsible for the good Government of the country upon questions of domestic reform and improvement. I say the eyes of our rulers are exclusively fixed upon the frontiers. The spectre of Russian invasion haunts their imagination. *(Laughter.)* The gentlest breeze wafted across the Hindu Kush suggests to their excited imagination the Cossaks and their little ponies. The Russians have not come. They never will come, and if we are animated, as I hope and trust we shall always be, by sentiments of warm attachment to the British connection, then let them come—the brave hearts of a loyal people will offer the strongest bulwark against foreign invasion. *(Cheers.)* The frontier craze has assumed the proportions of a disease. It was not so fifteen or twenty years ago.

It was not so ten years ago. Lord Ripon devoted the whole of his time and attention to the grave considerations of domestic policy and internal improvement. He repealed the Vernacular Press Act, extended the great principle of Lord Self-Government, and gave a wider impetus to the employment of natives of India in the higher offices under Government by appointing a distinguished countryman of ours, Sir R. C. Mitter, to the high office of Chief Justice of Bengal. When Lord Dufferin came, the frontier fever had taken firm possession of our rulers. *(Laughter.)* But still he found time to appoint the Public Service Commission, and also to recommend the expansion of the Legislative Councils. In the clays of Lord Lansdowne the fever had reached almost its culminating point. None the less Lord Lansdowne was able to give partial effect to the recommendations of the Public Service

Commission and to enlarge the Councils and reconstitute them upon a somewhat representative basis. Show me a single measure of domestic reform or improvement which has distinguished the reign of the retiring Viceroy. I am unable to find it. (Cries of " No, No') You may, but I am unable to find it. (" No, No.) I road the newspapers and the current events with considerable interest and attention, because I am paid to read them, being the Editor of a newspaper. I do not make this a matter of complaint. Far be it from me to say one word by way of disparagement in relation to the noble man for whose personal wroth I have the greatest possible respect and who in the course of the next few days will have laid down the reins of his great office. But there is the broad fact that not a single measure of reform has distinguished the Viceroyalty which is about to close.

No doubt there were great difficulties in his way—difficulties created by the famine and the plague —but the spirit of reform is always watchful and always ready to assert itself at the earliest possible opportunity, and let it be borne in mind that is was amid the dark clays of the Indian Mutiny, when the Empire was being shaken to its very foundations by one of the most direful tragedies enacted on the stage of Indian History, that the Universities of Calcutta, Madras and Bombay were established by the orders of Sir Charles Wood, who was then Secretary of State for India. Our hope and prayer is that Lord Curzon may devote greater attention to the internal Government of the country with the result that it may be his lasting glory and honour to settle once for all the grave financial complications which are fast gathering round the Government of India; for the fact cannot be too often repeated that it is upon the soundness of the financial position —my friend Mr. Wacha sympathises with me—the structure of national prosperity must be made to rest.

The financial test is the crucial test. "Tell me" said Sir John Bright in one of his speeches, "what the financial position of a country is and I will tell you all about its Government and the condition of the people". Judged by this test we are deplorably wanting. Our resources are frittered away on the frontiers. The commonest domestic improvements have to be starved. The cash balances of the Provincial Governments have vanished almost to nothing. You know perfectly well—I am speaking of Bengal—that under the orders of the Secretary of State, the cash balance of that Province has to be maintained at the sum of 20 lakhs of Rupees. Last year what was the cash balance we had? Five lakhs, not twenty. Bombay was still worse. It had a big cipher as balance. (Laughter.) What does all this mean? It means the utter blasting of all hopes of improvement upon which the happiness, the contentment and the prosperity of the people depend. No amount of the financial jugglery in connection with the currency question will avail to remove the gravity of the situation. *(Hear, Hear.)* Firmness and decision and the comprehensive grasp of genuine statesmanship are the qualifications that are needed; and Lord Curzon promises to deal with this grave problem in this spirt, for I will quote what he said at one of the recent demonstrations held in his honour.

He said, "India is ill-equipped with the material, industrial and educational resources which are so necessary to her career, and the Government should be so conducted that she may by slow and sure degree, expand to the full measure of her growth.' She can only expand to the full measure of her growth if the financial position permits it. Well, Gentlemen, I will not take up much more of your time. We pray that a policy of beneficence and confidence in the people may be inaugurated under Lord Curzon's auspices, We pray that the policy of reaction which finds favour with the Government of India at the present moment may be reversed. A wave of reaction is sweeping across the high places of the Government and is infecting the Councils of the Empire. Even in England the same spirit has made itself felt. It is visible in the extinction, the practical extinction, of the Liberal party. In India, this spirit of reaction has inscribed one of the darkest chapters in our History, a chapter as black as any to be found in the dismal records of India, a chapter marked by such events as the incarceration of Mr. Tilak *(Shame)* the deportation of the Natu Brothers, the enactment of the Sedition Law, the installation of the Poona Press Committee, and last but not least, the preparation of the Calcutta Municipal Bill. *(Shame)* Gentlemen, I think I express the sense of the Congress and, I may add of the country too, when I say that we all rejoice that Mr. Tilak has been released (Loud Cheers).

We should have still more rejoiced if he had not been convicted at all (Cheer), if that travesty of law and justice which was enacted 18 months ago had never been enacted. You will have a Resolution regarding the Natu Brothers and repeal of the Sedition Law. I call upon this Congress to repeat those resolutions year after year until the Act and the Regulations have been wiped off the Statute Book. *(Cheers).* As for the Poona Press Committee I know very little about it, except that it has been whispered to me that the object is a very noble and beneficent one. It is to pour into the ears of the benighted editors of the Native Press of Poona all the knowledge, all the information, all the wisdom which we know flows so spontaneously so gratuitously from official sources. *(Laughter).* If that be the object, why should we not have such committees in Madras? What have we done, what sins are we guilty of, that we should be thus condemned? But jest apart, the object is, I understand, not to instruct or to enlighten but to muzzle and to gag. If that be the object, we ought to protest against the measure in season and out of season. We do not want these committees. We can do without them. We have done without them for the last too years, and we shall be able to do without them for the next 100 years.

Now, Mr. President, with your permission and only for a few minutes let me draw your attention to the Calcutta Municipal Bill, in which I feel the strongest possible interest. Brother-Delegates, who enjoy the boon of Local Self-Government, we want your sympathy in our misfortune, your cooperation in the great struggle for civic freedom in which we are engaged at the present moment, and I am sure you will extend to us both that sympathy and that cooperation in the terrible crisis which has overwhelmed us. The Bill has filled the citizens of Calcutta with alarm and anxiety. Sir John Woodburn said from his place the other day in the Council Chamber that it is a perfectly innocuous measure and that it only means the re-adjustment and not the extinction of the system of Local Self-Government in Calcutta. For Sir John Woodburn personally I have the greatest possible respect. His is a charming personality. It is impossible to meet him without being impressed by the many great qualities of his head and heart. But, in justice to myself I am bound to enter my protest against this view of the matter. What does Local Self-Government mean? If it means anything it means this—the administration of local concerns by the representatives of the local community. But when you take all power away from these representatives and vest it in the hands of the officials and their friends, what becomes of Local Self-Government? It is gone. It has ceased to exist. The object of the Bill is to transfer all authority from the representatives of the people and vest it in the official head of the executive who is a Government nominee, and in a General Committee the vast majority of whom—two thirds—are to be nominated by the Government and by the trading and mercantile communities. What is the justification for this revolutionary measure? Absolutely none. Have the Commissioners been tried and found wanting? On the contrary successive Lieutenant-Governors belonging to the most opposite schools and professing party. He stands high above all parties, reconciling the jarring conflicts of opposing factions. No matter whether he is Whig or Tory, Liberal or Conservative, he stands pledged to no creed, no dogma, no doctrine, and save and except that which will preserve immaculate the sacred interests of India. . He is above all the repository of British justice and British honour. Therefore with confidence do we appeal to Lord Curzon, that he will not permit a departure from the traditionary policy of this realm, that he will preserve in the true spirit of Conservatism those canons of statesmanship which lie embalmed in the lives of distinguished Anglo-Indian rulers, and which, more than the armies of England more than her navy, more than her illimitable resources, have contributed to build, to expand and solidify this vast, this stupendous, this colossal fabric of imperial sway which while it excites the envy and admiration of foreigners, is regarded by us, the children of the soil, as an inscrutable dispensation of divine Providence ordained for the wisest, the noblest and the truest purposes of human history. *(Loud and continued cheers).*

Speech at Ahmedabad Session

[Extracts from the Presidential Address to the Eighteenth Indian National Congress.]

Today we begin our work for the 18th Session of the Congress. The mind is spontaneously carried back to the past—to the trials we have endured, the labours we have undergone, the disappointments we have suffered and the triumphs we have achieved. The time has not yet arrived for the final judgement, for the authoritative pronouncement of history, on the work of the Congress. "We are yet in the midst of our journey, our long, long journey, through the dreary wilderness, which is to carry us to the Promised Land. Many will not enter Cannan. Some choice spirits have already fallen in the grand march. Many more will yet fall before the journey is accomplished, and the darkness of night gives place to the dawning of the new day. Some of us who cannot promise to ourselves length of days can-only anticipate with the eye of hope and faith the blessings of the Promised Land. But the faith that is in us is strong and the hope that inspires us is proof against all disappointments—all reverses. . . . For myself, I believe the Congress has a divine mission. It is a dispensation of Almighty God for the unification of our peoples and the permanence of British Rule in India. Thus, we are gathered together under the aegis of an organisation, political in its character and in its scope, but drawing its strength and its inspiration from those ever-living fountains which flow from the footsteps of the throne of 'the Supreme. Sree Krishna—the divinely inspired Sree Krishna—who has his shrine at Dwaraka in the province of Gujarat, in his memorable admonition to Arjuna on the battlefield of *Kurukshettra,* said *Karma* is *Dharma* (good deeds constitute religion). Is there a holier *Dharma,* a nobler religion, a diviner mandate than that which enjoins that our most sacred duty, which has a paramountcy over all others, is the duty which we owe to the land of our birth.

What are trials—what are delays, what are disappointments—what is even the cankering worry of vexation in the presence of this consecrated task? They are the necessary incidents of the struggle in which we are engaged—the ordeal of fire through which we must pass—the purificatory stage which must qualify us for the rich blessings that are in store for us. They will strengthen our fibre, develop our manhood, ennoble our nature and call forth whatever is good and great in us. The chastening discipline of adverse circumstances is the necessary apprenticeship for the splendid heritage to which we aspire. We ought to thank God on our knees that the discipline is so mild—the sacrifice entailed so insignificant. Bead the ensanguined pages of history—note the trial of blood and the hecatombs of mangled corpses, with all their attendant horror and desolation, which mark the line along which victorious movements of reform have careered their triumphant way. We live in happier times, under more fortunate circumstances, under the beneficent protection of a rule which affords the widest tolerance for the widest differences of opinion and evinces the deepest sympathy for all constitutional struggles for constitutional liberty. Yet we have our trials and our disappointments. The forces of reaction are now in the ascendant. The cause of progress has met with a temporary check. For the moment we have been worsted. For the moment we have lost ground. But we Congressmen never confess to a defeat. We bide our time in firm conviction that the turn in the tide will come and the forces which make for progress will once again assert their undisputed supremacy.

New Imperialism

Imperialism blocks the way. Imperialism is now the prevailing creed. Imperialism has always been synonymous with autocracy—the rule of the despotic monarch or of the victorious general who has made his way to sovereign power; In ancient Rome, as in modern France, imperialism meant the supersession of popular authority and the establishment of one-man authority. British imperialism does not, indeed, imply the extinction of British democracy. It means Self-Government for Great Britain and her Colonies, autocracy for the rest of the British Empire. "What its latent possibilities are, it is impossible to say. "Whether in its further developments, it will lead to the curtailment of democratic power is one of those secrets, hidden deep in the bosom of time, regarding which even the most confident predictions may prove futile. But all history bears record that the extension of territory and power over subject-races is fatal to popular Government. Let us not however speculate about the future. British imperialism implies the closer union—the more intimate federation between the English-speaking subjects of His Majesty. We stand outside the pale of this federation. We are not admitted into this inner sanctuary of freedom. "We are not permitted to enter the threshold of the Holy of Holies. "We are privileged only to serve and to admire from a distance. As a part of the Empire, we sent out troops to South Africa, and they saved Natal. As a part of the Empire, we sent out troops to China, and our Indian soldiery planted the imperial standard on the walls of Pekin. Our loyalty is admittedly so genuine, so deep and so intensely realistic that oven the Secretary of State had no conception of it. All the same, we are not the children of the Empire, entitled to its great constitutional privileges We are Uitlandors in the land of our birth, worse than helots in the British Colonies. Our countrymen in Natal, whose splendid behaviour during the late war was the subject of unstinted praise, are still exposed to a degrading treatment which is galling to their self-respect and discreditable to those who permit it. British Imperialism, which is so sedulous in exalting British greatness, is not equally sedulous in opening up to us the possibilities of our greatness.

British Imperialism, which seeks to draw closer the bonds of union between the Mother Country and the Colonies, has literally done nothing to cement the loyalty or deepen the gratitude of the Indian people. I would welcome an Imperialism which would draw us nearer to Britain by the ties of a common citizenship and which would enhance out self-respect, by making us feel that we are participators in the priceless heritage of British freedom. But we are as yet very far from this blessed consummation. In India, imperialism has accentuated the forces of reaction and has engendered a love of pomp and show which is apt to encourage extravagance and to withdraw attention from the graver issues of domestic reform.

We are not, therefore, prepared to welcome the new imperialism in the form and garb in which it appeal's to us. Mr. Gladstone's sound liberalism, with its strenuous persistency in the matter of domestic reform, with its thorough recognition of England's grave responsibilities in relation to India, would be to us far more acceptable than the imperialism which indulges in expensive pageants, but which turns a deaf ear to the cry of the coolies in the tea-gardens of Assam, which often subordinates our interests to other interests and which relies for the justification of Imperial Rule upon the pomp and circumstances of Imperial grandeur rather than upon the solid and enduring basis of truly Imperial achievements a desponding view of the SITUATIONS. I have no doubt that the now Imperialism is a passing fronzy which the robust common sense of the English people will oro long discountonanen and that it will soon pass away, like so many of the varying fashions of the hour. But whether that be so or not, wo must bo sleepless in our vigilance and unremitting in our efforts to stem the tide and roll it back. We have no reason to bo discouraged. The p:tst ought to stimulate us and to stir us into now enthusiasm. Ours is a brilliant record. I claim for the Congress that it has never taken up a question which it has not brought within the range, of practical politics. You took up the question of the separation of Judicial and Executive functions.

The matter is awaiting consideration by the Government of India. You agitated for the reform of the Police. A Police Commission is now sitting to elaborate a scheme of Police reform. You insisted in season and out of season upon the wider employment of our countrymen in the Public Service. The Public Service Commission was appointed; and though much remains to bo done, the impetus you communicated to the movement will produce enduring results. Last but not least, your crowning triumph was the introduction of the representative principle into the government of the country. But your moral achievements, though less palpable and obtrusive, are a yet more enduring monument of your public spirit and your self-sacrificing devotion. You have created a now spirit and have infused a new life into our people. You have brought together the varied and multitudinous races and peoples of India upon the same common platform and have inspired them with a lofty sense of patriotism. You have established a new bond of sympathy among them and their leaders and have taught them the value of organised effort, with all the infinite possibilities of good attendant thereon.

Yet there are those who take a desponding view of the situation—who say that our methods are faulty, that we have wasted our time and our breath, or that at any rate the results achieved have not been commensurate to the sacrifices incurred or the efforts put forth. There are moments of despondency which cast their shadows over the noblest and most unselfish natures, when the spirit appalled at the sacrifices made, shrinks back at the contemplation of the disproportioned achievement. In the anguish of disappointment, the question is asked—what is the good of persevering in methods and in sacrifices, when the outturn of them all is so insignificant? I confess I have nothing but respect for those who, with the utmost goodwill for the Congress and ceaseless in their endeavours for the public weal, are sometimes apt to indulge in these sombre reflections. But I ask—has the time come for the final judgement? I ask—are the results inadequate? Even if they were—what are 20 years in the life-time of a nation? The triumphs of liberty are not won in a day. Liberty is a jealous goddess, exacting in her worship and claiming from her votaries prolonged and assiduous devotion.

Bead history. Learn from it the estimable lesson of patience and fortitude and the self-sacrificing devotion which a constitutional struggle for constitutional liberty involves. Need I impress these lessons upon a people who have presented to the world the noblest examples of these virtues? Every page of Indian history is resplendent with the touch of self-abnegation. In seasons of doubt and despair when darkness thickens upon us, when the journey before us seems to be long and weary and the soul sinks under the accumulating pressure of adverse circumstances, may we not turn for inspiration and guidance to those great teachers of our race—those master-spirits—who, with their hearts aglow with the divine enthusiasm, triumphed over the failing spirit, faced disappointment and persecution with the serenity of a higher faith and lived to witness the complete realisation of their ideals? Chaitanya and Nanak, Tukaram and Ram Das lift the mind high up to the sublimer eminence of the divine ideal.

India of the past is rich in these examples. May we not hope for their successors in the India of the present, in the India of the Congress, in the India under-British Rule, with all the stirring influences of Western life and civilization? The responsibilities of the present, the hopes of the future, the glories of the past ought all to inspire us with the noblest enthusiasm to serve our country. Is there a land more worthy of service and sacrifice? Where is a Land more interesting, more venerated in antiquity, more rich in historic traditions, in the wealth of religious, ethical and spiritual conceptions which have left an enduring impress on the civilization of mankind? India is the cradle of true religions. It is the holy land of the East. Here knowledge first lit her torch. Here, in the morning of the world, the Vedic Rishis sang those hymns which represent the first yearnings of infant humanity towards the divine ideal. Here was developed a literature and a language which still excites the admiration of mankind—a philosophy which pondered deep over the problems of life and evolved solutions which satisfied the highest yearnings of the loftiest minds. Here man first essayed to solve the mystery of life, and the solution wrapped in the rich colours of the poetic imagination and clothed with the deeper significance of a higher spiritual idea, bids fair, thanks to the genius of the greatest Hindu scientist of the age, to be accepted by the world of Science. From our shores went forth those missionaries who fired with apostolic fervour travelled the wilds of Asia and established the ascendancy of that faith which is the law and the religion of the nations of the Far East. Japan is our spiritual pupil. China and Siberia and the islands of the Eastern Archipelago turn with reverend eyes to the land where was born the prophet of their faith. Our pupils have out-distanced us; and where are we, hesitating, doubting, calculating, casting up moral results to satisfy ourselves that our gains have been commensurate to our sacrifices. Such, indeed, has not been the Royal road to political enfranchisement. The triumphs of liberty have not thus beet) won. Japan is an object-lesson which thrusts itself upon the view. Read her history; note her wonderful self-sacrifice, her marvellous power of adaptation, her patience, her fortitude, her indomitable energy and persistency, and let the most ancient of Eastern nations derive inspiration and guidance from the youngest which has solved the riddle of Astatic life and has harmonised the conservatism of the East with the progressive forces of the West.

Our Constitutional Struggle for Constitutional Liberty

In the constitutional struggle in which we are on gaged, we need the cooperation of Englishmen and the sympathies of civilized mankind. It is England which has created in us those political aspirations, the fruition of which we now claim. Our minds are steeped in the literature of the West. Our souls have been stirred by the great models of public virtue which the pages of English history so freely present. Where shall we find the like of them? Their sobriety, their moderation, their lofty enthusiasm for the public good, their scrupulous regard for constitutional principles, even amid the fervour and heat of revolutionary agitation, place them in the front-rank of political leaders for all times and all countries. Englishmen must accept the consequences of their own policy—they must cheerfully face the results which are the outcome of their own beneficent administration. They must gratify the ambitions which they have roused and adopt their administration to the altered conditions which are of their own creation. They have taught us the principle of adaptation to the environments of our situation, and they must not complain, if we, as their apt pupils, invite them to reduce to practice what they enforce by precept. We have no higher aspiration than that we should be admitted into the great confederacy of self-governing States, of which England is the august mother.

We recognise that the journey towards the destined goal must necessarily be slow and that the blessed consummation can only be attained after prolonged preparation and laborious apprenticeship. But a beginning has to be made, and there seems to be no more suitable time for inaugurating this new departure, for 'commemorating the new epoch which is to mark the birth of an emancipated people than the commencement of the new reign. The Victorian epoch, memorable in its achievements, is still more memorable' in the generous impulse to human freedom which it communicated in all parts of the world.

We shared in full measure the beneficent influences of that epoch. Our disabilities were removed, our rights were extended, higher ideals of Government were recognised and a loftier conception of Imperial duty enforced. A succession of illustrious Viceroys imparted an impetus to this beneficent movement. To the now sovereign, to whom on his Coronation we offer our respectful salutation, we appeal to commemorate his glorious reign by the still further expansion of those great traditions of government which have been consecrated by the example of his illustrious mother and which more than British arms have contributed to the solidarity of the British Empire. We have a special claim upon His Majesty's sympathetic consideration. The recollections of his Indian tour are to us a grateful memory. We know him. Ho knows us. His Majesty's feelings in relation to us are those of personal goodwill. Our feelings in relation to him are those of personal attachment 'and devotion, emphasised by the recollections of his general warmth, his truly kingly benignity, his royal condescension, his generous concern for all placed under his authority. The words of the Proclamation are still ringing in our oars, consecrated by the breath of his illustrious mother, our late Sovereign. We have His Majesty's assurance that he proposes to follow the traditions of his great mother, that the happiness of the Princes and the People of India would be to him matters of the highest concern, and that he would endeavour to promote the general wellbeing of all classes of his Indian subjects, and thus merit their loyalty and affection.

We appeal to His Majesty to enthrone himself in the hearts of his people and to lay broad and deep the foundations of his Empire, by the practical recognition of the claims of the people of India to a just and adequate representation in the government of their country, by the gradual extension to them of that system of Self-Government which has been the invariable accompaniment of British power and civilization and which, "wherever it has been granted, has been the strongest bulwark of Imperial Rule and has evoked the affectionate gratitude of the people.

Under the beneficent influences of Self-Government, alien races, hostile to the British connection, have been transformed into loyal and devoted subjects of the Crown. We need no such transformation. We are already sufficiently loyal, sufficiently attached to the British connection. But we are anxious for the permanence of British rule—for our permanent incorporation into the great confederacy of the British Empire. The present system of government necessarily represents a transition. All history proclaims the truth that autocratic power is devoid of the elements of permanence, and that authority to be permanent must be planted deep in the affections of the people and derive its sustaining breath from the vitalising springs of popular enthusiasm. The voice of the people is the voice of God and the right divine to rule is based on the unchangeable foundations of the love, the gratitude, the devotion of a people, evoked by the consciousness that they share with their rulers the responsibilities of government. Despotic rule represents a stage of transition, the period of which should not be unnecessarily prolonged. But transition must give place to permanence. All signs point to the conclusion that the period of reconstruction has now arrived. The forces are there; the materials-are there; they lie in shapeless masses. Where is the man of genius who will communicate to them the vital spark and transform them into a new and a higher and a grander organisation, suited to our present requirements and fraught with the hopes of a higher life for us and a nobler era for British Rule in India? The statesmanship of Mr. Chamberlain, bent upon work of reconstruction and consolidation in South Africa, will pale before the splendour of this crowning achievement. We plead for the permanence of British rule in India. "We plead for the gradual reconstruction of that ancient and venerated system, which has given to India law and order and the elements of stable peace. We plead for justice and liberty—for equal rights and enlarged privileges—for our participation in the citizenship of the Empire; and I am sure we do not plead in vain; for the Empire thus reconstituted and reorganised will be stronger, nobler, richer far, in the love, the gratitude, the enthusiastic devotion of a happy and contented people, rejoicing in their indissoluble union with England and glorying in the rich promises of steady and uninterrupted progress towards their high destinies, under the protection and guidance of that great people, to whom in the counsels of Providence has been assigned the high mission and the consecrated task of disseminating among the nations of the earth, the great, the priceless, the inestimable blessing of constitutional liberty.

Speech at Lucknow Session

Calcutta Municipal Act

Mr. President, Brother-Delegates, Ladies and Gentlemen,—I have the honour to move this resolution:

Resolution VII.—That this Congress expresses its disapproval of the reactionary policy, subversive of Local Self-government, as evidenced by the passing of the Calcutta Municipal Act, in the face of the unanimous opposition of the people of India, and by the introduction into the Legislative Council of Bombay of a similar measure which will have the effect of seriously jeopardising the principle of Local Self-government.

Sir, when last year we met in Congress in the town of Madras we ventured to express the hope that it might be our privilege to associate the name and fame of Lord Curzon with the reversal of that policy of repression and reaction which is now in the ascendant in the Councils of the Empire. I cannot say that hope has been realised, I am bound to say that hope has not been realised. For within the last twelve months we have had two notable illustrations of this policy of repression in the enactment of the Calcutta Municipal Bill and in the introduction into the Legislative Council of Bombay of a measure which will emasculate the principle of Local Self-government in the towns of Western India *(hear, hear)*. But, Sir, I think I speak the sense of this great Congress, the sense of the representatives of educated India, when I say that we distinctly decline to associate Lord Curzon with that policy which our conscience has disapproved and our judgement condemned *(hear, hear)*. In free and constitutional countries the sovereign stands isolated and apart from the conflict of parties and the bitterness of feelings which these conflicts awaken.

The sovereign belongs to no party, is identified with no class interest *(heat, hear), the* sovereign stands high above all parties, the jarring note of party strife does not reach his ears *(cheers)*. From his exalted position animated by that inspiration which such a position cannot fail to impart he holds the scales evenly and dispenses impartial justice between man and man and party and party, *(cheers)*. The position of the Viceroy of India is different. As the representative of the sovereign, he is the fountain of mercy, the repository of honour, the dispenser of justice *(hear, hear)* but there is also another side to his character. He is the first, the most trusted, the highest, the most responsible minister of the crown *(cheers)*, directing, guiding and controlling the policy of the State, infusing into it a large-hearted benevolence, relaxing the rigour of our cast-iron system, accentuating, deepening, and strengthening those forces which make for progress and which, though their career might be temporarily arrested are hound to assert themselves in this world of God's providence for all things tend steadily, though slowly, towards the approximation of that perfection which is the divine ideal *(cheers)*. We recognise the dual character of the Viceroy as the representative of the Sovereign, and also as the first minister of the crown. We are fully alive to the peculiarity of the situation. All the same we decline, distinctly decline on your behalf, to associate him with that policy which this resolution condemns. For, as the representative of the sovereign, it will be our duty later on to approach him for the redress of that grievance of which we complain in this resolution. We dissociate him from that policy, we separate the man from the ruler, *(hear, hear)*, the statesman from the politician, for we cannot bring ourselves to believe that a ruler so sympathetic in his utterances, so generous, so large-hearted in his views, so keenly appreciative of the situation, will countenance a policy opposed to the best traditions of British rule, repugnant to all that is highest, noblest and truest in British statesmanship. For the echoes of his great speech are still ringing in our ears, that speech which he delivered to an assembly of the Taluqdars of Oudh. Read that speech, contrast that speech with the policy. The speech, how noble, how generous, how sympathetic; the policy, how narrow, how illiberal, how un-English *(hear, hear)*.

English veracity, said the Viceroy, in language which I hope will be written upon the portals of Government House, upon the entrance to the Council Chambers, *(hear, hear)*, has done more to establish and preserve this Oriental Empire than English valour and discipline *(cheers)*. Never were truer things said in more felicitous languages and if English veracity has won this 'great Empire for India, might we not look confidently forward for a practical illustration of that principle in the policy of the Viceroy *(cheers)* Might we not hope for a reconcilement between principle and policy, and between word and action?

Might we not confidently look forward to that highest form of veracity which is the crowning glory of statesmanship, which has built, which has consolidated and which has extended this vast fabric of Imperial sway? Sir, if you will permit me for one moment as I am on this subject of the Viceroy, I will refer to a local application of that speech which seems to have a significant bearing upon the demonstration which seems to have taken place in this city. The Viceroy dealt with special emphasis, in that speech addressed to the Taluqdars of Oudh, upon the lesson, the great lessen of reconciliation, between those who, on the occasion of the Mutiny, fought on behalf of the British Government and those who took another part. Now, Sir, in this historic city, in this home of reconciliation, our hosts— for I conceive that we are the guests of the whole city, that Lucknow is treating to great act of hospitality, that is Hindus Mohammedans and even officials, Congressmen and anti-congressmen, we are all the guests of them, *(cheers)*—our hosts have raised a discordant note. They have ventured to record a protest against this movement. I am anxious and willing to speak of them in terms of the utmost possible respect. I am prepared to extend to them the courtesy and consideration which they have denied to us. But I will say this— that it is rather late in the day to record a protest against the movement which has now been fifteen years in existence *(cheers)*, to which official recognition has been extended and whose undying achievements are written in characters of gold in the enduring pages of modern Indian History *(cheers). There* never was a more striking personality among the Mohammedans of this generation than the late Sir Syed Ahmed.

Of Sir Syed Ahmed I desire to speak in terms of the greatest admiration and praise. We worship in opposite temples, we belong to opposing political systems whatever our differences might have been, they lie entombed in that crave where remain the illustrious dead *(cheers)*. Sir Syed Ahmed founded, a Patriotic Association with a view to oppose the Congress movement. He was supported by official and retired Anglo-Indian gentlemen. He had his supporters in England. Despite all his influence, all the official backing and all the weight of his striking personality, what has become of the Patriotic Association? *(laughter)* The ways of all things of evil is all sham, all show, all impositions, all possibilities of achievements; their counterparts in the eternal verity of things are bound to disappear in this world of God's providence *(cheers)*. That is written in the book of time with the pencil of the Almighty. One observation I wish to make with reference to the statement which was published authoritatively by the Raja of Mahmoodabad. He is a personal friend of mine. I have the honour of his acquaintance. I have not used the past tense because I hope he will consider me still a friend. He said that the Congress propaganda was a propaganda calculated to spread disaffection among our people *(laughter)*. Well Sir, if that was the case, we should have been taken under the merciful protection of the Government long ago, specially after the revision of the sedition law *(cheers)*. I wish to tell the Taluqdars of Oudh and all whom it may concern, I wish to remind them of what Sir Antony MacDonnel said *(cheers)* with reference to this movement in 1890. He was then Chief Commissioner of the Central Provinces. He was approached by the Chairman of our Reception Committee, and the words of Sir Antony MacDonell were repeated by the Chairman of the Reception Committee in his speech. Sir Antony MacDonnel said, "I will not think worse or better of anybody for having attended the Congress". Sir, who are the men who are bitterly disloyal,—the men, who say ditto to every measure of Government, who in season and out of season sing the praise of Government, who suffer and suffer in silence of bitterness of unknown and unknownable sorrow, or those who, like myself, give expression, frank expression, to our grievances, raise the danger signal and call the attention of Government and press for remedy? Sir, in these days I am perfectly sure the greatest bulwark of all the Governments, be they indigenous or be they foreign, is the contentment, the gratitude and the affection of the people *(cheers)*. How is the affection of the people to be won except by the removal of grievances, and how are the people to remove their grievances except by the adoption of constitutional means or the adoption of revolutionary measures.

We are the friends of Reform because we are enemies of Revolution *(cheers)*. We have made our choice, let our enemies make theirs *(laughter and cheers)*. Do they wish to belong to our camp, or do they wish to belong to the camp of revolutions *(hear, hear)*. There is no intermediary step between Reform and Revolution *(cheers)*. For you must enlist yourselves under the banner of Reform or you must take your place behind the standard of Revolt and Revolution *(cheers)*. I am certain of this that if the Congress existed in the early fifties there would have been no mutiny. I am certain of this for the educated India with all their influence and with all their knowledge would have enlightened the Government, and would have instructed and warned their countrymen and thus they would have averted the greatest danger of this century. Sir, I am afraid I must beg your pardon for making a digression *(cries of "go on" "go on")*. It is unavoidable. The Resolution condemns only the system. The Resolution condemns the Municipal Bill of Calcutta and also the Bombay Municipal Bill as being opposed to the principle of local self-government. Sir, local self-government is the gift of our rulers, but it is in entire accord with those deep-seated instincts which are fostered by the Panchayet system and by our village communities. These village communities, as you, Sir, reminded us the other day in your presidential speech, carry the mind back to the dawn of human civilization when the ancestors of the self-governing nations of the earth at the present moment were roaming in the primitive forests in a state of primitive simplicity.

The antiquity of this institution cannot be called in question. To them was accorded a measure of self-government which the British Government has not thought fit to confer upon the Municipalities of British India. They not only looked after the sanitations and conservancy of the villages concerned, but they administered justice and controlled the police. Therefore those village communities were complete self-governing unities. My point is this—that we enjoyed in ancient India a much larger measure of Self-Government than the British Government has given to us, and even what was given to us is to be taken away from us *(shame)*.

In 1881 the boon of Local Self-government was conferred upon the Municipal towns of India under the great resolution of Lord Ripon. *(Cheers)*. In 1876 the Corporation of Calcutta was reconstituted upon a popular basis. It is a remarkable fact, expressive of the irony of fate and the changes of opinion which are constantly taking place, that the great resolution of Lord Ripon appeared over the signature of Mr. Alexander Mackenzie, who as Sir Alexander Mackenzie was the author, originator, framer and inspirer of the Calcutta Municipal Bill which has destroyed civic rights of my native town *(Shame)*. I think it is a matter for unutterable shame. Sir Alexander Mackenzie is a name well-known to my friends of the Central Provinces, He is the author of the enhancement which they so bitterly, complain of. He is a man of universal fame *(laughter)*, well-known in Bengal, well-known in the Central Provinces. His fame spread even to the other side of the waters. He is well-known in Burma. Now he has retired. I am bound to say that the blessings of the community do not follow him or afford him any consolation in the clays of his retirement *(laughter).* It i equally remarkable, that it was a Conservative Viceroy and a Conservative Secretary of State who conferred the boon; of local self-government upon the people of Calcutta. It is a Conservative Viceroy and a Conservative Secretary of State who withdraw that right. These are changes to which even the best and the noblest of men are exposed.

Therefore, Sir, it comes to this—that we in Calcutta have been in possession of the boon of local self-government for nearly a quarter of a century. Why should it be now withdrawn from us? Sir Douglas Straight, who is now the Editor of the Pall Mall Gazette, said that a concession once made should never be withdrawn except under the stress of paramount necessity. Whether such a necessity exists in this case is the question. But on the very threshold of the enquiry, I am confronted with a difficulty, for we have it, on the authority of no less distinguished a personage than Sir John Woodburn, that the Calcutta Municipal Bill is a perfectly innocuous measure and that all it does is a re-adjustment and not entinction of the principle of local self-government.

Well, Sir, if that is so, I have no grievance. I am prepared for re-adjustment provided that in the process of re-adjustment the whole thing does not disappear (*laughter).* Is that readjustment or extinction? Let us examine the matter a little closely. What is local self-government such as the ordinary folks who do not breath the pure atmosphere of officialism in the heights of Olympus, conceive? What is local self-government? Local self-government is the administration of local affairs by the representatives of the local public. If all authority, all power, all patronage is withdrawn from the local representatives, and is vested in the representatives of official hierarchy and European merchants, I conceive local self-government is at an end. Is that the real state of things? What is the present Constitution of Calcutta? What was the old Constitution of Calcutta? Let us for a moment examine the matter. Under the old Constitution the Corporation of Calcutta consisted of 75 members, two-third of whom were elected—mark two-third were elected. Under the new Constitution, which is said to be a readjustment and not an extinction, not two-third but only half of the members are to be elected, and then there is to be an official Chairman who will have a vote and a casting vote in case of equality of votes. Therefore, Sir, we are driven to this position. There will be 26 members, official members, against 5 popular members, under the best of circumstances and conditions. In any case, the popular representatives will be in a minority. They may be in a hopeless minority, because at the ward elections some members might be returned who are officials.

Therefore, I am right in the contention that the effect of this transformation is transferring the entire authority from the hands of the representatives of ratepayers into the hands of officials of Government and their friends. Is that local self-government? *(cries of no,* no*).* Of course not. But the Government stands convicted out of its own mouth. Mr. Baker, the Municipal Secretary who was in charge of the Bill in the Bengal Legislative Council, not once, not twice, not thrice, but repeated!', as often as he opened his mouth, said that the main object of the Bill was to cut down the preponderance of Hindus in the Corporation.

What have the poor Hindus done to merit this treatment at the hands of the Government? Is this the reward for the devotion and faithful allegiance to the principle of local self-government in the capital of the Indian Empire? But the very proposal involves the extinction of local self-government, for the Hindus constitute the bulk of the population. They own the bulk of the assessable property in Calcutta and they pay the bulk of the taxes to the Municipal funds. Therefore, in accordance with the elementary principle of local self-government, they ought to have a preponderant voice in the deliberations of the Corporation *(cheers).* For John Stuart Mill, as the greatest exponent of representative institutions whom this century witnessed, has laid down this principle,—'that local representation is to be proportionate to the payment of local taxes'; and therefore the Hindus are entitled to a preponderant majority in the Corporation. But, Sir, we are made to the Outlanders in the city of our birth. The English people at the present moment are waging a war for the purpose of securing to the Outlanders of South Africa the inestimable boon of political franchise. We "citizens of Calcutta, had enjoyed that franchise for a period of 25 years and now the British government, with strange inconsistency, is about to deprive us of that franchise (*shame*) for which they are fighting at the point of the sword in South Africa. The Englishman newspaper, a great friend of the people of this country (*laughter*), said the other day in speaking of the Congress that it was like a band of Africanders in South Africa, with this difference, that it is less mischievous than the band of Africanders. We distinctly decline to be compared to the Africanders. We are the loyal subjects of the Crown (*hear, hear*), wedded, inexorably wedded, to the British connection, which is a pledge and guarantee of the attainment of justice and political freedom (*cheers*). We are no Africanders but we are Outlanders, and there is no Secretary of State of the type of Joseph Chamberlain to enforce our claims. That is the true state of things.

Now, Sir, let me ask what is the justification for this change of the law. Were the Commissioners tried and found wanting? Was it ever alleged that the Municipal administration of Calcutta had failed? If that was so, the position would be unassailable, but absolutely there is no evidence of failure. On the contrary, then, whatever evidence there is, it points to a distinctly opposite conclusion. Compare Calcutta when it was under the direct administration of Government with what it now is after quarter of a century of administration by elected Commissioners.

My opinion is of no consequence, I am under trial. I am a member—I was a member of the Corporation, but I resigned my seat—I am under trial, and my opinion is of no consequence. Let me place before you the opinion of an individual who attained the highest official position in these provinces, and who might be supposed to be rather partial than otherwise to the Government Mr. afterwards Sir John Strachey made a report on the sanitary condition of Calcutta when it was under the administration, of Government. And what did he say? It was one of the filthiest cities in Asia, a scandal and disgrace to civilized administration. That was the opinion of Sir John Strachey when Calcutta was not under direct administration of the Commissioners. Now let me quote another authority on my side. Sir Henry Fowler, speaking from his place in the House of Commons on the occasion of a recent debate, said he had failed to discover any evidence of failure on the part of the elected Commissioners in the charge of their duties *(hear, hear)*. Therefore, Sir, I am entitled to hold that the Corporation of Calcutta, the greatest self-governing institution in the Indian Empire, has been superseded without a shadow or semblance of any justification *(shame)*; and if the Government thought that it had 'a strong case, why did not put it to the test of scrutiny by the appointment of a commission of enquiry? *(hear, hear)*.

The greatest criminal with his hands wreaking with the blood of his murdered victim, is allowed a trial before a constituted tribunal of the land, but the most illustrious self-governing institution in the Indian Empire, with a brilliant record of past achievements is to be condemned without even a show or semblance of enquiry *(shame)*. Does that commend itself to your sense of justice? There was ample time for a commission of enquiry, for the application—I am afraid I am taking up too much of your time *(cries of "go on", "go on")*—to the Government "for the introduction of the Calcutta Municipal Bill was made in June 1897 and the Rill itself was introduced in March 1898, There was ample time. We prayed again and again but prayed in vain.

The Government treated our prayer with stolid indifference The same prayer was repeated from the floor of the House of Commons by Mr. Herbert Robert *(hear, hear)*, to whom we cannot be sufficiently grateful for his endeavours in this connection *(cheers)*; and then a reply was given which, I think, affords an apt illustration of the saying, that language was given rather to conceal than express one's thoughts in. What was the reply that Lord George Hamilton gave? I wish, Sir (Mr. President), you were a member of the House on that occasion. I wish Dadabhai Naoroji were there (three cheers for Dadabhai Naoroji were given) to point out the utter Hollowness and insincerity of that reply. The reply was this. It is no use instituting an enquiry into the Municipal administration of Calcutta; such a thing is being done by the select committee of the Bengal Legislative Council, and that it would be highly improper on the part of the House of Commons to take the matter out of the hands of a self-governing body like the Bengal Legislative Council. The only drawback about that statement is, that it is misleading and inaccurate from beginning to end *(laughter)*. In the first place, no enquiry was made by the Select Committee into the Municipal Administration of Calcutta. I was a member of that Select Committee *(laughter)* and therefore I know perfectly well what we were about. "But the rules of the council, the principle having been affirmed, all that the Select Committee had to do was to consider details. It was beyond the legal competence of the Select Committee to enter into the broader question of efficiency or otherwise of the Municipal administration of Calcutta; and I may say that Mr. Narendra Nath Sen and myself were the dissenting members on the Calcutta Municipal Bill and strongly protested against this observation of Lord George Hamilton. We have received no reply to that part of our statement. I wish to draw the attention of the Congress to the other part of the statement that the Bengal Legislative Council is a self-governing body. Against this statement I have the advantage of getting officials to fight with officials, and I am saved the trouble of saying one word or other. I am an impartial, unbiassed" spectator to the affray that goes on between officials.

In this connection we have again the statement of Mr. Baker, the Municipal Secretary in charge of the Bill. He said from his place in the Bengal Legislative Council that the Council was a subordinate legislature (my friend will bear me out), and that it was a part of the duty of that Council to register the mandates of the Supreme Government *(shame)*. What becomes of this glorious fabric of a self-governing body, enquiry into the Municipal administration of Calcutta? Well Sir, therefore, there was no enquiry at all, and we have been condemned unheard. We have a grievance. Our civic rights have been taken away from us. The other part of the resolution has reference to Bombay. I will not dwell on that part of the resolution, but I cannot help contrasting our fate with the fate of the people of the North-Western Provinces under the beneficent administration of the Sir Antony MacDonnell *(cheers)*. Here, instead of curtailment, there is to be an enlargement, so far as I have been able to understand the principle of local self-government, in the greater powers which it is proposed to confer upon the District Boards. Mark the difference which is shown to public opinion by Sir Antony MacDonnell in the matter of the Land Bill and contrast it with the contemptuous treatment which public opinion received in Bengal to the hands of the local authorities; and yet, Sir, if there is any measure more than another which needs the support of public opinion it is the Municipal measures. Municipal measures deal with the question of sanitation, and sanitary measures can never be carried out except with the aid of the public opinion unequivocally condemned the Bill. Lord Ripon said in one of his-speeches as Chancellor of the University that public opinion in India is destined soon to become the irresistible, unresisted master of the Government Lord Curzon, in that admirable speech which he delivered to the Taluqdars of Oudh, expressed himself in similar language. He said: "Indeed, to me, it seems that the times have passed by when the rulers can air way live with impunity amids the clouds of Olympus. They must descend from hilltops and visit the haunts of men. They must speak to the people in their own tongue, must be one in purpose and heart with the people.

Only then will they justify their high station. Only then will their authority be free from challenge, because it will be founded upon trust. " The rulers and the ruled must be one in purpose and one in heart. I ask is there solidarity of opinion and sentiment between the rulers and the ruled? Have we not again and again prayed for the release of the Natu Brothers? And it was not until the other day that the Natu Brothers were released! Have we not again and again prayed for the withdrawal of the Calcutta Municipal Bill? And the Calcutta Municipal Bill has been passed into law *(shame)*. I am afraid there is no renewal of confidence, no interchange of opinion between the rulers and the ruled. I am afraid both the rulers and the ruled stand isolated and apart in grim and solemn silence. The gulf is widening. That which ought to be regarded as the proudest memorial of British rule is considered to be a grievance; that educated natives of India should claim equality in political rights with Englishmen can only be due to the education which the English have been instrumental in introducing into our midst, which constitutes the noblest achievements of British rule in India *(cheers).* Our rulers seem to think differently. There is reaction in their policy, reaction in opinion, reaction along the entire line, reaction is the order of the day. But those great and illustrious men who founded the Anglo-Indian Empire, who preserved and consolidated it, were animated by different motives.

Miss Garland, in that admirable speech to which we all listened with so much interest and with no little admiration, quoted an extract from the speech—the memorable speech— of Lord Macaulay, delivered 60 years ago in the House of Commons, when with a gift of prophetic inspiration, he anticipated the advent of that day when the Indian subjects of the Crown, educated in Western learning, would crave for Western institutions; and Macaulay went on to say that, that would be the proudest day in the annals of England *(cheers),* Our rulers at the present moment seem to take a different view of the situation. They would fain undo the past They would fain roll back the tide of progress which has set in with such irresistible force. Shall we let them, shall we permit them to prove false to the noblest traditions of their own race? *(cries of "No" "No").* No, *servius Romanus sum* was the boast of the ancient world.

Our boast is a greater one. We are British subjects. We are part and parcel of the greatest Empire that the world has ever seen, an Empire over which the sun never sets. May the glories of that Empire in the domain of human freedom and justice never fade ! We are the subjects of this great Empire, over which floats the high flag of freedom. We are the subjects of an Empire where a bondsman can never breathe, and where the moment he sets his foot his chains burst around him and he stands forth a regenerated and emancipated being *(cheers).* Citizens of this great Empire, an Empire whose watchword is freedom, which has emancipated the Negro slaves, which has taught great lessons of constitutional liberty to the rest of the world-citizens of this great Empire, ought we to submit to our rights being filched away from us? Ought we to submit to our being reduced to the rank of hewers of wood and drawers of water in our own country *(No, No)?* Ought we permit the brand of the helot to be placed upon us and leave an ignoble bruise? *(No, No)?* Standing in this historic city within a measurable distance of that place which was the scene of the trials and sufferings, the ultimate triumph of the greatest hero of the Hindu legend and of his greater consort, let us resolve in our heart of hearts and do what lies in our power to check this current of reactionary policy, to win back our lost position, to continue our glorious and patriotic work until it culminates in the attainment by us in full measure *(cheers)* of the inestimable blessings of British freedom and British justice. I am certain of this; that in this holy endeavour we shall claim and we shall receive in full measure the active cooperation of our own countrymen, and even of our political opponents. We shall receive the sympathies of civilized humanity, and above all the blessings of Almighty Providence *(hear, hear).* I have an undying faith in the justice of our cause, a burning conviction that, though darkness may cloud our prospects, the day of deliverance and enfranchisement is near at hand *(cheers).* We may meet with a temporary reverse, a temporary check.

The flag which we hold aloft, the banner of the Congress, might drop from our sinking hands, but others will rise up who will take up that flag and lead us to triumphant victory *(hear, hear and cheers).* I am sure patience is what is needed—not the patience of despair and despondency— but patience which is born of faith consecrated by the living genius of self-sacrifice. What are 30 years, or even half a century in the lifetime of nations or communities? Read the histories of the great European living nations, mark the patience, the marvellous patience, fortitude, indomitable resolve to serve their country, to promote her honour, her glory, her truest interest. Remember that we are confronted with one of the gravest crises in our history. If we succumb to that crisis, the political enfranchisement of our people will be infinitely postponed, but if we rise above it, we shall have done a service to India, to England and to humanity, and shall have covered ourselves with undying renown. Act bravely before man and God, so that when you are dead and gone, and when you are beyond reproach or praise, it may be said of you that you were tried in the balance and not found wanting, that you overcame grave crisis, that you surmounted all difficulties and that you planted the Empire deep in the affections, love and gratitude of the people by securing to them the inestimable blessings of British rule, sanctified by the principles of constitutional justice and freedom, and then you will have done your duty to the country and to the Congress (*loud and continued cheers*).

Appointment of an English Agency

"That an Agency be appointed in England for the purpose of organising, in concert with the British Committee of the Congress, public meetings for the dissemination of information on Indian Subjects and that funds be raised for that purpose,"—said:—I have the honour to move the Resolution which has just been read out by the President. I will not read it again. It is unnecessary to do so; but, Sir, before I proceed with the Resolution it is necessary to clear my ground to make a few observations with a view to guard against any misconception which the circumstances of the case might suggest. It is not for one moment to be supposed that we desire to suppress or in any way interfere with or encroach upon the functions of the British Committee of the National Congress (*hear, hear*).

Sir, our feelings towards that Committee and its respected head Sir William Wedderburn (*cheers*) are feelings of respect, gratitude and admiration for the manifold services which they have rendered to us for the last 12 years or more. We are incapable, in Congress assembled, of passing any Resolution which would in any way interfere with those responsible duties that we have entrusted them with. That is not the scope of this Resolution at all Sir, if it were the scope of the Resolution, I, for my part would be no party to it; and that is not the scope of this Resolution will be further apparent from the fact that our respected President, Mr. Dutt, has undertaken to supervise and control the work of the agency for the coming year (*cheer*). The British Committee of the National Congress will bring questions before the Parliament and assist in the organisation work referred to in this Resolution. Sir, it is a matter of the first importance, the work to which reference is made in this resolution. It is a matter of the utmost necessity, that we should from year to year, if possible, send deputations to England with a view to address the electors. When I was in England in 1890 with my friend Mr. Mudholkar, we were asked in the different centres which we visited to come back again, and to repeat those deputations from year to year *(cheers)*. We were not able to do it. These deputations were given up. In 1897 I addressed some meetings. Mr. A. M. Bose *(cheers)* addressed some meetings in 1898. What is now proposed is to reduce this work to a system by the appointment of an agency like this and Sir, I cannot exaggerate the importance of this work. You hold these meetings here from year to year. You spend large sums of money, but your voice will be like that of one crying in the wilderness; unless and until the cry that you utter here is repeated from the platforms of the British meetings, through the columns of British newspapers, and from the floor of the House of Commons *(cheers)*. Our agitation here must be supplemented to the agitation in England. It is not enough for us to hold this demonstration once a year. It is necessary, it possible, to send deputations to England every year.

Sir, speaking of the British public I will say this, viz., that Indian gentlemen addressing British audiences cannot find more sympathetic listeners to their grievances anywhere in the world *(hear, hear)*. I have studied the English character such as that character in all its strength and all its weakness, and I will say that, if an appeal is made to their instinct of justice and freedom such an appeal is bound to meet with the warmest response *(cheers)*. The greatest reforms of this century have all been brought about by direct appeals to the British people. What has brought the home rule within the range of practical politics? I may say the Irish people held meeting in Dublin and elsewhere, but it was not until the agitation was transferred from Ireland to England and Scotland and meetings on the question held all over the towns of the United Kingdom of England and Scotland that the conscience of England was roused to do that measures of justice towards the Irish people to which they are entitled. We must follow the same methods, and Sir, if we are to follow the same methods money is needed for the purpose. You must come out with your subscriptions. Sir, there is something peculiarly appropriate in my making this appeal for funds. I am a Brahman. By instinct, by tradition, by association, I am a beggar *(laughter)*. The hereditary qualities which are in me have been perfected by practice *(laughter)*. I have been here upon this platform more than once appealing to you for funds, and now I extend my Brahminical hand in order that you may come forward with money, hard cash, not the plaudits with which you greet may speeches, hard cash in order that we may be able to start this agency at once. How many are you here—two to three thousand? *(a voice of " more ")*. The more, the better. Well is it difficult to raise ten or fifteen thousand rupees amongst us just now at the present moment? I made an appeal to a great meeting of the Congress and a sum of Rs. 6000 was subscribed on the spot. Is it to be said now that our enthusiasm is on the wane, that the men of 1899 are not the men of 1889, that instead of our feelings of patriotism being accentuated, being strengthened and deepened, these feelings are on the wane! I hope and trust not. I hope that the early fervour and the early enthusiasm which animated us in the early days of the Congress have not been spent, and that we are animated by that fervour and enthusiasm and that under its impulse—overwhelming impulse—we are capable of making those sacrifices which the interests, the supreme interests of our country, demand *(cheers)*. Come forward with your subscriptions.

Act like men before God and Man. It is no use recording resolutions. You must reduce speech into action. The charge that you bring against the Government of this country is that it makes promises which it never redeems. The charge that is brought against you is that you talk big, but that your actions any incommensurate with your profession. Disprove that charge; prove yourself worthy of this great National movement. There is no royal road to the attainment of political liberty. You must pay the price. Fortunate you are that you are under a Government so benign that a heavy price of blood has not to be paid. Pay therefore the price of money and thank God that this is the only price which you are called upon to pay. If you do not pay that price, then I will say this,—"Dissolve this Congress, go back to your homes" (*cries of no, no*). Don't talk of National movement, be helots that you are, and that you will always be, unless and until you have learnt the noble lesson of self-sacrifice. Come-forward with your subscriptions. Let each man subscribe what he can, and when you have set an example in that direction, then and only then you will have established your claim to that political enfranchisement towards which our hopes and aspirations are directed. I have to announce that Mr. Mudolkar has subscribed Rs. 50 *(Cheers)*.

Speech at Banaras Session

Mr. President and brother delegates, when I entered this hall I had not the smallest idea that it would be necessary for me to speak to any resolution of today. But the mandate has been laid upon me by your President that I should speak. Ten years ago when I was the President of the Poona Congress, I vehemently entered my protest against the mandate theory of Lord George Hamilton. By a bitter irony of fate the person who recorded that protest is now called upon to eat his own words and submit to the mandate of our worthy President I obey because I regard you, Sir, the elect of the people, as occupying, in my estimation, and I venture to think, in the estimation of the people of India, a higher and more responsible, and a certainly more affectionate place than the Secretary of State can ever hold (cheers).

I am in strong sympathy with this resolution. It used to be my own resolution on this platform from years' end to years' end. From the year 1886 up till the year 1892, if you turn up the Congress reports, you will find me either as a mover or seconder or supporter of the resolution in connection with the Expansion of the Councils. And in 1890, along with my friends Mr. Mubolkar, Mr. Joshi, Mr. Norton and one or two others, we went on a deputation to England. We held many public meetings and we had the high honour of a personal interview with Mr. Gladstone (cheers). Sir, as the result of that deputation, as the result of the persistent efforts of the Congress, the Statute of 1892 was passed (cheers). We are dissatisfied with that Statute. It is a halting measure; an imperfect and inadequate measure of reform. It was bound to be so. Who were the authors of that measure? Who was the arch pontiff of that occasion? The authors of that measure were the Tory Government of that day, and the arch pontiff and high priest who ushered it into existence was George Nathaniel Curzon (shame). For he was then the Under-Secretary of State in the India Office. If that were a measure which was introduced by a Liberal Government, if that was a measure which had behind it the inspiration of Mr. Gladstone's broad-minded Liberalism, I venture to think it would have been a very different piece of Legislation from what it has been.

Sir, for 8 years I had the honour of a seat in the Bengal Legislative Council. I know how hopeless a task it was to fight the battles of the people and the country against the solid phalanx of officialism arrayed against you in the Councils of the Empire. We had the Calcutta Municipal Bill. It was a very important measure. We introduced amendment after amendment What was the fate of these amendments? We lost most of them — 90 per cent of them. The so per cent that were carried were carried not at the point of the bayonet but by the grace and condescension of our rulers and in a moment of irritation, I will not conceal the fact from you—addressing the Lieutenant-Governor, Sir John Woodburn, I said from my place in the Bengal Council. "Sir, what is the good of our being here? We come and place before you amendment after amendment only to be thrown out of this Council. If you have made up your mind about passing the bill in its entirety you have only to intimate the fact and we say good-bye and depart from this place." That was what I said. After that indignant protest a few of our amendments were allowed to be passed. I think, Sir, we make a very moderate demand. We say we want a further expansion of the Councils. In Bengal, a population of seventy millions, is represented by how many members do you think? By ten. I suppose the same unsatisfactory state of things prevails everywhere, wherever we have a Legislative Council. We want better and a more adequate representation of the non-official element. I would like to suggest that a member should be taken from each district. I should like to suggest that we should have the right, as you suggest in the resolution, of dividing the Councils upon financial questions.

The financial debates of the Councils are of an academic order. We make speeches. They listen attentively sometimes, and sometimes impatiently. The matters are promised to be considered. Sir, as a matter of fact, very little attention is paid to them. Here is: our demand, but whether we shall have a further expansion of the Councils or not will depend upon ourselves. A noble people cannot have an ignoble Government and an ignoble people cannot have the gift of representative institutions. If you make up your mind, determined and resolved in the depths of your heart to emancipate yourselves from your present condition of serfdom, then rise to the height of your manhood, assert your rights as responsible citizens (cheers). If you are determined to do that, the Councils will be expanded, but not otherwise. If you hold this meeting and then go to sleep for the next 12 months, do nothing, think nothing about your country the chances of your political emancipation are remote. Therefore; brother-delegates, I ask you all once again to take the firm resolution in your mind that you will begin the agitation in this connection, continue the agitation through good report and evil report, determined to emancipate yourselves and obtain for your country and for your countrymen the priceless gift of representative institutions, then the blessing of God will be with you and your labours will be crowned with the success which they deserve (loud and continued applause.)

Speech at Lahore Session

Employment of Indians in Minor Civil Services

Mr. President, Brother-Delegates, Ladies and gentlemen, I have the honour to propose " That the Congress regrets the practical exclusion of natives of India from the higher appointments in the Police, the Public Works, the State Railways, the Opium, the Customs, the Telegraph, the Survey and other Departments and prays that full justice be done to the claims of the people of India in regard to their appointments." I rejoice that the Congress has taken up this question after having achieved if not a victory, something at any rate in the nature of a victory in regard to our agitation for the wider employment of our countrymen in the covenanted appointments. The three important questions which constitute the chief planks in the Congress platform may briefly be summarised as follows:—The wider employment of our people in the Public Service, the introduction of Representative element into the Government of the country and the purification of the system of the administration of justice by the separation of judicial and executive functions. The first of these questions stands on a different footing from the others. The first of these questions to which this resolution refers is to us a heritage consecrated by illustrious names not the least noble of which in Bombay are Dadabhai Naoroji, and Naoroji Fardunji, and in Bengal the late Kristodas Pal and the late Ram Gopal Ghose (Hear, hear and cheers). The policy of the English Rulers in regard to the wider employment of our people in the responsible offices of trust and responsibility, is, I regret to say, very different from the policy of the Roman Conquerors of old or from the policy of the Great Akbar. In the case of Akbar the grandsons of those who had fought against his grandfather became, the Captains of his army, the governors of his provinces, the confidential advisers of their sovereign. It was a policy of trust and confidence, a policy which was sanctified by the immediate successors of the great Moghul. I am sorry that in the case of the English Rulers of India it is no longer a policy of trust and confidence but a policy largely leavened by mistrust and suspicion (voices "shame"). Our fathers, as soon as their intellects were stimulated and their self-respect enhanced by the education which they received at the hands of Englishmen, commenced an agitation against their exclusion from these high offices. Therefore this question conies to us in the light of a heritage. In carrying on this agitation, we are performing an act of filial piety, rendering obeisance to the adored memories of our sires, for, what memories in Bengal are more loved or respected than those of Kristodas Pal and Ram Gopal Ghose, or what name excites greater reverence in Bombay than that of Dadabhai Naoroji.

This claim for the wider employment of our countrymen in the higher offices of state is not only founded upon considerations of justice and expediency, but upon the promises of our beloved sovereign. We take our stand upon the proclamation, the Magna Charta of our rights and liberties. The proclamation, the whole proclamation, and nothing" but the proclamation (Hear, hear)—that is our watchword and battle-cry (Cheers). Armed with the proclamation, we are invincible in battle, and undaunted in defeat Taking our stand upon the proclamation we appeal to the rulers of India in the name of our sovereign to redeem its gracious promises. We hold ourselves as the trustees of the honour and the dignity of our beloved *Empress* (Cheers). And those who defer the fulfilment of the sacred obligations contained in that proclamation do harm to the honour and the reputation of our beloved sovereign (Cheers).

That is our attitude; and Sir, the Queen was pleased to say in that proclamation in one of those passages which have often been quoted, "It is our further will that so far may be our subjects of whatever race or creed be freely admitted into all offices the duties of which they are qualified by their education, ability and integrity duly to discharge." And to add to the solemnity of this gracious promise, Her Majesty invoked the blessing of Almighty Providence:—"May the God of all power grant to us strength by which we may carry out these, our solemn declarations." These are the words, the concluding words of that proclamation; and yet, Sir, I regret to have to say there are people—they shall be nameless, who venture to be little this proclamation. I have read with amazement a discussion which took place not long ago at Simla in connection with this matter. It was said by a distinguished authority that if the Romans had ruled in India, the proclamation would never have been issued. I know not whether it would have been issued or not. It selves no useful purpose to speculate upon potentialities and possibilities.

But this I do know that if the Romans had ruled in India the inestimable boon of Roman citizenship would have been extended to the remotest corners of the Empire (Cheers). Further, I do know this—that if the Roman Emperor had issued a proclamation, no Roman proconsul would have dared to set it at defiance (Hear, hear and cheers) but I ask the question, "Is that proclamation to be regarded as merely a ceremonial document or as having a binding force upon the consciences and the, policy of our rulers?" In this connection we have the highest authority in support of the view which must be gratifying to every patriotic Indian, that the proclamation is obligatory upon the rulers of India and that as we consider it to be our great charter, the English Civil Service must regard it also as the table of their commandments. In this view I can do nothing better than quote to you the observation of Lord Lansdowne belonging to the party which is now in power. Speaking from his place in the Viceregal Council in 1893 he said. "The Proclamation I regard as being absolutely obligatory upon the Government of India" (Hear, hear). Lord Ripon, as you know perfectly well, went a step further. He said;—" It is not a ceremonial document, it is not a diplomatic instrument. If it is obligatory at all, it is obligatory upon those in respect of whom it is addressed." Sir, the other day at a banquet which was given to the Governor-Elect of Madras, Lord James Hereford, a name well-known to the legal world in England, called the attention of the Governor-Elect to the terms of the proclamation and said "it was the Magna Charta of the people of India in the highest sense. It was also the table of commandments of the Indian Civil Service." Therefore, it comes to this that the terms of the proclamation are obligatory upon the rulers of the land. Have they been fulfilled? I do not wish to say one word which would militate against the honour of my sovereign or the reputation of the British Government in India. But the fact remains that the highest Indian authorities have, from time to time, declared that the terms of the proclamation remain inadequately redeemed.

Lord Lytton, speaking as the Chancellor of the University of Calcutta, said that her Gracious Majesty's proclamation had not been fulfilled and in a document, a confidential letter which he addressed to the Secretary of State, letter no longer confidential, he used much stronger language. He said that the people of India had been cheated out of their dues and the Government had broken to the hope the words of promise which they had uttered to the ear. We are therefore justified in holding that the terms of the proclamation have not been carried out.

But if some thing like an honest effort has been made to secure the wider employment of our people in the ranks of the Covenanted Civil Service, little or nothing has been done so far as their employment in the higher offices of what are called the minor civil services is concerned. These minor civil services include the Postal department, the Telegraph department, the Police department, the Survey and Customs department, the State and other Railway departments. If you look at the statistics connected with these Departments you will find that the higher offices, the bulk of the higher offices—I should not be guilty of the smallest exaggeration if I say that at least 80 per cent of the higher offices—are filled by Europeans and Anglo-Indians (A voice " Anglo-Indian Imperialists "), Imperialists, somebody says. They may be imperialists or not, but, at any rate, these departments constitute the close preserve, the absolute monopoly of these gentlemen. We are excluded. And why? Because of our race. Our colour is our disqualification. (Loud cheers). And the terms of the proclamation, which lays down that merit is to be the sole test of qualification, are ignored. Let me give you some facts and figures in order to bring home to your minds the gross injustice done to our countrymen in the matter of their employment in these high offices. I will take in the first instance the figures for the Forest department. Do not be alarmed. I am not going to read all this (referring to a bundle of papers he had in hand). My figures refer to Bengal and what is true of Bengal is more or less true of other provinces. Bear in mind that in Bengal we are a race of talkers, we have carried agitation to the point of perfection (Cheers).

We have got our press, which is powerful, we have our various associations, and if anywhere Government is prone to defer to public opinion it is in Bengal, Therefore if this state of things is a scandal in Bengal, it must be a graver scandal all over the other provinces. Here are the facts. In the Forest department there are 24 high appointments in the Bengal Establishment. How many do you think of these appointments are held by Europeans, how many by Indians? Make a guess, you will never be able, to come near the mark, (a voice, "zero.") Only two are held by Indians and twenty-two are held by Anglo-Indians. And the Public Service Commission made a recommendation to the effect that the Government of India should keep in view the policy of training in India men qualified to take charge of the higher administrative appointments so as to avoid, as far as possible, the necessity for expanding the Imperial Branch of the Service. This was said in 1887. We are in the year of grace 1900. 13 years have elapsed and little or nothing has been done so far as this recommendation of the commission is concerned.

Now, Sir, let us take the Opium Department. This is a departments out of which you know Government derives a handsome revenue. There are 77 appointments in the higher grades of the Opium Department. Of these 77, only 8 are held by Indians. But the Public Service Commission recommended that the future recruitment of the department should be subject to the general principle of equality of treatment of all classes of Her Majesty's Indian subjects. Magnificent equality! (Laughter). Eight out of seventy seven appointments are held by native Indians.

Take again the Customs Department. There are 33 superior appointments in this Department. How many of these appointments do you think are held by natives of India? Of the 33, 31 are filled by Europeans and two by natives, and yet Sir Charles Trevelyan when he was Finance-Minister observed that the whole of the appointments of the Customs Department might be filled by Indians. Then there is the Preventive Branch of the Customs Department. There are 157 appointments in it. How many do you think are held by Indians? I now turn to my friend who made that guess on the last occasion. How many, Sir, do you think of these appointments are held by Indians? You will be right if you say zero (voices " shame "). It is an unutterable shame; it is a disgrace of the most scandalous kind that these 157 appointments should all be held by persons who are not Indians. Then we have got 100 apprentices in this branch. How many do you think of these are natives of India? Will you guess again, Sir? An Eurasian gentleman whose mother was European and whose father was Mohammedan holds one of these appointments. It is most interesting statistics.

Take again the Survey Department. How many of the higher appointments do you think are held by Indians in this department? I will turn to my friend again. All by Europeans, and none by Indians. Cipher is the order of the day here (Hear, hear, voices "shame"). Sir, in this connection, with your permission, I desire to read a statement which was made by the Head of the Survey Department, and which was laid before the Public Service Commission. It was a statement drawn up by Colonel Du Pre. Look at the attitude of this Head of the Survey Department in regard to the admission of Indians into his Department. This is what he says:—"I may here remark, that my numerous inspections show me that the tendency of the European surveyors is to stand and look while the natives are made to do" the drawing and hand-printing as if they thought themselves above it. This is a mistake and cannot be permitted for the future. Besides it is suicidal for the European to admit that natives can do any one thing better than themselves and they should of course claim to be superior in everything and only allow natives to perform subordinate duties. In my own old parties I never permitted a native to touch a theodolite or to do computation on the principle of the triangulation or scientific system. All this work must be done by Europeans". If that be the attitude of the Head of the Department, it is no wonder that there is not a single native gentleman filling any high appointment in that Department.

Take the Jail Department. Who are the inmates of Her Majesty's prisons? I suppose most of them are our countrymen. Some of us have some experience of Jail life (Laughter) My distinguished friend (pointing to Mr. Tilak) has more recent experience of it (cries of "shame"). My experience is somewhat antiquated. It dates so far back as the year 1883. Be that as it may, the bulk of prisoners in our Jails are Indians, be they respectable or otherwise; and yet the Jailors of the more important Jails and the Superintendents of Jails are all Europeans, absolutely unacquainted with the feelings and prejudices of the inmates of the Jails. Of course an anomaly of this kind was bound to make an impression upon the minds of members of the Public Service Commission and they accordingly made the recommendation that in future when Superintendents of Jails (Central and District) were not Medical Officers, more opportunity might be given to natives of India to show their fitness for these appointments. How has this recommendation been attended to? Not a single native of India is Superintendent of any Jail in Bengal (cries of "shame"). I do not know what the state of things is in the Punjab (a voice, none). Well, it is much the same in the Punjab. I should have expected it. I suppose it is the same everywhere else.

Next take the Telegraph Department. There are 29 superior appointments in the Telegraph Department. With 4 exceptions, all these are held by Europeans.

I will deal lastly with the Police. In the Bengal Police out of 102 superior appointments, only 5 are held by natives of India, and I believe there is only one Indian District Superintendent of Police; and in the Calcutta Police out of 10 superior appointments, only one, that of Detective Superintendent,—is held by a native of India. The Public Service Commission in this connection remarked 'that "endeavours should be made to introduce a reasonable proportion of natives of India, regard being had to the efficiency of the service." Reasonable proportion means 5 in a 100

(Laughter). And, Sir, in this connection, I cannot but advert with a sense of the deepest indignation to our exclusion from the competitive examination which is held in London for recruitment to the office of Assistant Superintendent of Police, on the ground of our race (cries of "shame"). We are permitted to compete at the open competitive examination for the Civil Service of India. We are permitted to compete at the examination in connection with Coopers Hill; we are permitted to compete at the examination in connection with the Telegraph and Forest Departments.

But from this particular examination, natives of India are excluded because they are natives of India. Just as I was about to speak to this resolution, a very important piece of information bearing on this point was given to me by my distinguished friend, Sirdar Mansingh. The representative of a distinguished family, inheriting the martial instincts of his race, he wanted to compete at this examination to qualify himself as Assistant Superintendent of Police in the Punjab. And what was the answer that was vouchsafed to his request? Natives of India are debarred from appearing at this examination (cries of " shame"). I think, Sir, it is a matter of unutterable shame. There ought to go forth from this Congress the strongest protest against, an exclusion based upon considerations which impose an indignity on our race. And are we an inferior race—we who have taught the nations of the earth a code of ethics and a system of morality which to this day excites the admiration of mankind. (Prolonged cheers and loud applause). I hope and trust that we shall continue this agitation. We have allowed ourselves, to sleep over this matter and the Government is only too ready to sleep when you allow them.

Let us resolve in our heart of hearts that this agitation for the wider employment of our countrymen in the higher appointments in connection with the minor Civil Services will be continued with all the enthusiasm, the earnestness, and the patriotic fervour of which this Congress is capable. Let us make it one of the principal plan! in the congress platform. Let it go forth that we are not content with our exclusion from these appointment. The victory will assuredly be ours. The history of constitutional agitation in India is full of inspiration and encouragement. We pressed for the repeal of the Vernacular Press Act and the Vernacular Press Act was repealed. We pressed for the reform of the Councils and the Councils have been reformed. Let us go on in this glorious work. It is a noble work; it is a sanctified duty, and the God of all nations will vouchsafe to us in his infinite mercy that triumph to which we are entitled. Is there any power on earth which can resist the onset of patriotic fervour? (Hear, hear). When our hearts are aglow with that divine enthusiasm which words cannot express, we are more powerful than even the most omnipotent Government in the world. The moral laws of governing the universe, under the guidance of an invisible hand, shape the destinies of nations and communities. None can ignore them. None can defy them. Relying on the supremacy of the moral laws and the righteousness of our cause, let us appeal to the Government for justice and justice will not be withheld. And when this great boon will have been conferred upon us we shall have done a great service to the country—we shall have vindicated the honour of the Government, we shall have broadened the self-respect of our community, added to the wealth of civic virtues which constitute the crowning heritage of all nations, be they ancient or be they modern. Let us then launch upon this holy crusade, this great and noble work, and I am sure that under the providence of God, the victory will be ours. (Loud and continuous cheers).

Speech at Calcutta Session

Wider Employment of Natives of India

Mr. President, Brother Delegates, Ladies and Gentlemen, — "That this Congress once again records its deep regret that the labours of the Public Service Commission have not produced the results which were anticipated and this Congress repeats its conviction that no satisfactory solution of the question is possible unless effect is given to the resolution of the House of Commons of the 2nd June 1893 in favour of holding the examination for the Indian Civil Services simultaneously in England and India.

That in this connection this Congress desires to express its profound disappointment at the policy of the Government in respect of the wider employment of natives of India in the higher offices of the Minor Civil Services, such as the Police, the Custom, the Telegraph, the Forest, the Survey, the Opium, as involving their practical exclusion from these offices and as being opposed to the terms of the Queen's Proclamation and the recommendations of the Public Service Commission; and this Congress prays that the Government will be pleased to take early steps to remedy the injustice thus done to the claims of the people of this country."

Brother Delegates. This is an old question which in substance has been included in the Congress programme ever since the Congress has come into existence. It is a painful necessity which compels us to renew this demand from year's end to year's end. But our rulers will not listen to us. Inaccessible to the voice of reason or of remonstrance, wrapped up in the sense of their own infallibility with regard to this matter they turn a deaf ear to our representations. But we must continue to repeat them in season and out of season, until we will win by our persistency what has been refused to the justice of our cause. We Congressmen never confess to a defeat (hear, hear). We are like the veterans of Waterloo who never knew that they had lost a battle.

With us defeat means a temporary reverse, the temporary frustration of our hopes and aspirations—perhaps the temporary suspension of our activities in a particular direction, but it never does or can mean the definite abandonment of a programme which we have deliberately resolved upon (cheers). Such a programme must be renewed again and again until the clamour of an irrational opposition has been hushed into silence and the moral forces which we have helped to create, to foster and to promote, working noiselessly it may be but steadily in the bosom of society and operating through the medium of an enlightened public opinion have established their complete and triumphant sway, (cheers). We believe in reiteration—we believe in persistency—above all we believe in the justice of our cause, We believe that so long as there is a God in Heaven, Who shapes and controls the destinies of men and nations, Who regulates the march of human affairs, Who compels rulers of men, be they autocrats or the representatives, or constitutional sovereigns, to conform to the paramountcy of the moral laws, our cause is bound to triumph; for it is founded upon the highest justice (cheers). If justice to individuals be binding upon Governments, justice to communities is of paramount obligation which no Government can set at naught with impunity to its highest and truest interests. In the intoxication of power—in the frenzy which is begotten of long continued and uninterrupted success—this elementary principle is apt to be ignored. But it is writ large on the pages of history, and the annals of mankind teach the impressive lesson that Governments are strongest when they are most liberal and most popular. Alexander conquered the world, less by the prowess of his arms, more by the liberality of his policy.

The master of Persia, with his feet planted upon the neck of the Persian people, he insisted upon Persianising himself and his great 'nobles. Rome, the mistress of the world (mistress even now in a wider sense, in the domain of religion, of law and jurisprudence), Rome retained her supremacy over men and affairs, not so much by the splendour of her military achievements, as by the generous extension of her much-prized gift of citizenship to the remotest parts of her conquered dominions (cheers). We invite the Government of India to accept this principle, not merely in theory, but as an integral, effective and permanent, of its policy. For we desire the permanence of British rule in India, for with it are bound up the best prospects of our political and material development But we cannot ignore the fact that British rule, as at present constituted, represents a foreign domination, and it is equally notorious that all foreign domination lacks the elements of stability and permanence.

Therefore is it that we are anxious to nationalise the Government, and so relieve it of these elements which are calculated to jeopardise its permanence, and broadbase the Empire of the King upon the gratitude, the love and the devoted allegiance of the millions of our population (cheers). Our position is enormously strengthened by declaration of the Government, above all by the Proclamation of Her late Majesty the Queen, the Magna Charta of our rights. I am happy to be able to say that there has been no disposition on the part of the illustrious men who from time to time have filled the high office of Viceroy to belittle the significance of this solemn document. On the contrary, they have always regarded it as a sacred injunction issued on a historic occasion, imposing a solemn duty upon the rulers of India in relation to the people of India. I will not trouble you with the opinions of preceding Viceroys. The latest pronouncement is that of His Excellency Lord Curzon. His Excellency observed that it was the golden rule of his conduct. We take our stand upon the Proclamation and call for its redemption. We take our stand upon the Proclamation and appeal to His Excellency to be guided by the golden rule of his conduct.

Sir, it has been proposed to inscribe the words of the Proclamation upon a brass tablet to be raised in the All India Memorial Hall. May the words of the Proclamation be graven deep on the hearts and consciences of our rulers ! May they be to them the table of their Commandments, to be obeyed by them unswervingly and faithfully for the honour of their late sovereign, the glorification of their country and the fulfilment of the highest ends of British rule in India! (cheers). We hold that the Proclamation will not be redeemed and justice will not be done to the people of India unless and until simultaneous examinations for the Indian Civil Services are held in India and England. In this view we are supported by high and distinguished authorities. So far back as 1862 a Committee of the India office was appointed, consisting of eminent Anglo-Indian officials, who held the view which has been put forth in this resolution. They were of opinion that the plainest considerations of justice to the natives of India demanded that simultaneous examinations should be held in India as well as in England. Their report was not unanimous but it was unanimous on this point. But we have yet a higher authority to quote. There was no more strenuous opponent of Indian aspirations than the late Lord Lytton, for he deliberately proposed to close the open competitive examination for the Indian Civil Services as against natives of India. Even Lord Lytton was constrained to admit that in the matter of their admission to high offices the people of India had been cheated of their dues, and that the Government had broken to the hope the words of promise which they had uttered to the ear.

We express dissatisfaction with the recommendations of the Public Service Commission, because they decided the question of simultaneous examination against the weight of evidence. The Public Service Commission examined 597 witnesses. Out of them 361 were in favour of, and 163 witnesses were against, simultaneous examinations; 73 witnesses were among the doubtful ones. Thus, nearly 70 per cent of those who were examined were in favour of the principle of simultaneous examination. And it is a very remarkable fact, perhaps not generally known, that there is a strong body of European opinion in favour of simultaneous examinations. I will now mention the names of those distinguished men who gave evidence in support of our view, and they were gentlemen who, during their official career developed no decided partiality in favour of Indian aspirations for liberal and generous treatment in the matter of high appointments. Amongst those in favour of simultaneous examinations were some names which are familiar to the people of these provinces, such as those of Sir *Alfred Croft,* late Director of Public Instruction, Mr. Tawney, late Principal of the Presidency College, and Mr. Kisch, late Postmaster General, now Municipal Secretary to Government. There were also distinguished personages outside these Provinces, such as Mr. Sime, Director of Public Instruction in the Punjab and Mr. Tupper of the Punjab Civil Service who supported our view. It goes without saying that the Hon'ble Mr. H. J. S. Cotton, the respected Chief-Commissioner of Assam, (cheers) and our great and good friend, Mr. Allen Hume, (cheers) were also in favour of holding simultaneous examinations.

Well, Gentlemen, we have heard a great deal about Mohammedan opposition to the Congress and that opposition is said to be founded on our adhesion to the programme of simultaneous examinations. Now, let us examine the drift of Mohammedan evidence as given before the Public Service Commission, at least in Bengal. Bengal is the one province in the Indian Empire which contains the largest level of Mohammedan population. Sixteen representative witnesses were summoned by the Public Service Commission to give evidence before them, and what was the drift of their evidence? Out of 16 witnesses, 10 were in favour of simultaneous examinations, two were doubtful, and four were against. And amongst these ten there are some whose names are names of honour amongst the Mahomedans of this Province, who will find a permanent place in the annals of Mohammedan greatness. Foremost among them was the late Nawab Bahadur Abdul Lateef who was not known to be a friend of the Congress, and yet when called upon to express an opinion on the subject, he gave evidence in favour of simultaneous examinations. Then, Sir, there was Moulvi Abdul Jubbar an honoured and respected name throughout these provinces, now Prime Minister of Bhopal. He was in favour of simultaneous examinations. Moulvi Khudabux, late Chief Justice of Hyderabad, vice President of the Reception Committee of the Congress, an extract from whose letter I read out yesterday, he, too, was in favour of simultaneous examinations. And last but not least there was Mr. Sharfudin, Barrister-at-Law, of Bankipur. Mr. Sharfudin belonged to us, but he now sits on the fence in an attitude of anxiety and suspense which is painful to his friends, and must be galling to his own sense of self-respect; (Laughter and cheers). It will thus be seen that those members of the Mohammedan Community who object to simultaneous examinations make it a ground of their abstention from the Congress, are arrayed in opposition to the views of the most illustrious of their co-religionists. Nay, more, they do a grave injustice to the great community to which they belong. They forget the past glories of their race. They forget that although the Hindus have had a start of fifty years over them in the matter of high education, our Mohammedan fellow-countrymen are rapidly coming to the front and are gallantly holding their own in honourable competition with the elite of our youth (cheers).

Sir, not many years ago, Mr. Tyebji, the bearer of an honoured name, was the first man of his year in the final examination for the Indian Civil Service. Another Mohammedan gentleman from the Punjab quite recently occupied a high place in the Cambridge Mathematical Tripos examination and won for himself an equally distinguished position among the selected candidates for the Indian Civil Service. I think it was only year before last when a Mohammedan student from Bankipur was the first man of his year at the First Arts Examination. All these circumstances ought to inspire us with hope as regards the future of the Mohammedan community in India. That hope has been accentuated by recent events. We Hindus, rejoice to find that our Mohammedan fellow-subjects have shaken off their political torpor (cheers). The apathy which paralysed their energies has given place to serious reflection on their present political situation. A visible wave of unrest is agitating the Mohammedan community in India. Out of a total number of about one thousand delegates attending the Congress there are as many as 100 Mohammedan delegates. The portals of the Congress are wide open for their reception *(cheers). We shall welcome them as brothers, animated by* a common sentiment, living upon a common hope and fired by a common enthusiasm (cheers). Who will sunder ties which nature has forged with her own hands? (Cheers) I know that some of your leaders—I will correct myself and say your so-called leaders—have essayed this impossible task. Vain effort. Success can never be theirs. The moral sense of the community will rise in revolt against an enterprise which is opposed to the mandate of nature, (cheers).

The second part of the resolution deals with the question of the Minor Civil Services. It deplores the policy of the Government of India which amounts to a policy of the exclusion of our countrymen from the higher appointments in the Minor Civil Services. As regards the Indian Civil Service, as the result of our agitation, we have gained some ground. As regards the Minor Civil Services, as the result of our apathy we continue to he excluded from the higher appointments. As regards the Indian Civil Service, one-sixth of the listed appointments have been thrown open to us, and I am thankful to be able to say that in Bengal the Government has made a real effort to carry out this policy. As regards the Minor, Civil Services, there We departments where we do not hold even one twentieth part of the higher appointments—there are departments from which our ostracism is complete, where the representatives of the dominant race hold all the loaves and fishes of office. Let us look at the figures:—They are those for Bengal. In the Forest Department the total number of high appointments are 24,—22 held by Europeans and 2 by our countrymen. In the Customs the total number of appointments are 33, 31 held by Europeans, one only by a native, the other which is vacant will probably go to a European. Preventive Service,—157 appointments; all held by Europeans. There is a big zero for us. (A voice from the delegates—" Preventive Service means the prevention of the children of the soil)", Yes, Preventive Service means prevention of the children of the soil. I accept that interpretation. Survey,—appointments 13; all 13 the monopoly of the dominant race. We are not even fit to be good surveyors. Jail,—total number of high appointments 18; all held by Europeans.

Police—H2-, including the Calcutta Police; of these, 103 are held by Europeans, 6 by natives and 3 are vacant. Telegraph—79 higher appointments, 75 held by Europeans, 4 by natives (shame). This is indeed a scandalous state of things. The gravity of the scandal is apparent to every one who is not blind to what is right Nothing could be more scandalous than the state of things disclosed by the figures to which I have referred. Well, this was the state of things to which the Indian Association called attention. The Government of India took about 12 months to cogitate the answer. The Government of India at last replied, and it replied with a big non-possumus. "We are unable to do anything in the matter, except that the appointments in the Appraiser's Department might be thrown open to you; but the higher offices in the other Departments must continue to be the monopoly of the dominant race"—so said Lord Curzon and his advisers. Well, gentlemen, with your permission, I won't take much of your time, I will refer to two or three extracts from the Government of India's letter with a view to show the reactionary character of the policy which is now in the ascendant in the councils of our rulers. With reference to the Salt Department not a single native of India holds any high appointment. But mark the anomaly. For sometime the head of the department was a native Civilian. The head could be native, the foot could be native, but the body must be European. I cannot understand it, but that is exactly the arrangement which was in force. The Government of India said in their reply to the Indian Association:

> "The Department is still in its infancy and the preventive operations now being introduced require an energy and physical capacity which ordinary natives of Bengal who would apply fur service in the Department do not possess *Here after, when the illicit practices have been repressed* and the work of the Department has been normal, it will, the Government of India anticipate, be found feasible as it is in Madras to employ a larger proportion of pure natives."

We Bengalis are told that we have not even the physical capacity requisite for the operation of this Department. Well, gentlemen, I do not know what extraordinary physical capacity is required for the purpose of suppressing smuggling carried on by a few Bengali villagers, when those who attempt to suppress it are armed with all the power and authority of the Law. But it seems to me that the remark involves a gross libel on the Bengalis. Of course, I cannot claim to be a fine specimen of the physical energy and of the physical capacity of my race (Laughter). You can find such specimens amongst your volunteers (cheers). There are many of them quite ready to fight as you have had some evidence since yesterday (Laughter). But in any case it must be held that we possess sufficient physical energy for the purpose of suppressing smuggling. The Government however seem to ignore the physical development—the marvellous physical development—of modern Bengal. Look at our Cricket teams, our Football teams, our Gymnasiums, our Circuses our Lion-tamers (Hear, Hear and cheers) who in point of endurance, physical strength and nerve are capable of competing with the bravest men of the same profession in other parts of the world (cheers). The reply of the Government involves a calumny upon the Bengali race. If the Government does not want to give us these appointments, let it say so. Why indulge in calumny? Why does it not tell us:—"This application of yours does not suit us? It is not in harmony with our reactionary policy." I think the Government of India has done us great injustice by refusing to as these high appointments, and has added insult to injury, by the reply given to the memorial of the Indian Association.

In the next place, Sir, the Government of India says in its reply that as regards the Jail Department the Government has ruled that Superintendents of Central Jails should be recruited from among members of the Indian Medical Service. I do not know that the much-gifted members of the Indian Medical Service have the exclusive monopoly of knowledge and wisdom which is not vouchsafed to others. These appointments are to be their monopoly; and you, Dr. Mullick, with all your learning, and you my friend Dr. Nilratan, with all your practical knowledge of the great profession to which you belong, you can never hope to be Superintendents of our Central Jails, because for sooth you do not belong to that heaven-appointed service which claims the monopoly and exclusive knowledge which the Government of

India credits the Indian Medical Service with. Nor is this all, the Assistant Deputy Superintendents of Jails are required by the terms of the letter to possess European qualifications.

Gentlemen, I know European goods. They are easily distinguished by their, trademark. But what are European qualifications, will you tell me? Are they specified anywhere? Are they not qualifications which are the gifts of a bountiful Providence, freely distributed amongst the entire human race, depending entirely on education, training and the environments of one's situation? Is it to be supposed that we do not possess the qualifications of Deputy Superintendents of Jail? If we do not, the fact implies the gravest reflection upon British rule—it means that under British rule we have become so degraded that we are unfit to be even Deputy Superintendents of Jails, but that under Mohammedan rule we were qualified to be the governors of Provinces, the commanders of armies and the confidential advisers of the Sovereign (cheers). Let our rulers look upon that picture and upon this and draw the moral (cheers).

Let me now pass on to the next and the last item, i.e., the Opium Department I am surprised at the observations of the Government. It is my respect, personal respect for Lord Curzon, which prevents me from giving expression to sentiments which rise uppermost in my mind and struggle for utterance. I restrain myself, because the dignity of this assembly requires the practice of self-restraint. At the same time the reply of the Government must be considered by us and the answer must be forthcoming. The Government say:—"This scheme of admitting natives of pure Asiatic descent to the Opium Department on a limited scale which was introduced experimentally in 1884 has not yet been found to be sufficiently successful, and the Government of India is, therefore, of opinion that the department must continue for the present to be recruited mainly from the European and Eurasian community." Now Sir, what does this mean? It means this—it means the complete reversal of the policy of Lord Ripon and of the recommendation of the Public Service Commission. Lord Ripon in 1884, by the terms of the resolution referred to, declared that one-forth of the appointments in the Opium Department should be recruited from among the natives of India. The Public Service

Commission went a step further. The Public Service Commission recommended that there should be equality in the treatment of all races, as regards the higher appointments in the Opium Department. Now the Government of India comes forward and says:—"You have been tried and have been found wanting, and we are not prepared still further to develop the principle which was accepted by Lord Ripon's Government."

Gentlemen, I dispute the position assumed by the Government. I say we have been tried but have not been found wanting, and I will ask you to say 'no' to this part of the reply of the Government. When you have heard me I am sure you will say no, an emphatic no, (voices of no, no) which will ring from one part of this hall to the other. There are 300 appointments in the Opium Department. Out of those 300 appointments, 12 are filled by the natives of India, and 288 are filled by Europeans. In the administration report of the Department, 8 officers were: singled out for honourable mention, and who do you think the officers were? Of these 8 officers, 4 were Europeans and the rest were natives. Now, Sir, it comes to this— that out of 288 European officers, 4 were qualified for honourable distinction, and out of only 12 native officers, 4 also were similarly qualified for honourable mention. Look at the facts here disclosed, and yet the Government of India says that we have been tried and have been found wanting. Sir, a more unfounded allegation has never appeared within the limits of a State paper. I am surprised that Lord Curzon, with his great capacity for work and his keen insight into details, did not observe the contradiction between the reply of Government of India and the facts stated in the administration report of the Department.

Upon such grounds as these our prayer has been rejected. We owe it to ourselves to renew it in season and out of season, until we get what we want. It is through failure that we mount to success. Failure is the school of discipline through which we must pass before we reach the destined goal of our aspirations. Look at the trials and tribulations of other nations. It is fortunate, thanks to the constitutional Government under which we live, that we are not called upon to face them, I have heard complaints of the comparative unsuccess of the Congress movement and of our waining enthusiasm. You, Sir, (referring to Mr. W. C. Banerjee) were pleased yesterday to refer to it in your eloquent speech. I will not go over the ground, so happily trodden by you. But even if there was the shadow of a substratum of truth underlying the allegation, I would ask what are seventeen years in the life-time of a nation? I am unwilling to enter into a comparison between the Irish people and ourselves. But Irish history teaches an impressive lesson which we would do well to lay to heart. The *Irish carried on an agitation for more than fifty years before they* got the Catholic Emancipation Bill, passed into law. They have now been agitating for Home Rule for more than one hundred years and they have not got it despite their perfect organisation, their limitless resources and their solid strength in the House of Commons.

Let us, therefore, possess our souls in patience in the certain conviction that the day is not far distant when the forces of liberalism will once again assert their ascendancy in England and a new impetus will be imparted to the cause of progress, not only in the united Kingdom but throughout the world wide dominions of the King-Emperor. You have the strongest motives to carry on the great work to which you are pledged. You are the descendants of a great race, the inheritors of illustrious traditions. Humanity owes a great debt to you. You were the instructors of mankind in the morning of the world. The hymns of your Vedic Rishis representing the first aspirations of infant humanity towards the divine ideal wafted through the distant ages, still linger in the air (cheers). Your country was the cradle of two religions, the nursery and the seat of the noblest ethical and spiritual conceptions (cheers). To the divinely inspired Buddha two-thirds of the human race still bent their knees in adoration (cheers). Will you not emulate the deeds of your sires? Will you not reconcile the past with the present, unite the past with the present—until they flow on a mighty stream converting towards the confines of eternity, fertilizing the unknown regions of the future, creating, fostering, stimulating a new, nobler, a grander civilization for Asia than any which the world has yet witnessed (cheers).

I have also an appeal to make to our Mohammedan fellow-subjects. You were the instructors of Europe in the Middle Ages. You held aloft the torch of learning and civilization at a time when the monks in their cloistered recesses were formulating, philosophical principles of doubtful utility to mankind. In India you were the inaugurators of a policy which remains unsurpassed for its beneficence and which has won for you the love, the respect, the affectionate gratitude of your Hindu fellow-subjects (Loud cheers). Hindus and Mahomedans, Parsis and Sikhs and Christians, let us all combine in a constitutional way to effect the political enfranchisement of our people and the great God of nations will sanctify our patriotic efforts.

I have a word to say to our rulers. Next year will witness the coronation of the King. The year after, there will be a Proclamation Durbar to be held at Delhi; the capital of the Hindu and the Mohammedan Kings of India. Whenever a Durbar has been held, associated with the Sovereign, it has been marked by an accession of popular rights. The first Durbar held by Lord Canning on the, assumption of the Government by the Crown witnessed the announcement of the Proclamation, the Magna Charta of our rights. The Imperial Assemblage Durbar of 1877 was associated with a proclamation which gave a new impetus to the wider employment of our countrymen in the more responsible offices of State. And last but not least, at the Jubilee Durbar of 1887, Lord Dufferin foreshadowed the expansion and the reform of the Councils. I hope and trust that the Proclamation Durbar to be held by Lord Curzon will not be an empty show, and idle pageant, a mere expenditure of the people's money with little benefit to the people, but that it will represent a new era in Indian history, and that it will be marked in the word of our first resolution, by the strengthening of free institutions, the expansions of popular rights and by a great and forward step taken for the gradual but complete redemption of the gracious promise contained in the Proclamation of Her late Majesty. (Loud and deafening Cheers).

Speech at Special Session at London

A Session of the Indian National Congress in London is by no means a new suggestion. It is an old idea which has often been broached and has as often been abandoned. Enormous have been the difficulties in the way of carrying it out, and no serious attempt has ever been made to face and overcome them. We have talked glibly enough; and have written on the subject with force and emphasis. But it has always remained a more or less pious aspiration to be fulfilled by a sturdier set of Congressmen, with their moral fibre strengthened by strenuous fight in the service of the Motherland. The late Mr. Caine would have rejoiced to have been the organiser of a session of the Congress in London, and Mr. Keir Hardie has been persistent in his appeals in this behalf, There are times and seasons for the fruition of great ideals; and to me it seems that the time has come for the holding of a session of the Congress in the capital of the Empire, with the highest benefit to our people. The British Public are now in an attitude of inquisitiveness about Indian affairs. Apathy has given place to a real desire for knowledge about Indian affairs. India is no longer a mere geographical expression which excites no interest or attention. Read the English newspapers and periodicals, and you will find that a much larger space is devoted to Indian considerations than ever had been done before in the life lime of this generation; and the English Press in all its branches is always keenly responsive to the trend of English opinion and sentiment. At such a time when the mind of the British public is so wide open to the reception of impressions about India, it seems to me to be our supreme duty to saturate it with our ideas and to give it an impulse and direction which would be beneficial to India.

The Englishman is slow to move, but his sympathies are entirely on the side of Justice and Liberty. Anglo-India has now the car of the British public through the numerous Anglo-Indian correspondents of English newspapers in this country who naturally reflect the views of their class. That we are not able to make our voice heard or felt in England or in Europe and America is our own fault. We have too often allowed judgement to go by default. We have never made an organised effort to present our standpoint of the Indian problem to the British public and the civilized world. Our opponents, the enemies of Indian progress, are the masters of the situation, the directors of the public opinion of the civilized world in regard to our affairs. Our efforts, in this direction, have been spasmodic, futile, lacking the persistency and organisation which alone can ensure success; Deputations sent by fits and starts, occasional telegrams despatched to the English newspapers, the upkeep of an organ of Indian opinion in London which we only half-heartedly support, exhaust the measure of our efforts to enlighten the public opinion of England and of Europe. There must, indeed, be more persistency and more strenuousness in the organisation of this branch of our work.

A regular Press Service between this country and England, setting forth the Indian standpoint, yearly deputations to England" and a session of the Congress in London seem to me to represent the supreme needs of the hour in our efforts to place our views before the civilized world. We cannot stand isolated in our national work. We need the sympathies of England and of civilized mankind. But we must instruct before we can awaken sympathy. And so just and righteous is our cause that we feel that we have only to rescue it from the misrepresentations of malicious critics, and the sympathies of civilized mankind will be infallibly enlisted on our behalf.

The success of our deputations in England has proved this truth. The deputations of the future would be even more successful than they have been in the past, if they were preceded by a session of the Congress in London. A meeting of the Congress in London in the present attitude of the British public would create a profound impression on British public opinion which would be reflected in the Press of Europe and America. It would dissipate a vast mass of misunderstanding which now prevails about India. It would curtail the illimitable facilities for misrepresentation which the enemies of Indian progress now enjoy. It would awaken deep sympathy and a deeper desire for knowledge. Altogether a session of the Congress in London would constitute a notable event in the history of our political activities.

The effort itself would be a great lesson in self-help. For every day in our lives, we have to help ourselves by calling in the aid of our neighbours and others. What is true of individual life is in a greater measure true of national life. For the nation today does not and cannot stand apart from the great federation of mankind—the brotherhood of humanity. For the session of the Congress we want the men—we want the money. There will be no difficulty about the money. If the idea is approved of by the nation, the money will as surely be forthcoming. There may be some difficulty about the men, in the United Provinces and Madras where the observance of caste-rules is perhaps stricter than in other parts of the country. But large numbers of young men have gone to England from Madras and the North-Western Provinces; and surely the leaders may follow the bright example set by their younger compatriots. Nor do I think would it be difficult, to charter, if need be, a special steamer which may facilitate the observance of caste-rules. The ways and means do not, I think, present an insuperable obstacle. What is wanted is that the nation should definitely resolve to hold a session of the Congress in London, and the earlier the better. I appeal to the nation in the name of our most sacred interests to form this resolve.

No time could be more opportune. Let us take advantage of it and sow the seeds which in the fullness of time will enable us to reap an abundant harvest of good. We owe this duty to posterity.

6

Addresses to the Imperial Council

Press Act

[*In moving the Resolution for amending the Press Act at a meeting of the Imperial Legislative Council at Delhi on January* 9, 1914, *the Hon'ble Babu Surendranath Banerjee said:*—]

Sir, my Resolution refers to the Press Act of 1910 known as Act I of that year. I have no desire to revive the memories of a controversy now passed and I hope forgotten, but it is useless to disguise the fact that the Bill was passed amid some opposition in this Council and considerable opposition in the country. Reading through the reports' of the debate which took place in February, 1910, I find that there was a general desire evinced by the non-official Indian Members that it should be a temporary measure and should not find a place among the permanent statutes of the land. That view, however, did not commend itself to the majority and the Act has been added to the stock of our permanent legislation. Sir, the Act has now been in operation for a period close upon four years, and We' are in a position to judge of its character. How it has worked, what are its defects and how they may be remedied—these seem to me, Sir, to be pertinent and relevant issues. They force upon our minds the conviction that the Act should be repealed, or, at any rate, should be modified, and that, if it is to be modified, it should be at least upon the lines of the suggestions contained in my Resolution. That, Sir, represents what I may describe as the 'irreducible minimum' which the opinion of the educated community demands, as the first definite step towards what they hope will lead to the final annulment of this Act. Sir, that this Act is bound to be repealed sooner or later-sooner I hope than later—is as clear as the noonday sun; for it is inconsistent with the great traditions of British rule and those noble principles of government which are incarnated in British administration. No concession to popular freedom has been made by the British Government in India which has ever been withdrawn. The Jury Notification was cancelled; the Vernacular Press Act was repealed; and so will it be with this Act in the fullness of time. I submit, Sir, that the Government of India, standing at the head of the nation, becoming every day more and more nationalistic in its views by the breadth and liberality of its policy, ought to show us the way.

Sir, the Act gives very large powers to the police. Under the provisions of section 8 of the Act, the magistrate is empowered to ask the publisher or printer of a newspaper, when he applies for registration, to find security. This power is exercised practically by the police. The magistrate in this case is the police and the police is the Criminal Investigation Department. Only the other day, in the case of the *Habul Matin,* a Persian journal published in Calcutta, it was not the Local Government but the magistrate which demanded security at the instance of the Commissioner of Police. That surely was not the intention of the original framers of the Act. The interposition of the magistrate meant the exercise of judicial discretion and was intended to be a safeguard against the aberrations of executive authority. One of the greatest anomalies of the Act is that whereas a right is given to the aggrieved party to make an appeal against an order of forfeiture, no such right is allowed when the order for deposit of security is given, and the High Court has recently held in the case to which I have referred that even its revisional powers are not available in a case of this kind. Sir, thus in the absence of any safeguard of this kind, the result has been that many newspapers which were called upon to find security have ceased publication. I hold in my hand a statement giving the names of some of the newspapers thus dealt with. I find that 17 newspapers were asked to give security. Of these 3 were Hindu papers and 14 Mohammedan; and not having been able to give security, they all ceased publication. The case of one of these papers, the *Ahli Hadis* of Amritsar, is very peculiar. It published a letter replying to certain strictures which had appeared in a Missionary organ reflecting upon the Mohammedan faith. This newspaper was asked to furnish security, but it does not appear that the book which published the strictures upon the Mohammedan faith was at all taken notice of. Then, Sir, passing from the papers which ceased to exist, we have a number of those which gave the security. The number according to the list which I have in my hand is 15—9 Mohammedan, 4 Hindu, I Sikh and Anglo-Indian. The case of the *Zamindar* of Lahore calls for notice. It has been required to give security to the extent of Rs. 10,000. The head and front of its offence was that it protested against the removal of a mosque.

The justice of the complaint was admitted; the mosque was restored-; but in consequence of certain remarks which it made against the respected head of the Government of the United Provinces, the paper was asked to give a security of Rs. 10,000. I will say this at once, that I have seen these remarks; I deplore them; I consider them to be very discourteous, very disrespectful, very objectionable; but at the same time, it seems to me that it would have been quite worthy of a great Government, if, instead of demanding security to the extent of Rs. 10,000, the Editor was sent for and sharply reprimanded. There is one other case to which I want to refer. Amongst those that were required to give security, there was an Anglo-Indian newspaper named the *Cawnpore Herald*. Somewhere about the year 1912 an article called 'A Dramatic Scene' appeared in that paper. The Deputy Superintendent of Police called upon the proprietress of the paper, and wanted to know who the writer was. Naturally enough, she declined to give the name. Then she called on the magistrate; the magistrate said that it was very improper on her part to permit her newspaper to be the means of criticism directed against the police and the municipality, and that she had no business to have the press moved about from place to place. The upshot of it all was that she was required to find security to the extent of Rs. 500. She submitted a memorial to the Government of India somewhere about the year 1912. My information is that up to this time, she has not received any reply of any kind.

Passing from these cases, let me note the vigour with which the Act has been worked under the different Governments. Through the courtesy of my hon'ble friend, the Home Secretary, I have been furnished with a statement. I find from it that for the three years during which the Act has been in operation, there have been 807 cases altogether dealt with under the Act. OF these, 239 were cases under sections 8 and 8, in which deposit of security was required; and the other cases-were under section 12, in which certain publications and pamphlets were declared to be forfeited. If we take the figure 807 for three years, it comes to this, that there was an action taken almost every day of the year. This seems to me to indicate very great vigour on the part of the different departments superintending the operation of this Act. All this indicates the urgent need there is for the supervision of public opinion over the operation of this Act.

Passing from facts, let me come to the authoritative-expression of opinion. I will not refer to the popular verdict, for that may not commend itself to gentlemen on the other side of the House; but I will cite an authority of unquestioned weight, whose pronouncement, I am sure, will command the implicit acquiescence of all members, be they official or non-official. Let me quote the opinion of the Chief Justice of the High Court of Bengal when delivering judgement in the *Comrade* case. This is what Sir Lawrence Jenkins said:

> 'The provisions of section 4 are very comprehensive, and its language is as wide as human ingenuity could make it. Indeed, it appears to me to embrace the whole range of varying degrees' of assurance from certainty on the one side to the very limits of impossibility on the other. It is difficult to see to what lengths the operation of this section may not plausibly be extended by an ingenious mind. They would certainly extend to writings that may even command approval. An attack on that degraded section of the public which lives on the misery and shame of others-

> would come within this Widespread net, the praise of a class might not be free from the risk. Much that is regarded as standard literature could undoubtedly be caught.'

That is the Chief Justice's opinion about section 4 of the Act. Sir, my Resolution does not cover it at all. It is a very modest one. I ask, is it possible to conceive of a condemnation of any measure more restrained in its tone yet more emphatic in its reference? A law so dangerously comprehensive in its scope naturally needs many safeguards for its proper working. The Government of India recognised the necessity of such safeguards and wisely provided them. The Hon'ble Mr. Sinha, late Law Member to the Government of India, speaking from his place in this Council, speaking on behalf of the Government of India, referred to these safeguards in clear and explicit terms, I will read an extract from his speech. He said:

> 'It is of no use to attempt to convince us that it is a very drastic measure, because we have put in all kinds of safeguards. I will mention another which my Hon'ble friends seem to have forgotten in their hasty perusal of the Bill. When the Local Government makes the order of forfeiture the Bill provides that it must state or describe the offending words, or articles,' or pictures, or engravings, or whatever it is, upon which it bases its order. No making an order which is vague, which is indefinite. No order without allowing the man to know what he is being punished for, but a definite order sluing the very words of the article or describing it as that which the man is being punished for. Is that not a safeguard? Apart from the Tribunal of Appeal, is it not a safeguard to provide that a man will not have his security forfeited without" being told exactly what he has written that is taken exception to.'

I think, Sir, there could not be a clearer exposition of the intentions of the Government in regard to this matter, and I understand that Mr. Sinha's speech on that occasion was endorsed wholeheartedly by the then Viceroy, Lord Minto. The question is whether these safeguards have been effectually provided, whether the promises then made have been redeemed. Let us examine the matter a little. Section 4 of the Act lays down that when a Local Government has decided to forfeit any deposit in respect of a printing press, it has to issue a notice in writing stating the grounds of the forfeiture—the words, signs, visible representations, to which exception is taken. Section 6 lays down that when a deposit has been forfeited and a fresh deposit has been made and the Government decides again to forfeit the deposit in consequence of the contravention of the terms of section 4, a notice is to be issued in writing again stating the grounds for the forfeiture. This is as regards printing presses. The same provisions *mutatis mutandis* apply to newspapers. Therefore it comes to this, that wherever a Local Government is invested with the right to forfeit a newspaper or a printing press, the obligation is cast on the Government to state the grounds for the forfeiture. But, Sir, unfortunately, all this is annulled by the provisions of section 22; that at any rate is the opinion of the High Court. It is necessary for me to read section 22. That section declares:

> 'Every declaration of forfeiture purporting to be made under this Act shall, as against all persons, be conclusive evidence that the forfeiture therein referred to has taken place, and no proceeding purporting to be taken under this Act shall be called in question by any Court, except the High Court on such application as aforesaid, and no civil or criminal proceeding, except as provided by this Act, shall be instituted against any person for anything done or in good faith intended to be done under this Act.'

This is the opinion of the Chief Justice in regard to this section:

> 'The notification therefore appears to me to be defective in a material particular and, but for section 22 of the Act, it would in my opinion, be our duty to hold that there had been no legal forfeiture.
>
> 'That section, however, provides that every declaration purporting to be made under this Act, shall, as against

> all persons, be conclusive evidence that the forfeiture therein referred to has taken place. " The result is that though I hold that the notification does not comply with the provisions of the Act, still we are, in my opinion, barred from questioning the legality of the forfeiture it purports to declare.'

Is it possible to hold in the face of this clear expression of opinion that the safeguards which were promised by the Hon'ble Mr. Sinha have been provided? Be it observed that these pledges were given in order to allay the great public excitement that was caused by the enactment of so drastic a law as the Press Act. What was given with the one hand is practically taken away with the other. This was not, this could not have been, the intention of the Government of India, for apart from its high-mindedness, and even its sternest critics must give it credit for that, there is internal evidence to show the anxiety of the Government of India to incorporate in the Act the declaration of Mr. Sinha; and section after section reproduces the safeguards promised by him. But all of a sudden they are nullified by the provisions of section 22.

It seems to me that there must have been some" error, some mistake in the drafting. I am confirmed in this view by an examination of the Act. Section 17 gives the aggrieved party a right of appeal to the High Court; that however becomes nugatory and meaningless if the aggrieved party is not furnished with materials on which the High Court is to form its judgement, or the High Court is barred from considering these materials for the purposes of reviewing the decision of the executive authority concerned. It is preposterous to suppose that the Act deliberately nullifies in one part what it has deliberately conceded in another, or that it has thrown an impossible burden of proof upon the aggrieved party. I will quote the opinion of the Hon'ble the Chief Justice:

> 'The Advocate-General has admitted, and I think very properly, that the pamphlet (that is the 'Comrade') is not seditious and does not offend against any provision of the Criminal Law of India. But he has contended, and rightly in my opinion, that the provisions of the Press Act extend far beyond the Criminal Law; and

he has argued that the burden of proof is cast on the applicant, so that, however meritorious the pamphlet may be, still, if the applicant cannot establish the negative the Act requires, his application must fail.'

'And what is this negative? It is not enough for the applicant to show that the words of the pamphlet are not likely to bring into hatred or contempt any class or section of His Majesty's subjects in British India, or that they have not a tendency in fact to bring about that result. But be must go further, and show that it is impossible for them to have that tendency either directly or indirectly, and whether by way of inference, suggestion, allusion, metaphor or implication.'

Well, Sir, it is impossible for any person to prove a negative, and the difficulty of the task is enhanced by the comprehensive nature of the obligation of proof that is cast upon him.

The second part of my Resolution follows as a matter of course from the first. It is no use placing materials before the High Court for a review, if the High Court is debarred from considering these materials. The High Court says that it is debarred. Therefore I submit that section 22 ought to be amended in order definitely to empower the High Court to set aside any order not made: in conformity with the provisions of sections 4, 6, 9,11 and 12. It may perhaps be held that the first portion of the Resolution is a surplusage, that it is already the law and that therefore no amendment is necessary. If this contention holds good, it constitutes an overwhelming argument in favour of the amendment of section 22 in accordance with my suggestion. If it is already provided in the Act that the grounds of the forfeiture must be set forth in the notes of forfeiture, you are bound to makes the law operative and to give it effect. Therefore you must modify section 22 upon the lines suggested by me.

Sir, it is admitted on all hands that there has been a sensible improvement in the situation; the highest authorities in the realm have borne testimony to this effect. It is also admitted that there has been a change for the better in the tone and temper of the press. Our critics hostile to our interests and aspirations have ungrudgingly admitted the fact; that being so, I feel that I should be justified in demanding the repeal or, at any rate, a substantial modification of the Act, but I go no further than to invite the Council so ' to amend the Act as to remove a just cause for complaint, to carry out its declared intentions and to redeem the pledged word of the Government. In making this appeal I speak not only as a Member of this Council but as one with whom journalism has been the cherished vocation of his life. We journalists feel as if the sword of Damocles was hanging over our heads. We may be right or we may be wrong, but that is our feeling. Ours is a noble calling and we are entitled to the wholehearted support and sympathy of the Government. The newspaper press is the great organ for the ventilation of popular grievances, it is the safety-valve of the State, it' is an instrument of popular and political education, it is the gift of British rule and we cherish it with affectionate ardour. Its liberty may degenerate into license, but I venture to hold that the arm of the law, such as it is without being reinforced by the Press Act, is long enough to reach it and strong enough to deal with it. The amendment of the Press Act which I pray for—and after all it is not an amendment but is in entire conformity with the intentions of the framers of the Act—will, if accepted, go some way to soften the rigours of the law and remove a just source of anxiety and of uneasiness felt by the great body of Indian journalists, and above all, Sir, it will proclaim to the world the unalterable determination of the Government to redeem its pledged word and to make justice to the aggrieved party the keynote of its policy, even when enforcing a measure of some severity, deemed necessary by the Government in the supreme interests of the State.

With these words, Sir, I beg to move the Resolution that stands against my name, namely:

> That this Council recommends to the Governor-General in Council that an amendment of the Press Act of 1910 be introduced in the Imperial Legislative Council so as to provide that when any order of forfeiture is made under the Act, the order must state or describe the offending words or articles or pictures or engravings or whatever it is upon which the Local

Government bases its order, and that section 22 of the Act be so modified as to definitely empower the High Court to set aside an order of forfeiture not made in conformity with the provisions of sections 4, 6, 9,11 and 12 of the Act.— *[At the close of the discussion before the Council divided on the motion, Bubu Surendranath said:*]

Sir, I will not, at this hour, take' up many minutes— especially in view of the criticisms which have already been offered by my Hon'ble friends over thereon the speech of the Hon'ble the Home Member and of the Hon'ble the Advocate-General. Sir, it is abundantly clear from the discussion that has taken place, that, barring one exception, of course, there is a general consensus of opinion as regards the course that should be followed in connection with the Press Act. I think we are all on this side of the House agreed that if there are safeguards provided in the law, those safeguards are inoperative and that they should be made effective. I am sorry that there was a disposition on the part of the Hon'ble the Home Member to go back upon the declarations of the past and discard the safeguards provided in the law itself. For the Hon'ble the Home Member observed that there was a danger in publicity. I am afraid it is too late to make that complaint at this hour. Section after section explicitly says that where notice of forfeiture is issued the grounds should be *slated.* I hope the Government of India and the various Local Governments will give effect to this part of the law, such as that law is. We ware expecting some kind of assurance from the Hon'ble the Home Member that in future when a notice of forfeiture was issued the notice would contain the grounds—would contain a statement of the words, signs or visible representations as indicated in the law. I must confess to a sense of disappointment that an assurance to that effect was not forthcoming.

But the Hon'ble the Home Member must have been convinced of the trend of public opinion as regards this matter. There is practically unanimity in our ranks, amongst the non-official Indian Members, that the law should be amended, so as to render operative the safeguards .which have been provided; and if on this occasion there is to be an adverse vote, as I fear there is likely to be, I feel that the Council have not heard the last of this matter; because there is a body of public opinion in favour of an amendment of this Act, and we, as representatives of the public voicing the public sentiment, will feel it our duty to give expression to that sentiment within the walls of this Chamber. Whatever may be the outcome of this debate, I am sure, I fear, that the matters, will have to be brought before this Council again.

Separation of Judicial and Executive Functions

[In moving the resolution relating to the separation of judicial and executive functions in the Imperial Legislative Council, in March 1913, *the Hon'ble Babu Surendranath Banerjee said:—]*

Sir,—I have the honour to move the following resolution:— " That this Council recommends to the Governor-General in Council that the grants made to local Governments be increased by such allotments as the Government of India may think fit with a view to enable them to carry out the experiment of the separation of judicial and executive functions in the administration of criminal justice in areas to be selected by them with the approval of the Government of India." Sir, the resolution is a financial one involving however administrative issues of great moment. I have tried to make the resolution as moderate as I' could. The resolution speaks of the separation of judicial and, executive functions as an experiment. It is to be in the nature of a tentative measure not to be definitely incorporated into the regular administrative machinery unless and until it has been tried and has been found successful. If it is attended with results, other than those which are anticipated by its supporters the experiment will have to be abandoned. The point upon which I desire to lay particular stress is this that the dominating note of the resolution is that the separation is to be an experiment for the present and that its further extension and development is to depend upon the results obtained and the experience gained. Nor is this all. The experiment is not to be tried all over the country, nor even in the regulation provinces, but only in such areas as may be selected by the Local Governments, subject to the supervision of the Government of India. Therefore,. Sir, all that the resolution seeks to secure is the acceptance of the principle in a definite "and practical form leaving the areas to be selected such as Government may decide.

I claim, therefore, on behalf of this resolution, that it is fenced round by conditions which ought to allay the fears and anxieties of the most cautious among administrators. Sir, not for one moment do I lay aside my own strong personal conviction on the subject, my sense of the unspeakable boon which this reform will confer upon all those who may have to appeal before our criminal courts; but at the same time, I feel that I have no right to thrust my convictions, however deep-seated they may be, upon a great Government weighted with a sense of responsibility and naturally anxious to proceed with due caution and circumspection. Sir, no Englishman can regard this combination of judicial and executive functions, this lumping up of the prosecution and the judge in one and the same person, without violence to his own inborn instincts and the traditions and environments in the midst of which he has been brought up.

Accordingly we find from the" earliest days of British rule many distinguished Anglo-Indian administrators to whose testimony I shall presently refer expressing themselves in terms of strong disapprobation of this defect in the administrative machinery and urging this modification. So far back as the year 1792, in the days of Lord Morris under a regulation of that year, it was declared that the combination of these two functions was extremely undesirable. That view was expressed 40 years later by a distinguished Anglo-Indian administrator. Mr. Frederick Halliday who as the President of a Committee that was appointed to enquire into police organisation, said that it was most undesirable and the same opinion was endorsed by his colleagues.

[After alluding 'to the opinion of Sir F. Halliday and others, the Hon'ble Mr. Surendranath Banerjee said:—]

Lord Cross", the Conservative Secretary of State for India and Lord Kimberley, the Liberal Secretary of State for India, in the discussions that took place in the House of Lords, declared their adhesion to this principle. In 1899, a very important memorial was addressed to the Secretary of State for India, Lord George Hamilton, by distinguished persons including Lord Hob-house who one time was Law Member of this Council, Sir Richard Garth, Sir Richard 'Couch, late Chief Justice of the High Court of Bengal, Sir Raymond West or Bombay Civil Service, Sir John Bartle Frere,

Sir William Markby, Judges of the High Court and Mr. Reynolds of the Revenue Board of Bengal. Nothing came of this memorial at that time beyond a pious-expression of hope that the needful would be done at some future time. Sir, the question received an added impetus by the discussions which took place in this Council in March 1908 and then Sir Harvey Adamson, the Home member made a very important pronouncement on behalf of the Government. With your permission, Sir, I will read that pronouncement I fully believe I am quoting from his speech delivered, I think, on the 27th March, 1908 though I am not quite sure of the date. ' I fully believe that subordinate magistrates very rarely do an injustice wittingly but the inevitable result of the present system—the combination of judicial and executive functions—is that criminal trials affecting the general peace of the district are not always conducted in that atmosphere of cool impartiality which pervades a court of justice. Nor does this completely define the evil—he calls it an evil which lies not so much in what is done as in what may be expected to be done— for it is not enough that the administration of justice should be pure. It can never be the bedrock of our rule unless it is also above 'suspicion.' I do not think it is possible to add to the eloquence of these words. I therefore, claim, Sir, that we have a vast body of officials of the highest position impregnated with a lofty sense of their responsibility as members of this great Government in support of the principle underlying the reform which I have ventured to place before this Council. Not only that, Sir, we have passed the stage of discussion. We are about to enter upon the stage of practice. On this occasion in the course of this debate, Sir Harvey Adamson declared that the Government of India had definitely decided to introduce the reform. It may be in a cautious and tentative way. I will quote his words; he said:—' The Government of India have decided to advance cautiously and tentatively towards the separation of judicial and executive functions, in those parts of India where the local condition render that change possible and appropriate.'

Sir, the local Governments take their cue from the Supreme Government. This was said in March 1908. As I have just observed the local Governments take their cue from the Supreme Government and in the Budget discussion which took place in the

Bengal Legislative Council in April 1911, Sir William Duke, now member of the Executive Council of Bengal, then Chief Secretary to the Government, held out distinct promise that the reform would be introduced at an early date. I will quote his observations. .' The scheme for the separation of judicial and executive functions is continuously under consideration.

The Government of India decided that an advance should be made in a cautious and tentative way' and the Chief Secretary to the Government of Bengal with a due sense of the responsibility of his utterances says that 'the scheme is continuously under the consideration of the Government and no doubt proposals regarding it will be brought forward as early as possible.' These, are his words. But a scheme of that kind is one which requires mature consideration not merely of the Provincial Government and it is certainly unlikely that anything will take place even this year, the year to which the Budget refers. That was said, Sir, in April, 1911. We have a still later pronouncement in September,. 1912, round this table though certainly not in this hall. I think it was the Home Member, I am not sure, but it was a member on behalf of the Government of India, who said in reply to a question asked by the Hon'ble Mr. Sachidananda Sinha that, the matter was under the consideration of the Government of India.

Therefore, Sir, we have three outstanding facts to be gathered from the 'three pronouncements to which I have called your attention. In the first place, that the Government of India have decided to inaugurate this experiment tentatively or cautiously is immaterial but that the Government have decided to inaugurate this experiment. Secondly, we have it from the lips of the Chief Secretary to the Government of Bengal speaking on behalf of that Government that the experiment would soon be introduced and lastly we have the statement made on the floor of this Council by a responsible member of the Government of India that the matter is under consideration. Therefore, Sir, I take it that the question has emerged from the stage of discussion and has entered the stage of practical politics and, Sir, it seems to me that one of the immediate effects of this separation would be an effect highly beneficial to the interests of the Indian Civil Service. We have heard a great deal about the necessity of judicial training on the part of - the Indian Civil Service—I have no opinions of my own on that subject; because myself I am not a lawyer and have never been a lawyer; but, Sir, it is clear that the effect of the separation of the executive and judicial branch would be a severance of that alliance between the executive and the judicial branches which, I think, does not improve the tone of the judicial branch and a concentration of the attention of the judicial branch upon its own appropriate duties. Therefore, Sir, it is clear that the Government, have decided to introduce this experiment cautiously and tentatively and the question is when is that to be done. In 1911 the matter was under consideration. It is time that the deliberations of Government should bear fruit in some practical scheme inaugurating this experiment The only possible objections that I have heard against the inauguration of this experiment are prestige and cost. Sir, with reference to the question of prestige I will say this, that indeed is a poor sort of prestige which is associated with a system that in theory is indefensible and in practice is attended with miscarriages of justice. Such prestige is no aid or source of strength to the Government. On the contrary it is a source of weakness and embarrassment to the Government.

With regard to this question of prestige again I have the high authority of Sir Harvey Adamson, and I venture to quote him. He said on the 27th of March, 1908, ' Can any Government be strong whose administration of justice is not entirely above suspicion. The answer must be in the negative. A combination of functions is in such a condition of society a direct weakening of the prestige of the Empire. This question of prestige in the larger sense has been altogether discarded and no longer forms an operative part of the policy of the Government of India.' Here again I may quote a very distinguished authority, Mr. Montagu, the present Under Secretary of State for India.

University and Secondary Education

[*At a meeting of the Imperial Council on January 6, 1914, the Hon'ble Mr. Surendranath Banerjee moved the following Resolution and said:*]

My Lord, I have the honour to move the following Resolution:

'That this Council recommends to the Governor-General in Council the publication of:

(a) all official papers in the possession of the Government of India, including correspondence, if any, with the Senate of the Calcutta University and His Excellency the Rector, relating to the affiliation of the Ananda Mohan College up to the B.A. standard, and the orders of the Government thereon, together with the replies, if any, to the representations of local public bodies and meetings:

(b) all official papers in the possession of the Government of India, including correspondence, if any, with Provincial Governments and Local Administrations leading to the announcement made in paragraph 25 of the Government of India Resolution, dated Delhi, 21st February, 1913, regarding the desirability of introducing the School Final Examination in Provinces where it has not been introduced, and in paragraph 47, of placing the recognition of schools for purposes of presenting candidates for Matriculation in the hands of the Local Governments, and all subsequent correspondence relating thereto.'

My Lord, my resolution is an exceedingly simple one. It is a mere request for information, an appeal to Your Excellency's Government to take the public into their confidence in regard to certain educational proposals which have excited considerable controversy and which, in my Province, have awakened a general feeling of alarm and anxiety. My Lord, in matters educational, there are, and there can be no secrets; for if there is one department of the State more than another in which the confidence of the public and their cooperation are indispensable for the ends of efficient administration it is the Department of Education. Lord Curzon is my authority for it and be it remembered that it was during His Lordship's time that the Official Secrets Act was passed. Addressing the Educational Conference, which met at Simla on the eve of the Constitution of the Universities Commission, Lord Curzon said ' Concealment has been no part of my policy since I have been here in India, and the education of the people is assuredly the very last subject to which I should think of applying any such policy.' My Lord, backed by this high and distinguished authority, I appeal with some confidence to Your Excellency's Government for the publication of the papers referred to in my Resolution.

'My Lord, in dealing with this resolution, I feel that I ought to clear my ground and guard against any misapprehension which the situation might give rise to. I wish to state as distinctly and as clearly as I can that I have introduced this resolution in no spirit of controversy or contention and that I have been inspired by a genuine desire to remove any misunderstanding or misapprehension, and to secure thorough cooperation between the representatives of the people and the representatives of the Government in regard to those vital issues raised in the resolution which forms the basis of my motion.

My Lord, in the first place, I feel that I owe it to myself and to my educated countrymen to express our deep sense of gratitude to Your Excellency for the impetus which the cause of education has received during Your Excellency's administration. If education and sanitation are the watchwords of the educated community, they have also, in the words of Sir Guy Fleetwood Wilson, become the watchwords of the Government of India. An Education Department has been created and now forms a part of the Government of India. The educational expenditure has steadily grown, and as Your Excellency was pleased to remind us in the speech with which Your Excellency closed "the Simla session, the words of which are still ringing in our ears, the educational expenditure under Your Excellency's administration has risen from 4 to nearly 6 crores of rupees a year. His Majesty's visit to India and the deep solicitude which His Majesty evinced for the spread of education among his Indian subjects, have helped to place the educational problem in the forefront among public considerations. His Majesty's message of hope and sympathy combined with the active and living interest awakened in educational problems among the Indian community and the highest circles of Government, have opened up vast possibilities of educational growth and expansion.

May I express the fervent hope that nothing may be done, that no policy may be followed, which may mar or even dim this fair and beautiful prospect. My Lord, the first part of my resolution refers to the Ananda Mohan College. Hon'ble Members may perhaps like to know something about this College. It is a second grade college at the headquarters station of the Mymensingh

District. Mymensingh is one of the biggest, one of the richest, one of the most populous districts in East Bengal. It has a population of 4½ millions and comprises an area of 0,382 square miles. My Lord, there is only one single solitary second grade college to meet the requirements in respect of high education of this vast and multitudinous people—a people as large as was the population of England in the time of Charles the First.

The Ananda Mohan College is so called after the late Mr. Ananda Mohan Ghose, who was a native of this district, and who was one of the foremost men of his generation. Religious, social and political reformer, Mr. Ananda Mohan Ghose rightly regarded education" as the great instrument for the elevation of his countrymen. He was one of the founders of the City College in Calcutta, which, I think my hon'ble friends in charge of the Education Department will admit, has for the last 30 years been doing admirable work. He founded a branch school in the Mymensingh District and raised it to the status of a second grade in situation. His death in 1906, combined with the exacting requirements of the recent University regulations, which have made heavy demands upon the financial resources of College authorities, led to the abolition of this College in 1908.

But, my Lord, the people of Mymensingh had tasted the fruits of the tree of knowledge, and not death but life and an awakened educational impulse was their reward. A movement was set on foot for the establishment of a second grade college. The local public, be it said to their lasting credit, raised a subscription-of Rs. 1, 23,000. The Government, with a generosity which was truly admirable, made a grant of Rs. 50,000 and also offered a grant-in-aid of Rs. 6,000 a year, and the college was re-established. Judging by its results, judging by the growing number of its pupils, it must be held that the college has been a highly successful institution. But, My Lord, things in Mymensingh and in India are not stationary, any more than they are in any other part of the civilized world. Things are moving fast, very fast, under the impetus of worldwide forces of irresistible potency and the inspiration of progressive ideals created by education and fostered by a wise and beneficent Government. My Lord, I have already referred to the profound influence of the Royal Visit and the stimulus which it has communicated to the educational impulses of our people. I will say this, and I think without fear of challenge or contradiction, that the movement for the creation of a Hindu University at Banaras, and also that for the establishment of a Mohammedan University at Aligarh, had their roots in the awakened educational enthusiasm which the Royal Visit had evoked. In Mymensingh the feeling manifested itself in an eager demand for a first grade college.

In January, 1018, the College Council, at the head of which is the Magistrate and Collector, Mr. Blackwood—a name he loured in Eastern Bengal for the liberality of his views and his deep sympathy with the people—submitted an application to the Senate of the Calcutta University for raising the status of the Institution to that of a first grade college, for affiliation up to the B.A standard in Arts. The movement was warmly taken up by the Magistrate-Collector as well as the Commissioner of the Division. The Government promised an initial grant of Rs. 50,000 and offered to raise a grant-in-aid to Rs. 11,000 a year if the local public would raise Rs. 50,000. The district was ablaze with enthusiasm. I am not guilty of the slightest exaggeration of language.

Facts are more potent, more eloquent than any testimony which I might bear to the public spirit of the people of Mymensingh. In a few hours' time—not days or weeks, but a few hours' time—a hundred of the leading men of Mymensingh signed a legal document, accepted by the Commissioner of the Division and the Magistrate-Collector, by which they held themselves responsible for a sum of Rs. 50,000. The Government was responsive and the Government was sympathetic. Two Directors of Public Instruction,, one after another—Mr. Kuchler, late Director of Public Instruction, and Mr. Hornell, present Director of Public Instruction—both were in favour of raising the status of the College. The University Inspectors visited the College, reported favourably upon the application of the College Council, the University recommended its affiliation up to the B.A. standard in Arts, limiting the number of subjects to be taught; and now, My Lord, a shadow was thrown over the patriotic efforts of the people of Mymensingh. The Government of India declined to grant the affiliation. The Senate had made the recommendation, the University Inspectors had supported it, the Government of Bengal was in sympathy with it, but the Government of India declined to sanction the affiliation of the College on the ground, as I understand—I am speaking without chapter and verse, but I have tried to test my information as far as I could —that the college building was not ready and the staff had not been appointed.

My Lord, I claim on behalf of the private Colleges, and I claim with some little warmth of feeling, having been for the past 40 years-connected with a private college, that they are entitled to the sympathetic consideration of the Government, in view of their limited resources and the arduous nature of the difficulties with which they have to grapple. The Education Commission of 1882 recommended the encouragement of private enterprise in matters educational on the ground that the effect of it would be to foster educational institutions of different types. My Lord, I hope and trust that the papers which will be laid on the table in response to my appeal will disclose some reason for this differentiation between Government and private colleges. But there seems to have dawned at last a ray of light and hope on the situation, for I understand that an assurance has been given that the first B.A. class in connection with the Anand Mohun College will be opened in July, 1914, and I hope my Hon'ble friends in charge of the Educational Department would be in a position to repeat this assurance from their places in the Council Chamber.

My Lord, the next part of my resolution has reference to the School Final Examination. Facts and figures are given in the Government Resolution. From those facts and figures I gather that in Madras the School Final has been making steady progress. The same cannot be said in respect of the other provinces. But even if the success of the experiment was much more assured, and the system was much more popular in Madras and in other parts of the country, that would not be an argument in favour of its application to-Bengal, for as the Government itself has observed in the Resolution which we are discussing, the educational systems of the different provinces vary and a system which may suit Madras may not be applicable to Bengal. My Lord, whatever presumption may be raised in favour of the extension of this system to Bengal from its success in Madras, it is negatived by the experience that we have had in Bengal itself. I will give some facts. The School Final was introduced in Bengal, in Western Bengal not in Eastern Bengal, in connection with primary schools and the middle schools, English and Vernacular. They have been in operation there since 1904. On the 4th February, 1913, the Director of Public Instruction declares in a circular note, from which I shall presently read an extract, that it has absolutely failed and that the system should be discontinued. The circular letter was addressed by the Director of Public Instruction to the Inspectors of Schools in the Rajshahi Division, the Dacca Division and the Chittagong Division. This is the extract:

> 'Observation of the system that has been at work since 1904 has convinced the Educational and Executive Officers and the general public of West Bengal of its inefficiency and unsuitableness to prevailing conditions. It is therefore proposed to revert to the old system and once more conduct the final examination of Standard VI as a public examination, upon whose results the Middle Scholarships and Middle Vernacular and Middle English certificates will be awarded. Before, however, addressing Government the Director of Public Instruction is desirous of ascertaining the views of Educational and Executive Officers of Eastern Bengal, where the same system of examination as outlined above prevails.'

My Lord, the educational system of East Bengal and that of West Bengal do not materially differ. Therefore this pronouncement though applicable to West Bengal is really also applicable" to East Bengal. My contention is this, that if in the primary schools and in the middle schools," vernacular and English, the system of school final has failed, have we not an overwhelming presumption in favour of the contention that it is doomed, foredoomed, to failure when applied to the high schools? But, my Lord, there is another consideration which has to be weighed in the balance in this connection, and it is this: those who believe in University education, who regard it as having been one of the most potent factors in making modern India what it is today, must view with grave-alarm and misgivings the operation and growth of a system which must encroach upon the ground covered by the University and eventually seriously restrict it. Speaking for the people of Bengal, and I hope that the sentiment will be re-echoed by my friends from the provinces, I say that we view with the gravest anxiety the proposed extension of this system to the high schools in our Presidency.

Now, my Lord, I pass on to the third and last branch of my subject, viz., the recognition of schools. Paragraph 47 of Government of India Resolution says that in Provinces where it does not exist the Government of India think it desirable that the power of recognition of schools should be vested in the Local Government. In Bengal, my Lord, this power is now exercised by the Senate, and if this proposal were carried out the effect of it would be to transfer this" power from the Senate and vest it in the Local Government. My Lord, the proposal has caused widespread alarm and anxiety throughout Bengal. Meetings have been held all over the Province culminating in a great demonstration at the Town Hall under the presidency of the venerable Raja Peary Mohun Mukherjee, the Nestor of the Bengal Zemindars and himself one of the most brilliant products of the Calcutta University. Speaking from his place as President of the Town Hall meeting, he voiced the public sentiment when he said that he was there as a representative of the past to join hands with the representatives of the present and invoke the Divine blessing upon their endeavour to rescue from peril their bounteous mother, the University of Calcutta, and the cause of education generally. My Lord, next to religion, education is our most sacred concern. It touches our deepest instincts.

Throughout our long and chequered history, despite its many vicissitudes, religion and education have gone hand in hand. Our holiest shrines of worship are our noblest temples of learning. Banaras stirs the religious fervour of the Hindu world. Banaras evokes the admiration by the profundity of its learning. Rightly or wrongly, rightly from my point of view, we regard this proposal, if it is to be extended to Bengal, and perhaps to other parts of India, as constituting a grave menace to the cause of higher education. And what is the justification for it? Has the Senate of the Calcutta University asked to be relieved; or has the efficiency of the work suffered by reason of this power being vested in the Senate? I think, my Lord, both these questions must be answered in the negative. The Government of Bengal the other day, with the full concurrence of the Government of India, consulted the Senate of the Calcutta University, and I understand that a weighty protest has been recorded against this proposal. In any case, the Senate do not want to be relieved. They feel that they can bear the burden and discharge the responsibility. Has there been any lack of efficiency? I say 'No,' and I think that Hon'ble Members will also say 'No,' when they have heard me. The highest official authority has borne testimony to the character of the work which the Senate of the Calcutta University have done in this respect. The Bengal Administration-Report is the voice and organ of the Bengal Government, and this is the testimony recorded in the Bengal Administration Report for the year 1911-12, as regards the character of this work:

> 'Another important task of the University is the inspection of the High English Schools. The number of these schools recognised by the University is 619, of which 63 are under the management of the Government. During the last five years the Syndicate has made a systematic examination of these schools and has succeeded in remedying many of the defects that were discovered. It has laid down that each recognised school must have on its staff at least two graduates and two F.A. or Intermediate passed teacher", a minimum scale of pay for teachers has been fixed; sufficient accommodation and equipment have to be provided, libraries maintained and arrangements made for physical exercise.'

Then comes the most important sentence of all:

> 'The granting or refusal of these privileges of affiliation or recognition is the foundation of the disciplinary power of the University'

My Lord, it is now proposed to weaken the foundation of this disciplinary power by withdrawing the right of recognition from the Senate. Is that conducive to its efficiency, its prestige, or its dignity? Here we have the highest testimony possible, coming from the Government of Bengal itself, in favour of the continuance of this' power in the hands of the Senate as being essential to' its disciplinary jurisdiction. I hope, my Lord, that with this testimony, coming from the highest official source, the Government of India in the Education Department will pause before it proceeds to extend this measure to the Province of Bengal. The Resolution says that the object of the transfer of this power from the Senate to the Government is to free the Universities for higher work and for the more effective control of the affiliated colleges.

The effectiveness of the control exercised by the Calcutta University over its affiliated colleges, has never been questioned. I am connected with one of the affiliated colleges, have been so for the last forty years, and I say this, and I think I echo Bengal feeling on the subject, that the effectiveness of the control is carried a little too far and that it is a trifle too meddlesome. We should like to have a little less of this control and a little more independence given to these colleges. Let us discuss another consideration.

The schools are the feeders of the colleges and it is obvious that the institution which controls the colleges is best fitted to control the system of instruction which is to qualify for college education. I think, my Lord, that this is a truism so palpable that I need not further elaborate the point. I cannot disguise from myself the conviction that behind this all is the old, old plea of efficiency about which Lord Morley has said that it had been carried a little too far in the administration of this country. Speaking from his place in Parliament, I think it was in connection with the Budget Debate of 1906, he observed 'our Government would be more popular if it was a little more elastic and a trifle less, efficient,' But, my Lord, not only is there no justification for this proposal, but I venture to contend that the whole weight of argument is on the opposite side. Let us examine the matter a little closely. When an application is submitted to the University for the recognition of a school it is forwarded to the Director of Public Instruction for report The Education Department has thus the fullest opportunity of recording its views upon the application. But the final authority is the Senate. Now the Senate, like all public bodies, deliberates in public, decides in public, and, although largely official in its

Constitution and personnel, it decides with the aid of popular representatives. Nor is this all; it decides on grounds that are purely educational. Now, my Lord, if this power were transferred to the Education Department, what would happen? The Education Department, like all other Departments of Government—I am making no reflection upon an)' institution or body, I am merely stating the facts—would deliberate in secret, and without the aid of popular representatives.

Further, what guarantee is there that its decisions will always be guided by educational considerations? Every Government, whatever else it may be, is unquestionably a political organisation, and every Department of Government, even that of pure study, partakes of a political flavour. What we fear is that if this power were transferred to the Education Department of the Local Government, in times of excitement the fate of our institutions would be determined by political, and, I was going to add, by police considerations. The past is a guide for the future. What has happened in the past may be repeated in the future. It is a matter of common knowledge that in the height of the excitement in Eastern Bengal some of our educational institutions escaped disaffiliation through the saving power of the Senate. The Brij Mohan College, one of the best institutions in Eastern Bengal, was recommended for disaffiliation by the Government of Eastern Bengal, chiefly on the report of the Criminal Investigation Department. The Senate appointed a Committee on which there were two European gentlemen, one of them now dead whose memory we honour, the late Mr. Cunningham. They visited the college, held a local inspection, and found that the report upon which the application for disaffiliation had been made was misleading or exaggerated in many" essential points. The college was saved, and is now doing useful and splendid work. I submit, my Lord, that our alarm and anxiety in connection with this matter is one that is well founded.

It has been said that ' the man who pays the piper has the right to call for the tune.' This is an argument that has been adduced by a high official of the Bengal Government; but it will not stand the test of scrutiny, so far as Bengal is concerned. It appears from the Administration Report that we have in Bengal

619 "schools recognised by the University. Of these 619 only 63 are Government schools, the balance of over 550 are private institutions, managed, controlled and financed by our countrymen; about one-half of them receive aid, the other half are entirely dependent on their own resources. Therefore, this argument of the tune and the piper does not apply to the conditions prevailing in our Province.

But, my Lord, there is another aspect of the question which arises from the view which I have presented to the Council. In almost every district town we have a Government school and there are one and sometimes two competing schools controlled by private management. Between these there is often rivalry and jealousy. A local feeling and local bias is thus engendered, the local education authorities are infected by this feeling.' It is these authorities, be it observed, who will report upon any application for the recognition of a school. Practically, therefore, it comes to this that you make over the decision of the question as to whether a particular school in any particular locality is to be recognised or not to the men who may have contracted a local bias" against private enterprise in matters of education. At the present moment and under existing conditions the controlling superintendence of an independent body like the Senate nullifies the operation of personal and local bias.

Therefore, I venture to submit that it would be exceedingly risky to introduce an experiment of this kind in a province like Bengal, where the vast majority of the high schools are controlled by the people. They, at any rate, ought to have a predominant voice in the matter of the recognition of schools, and if they have not, the fact will operate as a setback to educational progress. My Lord, what is it that has covered Bengal with her educational institutions? From the earliest period of our contact with our British rulers our people have evinced the most active interest in the spread of high English education. Our fathers founded the Hindu School in 1817, nearly a hundred years back, at a time when the Government had not entered the arena of high education, and only four years after the East India Company had budgeted the paltry and insignificant sum of 10,000 for the education of the whole province of Bengal. My Lord, it was at the instance of the great Raja Ram Mohan Roy that Dr. Duff, the Prince of Indian missionaries and the Prince of Indian educationists, came over to Bengal and established the Free Church College, now known as the Scottish Churches College. My Lord, it is trust that has covered Bengal with her educational institutions; Mistrust, or the semblance of a policy involving an abatement of the confidence which has hitherto been reposed in the people, will be disastrous to the cause of education in Bengal and in other parts of India. It will not add to the number of schools: it will restrict the educational area and may even nullify the gracious message of our august Sovereign. But I have no fears, no doubts, no misgivings. I am confident that this proposal will not be extended to Bengal and I am fortified in that confidence by the terms of the resolution of the Government itself. The resolution says: 'Each province' (I am repeating the exact words) ' has its own educational system. It has grown up under its local conditions and is' (very significant words) ' a part of its general wellbeing.' Then the resolution adds, ' The Government of India have no desire to enforce a uniform system amid divergent conditions.' That, my Lord, is my appeal. We are proud of our local institutions, our local environments, our local traditions. We have been nurtured in them, we have grown up with their growth. We have grown up, if not to the full height of our educational stature—which, perhaps, is a matter of future accomplishment—at any rate to our present stage of educational progress under the happy operation of local conditions and environments in the, creation of ' which the Government has had a supreme hand; We ' "love them, we cherish them with affectionate regard: they are a part and parcel of our very being. They are bound up with our happiness and contentment. It is now proposed, my Lord, to revise them, to modify them, indeed, to revolutionise them.

His Excellency the President said:—" I would ask the Hon'ble Member to conclude. I have already given him more than 40 minutes, so he must conclude at once please."

The Hon'ble Mr. Banerjee said:—I will, My Lord.

We of the East abhor great and sudden changes, whether in education or in Government, with all the warmth of our oriental natures. We are advocates of steady, normal, natural expansion, according to our requirements and the growth of an advancing public opinion. Public opinion in India, in Bengal, the opinion of a united community, of Hindus and Mahomedans alike, is arrayed in strenuous opposition to this proposal.

My Lord, we have had enough of contention, of-controversy, of agitation: we want peace; we pray for peace. Give us peace, My Lord, by suspending, at any rate for the present, the application of this proposal to the province of Bengal. If public opinion in its subsequent developments supports it, there will be time enough to try the experiment, and then, My Lord, it will be tried with the full moral support of the people of Bengal and under conditions which will conduce to its success. Such an experiment, so tried, will add another link to the golden chain of sympathy which Your Excellency's Government has been forging for the people of India, and it will afford another striking illustration of the policy of conciliation and cooperation with which Your Excellency's honoured name will always be imperishably associated in the pages of Indian history. In the meantime, My Lord, let us be permitted to walk in the old ways where our footsteps have been so sure, so safe, and so steady, and where on the whole the results achieved have been so triumphantly successful. That, My Lord, is our appeal to Your Excellency's Government, on behalf of the people of Bengal, whose interests in association with my colleagues I represent in this Council, and I am sure I do not make that appeal in vain.

Calcutta University

[At a meeting of the Viceregal Council the Hon'ble Mr. Surendranath Banerjee moved the following Resolution:—]

That this council recommends to the Governor-General in Council to consider the advisability of placing the University of Calcutta on the same footing with the Universities of Madras and Bombay in respect of the relations between the Calcutta University and the head of the Local Government for purposes of administration and control.

In moving the Resolution, he said:

> Sir, under the provisions of the Indian Universities Act of 1904, His Excellency the Viceroy is the

Chancellor of the Calcutta University, and large powers of control are vested in the Government of India. To us who are graduates of the Calcutta University, it is a matter of pride and honour that His Excellency Lord Hardinge should be the head of our University, and speaking for myself, I will say this, that but for the approaching retirement of His Excellency, I for one would not have brought forward this Resolution. Speaking as Chancellor of the University of Calcutta at the Convocation held on the 15th March, 1915, His Excellency was pleased to observe that his position as Chancellor of the University brought him in direct contact with the student community of India. In them and in their welfare, Lord Hardinge has always felt a keen and abiding interest We cannot forget the incognito-visit which His Excellency paid to some hostels in Calcutta, with a view to ascertaining for himself, after personal examination, the conditions under which the students lived in those hostels. Sir, nothing so powerfully appeals to the imagination of an Oriental people as when a ruler conceals his personality when doing good; and the memory of this visit will long remain an abiding possession with the student community of Calcutta. Lord Hardinge has always been a generous patron of the Calcutta University. The Government of India have paid a sum of over 42 lakhs of rupees for our hostels, besides other grants, the capitalised valuation of which would amount to about 36½ lakhs. Sir, I feel it my duty to make this public statement as some acknowledgment, however inadequate, of the obligation which we are under to our retiring Chancellor.

Sir, my Resolution has a constitutional bearing, and it is intimately connected with the raising of the status of our Province, to that of a Presidency Government. Bengal was made a Presidency Government by the Royal Proclamation of the 12th December, 1911. A part of that proclamation was embodied in a Parliamentary Statute in January, 1912—Statute 2 & 3 Geo. V, Chapter 6. I will read the first clause of the Statute, which is pertinent to the Resolution now under discussion. Clause I says:

> It is hereby declared that the Governor and Governor in Council of the Presidency of Fort William in Bengal shall, within 'that Presidency as so delimited as aforesaid, have all the rights, duties, functions and immunities which the Governors and Governors in Council of the Presidencies of Fort St. George and Bombay, respectively, possess, and all enactments relating to the Governors of those Presidencies, etc., etc.

Now, this is the important part:

> Provided that, if the Governor-General in Council reserves to himself any powers now exercisable by him in relation to the Presidency of Fort William in Bengal, those powers shall continue to be exercisable by the Governor-General in Council in the like manner and to the like extent as heretofore.

Therefore, Sir, it is obvious that, under the provisions of this Statute, the Governor of Bengal is placed exactly on the same footing with the Governors of Madras and Bombay, save and except in respect of certain powers and functions which are reserved to the Governor-General in Council, and which at the time were being exercised by him. Those powers and (unctions are two in number: (1) authority to fill temporary vacancies on the Bench of the Calcutta High Court, and (2) authority as Chancellor of the Calcutta University. Lord Crewe was then Secretary of State, and when introducing this Bill he made certain observations which, with the permission of the Council, I will read as bearing upon this particular proviso. I am quoting from Hansard. He said:

> I now come to the clauses of the Bill. The first clause (that is the clause I have just read) declares that the Governor of Bengal should have all the rights, duties and functions which the Governors of Madras and Bombay possess. The effect of the clause is to give the

> Governor of Bengal these extra powers given by the later enactments under which power was taken to apply to any new Presidency the powers which the Governors of the other Presidencies possess. Then, the House will observe this is the important part—that two provisions are attached to this first clause. These provisions depend upon the fact that the powers of the Calcutta High Court are not, as matters stand, curtailed although the area of Bengal is changed and a new Lieutenant-Governorship is created. The power which is pointed to in proviso (a) is this: that the High Courts Act of 1871 gives the Governor-General in Council power to appoint temporary Judges to the High Court of Calcutta..

Nothing is said about the Calcutta University, for the simple reason that the same grounds apply. The size of the Province of Bengal was curtailed, but the jurisdiction of the Calcutta University remained the same as before, extending over the new Province of Bihar and Orissa, over Burma and Assam. It was not thought desirable at the time that a local Governor should exercise authority over areas' outside his territorial limits. The same objection, of course, would not apply to the Governor-General in Council. The Governor of Bengal, who succeeded the Lieutenant-Governor of Bengal, stepped into his position as Rector of the Calcutta University. That is a new office altogether in connection with the Calcutta University, which does not exist in any other University.

The powers and functions of the Rector are defined in section 28 of the Universities Act. Clause I says that the Rector shall take precedence at Convocations next after the Chancellor, but before the Vice-Chancellor. Clause 2 says that the Chancellor may delegate all or any of his powers to the Rector. Sir, I do not know whether any powers have been delegated. My own impression is that they have not been; but I should like to be corrected if necessary. This I do know as a matter of fact, that from time to time in reference to important considerations, the opinions of the Rector are invited by the Government of India. These opinions— I am not a lawyer," but I venture to think that I am right in making the observation—these opinions have no statutory force, but they have a moral value, as coming from the Governor of a great Province and a Governor of such great popularity and 'One held in such high, esteem and regard as Lord Carmichael.

Sir, I have dwelt upon the constitutional aspect of this question in order to indicate that the conditions which led to the acceptance of the Constitution at that time are now in process of change and transformation. I take it, Sir, that the new province of Bihar and Orissa will soon have a University of its own. I presume that the Bill is nearly ready; and with Sir Harcourt Butler, our ex-Education Minister, as Lieutenant-Governor of Burma, I take it that within a measurable distance of time, Burma too will have a University suited to its own requirements. Sir, the Governor or the Lieutenant-Governor of every province in India is the Chancellor of the University belonging to that province. Why should an exception be made in the case of Bengal? I urge this proposition, not indeed on the ground of administrative symmetry. Administrative anomalies may and do exist, and they are tolerated so long as no inconvenience is caused, no injustice is perpetrated; but I rest my case upon far higher grounds. My submission is this, that the University system of a province should be in direct touch with and controlled by the public opinion of that province, and for this purpose the head of the Government should be the Chancellor of the; University.

Sir, I look forward to a time—it will not perhaps be within our lifetime, it may be a dream, but many of our dreams have become realities—when the Chancellors and Vice-Chancellors of our Universities will be elected by the members of those Universities, and I think we who are here working for the future, may prepare the ground for this consummation. I do not indeed place my Resolution upon that exalted basis. But I give expression to a suggestion which occurs to me as I am speaking upon this matter. Sir, the Government of India, when it was located in Calcutta, was in direct touch with the sources of local public opinion; but that is not and cannot be the case now. I will say this, that I can conceive of no possible objection to the acceptance of my proposition except this, that the Governor of Bengal as Chancellor of our University may exercise authority over areas outside his jurisdiction. I ask, are there not Governors and

Lieutenant-Governors who are doing that now?" The Lieutenant-Governor of the United Provinces is the Chancellor of the Allahabad University, and as such he exercises authority over affiliated institutions in the Central Provinces and in Ajmer, which are distinct and separate administrative units. Take another case, which is even more pertinent and apposite. The Governor of Madras as Chancellor of the University exercises authority over affiliated institutions in Ceylon, which is not a part of the Government of India, and is not even subject to the jurisdiction, of the Secretary of State for India. Yet, Sir, no-catastrophe, no cataclysm has occurred.

The authorities in Ceylon have not complained of the curtailment of their power or of the loss of their dignity. Educated Ceylon goes to sleep without any perturbation of conscience or loss of self-respect. In view of these cases, may I not ask those who are opposed to this proposition, to reconsider their views in the light of the facts to which I have referred? But, Sir, I desire to place my case upon a still higher ground. We have been promised provincial autonomy by the great Despatch of the 25th August, 1911. Attempts have been made to whittle down the significance of that message. What has been written, however, cannot be unwritten, *scriptummanet;* and we as the representatives of the people will see to it that this beneficent message is redeemed in the fullness of time.

Provincial autonomy is bound to come sooner or later. I hope it will come in the train of those political readjustments that are inevitable after the war. Provincial autonomy, if it means anything, means this, that each province should be self-contained, self-dependent, self-governing. If my Resolution is accepted and given effect to, it will be a distinct step towards the fulfilment of the pledge which is contained in the Despatch of the 25th August, 1911, and which will for ever be associated in the annals of Indian administration with the name and fame of Lord Hardinge. Sir, it does not seem to me that it is necessary that there should be immediate legislation upon this point, if my proposition is accepted. The Chancellor may delegate his powers, under the section to which I have referred, to the Rector. The Rector, without the name, will then become the *de facto* Chancellor. The experiment may be tried; and if it is found successful, legislation may be undertaken afterwards. My proposition is an exceedingly moderate one. All that I ask the Government to do is not to jump to a conclusion or to come to a finding with regard to the great issues which I suggest All that I ask the Government of India to do, is to consider—mind you, nothing more than to consider—the advisability of carrying out a reform which will make the head of the local Government the responsible head of the University. I do not want that my Hon'ble friend should get up in his place and say we are not in a position to accept that proposition, and we cannot make Lord Carmichael at once Chancellor of the University.' I do not want that I want you to consider the proposition. I want you to consider it from the standpoint which I have suggested, in the light of the facts, which I have mentioned. I want you also in justice to those who are opposed to me, to consider the objections that may be raised. I do" not think that any proposition can be more modest, or more reasonable, and therefore it is with some confidence that I submit this Resolution for the acceptance of the Council.

[After some discussion the Hon'ble Sir C. Sankaran Nair accepted the Resolution with some reservations, on behalf of the Government. Mr. Banerjee spoke as follows in reply.]

Sir, I thank the Hon'ble Member in charge of the Department for accepting the Resolution. Bengal opinion would have been more pleased if he could have seen his way to accept the Resolution without the reservations to which he has referred. There has been an animated debate over this mater, but, really, if we look to the bottom of the whole thing, there is perfect agreement and unanimity in regard to it.

I do not think my Hon'ble friends, the official members—and I congratulate them on having broken their golden silence on this occasion—really object to our Governor being the Chancellor of our University. What they are apprehensive of, and what they object to, is that their University affairs would come under the direction of the Government of Bengal and would, pass away from the control of the Viceroy of India. They do not object to our being autonomous in this matter, but they want to safeguard their own interests. I think they are quite right. I confess that if I were in their position, I would take precisely the same view. I have no quarrel with them, but I have a quarrel with the Government in regard to this matter. I desire to call the attention of my Hon'ble friend Sir Sankaran Nair, to section 28, clause 2. Of course he was an eminent Judge, an ex-Chief Justice, and my reading of the law must be subordinated to his interpretation of it. But this is, so far as I can make out, a matter of common sense. This is what section 28, clause 2, says—

A Voice:—What Act?

The Hon'ble Mr. Surendranath Banerjee:—It is the Universities Act of 1904.

This is what section 28, clause' 2, says:—

The Chancellor may delegate any power conferred upon him by the Act of Incorporation or this Act to the Rector.

Since, therefore, the Chancellor is at liberty to delegate any or all his powers, my submission is this. Let the Chancellor delegate his powers in respect of colleges within the territorial limits of Bengal to the Governor, and let him retain control over the other provinces. I think that section justifies that. So far as Bengal is concerned, let the Chancellor delegate the powers that are vested in him—and the section gives him the authority—in respect of the affiliated institutions in Bengal—and they are 41 in number, Sir, out of 48—retaining his power in respect of the institutions outside the territorial jurisdiction of Bengal. That seems to me the obvious solution of the problem. These institutions, in the outlying areas of Burma, of Assam and of the new Province, will continue as now, under the authority of the Governor-General. There will be a change so far as we are concerned, and our Governor will be *de facto* Chancellor though not in name. The Viceroy will continue to be the Chancellor in name, but by this delegation, the Governor of Bengal will become the *de facto* Chancellor for the affiliated institutions in Bengal. This, Sir, seems to me to be a solution of the question that will reconcile conflicting interests, and divergent views, conciliate Bengal opinions and the opinions which have been expressed in this Council Chamber today. I think that is the solution, and I really do not know why the Government should not see its way to accept it. But, if, for reasons with which I am unacquainted, Government is not able to adopt it, then my submission is that it should expedite the creation of these different Universities. I am entirely in favour of the creation of a University in Assam. Why should not Assam have a University of its own and work out its educational destinies in its own way, according ±o its lights and according to its requirements? I do not at all share the cynicism—if I may be permitted to express myself in that way—of the Hon'ble Colonel Gurdon who asks 'What do the Calcutta lawyers know about the educational requirements of Assam?' The Calcutta lawyers are not the masters of the University. 80 per cent, of the Fellows are officials or non-officials nominated by the Government. If I am excused for using strong language, I will say this, that they are the creatures of the Government And what have the Calcutta lawyers to do with the matter? Over and above the Calcutta lawyers there is the Government of Bengal and the Government of India.

Assam has done wonderfully in the matter of educational development. And let those who malign the Calcutta lawyers bear in mind that these lawyers have had a large hand in helping forward the educational development of Assam. My Hon'ble friend Mr. Dadabhoy quoted the opinion of the Hon'ble Sir Ashutosh Mukerji. That opinion is a matter of antiquarian history today. The opinion is as old as the year 1912. I am not permitted to disclose the secrets of conversations which I have had with Sir Ashutosh Mukerji, who is a high educational authority, but I imagine that the spirit of his dreams has undergone a change and that the opinions which were paraded before us in that ostentatious fashion, so peculiar to my Hon'ble friend over there are not admitted by him at the present moment. They may be relegated to a museum of things ancient and when the biographer of Sir Ashutosh Mukerji attempts to write his life he may refer to it and may draw the lesson that even the greatest amongst us are sometimes apt to be versatile.

I say, Sir, once again, with all the emphasis that I can command, that we in Bengal—and I represent the public sense and the public conscience of Bengal in this matter—do not in the smallest degree desire to stand in the way of the creation of the Universities in Assam, in Burma and in Bihar and Orissa. We shall welcome them with enthusiasm because we shall recognise them as the products, the children, the progeny of the Calcutta University. We shall have the satisfaction of knowing that we have helped forward the educational development of these Provinces. No jealousy, no malice, no feeling of antagonism will mar the beautiful prospect that will open out to them and to us. We are anxious that they should have Universities of their own, but we are also anxious that justice should be done to us, and that the head of our Government should also be the Chancellor of our University. There is no mistake as to what official opinion in Bengal is. My Hon'ble friend to my right, Mr. Cumming, in that quiet, dignified but firm way which is characteristic of him, stated plainly what the views of the Government of Bengal are. And then there are the representatives of public opinion in Bengal.

Official and non-official opinion is united in the demand which I have ventured to put forward today before this Council. And that demand affects 41 of the colleges and schools of the Calcutta University, as against seven in the other Provinces. We do not want to stand in their way: give them their Universities, but do not bar the way against us. . Do not flout public opinion in Bengal by refusing to us the reform which we are entitled to have because we are a Presidency Government. My Hon'ble friend Mr. Setalvad, has asked: 'Why have you not brought forward cases to justify your motion V My friend is a lawyer; I am not, but I understand the tricks of lawyers. And I will tell him this, that I did not want to prejudice this controversy or handicap it by creating irritation and bad feeling at the commencement. I had a bundle of cases in my pocket, and I could produce them just now, of mandates issued by the Government of India, being carried out in defiance of the wishes of the Senate. I do not want to refer to them because I deem it inexpedient to injure my case or handicap it by creating irritation. Therefore, my friend will pardon me if he thought there was a flaw in the arguments that I ventured to bring forward. I am grateful to my friend the Hon'ble Sir Sankaran Nair for accepting the Resolution, but I hope he will give effect to the section to which I have referred. And if, for legal reasons with which I am unacquainted, he is, not able to do so, I earnestly appeal to him to expedite the creation, of those Universities which may enable us to place the Governor of our Province at the head of our University. That would be the first step towards freeing the University from that official control to which my Hon'ble friend Mr. Setalvad referred; and as popular opinion in Bengal is a growing power, we shall soon bring the Chancellor of our University under our own control. The Resolution was put and agreed to.

Decentralisation Commission

[*In moving the Resolution re: recommendations of Decentralisation Commission with regard to Municipalities, at a meeting of the Viceregal Council held on March 18, 1914, Babu Surendranath Banerjee said:—*]

Sir, I have the honour to move the Resolution which stands against my name, namely:

"That this Council recommends to the Governor-General in Council the adoption of the following recommendations of the Decentralisation Commission, namely:—

(a) that subject to the maintenance of prescribed minimum balances, municipalities should have a free hand in respect of their budgets;

(b) that Municipal Councils should usually elect their own Chairmen;

(c) that District Boards should contain an elective majority chosen by the non-official members of the Sub-District Boards;

(d) that village *Panchayats* should be formed where local circumstances and experience permit with power to carry out projects regarding village sanitation, village schools and minor village works."

My Resolution covers a wide surface of our system of local self-government Ever since the days of Lord Ripon the encouragement of local self-government has been a prominent feature of the administrative policy of the Government of India. In one of his earliest utterances Lord Ripon, whose memory we the people of India cherish with affectionate gratitude, declared that he had it in charge from Her Gracious Majesty, the late Queen Victoria, to foster the growth of local self-government in India.

This message was followed by the Resolution of the 18th May, 1882, which authoritatively laid down the principles of local self-government, and which we regard as our Magna Charta in that matter. Lord Morley, in his despatch of the 27th November, 1908, endorsed the principles of this Resolution. He regards local self-government as an integral part of his scheme of constitutional reform, which he thinks ought to be presented as a whole; and he urges the Government of India to adopt speedy measures for the effectual advancement of local self-government With your permission, Sir, I will quote an extract from the despatch of the 27th November, 1908; 'It is desirable,' says Lord Morley,' to present our reformed constitutional system as a whole,' and he adds, ' from this point of view, it is necessary to attempt without delay an effectual advance in the direction of local self-government.' All that my Resolution seeks to bring about is an effectual and speedy advance of local self-government. Sir, I am confident of the sympathy and support of the Government of India in this matter: for His Excellency the Viceroy was pleased to say the other day, the 23rd December last, in reply to an address that was presented to him by the Corporation of Calcutta, that it was the earnest desire of the Government of India to advance the cause of local self-government, wherever possible.

Sir, the first part of my Resolution recommends that municipalities should be permitted a free hand in framing their budgets, subject to the maintenance of a prescribed minimum balance. This free hand they have not at present. Let me explain, Sir, the law and the practice, as the law and practice are in Bengal, and I presume that the law and practice, having regard to the considerations to which I shall presently refer, cannot in other provinces be materially different. In our province in the month of February, the Commissioners, at a meeting held for the purpose, frame and adopt their budget The estimates are then forwarded to the magistrate of the district. The magistrate of the district with his remarks sends back the estimates to the Commissioners or forwards them to the Commissioner of the division. The Commissioner of the division either sanctions the estimates or makes his remarks and sends them back to the Commissioners for consideration. Sir, the suggestions of the Commissioner of the division are in the nature of mandatory instructions. The Municipal

Commissioners are bound to carry them out. That is the law on the subject. My complaint is that this control of the Commissioner of the division extends to the minutest details of municipal administration. The Municipal Commissioners cannot add a rupee to the pay of a clerk, or even of a peon, without his sanction; and I" know of instances where such increments have been disallowed. Sir, the power of the purse is the test of all real power; and where it exists in name or under sufferance, there can be no sense of responsibility.

We have heard a great deal about the apathy of our ratepayers; but how can the ratepayers feel a living interest in their municipal affairs when they see that their representatives are thus treated in the supreme and crucial matter of finance. Our Conferences and our Congresses have again and again called attention to this matter and have addressed the Government to relax the rigours of executive control; but all in vain it was not until the Decentralisation Commission had come to our rescue that the Government of Bengal felt itself called upon to move. On the 20th April, 1910, in the time of Sir Edward Baker, a circular letter was issued over the signature of the Hon'ble Mr. Wheeler, who was then our Financial Secretary, giving a free hand to four municipalities, subject to certain restrictions to which I shall presently refer.

These restrictions were that they should maintain a prescribed minimum balance, that they should make adequate provision for the service of loans, and lastly that they should observe the Act and the rules and regulations of the Government. These are perfectly reasonable conditions. The municipalities, thus exempted from the rigours of executive control were the four biggest municipalities in the province— with the exception of the Corporation of Calcutta—each-having an annual income of over a lakh of rupees. This circular letter indeed went a little beyond the concerns of these municipalities. It laid down the general principles subject to which Commissioners of divisions were to exercise their control. Sir, with your permission,. I will read an extract from that circular letter:

> While it is only in the four municipalities specified that the Lieutenant-Governor is at present prepared

> to dispense with the supervision of the budget now enforced by the District Magistrate and Commissioner, it should be recognised generally with reference to all municipalities that, so far as possible, interference with details should be avoided; the three important points to be scrutinised in connection with the budget are enumerated above. Otherwise, Commissioners, when examining municipal budgets, should endeavour rather to guide the municipalities concerned by friendly advice than to control their discretion by explicit direction to take or forbear from particular action-; municipalities should be made to recognise that they are primarily responsible for the 'efficient and economical administration of their finance's, and if they misuse the discretion vested in them, they must bear the result of their own mistake.

Well, Sir, this was a circular letter issued in 1910. I was chairman of a suburban municipality in 1910. I am chairman of the same municipality in 1914. I find no improvement in my position. It is just as good, or just as bad now, as it was then The control is as minute, as searching, as all-embracing now, as it was in 1910. What then is to be the solution? Well, Sir, I venture to submit that all the municipalities in Bengal should be placed upon one and the same footing with these four municipalities, and that the recommendation of the Decentralisation Commission in regard to municipalities should in this respect be given effect to.

If Government should hesitate to take what may appear perhaps to some to be a big jump into the unknown, I venture to suggest a compromise, namely, that the municipalities having an income of Rs. 10,000 a year may be exempted. I think such a measure would be on the lines of Sir Edward Baker's policy, it would be in conformity with the spirit of the recommendations of the Decentralisation Commission, and would represent a further advance in the direction of local self-government. Sir, my remarks apply primarily to Bengal, but I venture to submit that the condition of other municipalities in other provinces is very much the same, if not worse. Therefore, these remarks apply equally to municipalities in other parts of India.

Now, Sir, I come to the second part of my Resolution, namely, that Municipal Councils should elect their own chairmen. I take my stand upon the great Resolution of 18th May, 1882, which says that whatever official control is to be exercised over local bodies should be exercised from without rather than from within. Lord Morley, in the despatch to which I have referred, thoroughly endorses this principle; and, indeed, he goes a step further. He says that the partial non-success of the system of local self-government in India is largely due to a departure from this which he regards as the true and vital principle of local self-government, and he invites the Government of India to affirm the principle and actively shape its policy in accordance with it. I will read an extract from Lord Morley's despatch. He says:

> If Local Self-Government has so far been no marked success as a training ground, it is mainly for the reason that the Constitution of the local bodies departed from what was affirmed in the Resolution to be the true principle that the control should be exercised from without rather than from within. The Government should revise and check the acts of local bodies, but not dictate them. I have no doubt that the Government of India today will affirm and actively shape their policy upon the principle authoritatively set forth by their predecessors in 1882.

That, Sir, is what I urged, namely, that the Government should affirm and actively shape their policy in accordance with the principles laid down by their predecessors. Sir, what is the state of things today? Here is the true, vital principle of local self-government laid down in the Resolution of the 18th May, 1882, supported by the high authority of Lord Morley. Why not apply that principle to the present situation? In reply to a question which I had the honour of putting yesterday, the Department over which you preside so worthily has kindly placed at my disposal a statement, a most interesting statement, throwing a flood of light upon the development of local self-government. It appears from that statement that there are 526 municipalities in all India. Of these 198 municipalities have chairmen appointed by the Government, that is to say, they do not elect their chairmen. I ask the Council to deduct 111 municipalities in Bengal from this figure, for the reason that I shall refer to the Bengal municipalities later on; for the present I hope the Council will have sufficient confidence in me to permit me to make this deduction. Therefore, we have a balance of 415 municipalities outside Bengal. Of these, 178 municipalities have chairmen appointed by Government, deduct 14 municipalities; because, although they have the right to elect their chairmen, they have not exercised that right: therefore, these municipalities should be deleted. Then we have these figures, out of 415 municipalities outside Bengal, 164 have chairmen appointed by Government— a departure from the principles laid down in the Resolution of 1882 and from the despatch of Lord Morley. In other words, Sir, after 30 years of local self-government, we have 89 per cent of the municipalities all over India, except Bengal, whose chairmen are appointed by Government. I think this is a situation which calls for immediate remedy. As far as Bengal is concerned, the situation is better, thanks to the statesmanship of a distinguished member of the Indian Civil Service, Mr. Herbert Reynolds. He is now in England, living in retirement; and the blessings of a grateful people follow him; he was the author of our municipal system. In Bengal, out of 111 municipalities, only 20 have their chairmen appointed by Government. In other words, whereas in the rest of India you have 39 per cent of the municipalities whose chairmen are nominated by Government, in Bengal there are only 18 per cent whose chairmen are appointed by Government. Nor is this all. I want to make a stand for my province and show that in this matter its policy is liberal to a degree, and should be extended to other parts of India. These 20 municipalities are included in the second schedule of the Act—we call it the black list. The Municipal Law in Bengal is so liberal that a municipality may be withdrawn from the schedule, but none can be added to it Furthermore, when a municipality which has the right to elect its chairman desires to forego that right and abandon its constitutional privilege, it can only do so, not indeed by a bare majority but by the vote of two-thirds of the entire body of Commissioners. It seems to me that there is no occasion for keeping this schedule at all, when the Government has such ample powers of the control from without, even to the extent of suppressing a municipality. There is, therefore, no necessity for exercising Us power from within by appointing a chairman. Sir, if there is to be an advance in this direction in respect of Bengal, *a fortiori* there should be an advance in respect of other parts of India.

I now come to the third branch of my subject, namely, that District Boards should contain an elective majority chosen by the non-official members of the Sub-District Boards. This is a recommendation of the Decentralisation Commission. There are 198 District Boards in India, having 5,013 members, of these 2,336 are nominated, in other words, less than half Thus, we have a majority of nominated and not of elected members, contrary to the recommendation of the Decentralisation Commission and to Lord Morley's despatch. Lord Morley says (I am not quoting the words, I have them here, I will reproduce them from memory) that non-official members of Local Boards must be made to feel that they have real powers and real responsibilities to discharge. What I want to ask is how can they feel that they have real powers and have real responsibilities to discharge, when they are in a standing minority in these District Boards, under the presidency of the omnipotent head of the district.

Now I come to the last branch of my Resolution, namely, that village *panchayats* should be formed where local circumstances and experience permit, with power to carry out projects regarding village sanitation, village-schools and minor village works.

Here again, Sir, I rely upon the authority of Lord Morley, who invites the Government of India to take active measures for the organisation of these village unions. He says:

> I desire Your Excellency in Council to consider the best way of carrying out a policy which would make the village the starting point of public life.

According to the same authority the village is the fundamental, the indestructible unit of the Indian Social System, which has survived the overthrow of dynasties and the fall of Empires. Sir, our village organisations carry the mind back to the dawn of human civilization and the early beginning of local self-government. They are dead" now, but the instinct is there, deep down in the national consciousness, and under the fostering care of a wise and beneficent Government, such as we now have, it may be revivified into a living flame. Our system of local self-government has been built up from the top. That, perhaps, was inevitable under the circumstances. But the time has now come when it should be strengthened from below and the foundations laid well and deep. I cannot help making the remark, Sir, that there has been a lack of enthusiasm, both popular and official, in the matter of these village organisations. Why, in India there are only 454 village unions, Madras carries off the palm in this matter with 393 village unions; Bengal comes second—a bad second, I am sorry to say—we have 56 village unions, and the other provinces, Bihar and Orissa, divide the rest. I think, Sir, the law should be revised. The power of these village organisations is limited, their funds are scanty. In Bengal, under the Cattle Trespass. Act, they get the proceeds of the pounds supplemented by the doles of the Local Boards. Well, Sir, I have no hesitation in saying that village sanitation will not thrive and primary education must fail of its purpose, if the villagers do not cooperate; for after all the nation dwells m the cottage and no surer basis of national prosperity can be laid than in the association of the residents of our villages in the great task of education and sanitation.

You, Sir, were pleases to observe the other day that the Government would soon issue a Resolution on local self-government. We desire that the Government should know our views before this Resolution is recorded. I hope and trust the trend of this discussion will place the Government in possession of the sense of the educated community as voiced by their representatives, Sir, the Government has evinced the most lively concern in the advancement of education. Local self-government rightly understood, is a part of our education. Lord Ripon regarded it as an instrument of popular and political education, and the Government of India have recognised the close interdependence that exists between them by placing the two departments under the control and guidance of the same Minister. Education is the hand-maid of local self-government; local self-government is the ally of education. They strengthen each other and help each other by their mutual interaction. I take it that the Government is most anxious to educate us in Western ideals, and not only in Western ideals, but in those practical activities which have their roots in those ideals. If I am right, I submit that a simultaneous advance in respect of education and local self-government is called for, and the first essential condition is that the leading strings should be relaxed, if not completely done away with; that a larger measure of independence, greater opportunities of initiative and self-reliance, should be accorded to the local bodies. I am sure, Sir trust will beget trust, kindle a new sense of responsibility and justify the great boon which is associated with the honoured memory of one of the most loved, and one of the most illustrious, of Indian Viceroys. When two such authorities as Lord Morley and the Decentralisation Commission call for an advance, I submit that the Government of India cannot stand still. Our goal, that of the Government and the people, is the same; we are journeying both towards the same destined end. If there is any difference of opinion, it is about the pace. We want the Government to quicken its pace, to move faster: a very significant request coming from an Eastern people. The East is indeed slow to move, but when it does move, it moves with all the passionate, but restrained and reasoned, fervour of the Orient. With these remarks I beg to move this Resolution.

Defence of India Act

[Speaking on the Hon'ble Sir Reginald Craddoc's Criminal Law Amendment Bill on the 18th March 1915, in the Imperial Council, Babu Surendranath Banerjee observed:—]

My Lord, I have listened with attention, I may add with respectful attention, to the speech of the Hon'ble Member in charge of this Bill and to the speeches that subsequently followed, including the lecture which my Hon'ble friend to the left read to our public men who are members of this Council. I will say this that I am not convinced as regards several of the provisions in the Bill, which to my mind do not seem to be justified by the exigencies of the country or by naval and military considerations. My Lord, we have been told, and I accept the statement in an unqualified form, we have been told that the situation in the Punjab is grave and the situation in Bengal also is serious, though perhaps not to the same extent. The object of the Bill is to improve the situation. The end is one which will commend itself to all, no matter to what school of politics he may belong, for we know that order—stable order—is the fundamental condition of all real progress. But when we come to consider the means to be devised for the purpose of attaining this object differences of opinion arise. My Lord, I say at once that so far as the provisions of the Bill are concerned arising out of the war and relating to naval and military considerations, it is the duty of every patriotic Indian to accord to them his wholehearted support, and I am sure that this will be the sense of the country.

But, My Lord, the Bill traverses ground beyond military and naval considerations, raises issues of a highly controversial character in regard to which many of us will not be able to see eye to eye with the Government. It has been stated by the Hon'ble Member in charge of the Bill that it is framed upon the English Act. Well, in many respects it traverses beyond the English Act, and I will mention one or two points. I am not considering the sections in detail, but section 2 creates an offence which is not to be found anywhere in the English Act, namely, promoting feelings of enmity and hatred between different classes of His Majesty's subjects. That is altogether new in this Bill; it is nowhere to be found in the English Act, and I think the Hon'ble Member in charge recognises the fact.

Then, My Lord, there is section 3 which creates a particular tribunal and lays down specifically the offences which are to be tried by that tribunal.

My Hon'ble friend in charge of the Bill has said that the tribunal in England is the Court martial: here the tribunal is to be a Commission to be constituted by the Local Government. Undoubtedly the provisions of the English Act as regards this matter are far more drastic than the provisions of the Bill that is before us.' But, My Lord, an amendment was moved in the House of Lords the other day—and I believe the underlying principle of it was accepted by the Lord Chancellor and the Government,—under the terms of which, when members of the civil population would be affected, they would have the right of claiming trial by a Civil Court and by a jury. But what I desire to point out is this, that it is only specific offences that are covered by the English Act, whereas we have a large number of offences under the head of Public Safety included in the Indian Penal Code which find a place here and which are to be tried in a summary fashion by a specially constituted tribunal.

Therefore, My Lord, the contention that this Bill is framed upon the basis and the model of the English Act is only correct in a qualified sense. It is far more comprehensive than the English Act, and because it is so, I fear there will be a great deal of agitation and controversy in the country regarding its provisions.

My Lord, reference has been made to the growth of anarchism in Bengal, to the recrudescence of crimes of violence in our province. My Lord, we, the educated community of Bengal and the leaders of the moderate party, hold anarchism in absolute horror and detestation, and we are doing what we can to put it down so far as it lies in our power. On the 13th of this month we held a Conference in the rooms of the British Indian Association, presided over by the Maharajah of Burdwan and attended by many men of light and leading, including a European gentleman who is the Principal of an important College in Calcutta. My Lord, it was the unanimous sense of that Conference that restrictive measures would not be suitable, and that they would aggravate the situation. My Lord, that is the deliberate judgement of the people of Bengal. We feel that the effect of restrictive measures in Bengal would be to add to the uneasiness of the community and perhaps help the breakers of the law, who would welcome them. What is needed is not new legislation, but greater efficiency of the police. I freely admit that the efficiency of the police has been added to and improved in recent years, but a great deal more remains to be done. My Lord, it is the immunity of the offenders and the helplessness of the community who are defenceless and unarmed, that encourage these breakers of the law in the perpetration of their foul deeds I may remind the Members of this Council that there was a formidable conspiracy soon after the outbreak of Fenianism in London, the object of which was to blow up the public buildings with dynamite. In one year's time the London police shadowed every conspirator, hunted down the gang, and the country was purged of the scourge. Of course I know India is not England, but still, what we feel is that if the Government is to deal with the outward symptoms of these unhappy developments, the efficiency of the police has to be greatly improved. With regard to the root causes, my Lord, they have to be dealt with in that spirit of conciliatory statesmanship for which Your Excellency's Government has obtained a name and fame.

My Lord, I feel that in this matter the Government should have proceeded by Ordinance. Your Excellency was pleased to refer to this matter in the course of your speech. We of course bow to Your Excellency's decision, but what some of us felt, what I at least felt, was this, that in this matter the Government could not admit us into their fullest confidence, that they could not perhaps disclose to us, in all their details, the information upon which their judgement was based, and that, therefore, it was impossible for, us to record an intelligent vote. That being so, I felt that it was the clear duty of the Government to have assumed the entire responsibility of these measures by issuing an Ordinance. However, that may be, my Lord, we are grateful to Your 'Excellency for the assurance which Your Excellency has given us today, that the crimes of a few fanatics, and this law which Your Excellency's Government thinks necessary to enact for their prevention, will not be regarded as a slur upon our loyalty. I hope and trust that this measure will in practical operation be administered with moderation 'and self-restraint. I hope and trust that it will not be a weapon in the hands of the enemies of Indian advancement for the purpose of blasting those prospects and frustrating those hopes which have been roused in our hearts by the loyal devotion of our countrymen consecrated by their blood on the battlefields of Europe. For the faults of a few fanatics the millions of our countrymen who are loyal to the core of their hearts should not suffer.

In Bengal Legislative Council

Calcutta Municipal Bill, Part I (1898):

"Sir,—My first duty is to congratulate the Hon'ble Member in charge of the Bill on the lucid and exhaustive statement with which he has prefaced his introduction of the Bill. Greatly as I differ from him with regard to his views about the Bill, and strongly as I condemn the measure, I am bound to recognise the tact, judgement and ability, and above all the conciliatory attitude, which are so conspicuous throughout the speech. My hon'ble friend rests his case not so much upon the failure of the Commissioners as upon the alleged inherent weakness of the system under which they had to work. It is the system rather than the men that he attacks. I commend this part of his speech. He has thus endeavoured, so far as it lay in his power, to dear the atmosphere and relieve the controversy of those personal elements which at one time threatened to darken the issues involved; for I can conceive no greater misfortune than that we should in approaching this grave consideration allow our minds to be perverted—our judgements to be warped—by any sentiment of personal or party bias or by any lingering recollection of a controversy which I hope and trust has now been forgotten. We should endeavour, in considering this question, to rise the height of judicial impartiality and level-headedness, for the issues involved are of grave and far-reaching importance. If this Bill should unhappily become the law of the land, and if its principles are to be engrafted upon the system of Local Self-Government which prevails in the Mufasil, then I have no hesitation in saying—I say it with regret, but say it I must—that one of the greatest blessings which we enjoy under British Rule, and with the inauguration of which, Sir, your name is so honourably associated—the inestimable boon of Local Self-Government—will have become a thing of the past.

Well, Sir, if I have rightly understood the attitude of my friend — and it is an attitude which challenges the system rather than the men—then the question which we have to ask ourselves is this—what are the grounds upon which he bases his conclusions? My hon'ble friend says in substance that the municipal system of Calcutta has been tried and has been found wanting, that the conservancy arrangements have broken down, that the Constitution does not ensure prompt and continuous executive action, and that it is unequal to the strain of a grave and sudden emergency. This represents the sum and substance of his indictment against the Corporation. Great as is the authority which undoubtedly belongs to my hon'ble friend as the Head of the municipal administration of these Provinces, I think we shall be guilty of no disrespect towards him, if we ask him to produce his evidence and to place before us the materials upon which he has based his opinion and upon the strength of which he invites this Council to endorse his judgement. Sir, if we examine the matter a little closely, we shall find that my hon'ble friend has undertaken a task beset with serious difficulties. It will not be enough for him to show that in regard to the municipal administration of Calcutta there has been a failure here—a defect there—a breakdown elsewhere. He must carry his evidence much further than that. He must show that the system has so completely failed—the situation is so desperate—that no partial remedy will suffice—that there must be a radical and fundamental change—that the system must be broken up, the site cleared for the erection of a new and a totally different superstructure. Nay more— he must advance a stage yet further.

My hon'ble friend must show that in the actual circumstances of Calcutta, menaced by the plague, the only remedy that is left open to us as sensible and wise men is to, adopt the discredited municipal system of Bombay which was not able to keep out the plague. A more desperate position—one more entirely at variance with the dictates of reason and sound sense—it would be difficult to conceive. My friend may well feel staggered, I will not say at the temerity of the enterprise, but at the gravity of the task which he has imposed upon himself, and if he is not able to do justice to it, his great ability will not be at fault-the badness of the cause will be responsible for it.

Sir, it is not for one moment to be supposed that I regard the present Constitution of the Calcutta Municipality as perfect. Far from it. It is capable of improvement, but it does not He in the directions indicated in the Bill. The Bill has been launched in the name of sanitation. Could we persuade ourselves to believe that it would promote sanitation and thus confer an unmixed benefit upon the people, what could be more natural than that we should support a measure, so wise in its scope—so beneficent in its intentions.

For Calcutta is the city of our birth—it is the city of our sires—it is the city of our children—and it is to be the destined city of our children's children. We have a far more permanent and abiding interest in its sanitary well-being than any other section of the community could possibly have. We would welcome any rational scheme of sanitation which would bring to our people an accession of health and all the blessings which the possession of health implies. But we are persuaded that this Bill will not promote this great object. It is not laws but funds that are needed for the structural improvement of Calcutta. We have had of recent years too many laws. We want rest, peace, the repose of peace, freedom from the excitement consequent upon new proposals for the enactment of new laws. It is money and not a change in the Constitution of the Municipality that is required for the sanitation of Calcutta. Sir, I speak not as an amateur or a theorist, but as one who has some practical familiarity with municipal work. I have spent the best part of my lifetime in the service of the Corporation. I entered it when young. I have grown grey in its service.

The work of the Corporation has been the pleasure and the pride of my life. I have behind me an experience of nearly 25 years. Fortified by that experience, I venture to make an earnest appeal to you, Sir, whose name is so honourably associated with the great scheme of Local Self-Government, to abandon or at any rate largely to modify a measure which has filled the ratepayers of Calcutta with alarm, which will not promote the ends of sanitation, which will depreciate the value of property, disorganise the work of the Corporation and wreck the best prospects of Local Self-Governments in the capital of the Indian Empire. Sir, I might put my case upon still higher considerations.

Municipal institutions, said Mr. Gladstone, are the seed-plots upon which and around which are developed that political capacity and those habits of political thought which ought to be the supreme concern of all Governments to foster and to promote. Our municipal institutions are the gift of our rulers. We owe them to their beneficence. But they have taken firm root in our hearts and our convictions, for they are in entire accord with our ancient traditions and the inherited instincts of our race, fostered by the *panchayat* system and our time-honoured village organisations. We cherish them with reverence.

The love and devotion of a people cling to them. They supplement our education; for what nobler school could there be than the school of public affairs! These noble seminaries inspire the people with a sense of responsibility, exercise a moderating influence upon their minds, and enlist their sympathies on behalf of the Government. It would be most unwise, most unstatesmanlike, in these days of political unrest and excitement, to do aught which would in the least impair the utility of these institutions or shake public confidence in them. We are the friends of sanitation; but the worship of sanitation may be carried to the verge of idolatry.

We agree with Sir Ashley Eden in thinking that a single case where native society is persuaded by conviction to adopt a sanitary reform is worth hundred cases where such reform is forced upon it by the pressure of external circumstances Sir, greatly as we value sanitation, we are not prepared to sacrifice our civic freedom for its sake, especially when such a sacrifice is unnecessary and uncalled for, and when it will prove disastrous to the fortunes of our people in other higher and nobler directions.

7

Lectures in England

Indian Press

[*At the meeting of the British and colonial journalists in the Imperial Press Conference in* 1909 *in London, Mr. Surendranath Banerjee made the following spirited defence in reply to Lord Cramer's attacks on the Indian Press:*—]

I am sorry to interpose with some observations which may not appear to be very pertinent to the question we are just considering; but an invitation was extended to us—I will not use the word challenge—by Lord Cromer that we should say whether in our opinion the anarchical developments which have recently taken place in Bengal are due to the irresponsible utterances of a certain section of the Indian Press. Sir, to that query to that question, my answer is an unqualified and an emphatic "No." I will not defend what has been said in the Press. I say to my brother journalists gathered from all parts of the Empire—let me put this question to them. Are they prepared to defend everything in the Press—that is written in the Press—on questions of public importance? Are we an infallible body? Do we not commit great and gorgeous mistakes which we have reason to deplore to the end of our lives? I am not here to defend the irresponsible utterances which unfortunately have found a place in some of the Indian newspapers. But, Sir, let me say this, that some of these newspapers form a very insignificant minority; their circulation is limited; their hold upon the people is circumscribed. Let me not for one moment be understood as standing up here in justification of these anarchical developments. I express the sense of my province, of the better mind of Bengal and of India, when I say that we deplore these anarchical developments; we have condemned them in our columns with all the emphasis we can command. They are in entire conflict with those deep-seated religious convictions which consciously or unconsciously govern our everyday lives. And without offence may I be permitted to say that anarchy is not of the East, but of the West? It is a noxious growth which has been transplanted from the West to the East, and I hope and trust that under the salutary and ameliorating treatment of Lord Morley these anarchical developments will be utterly crushed out. *(Cheers).* Sir, I am precluded from entering into controversial matters, or else I should like to say a word or two with reference to those circumstances which have led to these anarchical developments. But I recognise the fact that this is a non-controversial Conference, and I resist the temptation I exercise, the self-control of the East in this matter. *(Laughter and cheers).*

In conclusion, I desire to say this, that we regard the liberty of the Press as one of the greatest boons that have been conferred upon us under British rule. It was conferred on us not merely for political purposes but as an instrument for the dissemination of knowledge and of useful information. That was at any rate the conception of the great liberator of the Press, Lord Metcalfe, whose memory we cherish in our grateful recollections. Replying to a deputation which waited on him after the liberation of the Press, Lord Metcalfe said: " We are here not merely to collect taxes and to make good the deficit 5 we are here for a higher and nobler purpose, and that is, to pour into the East the knowledge, the culture, and the civilization of the West." *(Cheers).* That was the great aim, the great hope, the great aspiration of the liberator of the Press and that hope, that aspiration has been largely fulfilled. It is one of our greatest aims—I will claim this on behalf of my countrymen—that on the whole we have used it to; the benefit of the Government, to the credit of our race; 'and long may it be enjoyed to the mutual advantage of England and India, and to the glory of both countries. *(Cheers).*

Situation in India

[At *a meeting held at the Caxton Hall, Westminster, in July 13,* 1909, Sir *Charles Dilke, Bart., M.* P., *presiding, Mr. Surendranath Banerjee said:*]

Mr. Chairman, Ladies and Gentlemen,—I desire at the outset to associate myself, and I can also speak on behalf of my countrymen, with the observations which you, Mr. Chairman, have been pleased to make regarding the blessed and time-honoured memory of the late Marquis of Ripon. (Hair, *hear.)* In the illustrious muster-roll of Indian Viceroys he will take his place amongst the most illustrious. His memory will for ever remain enshrined in the grateful recollections of our people. The rulers of India who cling together In our grateful affections are Bentinck, Canning, and Ripon. *(Cheers.)* I do not think it necessary to repeat the observations which I have made at other public meetings to express the horror and detestation which, we have felt at the terrible tragedy which resulted in the deaths of Sir Curzon Wyllie and Dr. Lalcaca, for Indian public opinion in this country and in the homeland is clear and emphatic with regard to it. *(Hear, hear.)*

For various reasons, some of them not of the most pleasant character, the Indian problem at the present time looms largely into the public view. Our complaint —I mean the complaint of the people of India—is that so little interest is felt in this country regarding the affairs of that great dependency. *(Hear, hear.)* The apathy of the British public is one of our greatest grievances, because the fact remains, whoever might be our governors and administrators, the British democracy, the electors of Great Britian and Ireland, are the real rulers of India. *(Hear, hear.)* To them have been entrusted the destinies of 300,000,000 of my fellow-countrymen, not savages or barbarians, but representatives of a great and ancient culture which carries the mind back to the dawn of human history. *(Hear, hear.)* How is this awful responsibility discharged? I am reminded in this connection of an Eastern legend, historical in its character and based upon truth. Mahmood of Ghazni flourished in the eleventh century of the Christian era. His dominions extended far and wide. There lived in a part of his Empire an elderly woman who had suffered a grievous wrong, for one night she found her house burned down, her goods plundered, and her children massacred. Overwhelmed with the awful calamity, she set out to the capital of the Empire and sought her ruler's presence. She presented herself at the palace gates, was ushered into Mahmood's presence, and laid her complaint before him. Mahmood heard her case and its tale of sorrow and wrong, and then he remarked: "Woman, you live in a remote part of my Empire. How can you expect me to extend to you the protection of my power?" And the woman, with that promptitude of resource which characterises her *sex—(laughter)*—replied: " Sire, why then do you conquer countries to whose affairs you cannot pay sufficient attention, and for which you cannot hold yourself answerable at the Day of Judgement?" *(Applause.)*

Ladies and Gentlemen, I have no desire to enforce this lesson in its application to the British democracy, but I say this, and I think with your full concurrence, that the responsibility of these islands as regards their great dependency is not discharged by merely appointing your governors and your administrators and leaving them to the discretion of their own sweet wills. *(Hear, hear.)* I have no desire to make the smallest reflection upon the men on the spot. *(Hear, hear and laughter.)* I am sure they do their best according to their lights and opportunities; but after all, they are human beings, dominated with ideas and sentiments, and it may be with the passion of their prejudices. In the old days of the East India Company a Parliamentary Committee used to be appointed every twenty years to enquire into Indian affairs. The labours of this Committee were favourable alike to England and to India, and I do not understand why this practice should not be revived and the Government thereby exercise a beneficent sway over the people, caring for them and in turn being loved by them. There is nothing to lose but everything to gain by such an enquiry. *(Hear, hear.)* But Governments are slow to move. They will not prepare the materials or provide the grant for impelling progress without the irresistible pressure of public opinion being brought to bear upon them. *(Hear, hear.)* Yet this is what will have to be done. *(Hear, hear.)* I have heard it said that if such an enquiry were to take place the machinery of the Government would be dislocated. Well, all I can say is, I have a far greater faith in the stability of that machinery than apparently have those who work it and are responsible for its efficiency. *(Hear, hear and laughter.)* And this is justified by the lessons of experience. Only eighteen months ago the Decentralisation Committee was appointed to visit India and travel up and down the country, examining numerous witnesses and instituting the most searching investigation.

Ladies and gentlemen, will you believe it, the Government of India actually survived the catastrophe. *(Laughter.)* No dislocation nor any disturbance of the existing machinery of the Government took place. There was not the slightest deviation from the normal conditions of the administration of the Government, nor was there any deviation in the uses of Indian life and society. My own belief is that if this Committee were continued and their recommendations followed, the Government of today would not have been confronted with excitement and unrest and all the deplorable things which have followed in their train. *(Hear, hear.)* The Government would have been more in touch with the people. And that brings me to the subject of Indian unrest. What is the cause of that unrest, what are the circumstances contributing to it, and what is the solution of the problem? *(Hear, hear.)*

Ladies and gentlemen, I ask you to bear in mind that we in India area law-abiding and peaceful people. (*Hear, hear.*) Our instincts, traditions, and deepest religious feelings and affections are intimately bound up in the maintenance of law and order. Our ancestors developed a system of ethics and a code of laws upon that proclamation from on high, "Peace and good will among men," which today excite the admiration of mankind and constitute an enduring monument of their devotion to peace. What, then, is it that has plunged a people whose antecedents were such as I have described, so peacefully inclined, so adverse to all forms of excitement, into a vortex of unrest which is unparalleled? Edmund Burke has told us—and his dictum has never been challenged, for the reason that it cannot be challenged—that in all controversies between people and their rulers the presumption is that the rulers are in the wrong and the people in the right.

(Hear, hear). I say if the matter of this Indian unrest were carefully examined, and there is no tribunal more qualified for the task than the tribunal of the British public, it would be found that the responsibility for this unrest mainly rests, and I am sorry to have to say it, but say it I must, upon the Government of the country. *(Hear, hear.)*

I blame no one; I am not here to formulate charges against individuals. Even the most dazzling and brilliant of Viceroys fade out of my recollection before the issues involved. I am here to place the facts before you as they affect my countrymen and to vindicate their character as a peaceful and law-abiding people. *(Hear, hear.)* When you have heard those facts I know you will give your verdict in my favour. *(Applause).* I am happy to say from the outset England's great mission in the East was realised by the illustrious founders of the Indian Empire. It was not realised by every one, and certainly not by those who went out to India to make money or die of liver complaint—*(laughter)*—but it was realised by those great and illustrious men whose-genius and statesmanship founded the vast and majestic fabric of the Empire of India.

Macaulay, speaking, from his place in the House of Commons on the occasion of the Charter Act, used language which L for one have ever read with enthusiasm and gratitude. " It may be," said Macaulay, " that the public mind in India may so expand under our system that it may outgrow that system, and our subjects trained in Western civilization may pray for Western institutions. I know not whether such a day will come, but if it does, come it will be the proudest day in the annals of England." I venture to say that day has arrived, and great are the responsibilities of England. *(Hear, hear and applause.)* Lord Metcalfe the liberator of the Indian Press, used similar language when replying to a deputation which waited upon him. " We are not here," he said, "merely to keep the peace and collect taxes... we are here for a higher and nobler purpose, to pour into the East the knowledge and culture and the civilization of the West." (Hear, *hear.)* The Earl of Selburne, the great-grandfather of Lord Lansdowne, who opposed the insertion of Clause 3 into the Indian Councils Bill, said on the occasion of the debate in the House of Lords on the

Charter Act of 1833 that their lordships would be remiss in the discharge of their duties if they did not offer to the Indian people ample opportunity for developing the high moral and intellectual qualities with which they had been endowed. These utterances embodied a noble policy, rand such a policy pressed steadily into the view of the Indian Government by the most illustrious of Indian administrators has resulted in higher education being introduced into our midst, the Press liberated, local self-government, and the setting up of councils. But can you tell a people whom you have so liberally educated and plentifully supplied with the environments which stimulate public life that thus far shall they go and no further. *(Hear, hear).* Yet that has represented the attitude of Anglo-Indian government for the past twenty years.

There you have the beginning of Indian unrest, which has now assumed such vast proportions. Can we overlook the wondrous change which has taken place in Asia; changes have been brought about by the victories of Japan over Russia, which had strengthened the confidence of Asiatics in themselves. *(Hear, hear.)* We have a mighty wave sweeping over Asia which carries with it high ideals and aspirations. India would be false to herself, her ancient culture which she so largely imbibed, and the education she has received if she did not feel revivified in the example of oriental nations struggling for consideration and self-government. *(Hear, hear).* On the top of all this excitement came a period of reaction, in which the legitimate aspirations of the people were ignored and trifled with. The people were counted as nothing, we were counted as nothing, and we were to do nothing; everything was to be done for us. The generous policy of Lord Ripon was reversed. Local self-government was modified, and the universities, centres of humane and beneficent influence, were officialised, despite the protests of the people. Then on the top of all came the crowning piece of folly—the partition of Bengal. *(Hear, hear).*

It is true the situation has been somewhat eased by Lord Morley's reform, but this reform scheme has given rise to some considerable diversity of opinion amongst us. *(Hear, hear.)* There are those representing a section of Indian opinion who hold that it lacks the essential element of genuine reform; that it will serve no useful purpose, and that whatever merits it might have possessed have disappeared in the recommendation of a system of class legislation. *(Hear, hear.)* On the other hand, there are those who hold a different view altogether. They" declare that the scheme makes lavish concessions—concessions which were never before thought of, and which represent an entirely new and remarkable departure. As an Indian speaking on behalf of my countrymen, I say at once that I totally dissent from this view. The scheme contains no concessions which have not been sought for. So far from the scheme being lavish, I still say, that it does not come up to our expectations in regard to many matters which vitally concern the power of the purse. We want definite control at least over some of the great departments of the State; over sanitation, education, and the public works department. Are you not aware that hundreds of thousands of my countrymen die every year from preventible diseases, such as malaria and cholera? *(Shameful!)* Yes, I think it is very shameful indeed." We have been pressing the importance of the matter upon the Government for years. We have cried aloud, but who will listen to us? *(Hear, hear.)*

If we had some effective control over finance, or at least over sanitary measures to be' employed, I am convinced that we could prevent to some extent the appalling rate of mortality which desolates homes in Bengal. *(Hear, hear.)* The expenditure on education is inadequate.. The great bulk of it is not being spent for education at all but upon inspection. *(Laughter.)* As for elementary education, well, the less said the better. '*(Hear, hear.)* If we had any control over finances in regard to education we should devote the money to a useful and profitable purpose.

We want the power of the purse and a, definite and effective method of self-government. *(Cheers.)* This we have not got; all the scheme does is—and let me be perfectly candid in the matter—to provide machinery by which representatives of the people would be in a position to bring to bear upon the Government not a direct influence but an indirect moral pressure. *(Hear, hear.)* At the same time we have accepted the scheme as a beginning. We recognise that there is such a thing as the growth of public institutions. *(Hear, hear.)*. You cannot make a law, be it good or bad, which is not, at once subject to a process of transformation under the operation of immutable moral laws. These are hopes which have gathered round the scheme. They may be fulfilled, or dark clouds may gather, the force of reaction may be in the ascendant so that these aspirations which we have fondly cherished may fall away like shadows. All the same, we do cherish these hopes, and we pray that they may be realised. *(Hear, hear.)* In Bengal the situation has taken a somewhat strained and difficult aspect. In the firmament of that province there is a cloud which is no bigger than a man's hand, but which threatens to overshadow the beautiful prospect pointed out by Lord Morley's scheme.

Lord Morley has recently said that he will be no party to the withdrawal of the partition of Bengal. I hope that pronouncement does not preclude him from considering proposals for the modification of the partition.. *(Hear, hear.)* If any one were to tell me, no matter how high and exalted might be his position, that there is no hope for the modification of the partition of Bengal, I should venture to tell him, in the name of my countrymen, that then there is no hope for the conciliation of Bengal, or for the cooperation of our people in the working of the reform scheme. *(Applause.)* This partition is our greatest grievance, and in our judgement it is the root cause of, the present discontent in. India. *(Hear, hear.)* When it was first announced it invoked the united opposition of the Hindus and the Mahomedans alike.

The opposition was so widespread and so intense that it would have sealed the fate of any measure in this country. But the methods of the Government in India are different from the methods of the Government in England. *(Hear, hear.)* For this opposition the Indian Government had its revenge. A wider scheme of partition was announced, which had been deliberated on in the secret recesses of the Secretarial Bureau. It was resolved upon in secret and fell like a bolt from the blue upon the astonished people of India. It gave rise to an agitation the parallel of which I have never before witnessed. *(Hear, hear.)* It is four years since the partition was accomplished, but the wound today is as fresh as if it were only inflicted yesterday. *(Hear, hear.)* There are those who say that the feeling against the partition is on the wane, but we are in the position of unfortunate ' beings suffering from a painful disease. It has its moments of cessation, but the patient knows no rest or peace so long as the root cause of the disease lies ingrained in his system. The anniversary of the date of the partition is a day of mourning. The shops are closed, and all business is suspended. The people go about the streets bare-footed, interchanging amongst themselves the mystic ribbon of eternal love, and the vow to carry on the agitation from generation to generation until the partition has been abolished.

I ask you, ladies and gentlemen, is it right to allow a grievance of this kind to fester in the depths of a national life? The longer you permit if the wider becomes its mischievous operation and the deeper grows the discontent' *(Hear, hear.)* They say it is a sentimental grievance. Be it so. A sentimental grievance is one which is worthy of consideration. What I should like to know would be the feelings of the people of England, under the identical circumstances. But far more so is the question of sentimental feeling important when it is a question of governing an Oriental nation. *(Hear, hear.)*

But, ladies and gentlemen, this grievance is more than a sentimental grievance, and I desire to lay before you some of the most practical considerations which ought to operate for a modification of this partition. The partition was entered into in the name of efficiency. No finance, I venture to hope, is a crucial test for efficient administration. *[Hear, hear.)* What, however, do you find with regard to Bengal? It is a bankrupt province, unable to meet its demands, and compelled to rely upon subsidies from the Government of India in order to supply its most urgent needs. *(Hear, hear.)* If Bengal remained united she would have been financially prosperous, and financial prosperity means prosperity all round. *(Hear, hear.)* Let me take another consideration, and not a sentimental consideration. For generations the Hindus and Mahomedans have lived together in peace, but the partition has thrown the apple of discord into their midst, and has created an alienation of feeling which has led to great disturbances and breaches of the peace. Lord Ripon, of blessed memory, strongly condemned the partition on the ground that it had caused deep discontent among the population—meaning the population of which I have the honour to belong. Contentment of the people is the strongest asset of the British Government. Great Queen

Victoria taught us the utmost importance of this in the Proclamation of 1858, which she closed with these words: " In the contentment of our people lies the strength of our rule. " *(Hear, hear.)* It is useless for me to disguise the fact that universal contentment in Bengal has become a thing of the past. Any one who knows Bengal will tell you that it is a province of peaceful people. Why, then, is it now the centre of disaffection and discontent? It is the partition. *(Hear, hear.)* I have, ladies and gentlemen, the confirmation of official testimony. You will remember that the persons in the Alipore bomb case were charged with conspiring against His Majesty, and it was stated that the day fixed upon was October 16. That date is important because it happens to be the date of the partition of Bengal. *(Hear, hear.)*

I think, therefore, the partition stands confounded, from the mouths of those who support it. What does Lord Morley say? I desire to speak of him with the utmost respect; I have read his works again and again, and I teach them to my scholars and saturate their minds with lofty principles of political wisdom. *(Hear, hear.)* But if I respect Lord Morley, I love my motherland far more. *(Hear, hear and applause.)* Therefore, in the interest of my native land, I must enter into the arena and contend against my political guru. Lord Morley says it is merely a matter of the adjustment of boundaries, and yet he also says that the partition is a settled fact. *(Hear, hear.)* A statesman need not be logical, but he is bound to be reasonable and just, and cannot override the paramount claims of the people. Righteousness is the vital breath of Imperial statesmanship, and a single act of unrighteousness is more disastrous to British rule in India than a great reverse sustained upon an Asiatic battlefield. *(Hear, hear.)* I cannot conceive anything more disastrous to the credit of the British administration than such a proceeding as the partition. It is calculated to shake Indian confidence in the integrity and sense of fairness of the Government. *(Hear, hear.)* Lord Morley says the partition is a settled fact Then I say on behalf of my fellow-countrymen that we decline to accept it as a settled fact. We decline to accept what is admittedly a blunder and what we feel to be a cruel law and a wrong to the sentiment of the people. *(Applause.)* We will continue this agitation, and we want your sympathy in our great struggle.

(Hear, hear.) Will you extend to us the right hand of friendship and sympathy in this matter? *(Cheers.)* That this is a deplorable blunder has become obvious by the supplement of a policy of oppression which has become necessary to combat the feeling which has been evoked. Take away this partition and then the oppressive policy will become unnecessary.

So far as this policy of repression is concerned I say this, it came to us in the light of an unpleasant surprise. We are accustomed to associate English administration, especially control by the Imperial Government, with the most scrupulous observance of the rights of personal property. Your history and literature and poetry are saturated with the rights of personal liberty. *(Hear, hear.)* No one could read the glowing pages of English history without imbibing a passionate love for such liberty; yet it would seem that we are not to be allowed to enjoy it By-secret reports of a secret police the sanctity of our homes is invaded, domiciliary visits are made, and nine gentlemen, some of them men of light and leading, are wrested away from the bosom of their families and held in detention in gaol under personal discipline, without the purpose being communicated to them, any explanation given or a chance given of making a defence. (" *Shame* ".) And what is the character of these police? The most unscrupulous in the world. *(Hear, hear.)* Sir Lawrence Jenkins, the Chief Justice of Bengal, in the Court of Appeal, found that the police had deliberately put a bomb in the house of the accused with a view of fabricating evidence, and Mr. Weston, Magistrate of Midnapur, caused the arrest of the father of one of the accused with a view of extorting a confession. *("Shame* I") It is a shame, and it is a matter of bitter irony that these things should be done under a Government presided over by a Secretary of State of the pronounced liberalism of Lord Morley. *(Hear, hear.)* "Liberalism," said Mr. Gladstone, " was trust in the people, tempered with, discretion." Such proceedings as this, however, involve the gravest distrust of the people, and if you will not trust the people they will not trust you.

"Coercion is an evil instrument of Government," said Edmund Burke in the ' eighteenth century and so said John Morley in the nineteenth ! It exasperates and does not salve, but leaves wounds which take years of conciliatory administration to heal. How did you pacify India after the Mutiny? You did so by the rejection of all coercive measures and by the application of conciliatory methods. *(Hear, hear.)* With all the emphasis I can command, in the name of common sense, on behalf of the people of India and the credit of British rule, I do earnestly appeal to you to do all that lies in your bring about a speedy abrogation of this which sits like a nightmare upon the troubled bosoms of our people; and might I also be permitted to make another appeal to you, not to accept the official version that the feeling against the partition is on the wane. *(Hear; hear.)* The patient himself is the best judge of the painfulness of his malady, and we are the patients in this instance. *(Hear, hear.)* My countrymen are suffering, and in their name and upon their behalf I urge you to do all in your power to bring about a modification of the partition of Bengal. I am sure my appeal will not fall upon heedless ears, but will go forth from this meeting accompanied by a volume of sympathy which will have the effect of redressing our grievance and restoring many millions of my countrymen to contentment. *(Applause.)*

Lord Morley's Reform Proposals: I regard the new scheme as the beginning of Parliamentary institutions in regard to local administration. I don't think we have got all that we wanted, but we are thankful for what we have got and we shall continue to press far more in a thoroughly constitutional way.

We asked for definite and effective control over the finances and the Executive Government: I cannot say that we have got either. But we have obtained substantial concessions which will prepare the way for these great ends.

With reference to the financial question, the situation is less satisfactory. Members will be permitted to move amendments in Committee, but the Government is under no obligation to accept these amendments, and the functions of the members will therefore be more or less advisory.

There is a general feeling of disappointment that nothing is said about Partition.

We fervently hope that as the Government has embarked upon a policy of conciliation it will accomplish its work by reuniting the two Bengals under a Presidency Governor, for which the

Secretary of State proposes to take powers. I feel that the modification of the Partition and the raising of the two Bengals to the status of a Presidency Government should be the essential feature of the policy of conciliation.

An Interview with Mr. Stead: I travelled down to Lord Northcliffe's seat at Sutton with Mr. Banerjee when the editors of the *Empire* went down to lunch at that delightful place, and formed the highest opinion of his lucid intelligence, his marvellous command of English, and his passionate devotion to his native land. I had the honour of being one of the guests at the banquet given to him by his fellow-countrymen in England at the Westminster Palace Hotel, and was delighted to find in him an orator of brilliant eloquence and a statesman of comprehensive outlook, with a most practical mind. I invited him to my house and there in company with a dozen friends —American, Canadian, Irish and Indian—Mr. Banerjee kindly submitted himself to a process of composite interviewing the gist of which the readers will find condensed in this article. Mr. Banerjee has been twice President of the Indian National Congress, he has been once in gaol, he is the editor of the *Bengali*, and his repute is such that he was once said to have been crowned King of Bengal as a protest against the partition. He was the only representative of the Native Indian Press at the Conference, and none of the editors of the *Empire* excelled him in eloquence, energy, geniality, and personal charm.

Message to British Public

"If you were under sentence of death Mr. Banerjee, and the headman's axe was to fall in two minutes, what is the message which you would wish to address to the British public as the last words you were able to utter on behalf of your motherland?" Without a moment's hesitation Mr. Banerjee replied:— 'I would say this: (1) Modify the partition of Bengal; (2) release the deported patriots and repeal the Act which annuls *Habeas Corpus* in Bengal; (3) amnesty to all the political prisoners; (4) give the people of India financial control of their own taxes; and (5) grant India a Constitution on the Canadian model. That is what I would say, and having said that, I would go to my doom."

"Good!" said I. " Now let us condescend to particulars. I thought you wanted the repeal of the partition?"

Partition

"I wish that repeal were possible, but I recognise that Lord Morley, having been perhaps challenged prematurely for an expression of opinion, took up a stand from which he can hardly now be asked to recede. I am a practical man; I ask for modification, not for repeal." " But I suppose you want to modify it, lock, stock and barrel?"

"What I would like is to see Bengal placed under one Lieutenant-Governor with an executive council of six, of whom two should be Indians. You will have to come to this, for the new province is at present placed in a position of inequality with the old, having no executive council. The next proposal, and one which commanded from of old time the balance even of official opinion, was to divide Behar from Bengal. The people of Behar are distinct in race and language from the Bengalis. All administrative advantages claimed for, the original partition would be secured by this arrangement without offending national sentiment. So long as the Bengali nation is unnaturally cleft in twain by the sword of Lord Curzon, so long will agitation and unrest continue."

Deportees

"Now as to the deportees !"

"They ought never to have been deported without charge and without trial. They ought at once to be allowed to return home. I hope that will not be long delayed. They are good men, upright citizens who did not deserve deportation."

"And then?"

"Then Regulation III of 1818 should be repealed or declared illegal. This regulation, passed by a subordinate legislature, deprives the Bengali subjects of His Majesty of their inalienable rights as British subjects to the privilege of *Habeas Corpus.* I would like repeal outright, for if we bear the burdens and accept the responsibilities of British subjects we ought to have the privileges of freedom from arbitrary arrest, which no one has denounced more strongly than Lord Morley himself."

"Circumstances alter cases. India is not Ireland; to preach is one thing, to practise is another. Is no compromise possible?"

"As a first step," said Mr. Banerjee, " I would accept Mr. Mackarness's proposal that there should be no arrest without specification of the offence and that every accused person should be brought to trial within three months of his arrest."

"I propose as a compromise," I said, " that in future all Indians deported without charge or without trial should be sent to Great Britian in order that they might be at once elected to the House of Commons as Nationalist M. P.'s for Irish constituencies."

"I fear," said Mr. Banerjee, " that there might be difficulties in the way. But if a working alliance could be made, whereby one Indian Nationalist could be provided with an Irish seat, and the whole Irish party took up the Indian national cause, great things might be achieved."

"To return to your message. Do you want all the bomb-throwers, political cut-throats, etc., let loose to begin again their seditious practices?"

"There are no such persons in custody. I do not ask for an amnesty for the police who used bombs in a criminal conspiracy, in order to ruin innocent men. I only want the political prisoners released. There are about sixty of them, and many of them have been sentenced to monstrous sentences for very venial offences."

Mr. Banerjee then went on to instance Mr.Tilak's sentence.

Duma for India

"Do you want a Duma for India?"

"If you mean an assembly representing all India with financial control over the expenditure of India, I say yes. But I would say first give us autonomous provincial governments, with financial control over certain departments of provincial expenditure. Then build upon these provincial autonomies a central federal council or assembly. That is what we ask, and that is what sooner or later we mean to have."

So far Mr. Banerjee. That is his programme. And! " Surrender Not " is the nearest English equivalent to the pronunciation of his name, Surendranath. I do not think that he is likely to abandon any of the planks in his programme. John Morley, of the " Pall Mall Gazette" and of " The Life of Burke," would probably subscribe to them all. But as for Lord Morley—that is another matter.

Indian Unrest

The present unrest in India may be set down to the following causes:—(1) The utter disregard of Indian public opinion by the Government, of which the most notable illustration was afforded by the partition of Bengal. (2) The creation of racial animosities in at least two of the great provinces in India—the Punjab and East Bengal—by the introduction of racial bias into the administration. (3) The wide divergence between profession and practice on the part of the Government and the non-fulfilment of solemn pledges such as are given in the Queen's Proclamation and the consequent failure to associate the people in the Government of the country and to accord to them a recognised status in the administrations. (4) The contemptuous treatment of Indians by Europeans. (5) The hostile attitude of an influential section of the Anglo-Indian Press (whose views are listened to by the Government with respect) in regard to Indian aspirations and the violent and contemptuous language which often marks its utterances. (6) It may be added that the subsequent repressive measures have greatly intensified the unrest.

As regards the first of the aforesaid points, Lord Curzon's administration afforded the strongest illustration. The one end of Lord Curzon's policy was efficiency of administration to be secured by filling the higher offices with Europeans. Against this policy the Congress of 1904 recorded its protest. It was regarded as the practical reversal of the policy of the Queen's Proclamation. In carrying out his policy of efficiency, Lord Curzon treated Indian public opinion with open and undisguised contempt. On the top of all this came the partition of Bengal. It represents the deepest outrage upon popular sentiments which has been witnessed within the lifetime of this generation. When the partition of Bengal was first proposed, it evoked the strongest opposition from both the Hindu and the Mohammedan communities concerned.

Instead of modifying or abandoning the project, the Government, in the quiet recesses of the secretariat bureau and unknown to the public, enlarged the scheme, added the whole of North Bengal to the original project and, without giving the public the smallest hint of its proceedings, all on a sudden declared that the partition had been resolved upon. The indignation of the people was roused to fever heat, and an agitation was set up against it 'such as has never been witnessed. It is with us what Home Rule is with the Irish. We cannot give up the agitation against it.

The partition may be said to be the root-cause; and, as Mr. Gokhale has truly observed, the unrest of Bengal has caused the unrest of all India. There are new facts of the most convincing nature created by the partition of Bengal which call for the reconsideration of this measure. Before the partition was carried out, Hindus and Mohammedans lived in amity and good will. Since the partition considerable ill-will has been created between the two communities. The bulk of the inhabitants of the new province are Muhammadans and they have been taught to believe that the province has been created for their special benefit, and that they are a privileged class. The Government made no, secret of their intention that they wanted to create a Mohammedan province.

Among the fruits of the partition may be mentioned: (l) The unrest in the new province which has created the unrest in Western Bengal and all over India. (2) The policy of repression which followed the partition and has not yet been abandoned, adopted with a view to put down the unrest. (3) The ill-will between Hindus and Muhammadans, who had hitherto lived in peace and amity, which must be a permanent source of embarrassment to the administration. (4) The class bias which is apparent to the policy and the proceedings of the authorities.

The Queen's Proclamation was issued on the 1st November 1858. The proclamation had abolished race as the test of qualification for high office. The resolution of May 1904 affirmed that race connotes qualities and that the Imperial Service (which is the highest service in India) should be a *corps d' elite* to be filled for the most part by Europeans and that even in the technical branches of the public service, the higher appointments should be their monopoly. It is worthy of note that under the Mohammedan rule, race or religion was no barrier to employment in the highest offices, and that Hindus often' filled the most responsible offices in the State.

The contemptuous treatment of Indians by Europeans, and the hostile attitude of a powerful section of the Anglo-Indian Press are matters of public notoriety. Sometime ago the Indian Association of Lahore, in an official letter, called the attention of the Government of the Punjab to certain articles which appeared in the " Civil and Military Gazette" of Lahore, which constituted, to quote the words of the Government letter, "a campaign of calumny against the Indian community in general and the educated class in particular."

The reply of the Government (dated 1st November 1907) was interesting and instructive. It admitted the charges against the " Civil and Military Gazette," but declined to take any legal proceedings. Yet for offences of the same kind, the editor and the proprietor of the "Punjabee" (an Indian newspaper) were prosecuted by the Government, and sentenced to long terms of imprisonment by the Courts of Law. The law is thus held in abeyance against Anglo-Indian and Mohammedan writers, indulging in the fiercest racial provocatives. Against Hindu offenders of the same class, its terrors are enforced in all their rigour. Yet the fact remains that the Hindus form the bulk of the population in India.

The present unhappy lawless developments have undoubtedly their roots in the prevailing discontent.' When a whole community is discontented and exasperated, it is only natural that some people more excitable than the rest should lose their heads and do foolish and violent things. The anarchic development is only one of the outward manifestations of a serious distemper in the body politic, the causes of which are to be found in the reactionary policy of the last sixteen years and more, and which reached is climax during Lord Curzon's regime.

Lord Morley's reform scheme is a notable and distinct step towards conciliation. India is rapidly advancing; and the reform scheme represents an effort conceived in the spirit of sympathy and liberality to adapt the administration to the newly developed requirements of the situation. It is altogether a mistake to assume, as the special correspondent of the " Times" does, that the scheme makes concessions that are lavish and unsought for. On the contrary, it does not, in some important matters, come up to our anticipations. We have not got the power of the purse which we wanted, at least in some important departments of the State, and we have not got a definite or effective measure of self-government, which we have been urging from the Congress platform. But it is a beginning, and a good beginning, and our people welcomed it as such. In Bengal, however, there is a serious difficulty. The partition remains unmodified and Lord Morley has told us that he would be no party to the reversal of the partition. What Bengal wants is not the reversal but some modification of the partition.

How deplorable the blunder of the partition has been will appear from the policy of repression that has been followed in order to combat the feeling which the partition has evoked. There could be no stronger condemnation of the partition than the adoption of a policy which is in such entire conflict with British traditions of Government. The main features of that policy are: (1) House-searches; (2) domiciliary visits by the police; (3) suppression of societies by executive order; (4) deportations without trial. House-searches are most repugnant to Indian feeling In one case the High Court granted damages for Rs. 500 to a zemindar whose cutcherry (court-house) had been searched by the Magistrate of Mymensingh.

In by far the majority of cases the searches were fruitless, and only served to create irritation. They have created a sense of uneasiness among the Indian, community. At Dacca, the capital of the new province, about 200 young men are treated as suspects, and their houses are visited by the police almost every night No charges have been brought against them. The head and front of their offence seems to be that they were members of associations which have since been suppressed by order of the Government, but which were perfectly legal when they were connected with them.

Several associations have been suppressed by executive order, without their being allowed the opportunity of explanation or defence. Among them was the Bandhab Samiti of Barisal in East Bengal which did splendid work during the Barisal famine of 1906-7, and whose objects were: (1) The promotion of indigenous industries; (2) the settlement of disputes by arbitration; (3) the promotion of village sanitation. The suppression of an association like the Bandhab Samiti has naturally created very widespread dissatisfaction. As regards the deportations, Mr. Buchanan said from his place in the House of Commons that they were based " solely" on the report of the police and we know, from the judgement of Chief Justice Sir Lawrence Jenkins how unscrupulous the police in Bengal are, and how unsafe it is to accept their statements. In the case which Lala Lajpat Rai brought against the " Englishman " newspaper for stating that he had been deported for tampering with the loyalty of Indian sepoys, the Court held that the statement was " a malicious lie." The defence was that it was substantially the statement made by the. Government in Parliament. Damages amounting to £ 1,000 were awarded to Lala Lajpat Rai. All these repressive measures have intensified the excitement and unrest. To mix up coercion "with conciliation is to neutralise the good which conciliation may produce by the unhappy leaven of coercion.

I would suggest the following remedial measures:-- (1) That the partition of Bengal should be modified. It is the root cause of the unrest in Bengal, and, as Mr. Gokhale has observed, the unrest of Bengal means the unrest of all India. I may here point out that the Punjab was tranquillised by the redress of a local grievance—*viz.*, the vetoing of the Colonisation Bill by the Viceroy. (2) That the policy of repression should be abandoned and those who have been deported restored to liberty. The Indian public deplore the recent tragedy but they earnestly hope that it will not prejudicially affect the case of the deportees. (3) That the Government should observe the most rigid impartiality as between race and race and creed and creed. This has always been the strongest bulwark of British rule in India. Any suspicion on the part of the people that this policy has been departed from, would be a source of serious administrative embarrassments and of deep disappointment to a large class of His Majesty's subjects. (4) That a steady advance should be made towards the fulfilment of the pledges given in the Queen's Proclamation in the matter of the appointment of Indians to offices of trust and responsibility.

Meeting in Finsbury

[The first of a series of public meetings convened under the auspices of the British Committee of the Indian National" Congress, in furtherance of the movement for a reform on a partially elective basis of the nominated Councils in India, was held in the Forresters' Hall, Clerkenwell Road, on Monday, April 14th, 1890. The chair was taken by Sir William Wedder burn, Bart. Babu Surendranath Banerjee on being called upon to address the meeting, spoke as follows:—]

Sir William Wedderburn, Ladies and Gentlemen,

I appear before you, commissioned by the Indian National Congress to lay our grievances and to appeal to you for redress. I confess that I feel myself unequal to the magnitude of the task, and the greatness of the trust which has been reposed in me, but I am supported, and encouraged by the conviction which is deep in me, that feeble as the advocate may be, great is the cause which he has the honour to represent—*(Cheers)*—and that the claims for liberty and justice on the part of two-hundred millions of humans beings, whose destinies an all-wise Providence has entrusted to your care, cannot but appeal with irresistible force to the deepest instincts of the English people. I have read in a book, held divine by you, which affords consolation and comfort to the millions of your people, a book which is one of the noblest that adorn the literature of mankind, that, " Righteousness exalteth a Nation." I have read your history—read it with profit and delight, and if there is one lesson more than another which it enforces, if there is one truth more than another which shines forth in lines of light from every page of that brilliant record, it is again the grand old scriptural, text, "Righteousness exalteth a nation." *(Cheers).* I ask you, ladies and gentlemen, extend to us in relation "to the government of your Indian Empire that righteousness which has made you what you are, to enforce the fulfilments of solemn promises—*(Hear, hear)*—the redemption of sacred pledges, which have been uttered in your name and on your behalf by the Parliament of this country, and by the ruling authorities of India—

> Pledges and Promises,
> which I regret to say, up to this moment
> Remain Inadequately Redeemed,

and, I ask you, finally—and this forms the most important part of my appeal to you—to extend to us in part, at least, those representative institutions, which have followed in the path of English power and civilization, and which, wherever they have been established, have; inaugurated a new era of peace, prosperity, and happiness to the peoples concerned. *(Cheers).* It is with some measure of confidence that I appeal to you in respect to this matter, for you have already done the people, of India the great honour of nominating one of the most distinguished of pur countrymen as your Liberal candidate for representation in Parliament. *(Cheers).* Mr. Dadabhai Naoroji has won for himself, by his' devoted public services extending - through the period of a lifetime, the esteem, the confidence,' and the admiration of all classes of the Indian community, and he has set before, the men of a younger generation, an ideal, a lofty ideal, of public duty which it is impossible for us ever to hope to attain to. I only trust that you may lead him to victory—*(Cheers)*—and that it will be possible for him primarily to serve his constituents, and," in the next place, to serve the voiceless and unrepresented millions of India. *(Cheers).* Ladies and gentlemen.

England Has Done Great, Things for Mankind.. Unique is the record of her achievements not only in war and in diplomacy, but also in those higher spheres of human activity with which we are accustomed to associate the advancement of human civilization. Brilliant as this record is, permit me to say, and I am entitled to speak with authority upon a matter of this kind coming from the East, that its character is fully sustained by the nature of her Indian work. To have found a great nation sunk in the depths of superstition, to have raised them to a higher level of civilization, to have communicated to them the breath of a new life—the pulsations of a new civilization are titles to glory all her own. There was indeed a time when India was the cradle of civilization, the home of learning and of the arts; we look back upon the times even now with feelings of pride and affection. Long before the name and fame of Rome had been heard of, before Alexander had marched his armies to the banks of the Tigris and the Euphrates, while Babylon was yet in the height of her glory and her prosperity, our fathers had cultivated a language and had developed a system of morals and a system' of religion, which, whatever we may think of them now by the light of more advanced views on these subjects, still continue to excite the attention and to elicit the admiration of the civilized world. *(Cheers).* Those days are past and gone, centuries of misgovernment and of the domination of a priestly order to which, fortunately or unfortunately, I have the honour to belong, have produced their legitimate consequences. It was at a time of supreme national humiliation and misery, when our native governments were fast falling to pieces, when even the elements of social order were threatened with destruction, that England came to our rescue, not indeed through motives of philanthropy but impelled by the love of gain and the lust of conquest. *(Cheers).*

Nevertheless England has done a great deal for India but much more yet remains to be done. (Hear, *hear).* Under English auspices we enjoy the, blessings of peace and orderly government. *(Hear, hear).* England has conferred upon us the inestimable, boon of higher English education, the priceless gift of a free press and the right of free discussion. Our Universities are turning out year by year, thousands of graduates and undergraduates, men steeped in the literature of the, West, steeped in your political philosophy and your, political principles. Having become instructed in European knowledge they are craving for European institutions; and having lived for so long under these influences not only has a great change taken place in the outward and the material circumstances of the country, but a visible national awakening is to be seen on all sides *(Hear, hear).* A silent revolution has been effected, a bloodless revolution, indeed, but one which is unequalled in the annals of mankind, except by what is to be seen in your own history when the seeds of the Reformation were transplanted into this country and sown upon English soil. Such a consummation so noble, so creditable to the English nation had indeed been anticipated by those illustrious men who had founded the English Empire, those great men, the grand old men of a former epoch of whom I fear you have only one left, who realised not only the glories but also the responsibilities of Imperial sway. Macaulay, to whom reference has already been made by the Chairman, speaking on the occasion of the enactment of the Charter

Act of 1887, used language which reading it at this distance of time by the light of accomplished facts seems to me, as I am sure it will seem to you, to have about it the ring of prophetic inspiration. He said, " It may be that the public mind of India may so expand under our system as to outgrow that system; that our subjects being brought up under good government may develop a capacity for better government, that being instructed in European knowledge they may crave for European institutions. I know not whether such a day will ever come; but when it does come it will be the proudest day in English history... "This consummation so devoutly, so eagerly looked for, has now been accomplished, and it is our earnest hope and prayer as I trust it will be your deliberate resolve, that those who are in charge of the Government of India and who are responsible to you for that Government, will so administer its affairs as to be worthy of this historical occasion and of the duty which devolves upon them on such an occasion. Ladies and gentlemen, this change—in fact it is the groundwork of the demand which I am about to submit to you—has been so far-reaching, so vast, so significant in many ways, as to have even attracted 'the attention of a class of men who are not very much alive to considerations of this nature.

Our officials—and I desire to speak of them with the utmost possible respect—as a rule have no eye, no instinct, for the perception of those changes which take place deep in the inner strata of society. But it so happens that in our case there has been a fortunate exception, and Sir Auckland Colvin, Lieutenant-Governor of the North-West Provinces, was so impressed by the character and significance of this change that he felt himself called upon to use the pregnant phraseology of the Bible in describing it. In a pamphlet that he wrote in 1884, he said, " The dry bones in the open valley have become instinct with life," and he went on to ask, " Are we alone to remain stationary while all things else are moving forward in India? Are we not to adapt the genius of our Constitution to the genius of the altered time?" That is the question which he asks, and that is the question which I desire to put to you, and may the response come deep from your hearts, and may it be such as will be in accordance with the noble instincts of the English people and the great traditions of English rule. *(Applause)*. Ladies and gentlemen, the Indian National Congress, which has sent me here, is the highest expression and the noblest embodiment of this spirit of reform, this spirit of change which is manifesting itself in Indian society. In the words of a great Indian statesman, it is the " soundest triumph - of British Government." It seems to me marvellous that Englishmen should be found who view with suspicion and distrust a movement of this nature. I hope there are no such Englishmen at any rate in this kingdom, but I fear there are a good many in India. We have, however, no misgivings whatsoever with regard to the attitude of the British public with reference to this grand national movement The other day a discussion took place with reference to this matter in the House of Lords, and it is with a sense of gratitude that I refer to the sympathetic utterances of men like Lord Northbrook, Lord Kimberley, and Lord Ripon with regard to the Congress movement. *(Cheers).* But I have even a higher authority than these. Mr. Gladstone—*(Cheers)*—in a speech which he delivered at Limehouse some time the year before last, in referring to the National Congress, used language which at the present moment seems to be ringing in my ears. He said: " It is not right, it is not proper, that we should treat with contempt or even with indifference.

The Rising Aspirations of this Great People." Such is the language of the greatest of living statesmen— *(Cheers),*—and I am perfectly convinced that it represents the voice of the great body of the English people. Ladies and gentlemen, you may naturally ask me, what is this National Congress? Well, the Congress is a great gathering of delegates, which takes place once a year, about Christmas time, in some Indian capital, for the discussion of political questions and the settlement of a common political programme. The delegates are duly elected in the same way as I venture to think, your members of Parliament are elected: they are elected by constituencies in the various divisions of the Empire. It is computed that about three millions of the Indian population took part in the election of the delegates of the National Congress who attended at Bombay last year: (" *No, no*"). I' hear a dissentient voice; I should be glad if the gentleman who protests would be good enough to state his facts and figures which contradict this view—figures which I have the honour to lay before this meeting. For his edification, for the edification of all concerned, and for the information of the British public, I once again reaffirm the proposition which elicited that dissent, that no less than three millions of the Indian people took part in the election of the delegates last year—*(cheers)*—and the delegates thus elected as faithfully represent the views of those by whom they are returned as your members of the House of Commons reflect the sentiments and the ideas of their constituents. Yet there are men who tell us that we are unfit for representative government and for the elective system. (" *Shame* !").

We would point to this organisation of the Congress and tell them this: Here is this vast, this stupendous, this colossal organisation, with its thousands of members, with its branches and ramifications, extending from one part of the Empire to the other, all constituted upon a representative basis, and is it open to the Indian" Government after that to' say that their Legislative Councils are not capable of a similar treatment? *(Cheers)*. Well, the National Congress is an institution of recent growth, but I know of no movement in connection with modern India which exhibits greater vitality or a greater measure of strength, and a greater capacity for growth than this infant institution. Let me take you for a minute or two over the facts of the case.

The first National Congress was held in' Bombay in 1885, and the number of delegates present was only seventy; the second Congress was held in Calcutta, in the following year, and what do you think was the number of delegates present? Not seventy, but six times seventy, the number being four hundred and thirty-six. The third National Congress was held in Madras, and the number attending was over six hundred; the fourth National Congress was held in Allahabad and, in spite of the opposition of the local officials, the number went up to between twelve and thirteen hundred, while last year at the Congress held at Bombay, the numbers were nearly two thousand. And, gentlemen, in this connection there is an incident to which I desire to call your attention. On the last day of the meeting of the National Congress, we had placed before that body a resolution containing an appeal for funds to the extent of £4,000, and what do you think was the response which this appeal elicited? Instead of £4,000, £6,000, were subscribed in half an hour's time—*(cheers)*,—and £1,000 was paid down on the spot. And yet we have the veracious correspondent of a leading journal of this metropolis who has the effrontery to assure the British public that a movement which has behind it so much earnestness and so much enthusiasm, which is based upon the eternal and unchangeable principles of justice and liberty, was about to collapse. Much more likely that leading journals would collapse—*(cheers)*—than such beneficent organisations for the promotion of human good. Ladies and gentlemen, you may possibly want to know from me what it is we want; what is the question to which above all others we assign the foremost place—what is the chief plank in our platform? I think I shall best discharge my duty by telling you in a few brief concise terms what it is we do not want, because we have been credited with a great many things for which we do not deserve credit. Our trademark has been put upon a number of articles which really do not belong to us. *(Laughter).* Let me say at once very distinctly and very emphatically, on my own behalf and on behalf of the Indian National Congress, on behalf of the educated community throughout India, that we do not wish to see installed in our midst anything like a democratic form of government.

We do not think India is ripe for it yet: nor do we want Home Rule, though if we did I am sure a great many Englishmen would sympathise with us. *(Hear, hear).* We want something even much less than an English House of Commons, and therefore, with the assurance of absolute confidence, we appeal to the generous sympathies and the warm support of all sections, and all classes of the English community, Liberals and Conservatives, Whigs and Tories, whatever may be the character and the complexion of their political faith. We take our stand upon one of those maxims which you have taught us—" No taxation without representation." *(Cheers).* And we press for the reform of the Legislative Councils which impose the taxes and make the laws. Our Councils are absolute, utter, unqualified, unmitigated shams. I use very strong: language; I use it advisedly and deliberately with a full sense of the responsibility I incur. I say once again that our Councils are absolute shams. The members are all nominated by the Government. Not one of them owes his seat to the suffrages of the people, or to the confidence or esteem of his fellow countrymen. Not one of them has the right to ask a single question of the Executive Government with reference to any matter of finance or with reference to any matter of administration, foreign or, domestic. Ladies and gentlemen, I ask you what would you think if your Parliament, if all the members thereof were nominees of the Crown passed under the seal of the Lord Chancellor of England, if they were shorn of all their useful and varied functions, if there was no opposition worth the name, if their debates were of a formal and academic character, if their - conclusions were foregone conclusions which did not even serve to test the strength of the rival parties? Our members are indebted for their seats to the Government, and they look forward to their re-nomination by the Government I ask: Is it possible for men thus constituted to say anything which would be in opposition to the views and the opinions of the Executive Government? It is not in human nature to rise to such heights of self-denial, and our Councillors after all are human beings. They are not angels, emanations of the all-beauteous mind. The result is that laws are passed which would never be passed in any other country, except under strong protest and remonstrance.

Therefore, it is that we press for this reform. Let me give you one illustration in order to point out the absolutely worthless character of the legislative bodies. You know we have to pay a heavy salt-tax; I do not suppose you pay anything of the kind here.. It would be the same thing as if a heavy tax on meat were imposed by your Government. I am sure you would resent it very strongly. Well, we pay something like two thousand per cent as a tax on the cost of the manufacture of salt, and this is paid not only by the rich but also by the poor, millions of whom have only one meal a day, according to the authority of Sir William Hunter. ("*Shame!*"). Well, now not long ago it became necessary to obtain some money. The Government of India was in one of those chronic fits of bankruptcy which are the normal condition of the Indian Government. They wanted money, and the proposal was to raise the salt-tax. What do you think was done? The proposal was laid before the Council, and a scene was witnessed which would have been impossible in any other country, in any other legislative Government. A valiant knight from Bombay, now a worthy baronet was the first to offer his felicitations, to the Government for having proposed a measure which served to cut down the scanty and miserable subsistence of the poor man, and an equally chivalrous

Rajah from the suburbs of Calcutta followed suit. Not a single word of warning, not a single voice of protest, barring the feeble notes of a Mohammedan Councillor was raised in that Council against a provision which, in any other country, or under any other Government would have been impossible.

Now, We desire to remodel and reform this Council. We say that half the members of the Council should be elected, the other half to be nominated by the Government, the President also being a member of the Government, the Government, you will see, will have a majority in any case. But what does Lord Cross say with reference to this matter? He says, " No, the elective element is not to be introduced into the Legislative Councils of India." Further we ask that the right of interpellation, the right of asking questions of the Executive Government, should be conferred upon members of Council. Lord Cross says, in the Bill which he has introduced, "That right is conceded, but it is to be so whittled down that you will have only a semblance or a shadow of the real thing. No resolutions will be permitted upon official replies. "Lastly, we want that the Budget should be discussed in Council.

Even here, what is conferred with one hand is taken away with the other, because no motions are to be permitted upon the countless items included in the Budget. Well, I must say that I have read with very great interest the debate in the House of Lords in connection with this Bill, though I declare my inability to follow some of the arguments which have been adduced. I wish to speak with the utmost possible respect of Lord Salisbury, the Prime Minister, but I fear, having read that debate very carefully, that Lord Salisbury has not yet been able to overcome that racial prejudice of which there was such a conspicuous display in connection with the " black man " incident. *(Cheers).* My friend. " the black man," is on this platform—*(cheers)*—and I hope he will pardon me for this passing reference to an incident in his political career which he can now afford to forget and forgive. Lord Salisbury says that the Eastern races are unfit for the elective system, and he instances the cases of Greece, Egypt, and of Turkey. But as far as the people of India are concerned, this argument has been adduced somewhat late in the day, for ... our entire system of Local Self-government is based upon the elective system, and that system has been pronounced to be a conspicuous success. It is because we have been so successful in reference to the elective system in regard to our local matters that we ask you to extend it to the wider concerns of the Provinces and of the Empire. But Lord Salisbury is a little bit of an ethnologist: we are of the East, we are of Eastern lineage, and therefore the elective system is not suited to us. I desire to point out that though we come from the East, yet we are sprung from the same stock from which you are derived— *(cheers)*—the Indo-Aryan branch of the human family. We are, in fact, your distant kinsmen, and Lord Mayo in one of those admirable speeches which he made on the occasion of the introduction of local self-government in 1868 and 1869 remarked that self-governing institutions form an essential feature of the civilization of the Aryan. Indeed our Panchayat system and our village communities are as old as the hills, and are graven deep on the instincts of our race.

But suppose what Lord Salisbury says were to be accepted as conclusive: does not the fact imply a very grievous reflection upon British rule? It comes to this—that we, the descendants of the ancient Aryans, inheriting by our blood-relationship the instinctive traditions of self-government, have become so degraded by contact with English people that, after a century of British rule, we have become unfit for this small effort in the art of self-government. I am sure Lord Salisbury will not accept a position so unwelcome to the national sentiment and one so inconsistent with truth It is well that we should remind Conservative statesmen of a little fact which they are apt to forget.

In the year 1858 Mr. Disraeli was called upon to draft a Bill for the Constitution of the House of Commons, and he actually proposed that the Council of the Secretary of State, the highest Council in connection with the Indian Empire should be constituted upon a representative basis, and that half the members should be elected *(cheers)* and now, after a lapse of thirty years, after the lifetime of a generation has passed, after great changes have taken place in India, Conservative statesmen are unwilling to apply Mr. Disraeli's principle to Councils subordinate to those to which he himself was prepared to extend it. Am I to understand that Conservative statesmen have forgotten the noble traditions consecrated by the name and fame of the most illustrious Conservative statesman of his generation; or have they forgotten those nobler principles embalmed in that remarkable document which we regard as the Magna Charta of our rights and privileges, the Proclamation of the Queen which was issued by a Conservative Government and embodied the views of a Conservative Ministry. But, ladies and gentlemen, I have no fear. From Conservatives and from Liberals alike we appeal to the ruling democracy of England. We have great confidence in the justice and the generosity of the English people. We have abounding faith in the liberty-loving instincts of the greatest representative assembly in the world—the British House of Commons, the mother of Parliaments, where sits enthroned the newly-enfranchised democracy of those islands.

To whatever party you belong, Liberals or Conservatives, Whigs or Tories, you all owe an indefeasible allegiance to that which forms the keystone of your Constitution, the representative principle, the right of the people to have a voice in the government of their own country. *(Cheers).* Your history is the history of the growth, the progress and the triumph of the representative principle; your literature is pervaded by the same lofty spirit of freedom. Wherever Englishmen have gathered together, wherever they have formed their colonies—whether it be amid the blazing heat of the equatorial regions, or in those distant continents watered by the Southern seas—wherever Englishmen have raised their flag and have formed their governments they have formed them upon the representative model and the representative basis.

We are not of English lineage, or of English blood, but we have been nurtured upon the strong food of constitutional freedom. You have taught us to admire the political philosophy of Burke, the eloquence and genius of Fox, Pitt, and Sheridan. We have been brought face to face, and in contact with the struggles and the triumphs of your Puritan fathers. We have read, with great admiration, the stately and triumphant march of constitutional freedom, culminating in the revolution of 1688. *(Cheers).* And you must take us to be something less than human, you must deprive us of that warm sensibility of our Eastern natures, if you think that after having lived under these influences and imbibed these impressions, we were not fired with a lofty ambition and a noble enthusiasm to transplant into our own country the spirit of those free institutions which have made you what you are. *(Cheers).* We ask, are you prepared to stifle in our breasts those ambitions and those aspirations which you have kindled in them— are you prepared to extinguish in us that noble ardour for freedom and free institutions, which is of English origin, and has on it the impress of its English parentage? Ladies and gentlemen, you have raised for yourselves a mighty Empire in the East—an Empire which has been won by the valour of your soldiers, and the statesmanship of your administrators. But there is an Empire nobler far than that, an Empire which is graven deep on the affections, the gratitude, and the contentment of a great and prosperous people. I ask you to aspire to this imperial sway in India, which will be worthy of a great and Christian people, and which will throw in the shade your proudest achievements in history. Let me say, once again, before I sit down, that I plead for my voiceless countrymen; I plead for liberty and justice, and if these words have any import, any weight, any signification among a Christian people, I am sure I shall not have pleaded in vain— I am sure your best efforts will be put forth on behalf of those vast and multitudinous races of the East, of whose well-being you are responsible to Providence, and who know so higher tribunal than the tribunal of the English people. Ladies and gentlemen, lead them along the path of progress which you have sketched out for them. Confer upon them the inestimable boon of representative institutions. Discharge your duty to India, the noblest duty that ever fell to the lot of any nation, Christian or heathen, ancient or modem, and then you will not only have performed a great national duty, which yet remains unfulfilled, but you will have consolidated the foundations of British rule, and placed it broadbased upon the affection, the gratitude, the contentment of a vast and multitudinous people. *(Loud and long continued cheering).*

Debate at the Oxford Union

[Question for debate " That this House views with regret the non-recognition of the elective principle in the Indian Councils Bill now before Parliament." Moved by Mr. Eardley Norton, B. A., Meston, opposed by Mr. F. F. W. Galbraith, Oriel, Secretary. The debating Hall

of the Oxford Union Society was well filled on Thursday, May 22nd, 1890, to hear Mr. Eardley Norton and Babu Surendranath Banerjee, the delegates from the Indian National Congress, upon the subject of Indian reform. The chair was taken by Mr. F. H. Coller, Christ Church, President of the Society.]

Babu Surendranath Banerjee, who met with an enthusiastic reception, said he was greatly indebted to the House for the cordial reception which had been accorded to him, and he could assure the House that the reception would be to him a source of encouragement and inspiration in the somewhat difficult task which he had undertaken that night. He craved the indulgence of the House for a few moments—he was afraid he would take some little time of the House—in discussing the numerous points which had been raised. He thought he would best discharge his duty by stating in the first place in a few plain words the situation in India, and the demand that they made in conformity with the requirements of that situation. What they said was this. The English Government had given them high English education, it had conferred upon them the inestimable boon of a free press, and last but not least it had conceded to them the gift of local self-government based partially on the representative system. *(Cheers).*

They had now for a period of more than fifty years lived under these influences. For more than fifty years they had enjoyed, these blessings, and he thought the House would think they must be something less than human, if after living under these influences and imbibing these impressions, they were not inspired with a lofty enthusiasm to transplant into their country something of the spirit of the constitution which they had learnt to adore in the noble literature and noble history that England had taught them *(Cheers).* They asked England and the English people to gratify those aspirations which they had kindled in their breasts, and they made that demand not only upon purely sentimental grounds— grounds of emotion, grounds of sensibility, grounds of vague, undefined feeling—but because they were distinctly of opinion that the result of such a concession would be to add sensibly and visibly to the efficiency, and he was going to say, the stability of British rule in India. *(Cheers).* Such was the case, such were the grounds upon which their appeal was made to this

House. *(Cheers).* He was somewhat surprised at some of the statements that had been made *(laughter)* by the gentleman *(Lord Hugh Cecil)* who had opposed the motion. He was somewhat in sympathy with him in his ignorance *(hear, hear);*—at the same time he felt it his duty to point out to him that he was grievously mistaken in some of the statements which he made he knew not upon what authority. He thought he did no injustice in that statement. *(Laughter).* The hon'ble gentleman said, in the first place, that English education was introduced into India in 1835. As a matter of fact, a Hindu College had been established in Bengal in 1817. Not only that, but he would fall back on an authority held in high esteem by the hon'ble gentleman himself. He would, quote Macaulay. Macaulay speaking in 1853 from his place in the House of Commons on the occasion of the enactment of the Charter Act referred to this wise step which had been taken by the Government. Let him quote the words because he had them in his memory. Macaulay said from his place in the House of Commons—Sir Robert Peel, Lord Lansdowne, and others taking part in the debate—Macaulay said,

> It may be that the public mind of India may so expand under our system that it may outgrow that system, and our subjects having been brought up under good Government may develop a capacity for better Government.

And this is the most important passage—

> That having been instructed in European learning, they may crave for European institutions. *(Cheers).* I know not whether such a day will ever come but if Undoes come it will be the proudest day in the annals of England.

On the authority of Macaulay, on the authority which the hon'ble opposer himself claimed, he maintained that the noble day which had been so longingly looked forward to, the proudest day in the annals of England had arrived, and it was for the English people to prove themselves worthy of the occasion *(cheers),* and he hoped and trusted their vote tonight would be a vote which would strengthen that public opinion which was after all the moral support of all Governments. *(Cheers).* He was somewhat amazed at some of the figures which were quoted by the gentlemen who opposed. He expected some such opposition, and he came armed with all the facts. *(Cheers).* He was glad he had got his authorities before him. Here he would quote the figures and they would tell a tale which no amount of rhetoric would ever do. The fact was this, that at the present moment they had more than three millions of their population who attended schools and colleges. And the English people who had representative institutions in such a perfectly developed form at the present moment, and have had representative institutions of that form for a period of fifty years and more, could only put forward three millions of students in 1881. In 1881 they had full-blown representative institutions, and they were in a position to send 670 members to the House of Commons. In India they had no representative institutions whatever, nothing ' even worthy the name of even elementary representative institutions, and yet their people were highly educated on the basis of these facts. Let him read a quotation from a speech of Mr. George Yule:

> Since 1858 about twenty millions of pounds have been spent on educational institutions.' The number of these institutions at the present time is 122,000 attended by upwards of 3,300,000 students. The number of schools in England in 1821 was only 18,467 and the scholars 650,000. These, however, have rapidly increased during the last twenty years, but it was not till 1881 they reached the number of the schools and scholars in India.

And to go to another official authority, here is Mr. Growse, a very eminent antiquarian, who says:

> My own opinion in which I am yearly more and more confirmed, is that the 'average of happiness, intelligence, culture, and general information is as high in an Indian as Indian English village." *(Cheers).*

He thought as far as the educational aspect of the question was concerned it might be taken for granted that they were not the barbarians they were represented to be." *(Cheers).* The statement was made in the course of this debate that the Indians before the advent of the English were a pack of barbarians or semi-barbarians; he believed that was the language that was used. Let him remind this House that they came—the Hindus of India, the race to which he had the honour to belong — *(loud cheers)*—they came from a great and ancient stock, that at the time the ancestors of the most enlightened European nations were roaming in their native woods and forests, their fathers had founded great Empires, established noble cities and cultivated a system of ethics, a system of religion, and a noble language which at the present moment excited the admiration of the civilized world, *(loud cheers)*. They had only to walk across the way, and place themselves in the Bodleian library to witness the ancient records of Indian industry, Indian culture, and Indian ethics; therefore it seemed to him the remark was somewhat out of place. *(Cheers)*.

If the remark was made to prejudice the claim which they had now the honour to put forward, to prejudice their claim for representative institutions, never was it more misplaced, for the simple reason that self-governing institutions formed an essential feature of the civilization of the Aryan race, and they came from the Aryan stock. *(Cheers)*. The hon'ble opposer of the motion was pleased to refer to the authority of Sir Henry Maine in reference to certain quotation he made. He (the speaker) was prepared to bow to that authority, and accept him as an authority on Indian matters. What did he say in reference to India? The first practical illustrations of self-governing institutions were to be found in the early records of. India. Their village communities were as old as the hills. *(Cheers)*. When they asked for representative institutions, or a partial concession of representative institutions, they asked for something which was in entire accord with the genius and the temper of the people of India, in entire accord with the traditions of their history, and in entire accord with the tenor of British rule in India. What had they done? As he had already remarked the British Government had conceded local self-government on an elective basis. They had a system of local self-government, based on the representative model, in Bengal, Madras, Bombay, and the North-West Provinces; the whole country was scattered broadcast with municipal institutions based on the representative model, and what was the official opinion with regard to them? They had been pronounced to be a conspicuous success. *(Cheers)*. And what they said was this, they took their stand upon the achievement that had already been made upon the success that had already been attained—they said to the Government, " You have applied the representative principle, the elective system, to the administration of our local affairs, and the administration of our local affairs has been pronounced to be a conspicuous success, and therefore on the basis of past experience we appeal to you to extend the elective system, the representative principle, to the wider concerns of the Provinces and the Empire at large." *(Cheers)*. He asked that House, was it possible by any show of reason or plausibility to dislodge them from a position so logical, so consistent, so unassailable'? *(Cheers)*. They had been tried, and they had not been found wanting. *(Loud cheers)*.

Therefore upon the basis of past experience they asked them to extend, the representative system *(Cheers)*. He found another misconception in the speech of the hon'ble opposer of this motion (Lord Hugh Cecil), in fact, the speech bristled with misconceptions. The words "democratic government" occurred at every third line of his speech. They did not want democratic government: *(Cheers)*. When they were fit for it they would come and pray for it. At the present moment they did not consider themselves qualified for democratic government, or for Home Rule, or for Parliamentary institutions. Their demands were exceedingly moderate. He had only to state them before an English audience in order" to point out how exceedingly cautious they were in their proposals. At the present moment their Councils were entirely nominative. He should have something to say with reference to the sham character of these Councils by-and-by: They were entirely nominative—the members were all nominated by the Government, and they told the Government they had tried that experiment long enough it was pronounced to be a failure from one end of the country to the other. *(Cheers)*.. Even, the official organs, of public opinion said that, and therefore they asked to have half the members nominated, the other half to be elected. And not only that but the President would be a Member of the Government, and therefore in these-Legislative Councils the Government would always; and infallibly have a majority. Not only that, they were so anxious that nothing should be done to hamper the Government in any way or to relax the: bonds, of Executive authority, that they actually reserved the power of veto to the Government, so that the Government might supersede or set aside any decision arrived at by a majority of the Council.. All they required in such cases was that the reasons for the supersession must be stated. Was there in this demand any approach to democratic Governments, to Home Rule, or to Parliamentary institutions? *(Cheers).* And was it not desirable to consider the great advances that had taken place in the circumstances of the Government and of the country, and was it not necessary that some reform of this kind should be made? (Hear, hear). He said that the English Government could not stand still where it was at the present moment. *(Cheers).*

It would be dangerous to stand still; it would be positively mischievous to fall back. There was one course of policy open to the English Government in India, namely to advance steadily, cautiously, wisely, deliberately, along the line of prudence and beneficence which had been marked out by the former policy of illustrious Anglo-Indian administrators. *(Cheers).* They asked the Government " to do this and no more. Reference had been made to their divergent religious beliefs. Had they not that in this country, might he ask? Protestants burnt Roman Catholics three hundred years ago, and the Roman Catholics paid back the compliment in the same way, and not very far from the place where they had met that night. They in India had never done that. *(Cheers).* They occasionally had some little controversies, but nothing equal to the bitter controversies that they had had in this country.

Let him relate to them an incident, if he was not trespassing on the patience of the House (cries of " Go on") to show the harmony that existed between Hindus and Mohammedans. About two years ago there was a dispute between the Sunnies and the Shias. These were the two great sects into which the Mohammedans were divided and at a great meeting, for the purposes of settling the dispute, which was held in the capital of Mohammedan influence and power, the ancient capital of Mohammedan greatness, what did they think was the outcome of their deliberations? Actually four Hindu gentlemen were appointed for the purpose of settling the matters of dispute affecting the religious ceremonies of the Mohammedans. *(Cheers).* He should like to know how many Protestants would appoint Roman Catholics for the purpose of settling any such differences. *(Hear, hear)*. Therefore, this religious dispute was a matter which had been vastly magnified, but only for a particular object, namely, to throw difficulties in the way of representative institutions in India. *(Cheers)*. But even if the differences were much wider, much deeper, much more bitter than what they were, he claimed upon the basis of historical facts that differences. In respect of religious matters were no bar to the introduction of representative institutions. *(Cheers)*. The Austrians and Hungarians fought with the utmost bitterness and animosity, but all their differences of opinion had been settled by the saving principle of representative Government He took it that this was really no argument to which any great importance should be attached. Lastly, as to social questions, it was said they paid no attention to social matters, but he was sorry to say here again there was a misconception, a misreading, a misinterpretation of Indian History.

The hon'ble gentleman who alluded to this subject seemed not to have understood that the National Congress movement was only a political manifestation of a great national upheaval, which had taken place not only in respect of politics, but also in respect of religion and social institutions. It must not be supposed that the National Congress movement represented the cackling of a number of educated Baboos or "much-speaking Bengalis," to use the language of the opposer of the motion. It represented something vaster than that, something far more comprehensive, far more significant, something which was likely to produce consequences of the very greatest importance as regarded the fortunes of the people and the Government.

In consequence of those agencies to which he had referred there had been a revolution in the national mind, and it had been felt in every department of human thought, in religion, in social questions, and in politics. In politics, fortunately or unfortunately as the case might be, they moved along the line of least resistance, and therefore the intensity had been most keenly felt there; but as a matter of fact it would be a mistake to confine its bearings to the National Congress, to overlook the influences which had been felt in the departments of religious and social thought. The National Congress was supplemented by a Social Conference, and not only that, but a revival of Hinduism was going on of which they had no idea, because it was not necessary for them to write their tracts in English for the edification of the British public They appealed to their people in their own language in order that they might be religious, but when they had to obtain political liberties they had to appeal to the English people, consequently they thought they ' were only politically engaged, whereas as a matter of fact they were engaged in matters of social as well as religious reform. *(Cheers).* He wished to tell the House that they were a deeply religious people. The religious reform movement was the first in point of time, as it was the first in point of importance. Rammohan Roy was the founder of Brahmoism, the monotheistic creed of new India. Rammohan Roy was the" brightest product of English education, and by a mysterious decree of fate England claimed his ashes; he lay buried at Bristol.

The religious movement preceded all other movements, then followed the social movement, inaugurated by Pandit Ishwara Chander Vidyasagar, and the National Congress came last, and therefore in point of logical sequence it was the last in point of importance, but as far their rulers were concerned it was the "greatest. That was really the state of things. He just wished to point out to that House, before he sat down, that this was really not a party question at all. *(Cheers).*

It was a question of national and Imperial justice. They bound themselves to no parties, they appealed for justice to all, and they had illustrious names on their side of the question belonging to both ranks of English party politics. That illustrious politician and diplomatist there—(pointing to a portrait of Lord Dufferin)—who was a President of that Union, had in a despatch recommended the recognition of the elective system in the Constitution of the Legislative Councils; the House Would attach very great importance to an expression of opinion coming from so illustrious a man, having behind him the weight of Indian experience. *(Cheers).* Not only that but another President of that Union, Sir Henry Harrison, was in favour of the elective system; and there were men, too, on the Liberal side of the House with them. *(Cheers).* Let him refer to some names on the other side. Take, for instance, Sir Richard Temple and Sir, Richard Garth, the late Chief Justice of Bengal. *(Cheers).* Thus, therefore, the matter was one in which no, party interests were concerned, which appealed to that common sense of justice and fair play, that found predominance in every English breast. *(Cheers),* Representative institutions were a consecrated possession which in the counsels of Providence had been entrusted to the English people. He quite admitted that it was for the English people to guard that possession, to spread it, and not to make if the property of this people, or that people, but the heritage of mankind at large. England was the home of representative institutions; from England as the centre, representative institutions had spread far and wide until this country had justly been called the august mother of free nations. The people of India were children of that mother, and they claimed their birthright, they claimed to be admitted into the rights of British citizens and British fellow subjects. He was perfectly certain that such an appeal made to the English people could meet with but one response— a response of sympathy, and a readiness to grant it. *(Cheers).* He pleaded before that House for justice; he pleaded for liberty not inconsistent with British supremacy, but tending to consolidate its foundations and he was perfectly convinced that so long as these words, these sacred words, had any weight, any meaning, any signification amongst Englishmen and in that House, they would record, by an unanimous vote, an emphatic vote, their sympathy with their aspirations, their desire that India should be governed according to those eternal principles of justice and liberty, which were engraved deep in the hearts, the convictions, and feelings of Englishmen to whatever party, to whatever creed, to whatever sect they might belong. *(Loud and prolonged cheering).*

India and English Literature

[In the course of a discussion at a meeting of the Imperial Press Conference in London in 1909, Mr. Banerjee followed Lord Morley's speech on "Literature and Journalism " with the following observations on the influence of the English language in India.]

My Lord and Gentlemen,—In the observations which your lordship was pleased to address to us, and which all listened to with great interest and attention, and if I may add for myself without impertinence, with very great admiration, you referred to the predominance of the English tongue. My Lord, nowhere is that predominance more marked than in my own country. The

English language has been the means of uniting the varied races and religions, the peoples and complexities of our multiform civilization in the golden chains of indissoluble union. It is our *Lingua Franca* and common means of communication, north, south, east and west. All are bound together by the common medium of the English language. Under the influence of the English language and English literature—and in this matter I am not guilty of the slightest exaggeration when I say that in India the dry bones of the valley have become instinct with life—English language and literature have brought about the most stupendous transformation in the lifetime of our generation. New ideas have taken possession of men's minds. New impulses have filled their hearts, and a new spirit is visible in the land. English language and English literature have communicated the Promethean spark which has galvanised us into a new life.

This is one of the most glorious achievements of the English race in the East. We had no newspapers before the establishment of British control. The first newspaper which was in India was published in 1817 and in Bengal. Thus, in this, as in other matters, I am proud to say that my province has taken a lead. The Press has controlled the judgement, the conscience, the mind, and the religion of all India. Being of British origin it partakes of the virtues and of the defects of its parentage. Its heredity is marked on every phase of the situation.

There is no quality for which the Britisher—and when I speak of the Britisher I include his kinsman over the seas there is no quality for which the Britisher is more noted than the variety of his grumbling. He is a past master in the art, and therefore it is no wonder that great authority, Sir William Hunter, has described the Native Press as "His Majesty's Opposition, always in Opposition." I dissent from that view completely. On the contrary, we are often proud to support the Government and accord to it a wholehearted measure of support. And, my lord, if I may refer to a personal event I hope and trust that I may be excused. The whole of the Indian Press welcomed with enthusiasm and gratitude your lordship's scheme of reform on behalf of India. For we felt it to be a distinctly genuine effort on the part of the Government to associate the democracy with the administration of India. We did not, indeed, get all that we want. For instance, we wanted the power of the purse, but we did not get it. At the same time, we believe that it was a notable advance in the process of evolution which is bound to give us a definite, effective, and real measure of self-government. We are not under any illusions. We knew perfectly well the limitations of the scheme. But the Government provided the machinery which would enable the Government to place itself in touch with popular opinion and would enable the representatives of the people to exercise an effective measure of indirect pressure on the Government and, therefore, we felt that it was a scheme which ought to be welcomed.

We felt that if we were patient and persevering, we should, in time, get what we wanted and be admitted into the great confederacy of free states acknowledging England as their august mother. Here at any rate there was no opposition, but absolutely wholehearted support. My lord, the Indian Press is the youngest branch of the Imperial Press and I claim for it that it is the promising scion of a noble stock. God grant that it may increase in power, in strength, and in usefulness and responsibility, to the great credit of ourselves and the glory of the great Empire to which we all have the honour to belong.

8

Miscellaneous Speeches

Indian Unity

[The following address on Indian Unify was delivered by Mr. Banerjee at a meeting of the Student's Association, held on the 16th March 1878, in the Medical College Theatre, Calcutta.]

It has been remarked by Tennyson, somewhere in his poems, that the path of human progress is, streaked with blood, that the car of human civilization rolls forward amid the corpses of men, women and children. This remark seems to me to be pregnant with truth. The history of the human race abundantly proves it. The Asiatic invasion of Alexander superficially considered seems but a long catalogue of wanton bloodshed, of indiscriminate slaughter. But if you examine the matter a little deeper, another feature of the case presently reveals itself to view. The Asiatic invasion of Alexander served for the first time to bring the East and the West into close and intimate contact, served for the first time to bring the Western mind into close and intimate communion with the Eastern mind. And what was the result of this contact, this communion? Eastern science with its amazing results, with its complicated method, with its marvellous developments, for the first time lay unfolded before the awe struck gaze of the Grecian people. From amid the blood and confusion of battle, from amid the clanging of martial music, from amid the groans of the dead and the dying, the Greek mind seized with wonderful grasp those cardinal principles of Eastern science, which were henceforth to become the regulating maxims of Western science, and which in the fullness of time were to confer such unspeakable and untold blessings upon the human race. A party of *savans* had accompanied the expedition of Alexander. These men were the intellectual beacons of the age in which they lived, men who have left the imperishable stamp of their genius upon the thought and culture of succeeding generations. These wise men of the West had access to the scientific records of the Assyrians and the Chaldeans. There they discovered that the two methods under which scientific investigations had been carried on in the East, were observation and experiment. Observation and experiment had been in the East the prolific mother of great discoveries. Nature, when questioned under the guidance of this two-fold method, had yielded up the hidden secrets that lay embosomed within her Observation and experiment had done great things for Eastern science. Might they not be made to perform a similar duty for Western science? So spoke, Aristotle and the band of illustrious, men by whom he was surrounded. A new era dawns upon the history of Grecian science. Observation and experiment were now to regulate Western science, as they had before regulated Eastern science. The blood, therefore, that was shed in the Greek expedition was not shed in vain. The treasure that was lavished in that expedition, was not lavished in vain. Out of that blood, out of that treasure, there rose the proud fabric of European science. There was thus, under the orderings of Providence, a distinct mission associated with the expedition of Alexander. That mission was to lay deep and secure the foundation-stone of the noble temple of Western science upon the firm and immutable basis of observation and experiment.

In the same way Roman Empire had a mission of its own to accomplish. Roman civilization followed in the path of Roman conquest. The legionaries of Rome bore aloft the banner of human progress. Under Roman influences, Europe emerged from her primeval barbarism. But the great mission of Rome was not accomplished, her predestined course in history was not run till Christ had appeared on the scene, till she had prepared men's minds for the acceptance of those great, those sublime, those eternal truth's for which the immortal founder of Christianity lived and died. What were those truths which Christ preached? What were those principles which he sought to impress on the minds of men and for which, when the hour came, he offered himself up a meek sacrifice on the blessed cross. The sum and substance of Christ's teachings is embraced in the simple but comprehensive formula of the Fatherhood of God and the Brotherhood of man. Christ taught that all men were equal, he taught that every man who drew the vital air was the equal of his fellow man. He taught that in Heaven's great book, in the eternal rolls of light, there was no distinction between the black man and the white man, between the European and the Asiatic, between the Roman and the barbarian. And the policy, the precepts, the maxims of imperial Rome had prepared men's minds for the admission of this great principle of equality. Roman Law admitted of no distinction between the Roman-born, and him who was not so born. In the eyes of the Roman Law, all Roman subjects were equal. There was not a right, not a privilege, not an immunity which a Roman enjoyed and which was not shared by the obscurest inhabitant of the most distant part of the Roman Empire. There was not an office in the state to which a Roman subject might not aspire. He might aspire to fill the senatorial rank, he might aspire to the governor of a province, the commander of an army or the confidential adviser of his sovereign. Rome's mission, then, was accomplished when under the shadows of her imperial throne, Christ first taught in his simple and noble eloquence, the great principle of equality, that principle which was to receive its last solemn seal and sanction amid the blood and smoke of the great French Revolution.

Rome then had mission of her own to accomplish. There was a mission associated with the expedition of Alexander. And am I to understand that England has no mission in the East to accomplish? Aye, she has a glorious mission to fulfil here, a mission far nobler than it ever fell to the lot of Greek, Macedonian or Roman to accomplish. It is England's mission in the East to save, regenerate, emancipate from the chains of ignorance, error and superstition, 250 millions of human beings, to heal the wounds that have been inflicted on them by the rapacity of their former rulers, to develop in them a self-reliant, manly, energetic character, to spread through the land the great blessings of peace, contentment and happiness, but above all its England's noble mission in the East to help towards the consummation of Indian unity, to reconcile the jarring conflicts of the diverse Indian nationalities to bring them nearer together, to evoke in them a sentiment of brotherhood and make them feel that, they have to make common cause for the redress of common grievances.

Gentlemen, I cannot help thinking that it is our proud privilege to live in one of the most interesting epochs in the history of our country, one of those epochs, which, if I am at all allowed to take a forecast of the future, will not be without its influence on the fortunes of after generations. Those fierce animosities, those bitter dissensions, those degrading passions which in the last and the preceding centuries had converted this beautiful country of ours into one vast ensanguined plain, have now happily subsided, and we live in an era of unexampled peace prosperity and happiness For this great result we are indebted to the British Government. If at this moment the semi-barbarous hordes of Afghanistan, bursting our barriers, are not sweeping across our country, it is because of the omnipotent might of the British Ruler. If, at this moment, happily the sentiment of brotherhood has been universally evoked in the minds of the Indian races, it is because under the auspices of British rule, the varied and diversified peoples that inhabit this great country have been welded together into a compact and homogeneous mass. But I ask, gentlemen, is this after all a season of unmixed gratulation? Have we no mournful reflections to darken the horizon of our thoughts? May we not, occupying the vantage ground that we now happen to occupy, emancipate ourselves from the present, look back into the past and question the past? May we not resuscitate the dying embers of a bygone age and endeavour to fan them forth into a living flame full of light for our future guidance? May we not, occupying the intellectual eminence that we have attained, invoke the genius of history and call upon her to declare what were the circumstances, what the incidents what the causes which' brought about our fall and have perpetuated our degradation? The Goddess of History thus questioned, is sure to return one answer, and it will be an answer at once decisive and unequivocal in its character. The Goddess will answer—" Indians, your dissensions, your jealousies, your animosities, have brought about your fall and have perpetuated your degradation. Learn to respect the holy principle of union. ' Learn to love one another as brothers. Learn to make common cause for the redress of common grievances, and the great God of nations, the Protector of the rights of fallen peoples may yet from his high place in Heaven look upon you with compassion, may yet in his infinite mercy ordain the dawning of a bright day for your country." So will speak the Goddess of History and she will point to facts in Indian History in support of her statement.

But, perhaps, it will be said that the question of Indian unity, of the intellectual, moral and social union of the Indian peoples, is a dream, is a chimera, the phantom of an excited imagination. It will be said that India throughout the long period of her chequered history, has presented the spectacle of a country, inhabited by peoples, separated by language, separated by religion, separated by manners, and customs, separated in short by everything that constitutes the distinctive difference between races and peoples. Why then, it will be said, at this time of day commit the monstrous absurdity of talking of Indian unity?

Gentlemen, I have stated the arguments against Indian unity as strongly as the case admits of, in order to point out that these arguments are not wholly unanswerable in their character. I invite your attention once more to' the terms of the proposition you are considering. India is inhabited by peoples separated by language, by religion, by manners, and customs. Is their intellectual, social, moral union possible? I say such a union is possible—is practicable; and I appeal to the facts of Indian history in support of the statement. Let us take the example of Switzerland, to begin with. Switzerland, you are aware, is a federal country, enjoying the blessings of a republican government Switzerland is divided into a number of cantons. Well, there are Roman Catholic cantons and there are Protestant cantons. There are French speaking cantons, and there are German speaking cantons. But in spite of these differences of language and religion, Switzerland in a united country, and never was the strength of Swiss union, the compactness of that homogeneity more strikingly exemplified, than on that memorable day when that great oppressor of our race, Napoleon Bonaparte endeavoured to wipe out this little republic from the face of Europe. Take again the case of Belgium. Belgium is a united country, and it would have been truly remarkable if it were not, considering how limited its area is. Well, in Belgium, there are the Wallons, and there is the Flemish speaking population, there are again Roman Catholic Belgians, and there are Protestant Belgians. But Belgium is a united country in spite of religious and linguistic differences. Let us now take the case of Germany. In Germany, we do not, indeed, meet with those strongly marked linguistic differences, we notice in the case of Belgium and Switzerland, but I know of no country where in modern times the spirit of religious difference, I had almost said, the spirit of bitter religious hatred, has been carried on to a greater or more extravagant length than in this confederated German Empire. And if it were not that this was the 19th century, that Germany was placed in the midst of the hallowed, the consecrated, the peaceful influences of modern civilization, Germany would today have presented the spectacle of a country, deluged with blood, shed on the altar of religious differences.

Germany is united in spite of strongly marked religious differences in her people. I shall take one more instance, and this time it will be Italy. Italy, you are aware, was united in 1870. But the idea was a very old one. Dante had sung of Italian unification. The highest minds in Italy had aspired to bring about the consummation of that great event. Again and again there rose up poets princes, philosophers and statesmen, with whom the great dream of their lives was the dream of Italian unification. But it was believed there were insuperable obstacles to the unification of Italy. The Italians had become a degraded people. They had forgotten the glorious memories of the past. They had forgotten the great deeds of their sires. They had forgotten the patriotism of Brutus, the eloquence *pi Cicero,* the martial achievements of Caesar. Differences of language added to the confusion. The Neapolitan understood not the Roman, the Roman understood not the Venetian. They were all brothers, born of the same illustrious progenitors, the inheritors of the same great memories, yet they knew not one another, understood not one another, they were strangers in each other's sight. But was there no hope for Italy? Was she for ever to remain in the grovelling depths of continued misery? Aye no. The day of Italy's deliverance was fast approaching. The fiat had gone forth, the celestial mandate had been issued that Italy was to he saved. The hour had arrived. The men were there. Under the guidance of Garibaldi and Mazzini Italy rose to the conception of Italian unity; and through acts of noble and unheard-of self-sacrifice, which have shed lasting glory on the honoured names of the martyred patriots of Italy, the Italian people brought about the unity and the independence of their country. The unification of Italy was effected notwithstanding dialectical differences.

Thus, then, gentlemen, from the instances I have just cited, we are naturally led to conclude that there may be religious differences, there may be linguistic differences, but they do not form insuperable barriers to the consummation of a national unity. A point has thus been gained in the argument. But it is my contention that the considerations I have just urged against national ' unity lose much of their weight when we bear in mind the wholly altered circumstances under which we now live. Modern India is very different from ancient India.

The conditions of life in modern India are very different from the conditions of life in ancient India. We may deprecate the change. We may regret the circumstance. But there is no denying the fact that we are in the midst of a great revolution along whose current we are irresistibly borne. English civilization has been introduced into our midst, and along with it have been introduced certain revolutionary agencies of mighty potency, which are operating with powerful effect upon the framework of Indian Society, thinning away its vital parts and greatly helping the cause of Indian unity. Foremost amongst these agencies, English Education claims our attention. The traveller who visits the cities of Delhi and Agra is struck with wonderment at the magnificent works of architectural beauty which still grace these once imperial capitals. They remind us of Moslem supremacy? They are the silent monumental records of bygone times. They remind us of the generosity and humanity of Akbar, of the splendour of Shah Jahan, of the religious bigotry of Aurangzeb.

England indeed cannot boast of such monuments of architectural magnificence; but her claims to the lasting gratitude of posterity will rest upon a surer, more permanent and durable basis, upon the conviction which is deep and earnest in us, viz., that under the auspices of English rule were, for the first time, sown the seeds of a civilization containing the germs of India's future greatness, of her political, moral and intellectual regeneration.

The question might be asked how is English Education helping the cause of Indian union. I have mentioned that one of the obstacles to national unity is the' diversity of dialects that prevails in India. English Education partly removes this difficulty by supplying a common medium of communication between the educated classes. I may not know Maharati. An educated, native of Bombay may not know Bengali. But we can hold intercourse with one another, correspond with one another-through the common medium of the English language. Nor is this all. English Education has uplifted all who have come under its influence to a' common platform of thoughts, feelings and aspirations. Educated Indians whether of Bengal, Madras, Bombay or the North-Western Provinces are brought up under the same intellectual, moral, and political influences. Kindred hopes, feelings and ideas are thus generated. The educated classes throughout India are thus brought nearer together Railways also are greatly helping to bring about a feeling of unity and sympathy between the Indian races.

Railways, have abridged distances. The distance between Calcutta and Delhi is not 1,400 miles but is only a question of about 44 hours. The distance between' Calcutta and Lahore is not 1,600 miles but is only a question of about 52 hours. The distance between Calcutta and Bombay is not 1,900 miles but is only a question of about 61 hours. The means of communication being so easy, we have taken more largely to travelling. We know one another now much more intimately than we ever did before. Those prejudices which had separated us for ages are fast disappearing, and the patriot sees in the distant horizon the faint streaks of that dawn which are to usher in the day of his country's regeneration and union. Railways are thus helping to promote Indian union. . The existence of a native Press is also calculated to bring about the same result. If I had addressed you day before yesterday, I should have said that the native-Press was a free Press. But within the last forty-eight hours a law has been hurriedly enacted which has put a gag into the mouth of the Vernacular

Press, has enveloped its fate in deep gloom, has dealt a terrible blow at the cause of Indian progress and enlightenment. The law which has been enacted, and the circumstances, under which it has been enacted strongly remind us of our degradation, of the stretches to which the exercise of arbitrary power might be carried in this country, and how it has become necessary that we should interpose an effective and at the same time a thoroughly constitutional barrier against the reckless exercise of such; great power. This is not the time nor the place to enter into a discussion of the merits of this most important measure of Law, but there are one or two remarks, which I feel bound to make with reference to a matter which must be uppermost in the minds of most of us here present. The Law has been described to be an "enabling" measure, a "preventive" measure, a "non-punitive" measure. Now, the concluding section of this non-punitive Act declares that nothing in that Act will exempt a person punished under it from being punished under the provisions of any other Act against which he may have offended. Now let us take the case of an unfortunate editor who has given security and who in the opinion of the Magistrate has been guilty of criminal intimidation. He forfeits his security and he is also liable to punishment under the Penal Code. Under this preventive, this non-punitive Law, a man may thus be punished twice.

The Law was passed at one and the same sitting, the standing orders having been suspended. The usual course is, when a measure is introduced into the Supreme Council, to refer it to a Select Committee. The Bill is also to be published in the Government Gazette, so that the public might have an opportunity of discussing the merits of the proposed measure of law. Nothing of the kind was done in the present instance. These formalities were quietly dispensed with, and the Bill became Law, the same day it was introduced. Now I ask what justification was there for this undue and precipitate haste. Was the atmosphere infected with treason? Were daggers floating about in the air? Were the Russians knocking at the gates of Peshawar? Was this great Empire, the embodiment of English justice and humanity in the East, this Empire resting upon the willing allegiance, the steadfast devotion and the fervent loyalty of 250 millions of human beings tottering to its foundations? If there is peace, happiness, contentment throughout the length and breadth of this great country, I repeat what need was there for this precipitate haste? But I forget Sir Alexander Arbuth not has told us that it was intended to avoid agitation and hence was it that the Bill became Law at one and the same sitting. The Government, I venture to think, is greatly mistaken if it really believes that by hastily carrying the Bill, it will avoid agitation. There will be an agitation on a vast, extensive scale, commensurate with the greatness of the occasion, and the importance of the subject There will be an agitation which shall extend from the Himalayas to Cape Comorin and from the Indus to the Brahmaputra, an agitation which shall be truly national in its character and shall include the varied and diversified races and peoples that inhabit this great country. And I declare I shall cheerfully bear my humble share in this great national work. It matters not who sympathises with us, and who does not. We shall do our duty manfully, fearlessly and courageously. It matters not if we are cried down as " stump orators." It matters not if we are described as " young men ambitious for fame and distinction." It matters not if our motives are misconstrued and we are held up to the ridicule and, it may be, the execration of our European rulers. I repeat, we shall do our duty fearlessly, manfully and courageously. We shall borrow a noble page from England's glorious history, that page wherein are blazoned forth in characters of glittering gold (O God! may the spirit of those words last till the end, of time) " England expects every man to do his duty." We shall borrow that page, from England's: history, fasten it on our banner, and unfurl that banner before the gaze of our own countrymen and of stagnant Asia. India too expects' every man to do his duty.

The Brahmo Samaj may also powerfully help to bring about Indian unity. Amongst the obstacles to national unity, difference of religion occupies not wholly an unimportant place. The Brahmo Samaj, by uniting Indians of varied creeds and beliefs under the bonds of a common faith,' may help to remove this great difficulty and foster and promote Indian union. 'And it seems to me that the Brahmo Samaj possesses special facilities for bringing about this great end. The creed of simple monotheism which it preaches and holds up for our acceptance has in all ages and times possessed an almost irresistible attraction for the minds of thoughtful Indians.

the question of the admission of our countrymen into the ranks of the Covenanted Civil Service. All India is of one mind upon this great question. And I am sure that with reference to all other questions affecting national interests, there is a similar unanimity of feeling among the educated classes throughout India.

But, gentlemen, I am not content to allow this question—the desirability and importance of promoting a feeling of sympathy and union between the different modern races and peoples—to rest upon mere intellectual considerations. I desire to place this question upon the exalted basis of the human emotions. Are not all Indians brothers, ought they not then to live and act as brothers? The ground which we tread is holy.. Hound us sleep our revered sires. Beware how we live in this land. Let us live in it as loving brothers. But if we cannot do so, then do thou, O God of nature ! hurl against us the thunders of thy wrath, for by living we desecrate and pollute the memories of our sires.

The cause of Indian unity stands in need of missionaries. No cause has ever prospered which has not had its missionaries, its apostles and prophets. The cause of Italian unity had its apostles and prophets, its Garibaldis and its Mazzinis. Who will be the Garibaldi and Mazzini of Indian unity? Who amongst us will emulate their self-sacrifice, their matchless patriotism, their unflinching devotion to the interests of their country? Their revolutionary spirit is not indeed needed for the benefit of India. The march of progress which has already commenced under English auspices must not be disturbed. May England long continue to rule India for the glory of England and the benefit of India. But we want the inspiration to noble actions to be derived from the blessed names and sanctified examples of the immortal apostles of Italian unity. I' repeat, who will be the apostles of Indian unity? . Young men, whom I see around me in such large numbers, you are the hopes of your families. May I not also say, you are the hopes of your country. Your country expects great things from you. Now I ask, how many of you are prepared, when you have finished your studies at the college, to devote your lives, to-consecrate your energies to the good of your country? I repeat the question and I pause for a reply. (Here the speaker paused for a few seconds. Cries of *"all, all"* from all sides of the gallery). The response is in every way worthy of yourselves and of the education which you are receiving. May you prove true to your resolve, and carry out in life the high purposes which animate your bosoms.

Gentlemen, I have a strong conviction and an assured belief that there comes a time in the history of a nation's progress, when every man may verily be said to have a mission of his own to accomplish. Such a time has now arrived for India. The" fiat has gone forth. The: celestial mandate has been issued that every Indian must now do his duty, or stand condemned before God and man. There was such a time of stirring activity in the glorious annals of England, when Hampden offered up his life for the deliverance of his country, when Algernon Sydney laid down his head on the block to rid his country of a hated tyrant, when English bishops did not hesitate in the discharge of their duty to their Fatherland to descend from the performance of their ecclesiastical functions and appear as traitors before the bar of a Criminal Court. These are glorious reminiscences in England's immortal history, which Englishmen to this day look back upon with pride and satisfaction. It is not indeed necessary for us to have recourse to violence in order to obtain the redress of our grievances. Constitutional agitation will secure for us those rights, the privileges which in less favoured countries are obtained by sterner means. But peaceful as are the means to be enforced, there is a stern duty to be performed by every Indian. And he who fails in that duty is a traitor before God and man.

In holding up for your acceptance the great principle of Indian unity, I do not lay any claims to originality. Three hundred years ago, in the Punjab, the immortal founder of Sikhism, the meek, the gentle, the blessed Nanak preached the great doctrine of Indian unity and endeavoured to knit together Hindus and Musalmans under the banner of a common faith. That attempt was eminently successful. Nanak became the spiritual founder of the Sikh Empire. He preached the great doctrine of peace and good will between Hindus and Musalmans. And standing in the presence of his great example, we too must preach the great doctrine of peace and good will between Hindus and Musalmans, Christians and Parsis, aye between all sections of the great Indian community. Let us raise aloft the banner of our country's progress. Let the word " Unity" be inscribed there in characters of glittering gold. We hare had enough of past jealousies, past dissensions, past animosities. The spirits of the dead at Panipat will testify to our bloody strifes. The spirits of the dead in other battlefields will testify to the same fact There may be religious differences between us. There may be social differences between us. But there is a common platform where we may all meet, the platform of our country's welfare. There is a common cause which may blind us together, the cause of Indian progress. There is a common Divinity, to whom we may uplift our voices in adoration, the Divinity who presides over the destinies of our country. In the name then of a common country, let us all, Hindus, Musalmans,. Christians, Parsis, members of the great Indian community, throw the pall of oblivion over jealousies' and dissensions of bygone times and embracing one another in fraternal love and affection, live and work for the benefit of a beloved Fatherland. Under English auspices there is indeed a great future for India. I am confident of the great destinies that are in store for us. You and I may not live to see that day. These eyes of ours may not witness that spectacle of ineffable beauty. It may not be permitted to us to exclaim Simeonlike, "Now Lord, lettest thou thy servant depart in peace." It may not be permitted to us to exclaim like the Welsh Bard on the heights of Snowdon, "Visions of glory, spare my aching sight" But is it nothing to know when you are dying, when you are about to take leave of this world, of its joys and sorrows, when the past of your life is unfurled before you, when eternity opens wide its portals, is it nothing to know at that last awful, supreme moment of your lives, that you have not lived in vain, that you have lived for the benefit of others, that you have lived to help in the cause of your country's regeneration? Let us all lead worthy, honourable and patriotic lives, that we may all live and die happily and that India may be great. This is my earnest and prayerful request. May it find a response in your sympathetic hearts.

Vernacular Press Act

[A public Meeting was held in the Town Hall, Calcutta, on the 17th April 1878, to consider the desirability of petitioning Parliament, on the subject of the Vernacular Press Act. The first Resolution having been moved, seconded and adopted, Babu Surendranath Banerjee on rising to move the Second Resolution spoke as follows.]

Gentlemen, I beg to move the Second Resolution. The Resolution runs as follows:

That having regard to the devoted loyalty and attachment of the people of India to the British Crown, to which willing and ungrudging testimony has from time to time been borne by many high and distinguished authorities both here and in England, to the peace and contentment that reign throughout the country, this meeting desires to record its emphatic opinion that a repressive and retrograde measure like the Vernacular Press Act is unnecessary and uncalled for, and is opposed to the interests of justice as it altogether dispenses with the usual safeguards of judicial investigation, and substitutes in their place the discretionary authority of executive officers.

Gentlemen, the Resolution which I have just read speaks of the devoted loyalty and attachment of the people of this country to the British Crown. It is rather a matter of regret that at this time of day, after having lived for more than a century under the fostering influences of English rule and English civilization, the task should have devolved upon us to speak on the subject of our loyalty, and not only that, but that it should also be necessary that we should endeavour to establish our loyalty by unimpeachable facts and unassailable arguments. But the necessity clearly exists. The new Act is a direct slur upon our loyalty. Where would have been the necessity for such an Act in the midst of a contented, happy, and above all a loyal people? Therefore, I repeat, gentlemen, the Act is a direct reproach, and a reflection upon our loyalty. The question, therefore, is, are we loyal, or are we not? Before I proceed to offer any observation on this most important subject, it becomes necessary that I should hasten to draw a distinction. Loyalty to the Crown is to be distinguished from subserviency, from obsequiousness, to this officer or that officer. We may criticise the measures of Government. We may criticise the acts of individual officers; but such criticisms are not incompatible with allegiance to British rule in this country. The question then is, are we loyal, or are we not? Are we wanting in loyalty, in dutiful homage, unswerving allegiance to the throne of her who rules over this country, whose matchless purity of character, whose generosity of disposition, whose keen and ardent interest in the welfare of her Indian subjects have created in our minds the highest respect for her person, and have planted deep her throne, in the affection of the teeming millions of this country. Gentlemen, I put the question, are we wanting in loyalty to this great, wise, virtuous, beneficent ruler—our beloved Empress? Let us appeal to facts. If we are to-be condemned, let it not be upon vague generalities, upon more assumptions, upon futile theories. You are all, gentlemen, familiar with the well-known maxim of English law,—-" The King can do no wrong." This is no more a cardinal maxim of English law than it represents a principle implanted deep in the inborn instinct of the Indian races and peoples. We are essentially a loyal people. By instinct, by tradition, by association, we are loyal. With us the King is a semi-divine personage. He is the embodiment Of justice, purity and truth. Given to the performance of his pledges, he claims the unconditional homage of his subjects. And some of the greatest of our poets—those master delineators of the prevailing sentiments of the age in which they lived,— have clothed this feeling in suitable form and appropriate diction.

Valmiki has taken advantage of this feeling in his immortal poem of the Ramayana. Witness the burst of grief that overpowers the good citizens of Ayodhya when their beloved heir apparent Rama, accompanied by his devoted consort, leaves the home of his father to retire into the wilderness. Witness again the waitings, the lamentations, the dolorous cries of mourning that fill the air on the death of the aged monarch, Dasaratha. Witness the transport of joy, the manifestations of rejoicings, that fill all hearts, when Rama returns home to take possession of the throne of his father. I say we are essentially a loyal people, and however much English education might have revolutionised our mental Constitution, it has not abated by one atom that character for deep and intense-loyalty which has marked the history of our race from the earliest times. Gentlemen, you have all read of the Pindari War, that war which England undertook in the first quarter of this century in the interests of civilization, to rid the country of those Pindari robbers the eternal enemies of progress and good government. When that great war was raging, when its flames had covered the firmament with their lurid glare, there was not a house, there was not a domestic circle which did not offer up its prayers to the God of battles, invoking his blessings for the success of British arms. This fact appears from a petition which the Native community sent up to, the Supreme Court in 1823. Our fathers prayed for the triumph of British arms, aye, the fathers of those who have met here tonight to vindicate their character for loyalty, and to hurl back with scorn and indignation the charge which is sought to be brought home to them—that they are disloyal and faithless to that Government under whose protecting shadows they have enjoyed the inestimable blessing of security of life and property, and have made such rapid strides in civilization and enlightenment. Great God I was it reserved to our iot Chat we should have to vindicate our character for loyalty, in the face of these instances of devoted allegiance to the British crown?

Passing over the Afghan War, we come to the dark days of the Indian Mutiny. It is essentially a military revolt, with which the people at large had no sympathy, and from which they sedulously kept themselves aloof. Not only did they not sympathise with that revolt, not only did they resist the temptation of joining their' countrymen in arms against the British Government, but when the hour came, they manfully stood by their English rulers, and rendered them important services. How many daring feats of valour were performed by the native soldiery, in arms against their own countrymen and in support of British supremacy; how numerous, how manifold were the services, rendered by native gentlemen for the maintenance of the existing order of things? Doe Narain Sing does not live, but we invoke his shade to bear witness to his trials and sufferings, his gigantic exertions to crush out the seeds of rebellion and restore peace and order. But for the memorable services of that great man, the last vestige of British power would, in the days of the Mutiny, have disappeared from the sacred and ancient city of the Hindus. Those were days when loyalty displayed itself the greatest advantage, and was appreciated most.

Now, gentlemen, let me draw your attention to a recent illustration of the same principle. Do the annals of a subject race present an instance of loyalty more cordial, genuine, earnest and enthusiastic than that with which the Prince of Wales was welcomed, when he did us the distinguished honour of visiting India? That manifestation of loyalty elicited from His Royal Highness the warmest expression of his heartfelt satisfaction and approbation. Is there a nobler instance of loyalty than that which was, displayed on the occasion of the Delhi Assemblage? While Englishmen were wrangling about the propriety of calling their Queen-Empress; while they were discussing, with no small amount of warmth and ardour, the constitutional question involved in this change of name, the people of India, from the Himalayas to the Comorin, from the Brahmaputra to the Indus, assembled by their tens of thousands in the capital cities of their provinces and districts to exchange congratulations and compliments, and to invoke the blessing of God on the new relationship which it had pleased Her Majesty to assume as regards her Indian subjects. These, gentlemen, are some instances of loyalty, which might be adduced in refutation of the charge which has been laid against us. But fortunately, loyal as we are our loyalty has received recognition from persons of the highest position, not excluding Her Most Gracious Majesty the Empress herself. I, therefore, beg to be allowed to read extracts testifying to our loyalty in the most glowing terms. I shall begin with the testimony of Lord Canning. I hold in my hand a book which contains a letter written to the late Maharajah Shirish Chander Roy Bahadoor, of Nuddea. The letter is dated 17th of December 1857. Thus, writes the Home Secretary to the Maharajah:

> The Governor-General in Council wishes you to rest assured that the Government of India will not forget, that England will not forget, that, if unhappily the mutineers and rebels of India are to be reckoned by thousands, the peaceful and loyal subjects of the Queen in India are numbered by millions

This is the testimony of that kind and humane Governor-General whose sense of justice and fairness has made his name a household word with us,

The next will be an extract from a message which Her Imperial Majesty was pleased to send to the Viceroy on the 1st of January 1877:

> We have witnessed with heartfelt satisfaction the reception which they have accorded to our beloved son, and have been touched by the evidence of their loyalty and attachment to our House and Throne.

This then is the testimony of that gracious, wise and good sovereign who rules over us. Lord Lytton was pleased to speak in similar terms, when the deputation from the Native Press Association waited upon His Excellency, on the auspicious occasion of the Delhi Assemblage. I have not been able to lay my hand upon the extract, but I was one of those who composed the deputation, so I am able to speak to the testimony His Lordship was pleased to bear. I shall, in the next place,' read an extract from the administration Report of Bengal for 1875-76.

This is what Sir Richard Temple says:

> At heart and in the truest and best sense, the Bengalis are thoroughly loyal. In this respect there are not in all British India better subjects of the Crown. And, under all circumstances, adverse or propitious, they evince a steady, industrious and law-abiding spirit which must command regard and esteem from every Englishman who knows them.

The remarks apply to Bengal alone, for Sir Richard was at the time Lieutenant-Governor of these Provinces. Gentlemen, if time allowed, I might produce such an array of extracts, testifying to our loyalty, as might detain you here all night.

We are then loyal, and ungrudging testimony to our loyalty has been borne by persons in the highest positions. But the Resolution also speaks of the peace and contentment that reign throughout the length and breadth of the country. There is peace; none can gainsay that. Rut, perhaps, it will not be so readily admitted, that there is contentment reigning throughout the country. Talk of contentment in the face of that rising at Surat; why, the people were in arms against the authorities only the other day, in one of the most important cities in the Western Presidency, and how could it then be maintained that the people are contented? I say, there is contentment as regards the existence of British rule in this country, though we may complain of the particular manner in which the administration is occasionally carried on. I do not believe that there is a single native of India who does not wish, from the bottom of his heart, that the English rule might continue long, for the benefit of India and the glory of England. We know full well the immense and endless debt of gratitude we owe to England. We know full well the incalculable blessings which English rule has been the means of conferring upon the people of this country. The English rule in this country is essentially a progressive rule. The Government of today is not the Government of 25 years back. What were the dreams of our fathers are realities with us. What are our fondest hopes and aspirations will be the cherished privileges with those who come after us and live to enjoy the benefits of British rule. We are loyal, we are contented. Why, then, bursts upon our heads this bolt of thunder in a cloudless sky!

It has been remarked by the immortal founder of modern jurisprudence that every law is an evil. It is an infringement of the natural liberty of man, an encroachment upon his innate rights and privileges. It, therefore, becomes the bounden duty of those who introduce any measure of law, to justify it by facts and arguments. Much more is this duty incumbent on those who introduce a repressive measure of legislation, like the one under discussion. Therefore, we are driven to the conclusion, that it is for Government to prove that the Act is necessary, and not for us to show that the Act is unnecessary and uncalled for. It must also be said, in justice to the Government, that they have made out the strongest case possible under the circumstances, and have brought forward all the facts and arguments in support of their position. But what are they? Let us examine the facts. The justification of Government is contained in the speeches of Hon'ble Members, the statement of objects and reasons, and above all, in the translation of extracts from the vernacular journals. I hold these extracts in my hand. The main objects of the law, as stated in the first paragraph of the statement of objects and reasons, is to empower the Government to suppress seditious writings more effectually than is practicable under the present law. Sir Alexander Arbuthnot remarks that, within the last three or four years, there has been a steady increase in the number of seditious writings in the vernacular papers, and that the evil has become worse than ever within the last 12 months. Thus, it has become necessary to pass a special law on the subject. But the question at once occurs, is there not already a section in the Penal Code to repress sedition? Why, we all remember that in the year 1870, when Sir Fitz-James Stephen was Law-member of the Supreme Council, a section was added' to the Penal Code, defining disaffection and punishing sedition. But that law is pronounced to be inefficient. I ask, have you tried it? Have you experimented with it? Have there been prosecutions under it? Have editors of vernacular papers been charged under its special provision? If not, what right have you to-assume that the law is inefficient? And, if inefficient and unworkable, why not rather amend and improve it than introduce a new law? But, gentlemen, the Government has strong objections to prosecute editors of vernacular papers for sedition, under the Penal Code. It has, therefore, thought fit to introduce this special law. Its grounds are not many. The chief of them runs somewhat as follows:—The ordinary criminal law punishes an offender after the crime has been committed; the "special law seeks to prevent the commission of an offence. The Government wants to prevent, not to *punish.* Hence, the special law. Gentlemen, I invite your attention to the terms of this argument, for upon this argument, rests the entire superstructure of the Act. The ordinary criminal law *punishes.* This special law prevents. I must at once pause to point out the fallacy of this reasoning, which seeks to draw a distinction between the criminal law that *punishes* and the criminal law that *prevents.* Why does the criminal law punish? Is it not to prevent the commission of an offence? The end and aim of the ordinary criminal law, therefore, is to prevent. The end and aim of the special law is likewise to prevent. What need is there, then, for the special law? But the analogy does not stop here. The modus operandi is in both cases the same. The ordinary criminal law prevents by means of punishment. The special law prevents also by means of punishment. For that law contemplates that the offending editor will be deterred from writing seditious articles through fear of forfeiting his bail bond, which amounts to a fine, and which is therefore a punishment. Hence, it will appear that the end and aim of the ordinary criminal law is precisely the same as that of the special law, and the modus operandi is the same in both the cases. What necessity what justification then is there, I ask, for this law?

There is another argument adduced in support of the measure. The Government is anxious to prevent the dissemination of the poison of sedition. If prosecutions for sedition were instituted under the Penal Code, the poisonous matter complained of, would be quoted in the various papers, and that would help to disseminate the poison. But what, then, if the poison were allowed to disseminate? . Why, the safety of the State, says Government, requires that the poison should not be allowed to spread. The supreme law of the safety of the State is invoked,, and we are asked to fall down before this dread divinity and to hold our tongues in sullen silence. If the safety of the State required such a law, I am sure, my countrymen would gladly vote in favour of it. But I ask, was there ever a time" in which the question of the safety of the State was more narrowly and anxiously considered than in the 'dark days of the Indian Mutiny? In those dark days, when the country was in flames, when the British Empire was tottering to its foundations, when the contagion of rebellion was spreading like wildfire over an American prairie; in those dark, stern and awful days, Lord Canning and his Council thought nothing of disseminating the poison, but boldly came forward when it became necessary to prosecute certain vernacular editors who had been guilty of writing seditious libels. In 1857, the editor of the *Durbin,* the editor of the *Samachar Sudhabarsan,* the editor of the *Sultan-ul-Akhbar* were prosecuted by Lord Canning for sedition. In those dark days of the mutiny, when the political system was most prone to succumb to the deadening effects of this poison, it had vitality enough to resist its baneful influences. And now we are told in times of comparative peace, contentment, and prosperity, and with a loyal and law-abiding people, that the gigantic fabric of British Empire, this colossal and imperial structure, resting upon the willing allegiance, the steadfast loyalty and the fervent devotion of two hundred and fifty millions of human beings, stands in danger of being wrecked and ruined by the miserable pratings of a few vernacular editors, who might take it into their heads to indite articles, not the most temperate or the most respectful towards the Government.

But there is another argument which, in the opinion ' of Government, makes it necessary that the poison should not be allowed to disseminate. It is assumed that the readers of vernacular papers are ignorant and uncultivated men, upon whose minds the seditious criticisms of the vernacular papers would have a most fatal and prejudicial effect, and sap the foundations of their loyalty. A paternal Government must protect them, and hence the law.

Now, I beg most distinctly to affirm that the readers of vernacular papers are not thoughtless, ignorant and uncultivated men. They are, for the most part, educated men. Primary education was introduced into our country only the other day, and we have not yet reached that state of blessedness, devoutly to be wished for, when the Bengal ploughman may be seen ploughing with the one hand, and holding the *Sulava Samachar* in the other. The vast masses of our people still continue in the grovelling depths of profound ignorance. They read no newspaper, vernacular or otherwise. It is educated people who read them. The *Hindu Patriot* confirms this view of the matter, and so does the *Indian Mirror;* and the *Shahachar,* whose mournful loss we deplored the other day, in that farewell letter of his which we all read with such melancholy interest, distinctly stated that all its readers were educated men and did not come from the uncultivated classes. But there is a higher authority yet who supports this view of the matter. Sir Richard Temple says as follows in his Administration Report for 1874-75:

> Generally speaking, it may said that the Vernacular Press has little or no influence on the majority of the people, who are agriculturists and labourers. *They do not see newspapers and are not influenced by them, either directly or indirectly.*

The arguments, then, upon which this measure of legislation is based, have fallen through, and the measure stands before us, in all its naked deformity, unjustified and unaccounted for.

But I contend that the law is unnecessary, and that the vernacular papers are not disloyal. A grave charge has been brought against the Vernacular Press, viz., that it is disloyal. This charge is broadly made. It runs through the speeches of the Hon'ble Members of the Council. It has, therefore, become necessary that we should discuss this question at length. I must crave the indulgence of this meeting to be allowed to confine my observations to the extracts from the Bengali papers, because I have not yet had time to compare the Urdu extracts with their originals. It is not for one moment to be supposed, that I do not sympathise with the vernacular editors of Upper India in their sore distress and trial. My heart bleeds as much for them, aye, indeed much more profusely than it does for the editors of Bengal, for they are poor, helpless, and alone in their trial, with no influentially organised association; with no powerful representative body to help them in this awful crisis. But the great God-who helps the distressed will help them too. The cause of justice is their cause; the cause of truth is their cause, and that cause will, in the end, triumph. Let me, gentlemen, begin with the remark that these extracts range over a period of twelve months, and are confined to the year 1877. There may be one or two extracts of December 1876, and one or two of January 1878, but, for all practical purposes, we may assume that the extracts are confined to the year 1877. The question at once occurs, what was the condition of the Bengali papers before 1877? Was their tone loyal or disloyal? Let us examine facts. Let me begin with the year 1874-75, when Sir Richard Temple was the Lieutenant-Governor of these provinces. Sir Richard Temple, in his Administration Report for 1874-75, Remarks as follows with reference to the tone of the Bengali Press:

> I have accordingly paid due attention to this subject, and my general conclusion is decidedly favourable in respect to the loyalty and goodwill of the Bengali Press towards the British Crown and nation, and towards the British rule in the main.

Later on, he says:

> The case on behalf of the British is put by the Bengali Press with a warmth and an impressiveness hardly ever surpassed, and seldom equalled by zealous advocates among ourselves.

In the following year, Sir Richard Temple sees no reason to change his opinion on the subject. In the Administration Report for 1875-76, he says:—

> The Vernacular Press maintains the same general tone as characterised it last year, and the Lieutenant-Governor sees no reason to modify the expression of opinion which was placed on record in the Administration Report for 1874-76.

Let us now come to the time when Sir George Campbell was Lieutenant-Governor. Now, in considering the opinion of that distinguished authority, we must bear, in mind that he was violently abused by the Bengali Press—in short, he was the best abused man of his time. Now Sir George Campbell says, in his Administration Report for 1872-73, that the Bengali Press is not really bad at heart. Thus, then for the two or three years preceding the year 1877, the tone of the Vernacular Press of Bengal was not only not hostile and seditious, but was absolutely loyal to the Government. Has it then all on a sudden become seditious? There is a' break in the chain of continued development.

Today the Vernacular Press is loyal and respectful to the Government. Tomorrow's sun dawns upon it, and all on a sudden, down goes its character for loyalty, and it becomes seditious, disloyal, spreading the taint and pollution of treason throughout the length and breadth of the land, and it becomes necessary to produce a Gagging Act This simple fact, this break in the chain of continuity, makes us hesitate to believe in the correctness of this charge of sedition against the Vernacular Press, and, as we wade through the extracts, we find this suspicion all the more strongly confirmed. From the last Administration Report, we learn, that there are thirty-five vernacular papers in Bengal; the so-called seditious extracts have been made from fifteen papers. I say "so called" advisedly, because the extracts are not really seditious. Out of the fifteen papers from which extracts have been made, one, the *Samaj Darpan* has ceased to exist for the last six or seven months. The gentleman who edited this paper received a notice from the Commissioner of Police, the other day, to enter into a bailbond for the good behaviour of his paper.

Poor unfortunate editor! Little did he know that the obloquy of having once edited a vernacular paper would stick to him through life, and that months after he had quietly buried his journal in its grave, its spectral form would once again rise and haunt him like the ghastly phantom of another world. There are fourteen papers then from which thirty-two extracts have been made, excluding four from the *Samaj Darpan*. Now, I contend, that several of these translations are misleading. I shall only instance three. I shall begin with an extract from the *Sadharani* of the 4th of March 1877, which speaks of the Fennua trial:— "It neither bespeaks," says the extract,' " a cultivated taste, nor is it agreeable, to have constantly to write against Government. But in view of the arbitrary acts which have become common in these days, we should be wanting in our duty if we passed them over without any protest. The people were hitherto proud of the justice administered in the High Court. In seeking to shield a rash, oppressive, and unprincipled European Civilian, Government has now brought that Court into contempt, and has struck a blow at the root of British justice. Government has thus worked its own ruin; and if after this the people are found to express discontent, the Anglo-Indian editors will brand the Bengalis with such epithets as ungrateful, disloyal, scurrilous, and what not." The translator has done injustice to the editor by omitting a passage which occurs in the same article, and the effect of which is to mollify the sense of the whole. The passage translated runs as follows:

> But it will not do for us to remain quiet any longer: there is no justice in the country; *now for sometime we must create an agitation* ON *this subject in the Parliament of Great Britain and Ireland.*

Could there be anything more loyal, anything showing greater confidence in the integrity, and honesty of purpose of the British nation and the British Legislature than the extract which I have just quoted. Justice may not be obtained in this country, but England will do us justice, so says the extract.

The next quotation will be from the *Shoma Prokash* of the 26th of February 1877. I may here add that I quote extracts from those papers only which have the greatest influence and circulation:

> The assertion so frequently made by our rulers that they never act contrary to law is seen to be utterly groundless, when we contemplate the illegal acts of Mr. Kirkwood, and the arbitrary treatment, which Baboo Lal Chand experienced at his hands. We are at such moments led to question the use of the Legislative Councils, the maintenance of which costs so much to India, and the equally expensive offices of Viceroy and Lieutenant-Governor. For what is the use of them when the officers in the Mofussil are all in all? They are the Viceroy and the Lieutenant-

> Governor; they are the Legislative Councils; their orders are law, and their acts furnish the rules, and their will is Government. Natives are wrong in regarding indigo planters as oppressions. These oppressors cannot compare with Kirkwood and his conferrers. If oppressions are necessary to the promotion of self-interest, the planters pledge themselves to resort to this means. Kirkwood and his brother officials (who ought to be officials of the same type) do the same, though they are sworn to put a stop to oppression.

Here is also an important omission, for in the very same article there are lines which translated run thus:

> Now we are eager to hear the opinion of the Governor General on this subject. His sense of justice has been clearly shown by his impartial minute on the Fuller case.

Now, I ask, could anything show greater confidence in the impartiality and sense of justice of the present Viceroy.

The third and the last extract Will be from the' *Shahachar*. I can scarcely conceal the feelings of indignation that rise in my bosom, when I come to speak of the manner in which the extract has been made up The extract is not the translation of any connected paragraph or article, but is made up of lines apparently taken at random. The *Shahachar* of the 2nd July writes the following in the course of an editorial, headed the Strength and Duty of England.

There are many points of resemblance noticeable between England and Carthage of the ancient times. In wealth, naval and commercial supremacy, and in military skill, both are alike". Carthage fell, and the causes which brought about her fall are in full operation in England at the present day. The fall of Carthage was due to her fighting with mercenary troops and the existence of fierce factions among the leaders of her people. Does not England present the same spectacle today? She is like Carthage, the home of liberty, and, like her, she is an eyesore to all despotic Governments. The supremacy of England in naval warfare is, however, now a matter of question, while it is almost certain that on land she is no match for the army of any of the great Powers of Europe. The present is a critical time for her, possessed as she is of influence, but without adequate resources of war.

Now there is a most important omission in connection with this extract. There occurs in this very article, a passage full of the most devoted loyalty and of good feeling to the English nation and the English Government, and which, curiously enough, does not appear in the translated extract. The passage runs as follows:— It is not because we are the subjects of England that we desire to see her great and powerful. Read the annals of the human race. No age, no *country, has ever witnessed any system of administration or government like that of the British. The downfall of the British Empire will be the precursor of many evils to the human race.*

Before I take leave of the *Shahachar* I may point out to the meeting a passage full of loyalty which occurs in another article, which is in the same issue, from which the condemned extract has been made. The passage runs as follows:

> We are the grateful subjects of Her Imperial Majesty. It is our incessant prayer that Her rule should be preserved intact.

It is upon extracts such as I have read to you that the Act is founded, and it is for you to consider whether an Act which rests upon extracts of this nature is justifiable or not. I may say that not one of the extracts made from the Bengali papers is seditious. Let me read an extract from the *Bharat Sanskarak* of 3rd September 1877:

> The *Bharat Sanskarak* observes with regret, says the extract Government has only two means, both imperfect and incorrect, of judging the tone of the native newspapers. These are—(1) the weekly report which is often a mistranslation of the views of native editors; and (2) the representations made to Government by men like Kirkwood, which cannot but be of a hostile character. Under these circumstances it has become a matter of consideration with Native editors how to keep the Government informed of the true views maintained on public questions by the vernacular newspapers. The Native Press Association should now be up and doing.

Now I ask could anything be more loyal, and respectful to the Government than what is stated in the above extract? The Advocate-General has taken the trouble of classifying the heads under which the several extracts may be placed. It would be interesting to know under which of those heads the extract I have quoted would come. The Vernacular Press is therefore not seditious. The Act, therefore, is entirely unjustifiable. It has been remarked by Sir Alexander Arbuthnot, in the course of his speech, that Sir Thomas Munro was against a free Press. Sir Alexander quotes Munro's minute dated 1822, but he says that he does not rely upon it. It is as well that Sir Alexander does not rely upon this minute. Sir Thomas Munro is opposed to a free Press, on what ground? Because he thought that the writings of a Free Native Press would have a most prejudicial effect on the minds of the Indian soldiery.

It is not even pretended that the articles of the Vernacular Press are helping to create disaffection in the minds of the native soldiery I, therefore, say that it is well that Sir Alexander does not rely on Sir Thomas Munro's minute. But Sir Alexander has likewise cited the authority of Metcalfe and Macaulay, in support of the new Gagging Act I am bound to remark that the honourable member has not done justice to Sir Charles Metcalfe. Sir Charles, no doubt, contemplated the possibility of circumstances arising, which might make it necessary to impose restrictions upon the liberty of the Press. But he thought that temporary or local' restraints would be sufficient to meet any case of emergency. Lord Canning and his Council understood Sir Charles Metcalfe's minute in this sense, as may be gathered from their Despatch to the Court of Directors on the subject of the Gagging Act of 1857. Metcalfe said, in reply to the address presented to him by the people of Calcutta:

> I entirely concur with you in the desire which you entertain that if, at any time, actual danger should render necessary temporary or local restraints on the liberty of the Press, the precautions applied by the Legislature may be only commensurate to the real exigency, and that no restrictions may be made permanent beyond those which are necessary to ensure responsibility; and I trust that all legislation, with a view to protect the community against licentiousness, will be in the true spirit of liberty.

While speaking on this subject, I cannot help remarking upon the manner in which the Act is being" worked. When the Bill became law, everybody thought it would be kept suspended like the sword of Damocles over the devoted heads of the vernacular editors. But, at last, these hopes have been blasted. Already several editors of vernacular papers-have been called upon to furnish security. Such demand has been made from the *Bharat Mihir* of Mymensingh; from the *Dacca Prokash* and *Hindoo Hitoysim* of Dacca, from the *Sulava Samachar* and the *Shahachar* of this city. And I ask, what offence have these papers been guilty of since the passing of the Act. We know of no offence which they have committed. Is the law then_ to have a retrospective effect? This call for security has told with fatal effect upon one at least of these papers. The *Shahachar* has ceased to exist And I have no doubt a similar fate will soon overtake many other vernacular papers. Gentlemen, there has been some irregularity in the practical working of the Act. Section 3 requires that it is the Magistrate who must take the " initiative in *calling upon editors to* furnish *security.* But in the case of at least three papers, it is the Lieutenant-Governor who has taken the initiative, and has called upon the Magistrate through the Commissioner of the Division, to require the editors to enter into their bail bonds.

It is melancholy to contrast the manner in which the Gagging Act of 1857 was enforced, with the manner in which the present Vernacular Press Act is being worked. The Gagging Act of 1857 was a much milder piece of legislation than the Press Act of 1878. Mild as it was, it was worked with far greater moderation and forbearance. Let me illustrate this by an instance. On the 23rd of June 1857, the Friend of India published an article, headed the Centenary of Plassey. The Governor-General was of opinion that it contained objectionable remarks. A warning was sent round to the editor. He look no notice of the warning. He published an article in the next issue of his paper, in much more violent language, in reckless defiance of the warning that had been sent. But even then the forbearing Governor-, General, whose memory we all cherish with so much-respect, did not withdraw his license, but on receiving an assurance from the proprietor of the *Friend of India,* that such objectionable matter would not be allowed to appear in its future issues, forgave the peccant journalist, and allowed the license to continue. A similar act of forbearance was shown as regards a letter which appeared in the *Bengal Hurkara* of the 13th September 1857, and this forbearance was shown at a time when it was a matter of question whether stern severity should not take the place of mercy and moderation.

It has been remarked, that the fact of the English Press having supported the Act ought to silence all criticism. I yield to none in my appreciation of the character for moderation, wisdom, and fairness which so eminently distinguishes the Press of England. The English Press, however, has decided the question exparte has not heard both sides of the case, and has certainly not heard the case for the defence. The English Press has likewise countenanced the Act, under a sense of imperious necessity. They are under the impression that the country is ripe for revolt, and that the seditious-writings of the vernacular journals constitute a source of danger to the Empire. But yet we are not without hopes of being able to appeal with success to the generous instincts of the English people. Our hopes and our confidence have been strengthened by what has already taken place in the House of Commons.

Before a breath of complaint was heard here, before a word of protest was publicly raised in this country, those ardent, advocates of human freedom and of liberty of speech, had already called in question, in the House of Commons, the wisdom, the policy and the justice of this most objectionable law. The question is, indeed, not an Indian question. It is essentially an English question. The question is not whether a certain number of Indians should have the right of free speech. The question is broader, vaster, deeper, far. The question is whether in any part of the British dominions, whether in any part of the world where floats the free flag of England—the flag which has " braved the battle and the breeze," the flag which has stood forth in all ages and in all climes as the beacon of human freedom and human progress—the question is whether in any part of the world acknowledging British rule, restrictions should be imposed upon the liberty of speech of any portion of Her Majesty's subjects. We claim-this privilege not as a matter of favour. We are no longer the conquered subjects of England. We are the incorporated citizens of a free Empire. Has not our Sovereign been graciously pleased to assume the title of Empress? And was not the act of assumption celebrated amid circumstances of pomp and splendour, which have left a deep and ineffaceable impression upon the minds of the Indian races and peoples? Was that act of assumption, of sacred incorporation, a fact or a myth? I appeal' to the princes, the chiefs, and the people of India—to the high officials who were present on that occasion—to bear witness to the solemnity of that ceremony and the sanctity of the pledges that were then given. We are British subjects, and are we to be deprived of an inalienable right of British subjects, in this summary and perfunctory manner? The Act is against the instincts of Englishmen, is against the genius of the British Constitution. The history of England is the history of freedom. It is the history of one long, continued, sustained effort to succour the distressed and to uphold the cause of oppressed nationalities. I cannot, for one moment, induce myself to believe that a nation so firmly wedded to the principles of justice and freedom, will sanction a measure which deprives a large portion of Her Majesty's subjects of an important privilege and an inestimable boon, which Englishmen prize above all things. It is England that has introduced into our midst the lamp of knowledge. Will she now put out that lamp with her own hands, and plunge us again into the depths of Cimmerian darkness? Under English influence, India was waked to life. Under English auspices, the pulse of life is beating fast within her. But the present Act has prostrated, paralysed, and overpowered her. Let us then appeal to the representatives of England, the custodians of her honour, the repositories of her name and fame, to repeal this objectionable law, to avert a great calamity from our country, and thus perform an act of duty which would redound to the glory of England and enhance that love, that respect, that veneration, which we all feel for the fair fame of England and her spotless name.

Appeal to the Mohammedan Community

[The following speech was delivered by Babu Surendranath Banerjee at the great Congress Meeting held at Dacca, ON *1st October* 1888:—]

Mr. Chairman and Gentlemen,

This is not the first time that I have had the honour of addressing a great assembly of my countrymen at Dacca. Ten years ago I was here, and you honoured me with a large measure of your attention. The kindly welcome with which I have been overwhelmed from all directions and all classes of the community from the moment that I set my foot in East Bengal is but the token of the renewal of your confidence in me and of your generous appreciation of my humble efforts in the service of my country. Next to the approbation of his own conscience the highest reward which a public man may claim and which he may receive is the applause of his own countrymen. This I have in an unstinted measure, so far as the citizens of Dacca are concerned. Encouraged and supported by it, it shall be the aim of my life in the future, as it has been in the past, to prove myself worthy of that confidence which has been bestowed upon me with such generous profusion. Within the last ten years, a great change has taken place.

Not the least noticeable feature of the change has been the introduction of Local Self-Government throughout the country. We owe it to the beneficence of perhaps the greatest Viceroy whom the wisdom of English statesmanship had ever sent out to govern the dominions of the Queen in this part of the world. Local Self-Government has been an unqualified success in all other parts of the country. I hope and trust it will be an unqualified success so far as Dacca is concerned.

But it has been with us a matter of constant complaint and of constant regret (pardon me for this reference) that the citizens of Dacca absorbed in their local politics and in the more exciting controversies nearer home have ceased to feel that degree of interest which might have been expected of them in regard to those questions of wider import and deeper significance which concern the welfare of the country at large, that in short the capital of East Bengal has abandoned her legitimate position as the leader of thought and the inspirer of public movements in this part of the country. I hope and trust this meeting is the augury of a better state of things, that the sleeping lion has shaken off its slumbers, and that Dacca means once again to reassert her ancient position as the leader of public opinion in East Bengal. If such be the significance of this meeting, I welcome it with gratitude; and God knows with what raptures of joy it will be welcomed throughout the length and breadth of the land. For at the present moment, the eyes of all our countrymen are strained with feverish interest and expectancy upon our proceedings here and your attitude will probably determine the attitude of other towns throughout East Bengal.

I have remarked that we are on the eve of a great change. We are on the threshold of a new epoch. The first streaks of the dawn of a new day are already visible on the firmament. The change is striking. It has even attracted the attention of men in high office who are less open to the influence of these changes. Sir John Strachey in a work of his has remarked that the India of Lord Ripon is no more like the India of Lord Ellenborough than the England of Queen Victoria like the England of Queen Anne." Sir Auckland Colvin, Lieutenant-Governor of the North-West Provinces, has quoted Biblical language to imply the significance of this change. " The dry bones in the open valley," says he, " have become instinct with life." There is a change deep, profound and significant. The National Congress is the visible outcome, the highest expression, the noblest embodiment of this newborn spirit of change. In the words of the greatest of Indian statesmen it is the soundest triumph of British administration and a crown of glory to the British Government.

England has done great things for India. She has given us peace and blessings of a settled Government. She has intersected the country with railways and telegraphs and other works of public utility. She has given us education, a free press, the inestimable right of free discussion, the handmaid of all knowledge and advancement. But all these pale and dwindle into insignificance when compared with the glory of her present achievement—the awakening of national life and the visible tokens of national revival among a people hitherto sunk in the torpor of ages. It is too often said that these Congressmen are seditionists, not surely by Mr. Kemp, the Editor of *The Bengal Times,* who sits opposite to me. But if we are seditionists, we are at any rate in very good company; for we claim among the friends of the Congress such men as Sir William Hunter, late Member of the Viceregal Council, Sir Richard Garth, late Chief Justice of Bengal, Sir Henry Harrison, Chairman of the Calcutta Municipality, and last not least Mr. Cotton, Secretary to the Bengal Government. We are not scditionisls at all. We are agitators and I am proud to belong to that class. We claim to be the best friends of the Government. A foreign Government such as ours is unaided by representative institutions, cannot possibly know all our wants and grievances, and we tell the Government what our wants are and thus seek to remove all legitimate cause for complaint. We are loyal and we are patriotic We are loyal because we are patriotic, because we know and we firmly believe that through the British Government and the British Government alone can we hope to obtain those cherished political rights which English education and English influences have taught us to hanker after.

The National Congress is the Congress of the nation. But who constitute the nation? Not surely the Hindus or the Mohammedans alone, but Hindus, Mohammedans, Parsis, Sikhs, Christians—the varied races that inhabit this vast Empire. I claim for the Congress that its programme is the most catholic, the most comprehensive, the most admirably suited to the varied requirements of the different sections of the great Indian community. Its concessions are such as will benefit Hindus and Mohammedans alike. I want to descend from the abstract to the concrete. I am a journalist, and journalists have a knack of taking a common sense view of things. I will quote chapter and verse.

The Congress prays for the separation of judicial from executive functions in the administration of criminal justice. If the concession is granted, will not the administration of justice in the country be improved and placed upon a satisfactory footing? And if so, will not the result be beneficial to Hindus, Mohammedans and all other sections of the community? The Congress advocates the repeal of the Arms Act, the enlistment of our countrymen as volunteers and the establishment of a Military College in India. Now—I ask—will not these concessions benefit all sections of the community? And I contend that they will benefit the Mohammedan a great deal more than the Hindu community, for it must be admitted that the Mohammedans represent a noble and a manly community. They still cherish the martial instincts of their sires; and to them far more than to their Hindu fellow-subjects the concessions to which I have referred will represent an unqualified blessing. But then it is urged that if in accordance with the programme of the Congress, the admission to the higher appointments in the Covenanted Service were to be regulated by competition, the Hindus would get all the appointments and the Mohammedan community would fare very badly. An argument of this kind implies an absence of faith in the future of Islam in India' and in the possibilities of its development which I for one am not prepared to share. I deny altogether that under a system of competitive examination the higher appointments in the Civil Service would be monopolised by Hindus and by them alone It is a matter of unalloyed satisfaction to me, as it must be to the great body of my enlightened Hindu fellow-citizens, to note the rapid advance which the Mohammedan community have made within the last few years in English culture and English education. Not long ago a Mohammedan gentleman stood first at the B.A. Examination of the Calcutta University: another was first in English in the M.A. Examination; and to a Mohammedan gentleman has been reserved a distinction which no Hindu has yet been able to achieve in any-competitive examination.

The worthy son of a worthy sire, Mr. M. Tyabji, the son of the Hon'ble Budruddin Tyabji, stood first at the final examination for the Civil: Service of India. With all these facts before me, is it possible to doubt the future of the Mohammedan community in India?—and I must say that it seems to me that those Mohammedan leaders do a distinct disservice to their coreligionists who would discard competition and in violation of the Queen's Proclamation would urge that any section of the community should be advanced to high offices, not by any definite test of merit, but through nomination and the avenues of official favour. Alone in respect of the question of the reconstitution of the Legislative Councils, can there arise any possible difference of opinion.

It may be said that if our Legislative-Councils were reconstituted upon a partially elective basis the Hindus being in a majority would completely swamp the Mohammedan minority. But here again the Congress, with that solicitude for the interests of all classes of the community which is its most distinguishing feature, provides a remedy. One-half the appointments are to be made by Government, and surely the Government might be trusted to safeguard the interests of the minority. But this doubt, this hesitation can only arise on the assumption of there being a conflict of interests between Hindus and Mohammedans. I deny there is any antagonism whatsoever between the two great races who inhabit this vast continent and who together form the Indian nation. I would appeal to this great gathering of my countrymen and I would appeal to Sir Syed Ahmed Khan himself. He is my authority in this matter. In the expressive language of Sir Syed Ahmed Khan, whose present views unhappily are in such direct conflict with the teachings of his lifetime—in the words of this venerable man—India is like a fair maid with two eyes, one representing the Hindu and the other the Mohammedan community. Are we who are her offspring—Hindus and Mohammedans—are we to deny to her the right of perfect vision? Is she to use only one eye when both are available? No, the advancement of India does not mean the advancement of one community to the exclusion of the rest.

It means the progressive development of Hindus and Mohammedans alike, bound together by the closest ties of goodwill and amity, and having in view the advancement of the interests of their common country. Our relations are no of yesterday's growth. Behind us looms the history eight hundred years of goodwill and amity. Tin records of the world do not present the instance of; wiser or a more beneficent sovereign or one more devoted to the interests of his people than Akbar.

Let me here relate an unwritten chapter of Mughal history. Having firmly established himself on the throne, Akbar sought a matrimonial alliance with a daughter of one of the princely houses of Rajputana. The offer was unique, but coming from the lord of Delhi, the Rajput Princes had no other alternative left than to give it their most serious attention. They at length resolved to accept the offer, but coupled it with conditions which they fully believed would be rejected with scorn. They agreed to enter into this strange alliance with a Mohammedan Sovereign but on the following express conditions:—(1) that the offspring of the marriage should be the heir-apparent and (2) that he should not be circumcised, (Jehangeer, Shah Jehan and Dara Sekoh were not circumcised) and lastly that the Mughals should give up-wearing a particular sort of headdress to which it appears the Hindus objected. Such were the conditions of the alliance, and to these Akbar unhesitatingly assented, and he thus paved the way for the complete unification of Hindu and Mohammedan interests which was the crowning glory of his rule as it added to the stability of his house. Thus, upon the basis of goodness and beneficence rose the majestic fabric of the Mughal Empire which lasted for 800 years, and which but for the fanaticism of Aurangzeb would have lasted for another 800 years. Raja Man Singh carried the Mughal standard to the frontiers of Afghanistan on the North West, to the wilds of Assam on the East and to the jungles of Orissa on the South. A Hindu by birth he was allowed by his Mohammedan Sovereign to rule over Moslem populations. Another Hindu, Raja Todur Mall, consolidated the Empire or a financial basis, while Beer Ball remained to the last moment of his life the favourite companion of his Sovereign. The policy of Akbar became the policy of the Mughal Empire and the policy of its Mohammedan subjects. The Mohamedans loved and trusted the Hindus and the Hindus reciprocated their kindliness with enthusiastic gratitude. The Mughal Empire has crumbled into atoms. Moslem-glory has for ever departed from India. But the cordiality between Hindus and Mohamedans has survived the wreck of an Empire and the downfall of a great and princely house. It has been truly said that the nation dwells in the villages and in the interior—away from the great towns and the busy centres of trade and commerce. If that be so, I would ask you to mark the relations which exist between Hindus and Mohamedans in the villages of Bengal. The most endearing terms of domestic relationship are freely interchanged. Brother, cousin, uncle, are the words which Hindus apply to Mohamedans, and Mohamedans to Hindus. Yet we are told in spite of these facts, in spite of the clearest evidence to the contrary, that the relations between the two communities are far from being satisfactory, and that there is a growing sense of estrangement between them. No such thing. We are brothers united by the closest ties which can bind man to man, and let no man seek to sever bonds which nature has fastened with her own hands.

I must say, however, that I cannot understand an argument which is sometimes brought forward in justification of the attitude of a section of the Mohammedan community in regard to the National Congress. A Nawab of Hyderabad in a conversation which he recently had with Mr. Gladstone gave him to understand that the Mohammedan community had abstained from joining the Congress, because they were unwilling to embarrass the Government Embarrass the Government by our puny representations ! Embarrass this mighty Government which has built up and which so admirably sustains this great fabric of Empire by any representation of grievances which you or I may make I Why I must say that I have a far higher opinion of the strength and the greatness of the British Government in India than to think that we should embarrass it by our representations. So far from doing so, it seems to me that we actually help the Government when we have any petitions to present or any representations to make.

But mark the inconsistency of the attitude assumed by the Nawab. What do our public bodies do—the *Anjuman* of this city of which your Chairman is the worthy President and the various Anjumans scattered all over the country? Why they seem to be a source of endless embarrassment to the Government, for they are constantly addressing the Government with petitions. If the views of the Nawab are to be accepted, every *Anjuman* in the country should close its doors and give up its appointed work. But perhaps what the Nawab means is that he has no objection to representations coming from particular bodies or associations, but a united expression of opinion such as what the Congress secures is likely to embarrass the Government. A single dose, the Nawab does not mind; but he objects to the dose being repeated.

Common sense and reason rise in revolt against an argument of this description. What is the object of any representation that you may desire to submit to the Government? Surely to obtain some concession or some reform. Is not the concession likely to be forthcoming when many voices pray for it instead of one? These are considerations so obvious that it seems to me a marvel that there should be any doubt with regard to them. But mark the answer that Mr. Gladstone" gave. That Prince of politicians, the far-seeing statesman, long the Prime Minister of England, quietly heard the Nawab and said that all legitimate and reasonable efforts of the people to represent their requirements to Government commanded his warmest sympathy. Therefore we have this fact that Mr. Gladstone himself approves of constitutional agitation. And the Congress aims at nothing more. I would once again earnestly plead for the sympathy of all sections of the Mohammedan community on behalf of the Congress. The Congress flings its portals wide open for the admission of all—it welcomes all. . The Mohammedan community have absolutely nothing to be afraid of from a Hindu majority.

Every possible precaution has been taken to safeguard the interests of the minority. A rule has been introduced at the instance, I believe, of Mr. Budruddin Tyabji which provides that if the Mohammedan Delegates unanimously or nearly unanimously object to any question, it shall not be taken up for discussion by the Congress. The voice of the minority will thus rule the majority in respect of the choice of any question for purposes of deliberation, when the minority have a pretty strong feeling on the subject. I must say that it appears to me to be extremely unreasonable on the part of any section of the community to object to the programme of the Congress and to find fault with it, when they deliberately stand aloof from it. The Congress is open to all; and if it goes wrong surely the only way of preventing it is by joining the Congress and not by criticising it from outside or by assuming a hostile position in regard to it In this connection I must observe that I deplore the language that has been employed by an important member of the Native Press in regard to the Mohammedan community of Bengal. I would give, words to recall that language.

It is as mischievous as it is wide of the truth, and I am perfectly certain that it does not represent in the remotest degree the sentiments of the Hindu community towards their Mohammedan fellow-countrymen. But let us not quarrel over mere words. Let bye-gones be bye-gones. I would ask you to forget and to forgive. Hindus and Mohamedans ! we are brothers; and as brothers sometimes quarrel, so too they always make up their quarrels in the presence of the larger interests of the family. I ask of you, Hindus and Mohamedans to forget your jealousies and your petty differences in the name of your common country and for the promotion of her dearest interests.

Government and Municipalities

[Speech at the Municipal Meeting in 1896 *.in connection with H. H. The Lieutenant-Governor's Speech at Entally.]*

Sir,—I have the honour to move the fast Resolution. The terms of the Resolution are as follows:—*(Here reads the Resolution.)* In moving this Resolution. I desire to guard myself against a misconception which the circumstances of the case may give rise to. The wisdom of holding this meeting has been doubted in some quarters, and our attitude has been misconstrued. I desire to say on my own behalf and I may add on behalf of those who have signed the requisition, that our attitude is not one of defiance but of defence—it is an attitude of explanation and of vindication. We are all here animated by a common sentiment of dutiful allegiance to the honoured Head of the Government of these Provinces by the belief—in my case I will add, the assured conviction that when we have stated our case as it ought to be stated, and have laid before His Honour the facts and arguments as they ought to be laid, and when upon the basis of those facts we appeal to him for justice and fair play, then we are sure His Honour with an Englishman's instinct will accord to us a sympathetic response.

In that hope and confidence we have convened this meeting. In that hope and confidence we desire to approach His Honour with the appeal that His Honour will be pleased to reconsider his judgement, at least, so much of it as involves a censure of the Municipality. Our case is so strong—it is so overwhelmingly convincing — that we have only to state it to carry home conviction to every unprejudiced mind and: to dissipate the' misconceptions which have gathered round His Honour's' speech. We fully recognise our position; in relation to the Government. It is a position of subordination strictly safeguarded under limitations, imposed by the law. In one sense we are the arm of administration. An important branch of public affairs has been entrusted to our care. But at the same time we cannot forget that we are also the representatives of the people. We are here, because our constituents, have sent us here. They can make and unmake us. Their confidence is to us the breath of our nostrils. Their approbation, next to the approbation of our own consciences, is the highest reward we can aspire to. But when our administration has been arraigned in the way it has been arraigned by the Head of the Local Government, then we incur the imminent risk of losing the confidence of our constituents unless we are able to vindicate our administration and justify it in their eyes. Duty to them and ourselves—duty to the public and the Government alike—renders it necessary that we should enter upon a formal and public defence of our administration. Such, however, is our faith in the justice of our case that we feel that we may rely with absolute confidence upon the approving judgement of public opinion.

The Resolution says that we have been condemned by His Honour—condemned unheard— condemned under circumstances which make the condemnation unmerited and inappropriate to the occasion. Have we been condemned or not? I heard Mr. Farr say that he was not aware that we had been condemned by the Lieutenant-Governor. I am sorry that Mr. Farr and his friends have left the meeting before they had heard all that we had to say. If we have not been condemned, such a meeting as this would be utterly out of place, and I should be offering an insult, a deliberate affront to your understanding, were I to ask you to accept the Resolution which I have the honour to move. Sir, as I listened to the speech of His Honour when it was delivered, as I read it in the newspapers in print, it seemed to me, as it must have seemed to all of you, that it involved a scathing unqualified condemnation of the Commissioners. Since then, however, an explanation has been offered.

The Hon'ble Mr. Risley, writing on behalf of His Honour the Lieutenant-Governor in a communication addressed to the Medical Board, has explained that His Honour has a perfectly open mind on the question of responsibility and that it is a mistake to suppose that he intended that the executive were blameless in the matter of the sanitary shortcomings of Calcutta, and that the Commissioners, alone were to blame. For my part, I am not prepared to accept the inference which underlies these remarks; and you are not prepared to accept the distinction which is sought to be made here between the Commissioners and their Executive. The Commissioners and the Executive form integral parts, inseparable elements of the Corporation. To condemn the Executive is to condemn the Commissioners. To condemn the Executive is to say that the Commissioners have been remiss in their supervision of their work Nay more, we are not prepared to permit an extraneous authority—however exalted that authority might be to interpose between ourselves and our employees and apportion the measure of responsibility between us. Nothing could be more demoralising to the Executive, more utterly subversive of official discipline. It has never been a part of the traditions of the Corporation to regard the Executive as separate from the Commissioners in the matter of responsibility. In the dark days of the Corporation when a Commission was appointed, the Executive under the guidance of Sir Henry Harrison cordially cooperated with the Commissioners in defending the menaced interests of the Corporation. I hope we are not going to depart from those traditions. I hope those traditions have not become matters of ancient history. I hope, Sir, you as the Head of the Executive will by your vote today once again affirm the principle that your honour or dishonour means our honour or dishonour.

Thus, then, notwithstanding the explanation which has been offered, we are driven to the conclusion that we have been condemned. The Resolution says that the condemnation passed upon the Commissioners was unmerited and inappropriate to the occasion and that it was "passed without affording them the opportunity of explanation or defence. The Lieutenant-Governor was the guest of the Commissioners. The Commissioners were his hosts. He was their honoured guest.

For the guest to turn round upon his hosts and to censure them is a proceeding which will not recommend itself to the approval of right-thinking men. Then again what was the occasion which had brought the Lieutenant-Governor to Entally? He had come to open the new drainage works—to preside at a function which associated with the inauguration of the most important sanitary work of the generation. It will occur to most people that such an occasion was singularly inopportune for censuring the Commissioners for their alleged neglect of the sanitation of Calcutta. The function itself was the most striking refutation of the charge. Even the *Pioneer* newspaper, the accredited organ of the official hierarchy, condemned the speech as being unsuitable to the occasion on which it was delivered. But we further complain that we have been condemned unheard. The Lieutenant-Governor based his remarks upon the Report of the Sanitary Inspectors; but the Report was never sent to the Commissioners for explanation. It is an eternal principle of justice that no man shall be condemned unheard. Is the Corporation along to be singled out for exceptional treatment? The veriest murderer caught red-handed in the act, reeking with the blood of his innocent victim, is allowed, such is the humanity of the law, the opportunity of explanation and defence. But this great Corporation, the greatest representative body in India, with a record which would bear favourable comparison with the record of any similar body in any other part of the world, is denied this privilege. And by whom?

The Head of the Local Government. And who is the Head of the Local Government? The distinguished administrator who was late Secretary to Lord Ripon's Government—a Government that placed the system of Local Self-Government in India upon a firm and durable basis and covered itself with ever lasting honour and glory. I am constrained to say—I say it with all reluctance but I must say it—in the words of the greatest of English poets that we are fallen upon evil times and upon evil tongues, and by darkness and danger compassed round.

But, Sir, we also complain that His Honour's speech was based upon a grave misapprehension of the facts of the case. The third Resolution in charge of my friend deals with the mistakes of fact bearing upon the conservancy of the town. I will not trespass into my friend's province. But there are mistakes of fact not covered by the third Resolution, and to some of these I desire to call your attention. We have been set down as a set of talkers wasting our time in talk. The charge of loquacity has been laid to our doors. With reference to this charge, I will say this that speech is governing the politics of the civilized world. I hope and trust that within a measurable distance of time it will govern the politics of the Indian Continent. Government by speech is the order of the day. Not even the omnipotence of autocracy will avail to arrest or postpone the slow, the steady," the triumphant development of these forces, working noiselessly in the bosom of society, which are hastening forward the accomplishment of this great end. However, that may be, is it true that we make speeches for the sake of speech-making—that we talk more than we should?. Is it the case that we are " an armoury of talk," to use the words of a late distinguished Secretary to the Government of Bengal? Those who are most familiar with the working of the Corporation are the best judges in this matter. In this case the saying is not true that the spectators see more of the game than the actual players. The spectators must see less for they have to rely upon hearsay evidence. In modern Indian history, there is no name more honoured than that of Kristo Das Pal, there never was a member of this body who rendered greater services to the Corporation and the town, or whose utterances are entitled to more weight. ' Speaking in 1881 of the elected municipality, then in its early years, he observed:

An examination of the Municipal debates in the past and present will, we doubt not, satisfy the most fastidious person that there is less talk now than before. It is superfluous for us to say that public question cannot be decided without talk, long or small, and that the character of the talk in public bodies is to a great extent regulated by the information possessed and the earnestness of convictions entertained by different speakers. Life itself is a long talk. If the world consisted only of mutes, then society would hardly exist. In all the walking moments of lite man spends much of his time in talk, whether for business, instruction or pleasure. Public life in the civilized world means a war of words.

But Kristo Das Pal was himself a greater talker. The most accomplished debater of his time, he might be presumed to be partial to speech-making. Further he laboured under serious disability that he was not an official, and to some minds, present company of course always excepted, official testimony has the force and validity of gospel truth. Therefore let me pass from unofficial to official testimony, and the testimony, which I am about to quote will be that of perhaps the most distinguished civilian who has ever held the office of Chairman. Thus, spoke Sir Henry Harrison in 1887:

> When large questions of principle came up for final discussion in general meeting, it could not but be expected that the men of leisure, who naturally took an interest in the work which they had helped to

> complete, would also naturally be prepared to discuss at length the questions which were under consideration; but the men of business would not like to sit for two or three hours to discuss them. It was unreasonable to suppose that this could be otherwise, and when European gentleman did take an interest in such matters, they themselves fell into the habit of making as long speeches as native gentlemen. Some of the longest speeches he had ever listened to were made by European gentlemen in debates in which they were taking a great interest.

But 1896 is not 1887, and that may make a difference. Let me therefore come to more recent times and quote a more modern authority. Let me quote the words of the late-lamented Mr. Lee whose early death was such a heavy loss to the Corporation and the town:

> Less frequently now than of old, because the outside public-is better acquainted with the facts, but still occasionally, we hear insinuations that much time is wasted in this hall by long speeches from the Municipal Commissioners. No charge could be further from the mark. In all my experience—and that has covered full three years—I have seldom listened to a speech that has not been useful and to the point. I can hardly recall a single instance in which I have made reflection that the speaker was throwing no new light on his subject, and was simply speaking to make a speech. The facts, indeed, are conclusive. In the course of the year you hold some thirty general meetings. All the proceedings of every committee meeting, of which some 260 ate held in the course of the year, come before you in this hall for review. A single Committee will frequently deal with 20 or more separate matters, and you have on the average to review proceedings of such Committees at each single meeting in this hall, so that you dispose of sometimes 120, seldom less than forty items of business at a sitting. How long do you take over it? As a rule between one and two

> hours I Who could say with fairness that, that is excessive? How many similar deliberative bodies in the world are there that would dispose of the work in less time? The general rule that we endeavour to observe is not to speak without special knowledge and clear opinion, and then to express our thoughts in language as brief as we can make it.

These words possess a pathetic interest for us; for they were the last words addressed by Mr. Lee to this Corporation—they form part of his valedictory address delivered on the 23rd March 1893.

From opinions let us pass on to the consideration of the facts of the case; and in this connection, I desire to congratulate my friend, Babu Nolin Behary Sircar, upon the admirable statement which he has drawn up, traversing the various points raised in His Honour's speech We find from the table in Babu Nolin Behary Sircar's statement, that in 3894-95 there were 239 items of business brought up before the Commissioners. Out of them 191 items were disposed of without discussion. There were 88 items in which short speeches were made, and there were only 10 items which gave rise to long debates.

In 1895-96, there were 328 items of business which were brought before the Commissioners, and so many as 249 items of business disposed of without any discussion. Further we find that in 1894-95 the attendance of Commissioners at a meeting was forty on an average, of whom only six spoke, 34 giving " silent, sensible votes." In 1895-96, the average attendance of Commissioners at each meeting was 41, of whom only 7 spoke on an average, 34 giving " silent, sensible votes." This charge has again and again been brought and as often refuted. Falsehood dies hard. It is a hydra-headed monster, which rears its head as often as you slay it. You have slain the monster this time. You may not be too sure that you will not have to repeat the operation. Then, Sir, our Constitution has been assailed.' For our Constitution we are not responsible. We do the best with it. It has been observed by Sir Alexander Mackenzie that the municipal Constitution of Calcutta is derived *en bloc* from the most advanced models in England, and that it has been determined without reference to the totally different circumstances of an Oriental city and a mixed community. The statement involves a serious misapprehension of facts. Point out to me the Town Council or Municipality in England the members of which are partly elected and partly nominated. Point out to me the Town Council or-Municipality in England the Mayor of which is nominated by the Government. Point out to me the Town Council or Municipality in England, which is subjected to the same measure of control to which we are subjected at the hands of the Executive Government. Then again it is not the case that the varied and diversified interests of an Oriental city and of a mixed community were not sufficiently borne in mind in framing the Constitution. Read the debates Which took place in Council in 1876 when the Constitution was framed, and again in 1888 when it came on for review (I will not tire your patience by quoting extracts) and you will find that the illustrious men who framed the Constitution and those who remodelled it, men like Sir Stuart Hogg and Sir Henry Harrison, paid special attention to the representation of the varied interests of our community, and took the necessary precautions to secure that end. But after all is our Constitution so bad?

It has been pronounced to be a success by distinguished men of the eminence of the late Mr. Colman Macaulay and others. A tree is judged by its fruits. Look at the achievements of the elected Municipality. The solvency of the Municipality secured upon a firm and durable basis, the increased and increasing credit of the Corporation until that credit is as good as that of the Government of India, the magnificent works of sanitation which have changed the face of Calcutta until it has become a sanatarium for all Bengal—these are the enduring memorials of the wisdom, the judgement, the sagacity and public spirit of the much-maligned elected Commissioners of Calcutta. I should like to know what department under the direct control of the Government could show such satisfactory results. You complain of the over-crowding of Calcutta. To what is it due? May I ask? People from the moffusil flock to Calcutta as to a sanatarium from their malaria-stricken homes. Within the last twenty years the price of land in Calcutta has been trebled. Has the volume of your trade increased threefold? No. What then is the explanation? The demand for land has steadily increased owing to the increasing healthiness of Calcutta. Why the elected Commissioners during the time they have been in office have spent nearly two crores and fifty lakhs of rupees upon works of permanent utility; the Justices spent only a crore and eighty lakhs during the time they administered the affairs of Calcutta.

It is too late in the day to criticize the Constitution. It has stood the stress or twenty long years. It has been pronounced to be a success by high authority. It has produced the magnificent results to which I have referred. It has secured the financial solvency of the Corporation and has improved its credit. Time destroys all shams and impositions. If ours was a bastard Constitution unsuited to the exigencies of the situation, it would have long ago gone the way of all things. I am obliged to say that never was there a grosser misconception than what pervades this part of the speech of His Honour, the Lieutenant-Governor.

Then, Sir, it has been observed that our executive is weak and can be easily upset. The suggestion is that we interfere unnecessarily with the executive. Sir, I appeal to you as the Head of the executive—I would like to appeal to Mr. Hughes as the head of the spending department of the Corporation—whether you have found any difficulty in getting on with the Commissioners—I should like to know whether any Chairman, any Health Officer, save and except Dr. Simpson, has ever experienced any difficulty in this respect. If Dr. Simpson had all his own way, I very much fear Calcutta would have been declared a plague-stricken city, quarantine regulations would have been enforced, the trade of Calcutta ruined, and the Municipality reduced to bankruptcy.

One word more, before I conclude. His Honour has-been pleased to observe that as regards many of us our individual stake in the town is small, that we represent ourselves in the first instance, and a mass of heterogeneous interests in the second. We cannot very well help representing ourselves. That we represent ourselves and that we represent a mass of heterogenous interests (by which I understand the interests of our constituents, who are Hindus and Mohamedans) may be our misfortune, but is certainly not our fault. But I deny altogether that we have little or no stake in the town. I will venture to say that we have much greater stake than the birds of passage who come here to shake the pagoda tree and run away with our gold. We have a small stake in the town

I Why the dust of our homesteads is consecrated by the ashes of our sires. Calcutta is the home of our ancestors—it is the home of our wives, our mothers and our daughters—it is the destined home of our children and our children's children. I£ ever the plague were to break out here—may God avert such a calamity—where would the birds of passage be? We shall, however, continue to cling to the habitations of our ancestors with fond and devoted affection. Nothing in history, nothing in fable exceeds, the love and devotion which the Hindu feels for his homestead. It is the centre of all his joys—round it gather the noblest and the tenderest of his domestic associations. They cannot indeed be transformed into gold—what gold can measure them I But are sentimental considerations of no weight in the concerns of life—are they to count as a feather in the balance in dealing with a people who are largely governed by' sentiment? I will not detain you any longer. I trust our vote today will be an unanimous vote.

This Corporation recognises no distinction of race—no difference between official and non-officials, between the Commissioners and the executive. Here we are all members of a common body, animated by a common sentiment and" a common desire to maintain untarnished the honour, the reputation and the dignity of this great Corporation which it is our privilege to serve. We remember with pride that when the Corporation was assailed by popular clamour and placed on its trial, Europeans and Indians; the Executive and the Commissioners stood shoulder to shoulder, firmly knitted together as one body, resolved to defend the menaced interests of the Corporation. Are we now going to prove false to our traditions?

No mistake; we are in the midst of a grave crisis, as grave as any one which has ever occurred in the history of the Corporation; for only the other day—I think it was on Saturday last,—His Honour the Lieutenant-Governor observed from his place in Council that a considerable amendment of the Calcutta Municipal Act might be expected. I do not take it in the light of a threat, but as the serious pronouncement of a deliberate opinion on the part of a responsible statesman. However, that may be, I will say this on my own behalf, and I will venture to add on your behalf, that so long as we are members of this Corporation, so long as we are entrusted with the municipal administration of this city, so long as the safeguarding of the Constitution under which we work is in our hands, as long we shall manfully endeavour to perform our duties, undaunted by the frowns and unseduced by the smiles of power. In order that we may thus perform pur duties, and in a manner that will redound to our own credit and to the benefit of the Corporation, the most perfect accord, the most cordial unanimity should subsist between us. In this as in other matters, united we stand, divided we fall.

On Social Reforms

Babu Surendranath Banerjee while moving the following Resolution at the Ahmedabad Social Conference that "this Conference is resolved that with a view to carry out the objects mentioned in the above Resolution each Provincial Reform Association should endeavour to raise a fund which the Conference recommends should be called the Ranade Memorial fund in order to perpetuate the memory of the late Mr. Justice Mahadev Gobind Ranade M. A., C. I. E., for the very valuable and untiring services rendered by him to the cause of Social Reform in India," said:

> Mr. President, Ladies and Gentlemen,—I have been asked to owe this particular resolution. I have always felt the deepest possible interest in the Social Conference movement (Hear hear.) I confess that I have not been able to actively take part in the furtherance of its objects. Several circumstances of my life have compelled me to devote myself to the prosecution of the Political aims, purposes and aspirations (hear, hear), but I regard the Social and political movements as indissolubly linked together. (Hear, hear) I regard them as being interdependent. (Hear, hear) I will go further and say this that, I hold that political reform is impossible without social regeneration (hear, hear) and moral enfranchisement.

We must cleanse the temples of our homes and our hearths. We must purify and elevate the social and moral atmosphere before we can aspire to those political rights which it is the aim of the Congress to secure and promote. (Hear, hear). It has always been my firm and steadfast conviction, and I have never hesitated to give expression to it and in my own humble way to reduce it to practice. (Hear, hear) I am not in favour of precipitate reform. (Hear, hear) I call myself a Hindu (Hear, hear) I am a Brahmin. (A voice 'oh') I hear a passionate expression of surprise (Laughter). I have not yet come to the end—to the climax. (A voice, "come then"—laughter) I am a Brahmin, a Brahmin of Brahmins at heart. I come from the highest class *of* Kulin Brahmins in Bengal (Hear, hear). And I venture to tell you that I have done nothing or said nothing to disenfranchise me from my Brahminical rights. (Hear, hear). In thoughts, in action, and in the prosecution of the purposes of my life, I am a Brahmin of Brahmins. (Hear, hear). I am not disenfranchised of my rights. I therefore feel that, if any reform is to be carried out it must be carried out upon the old lines (hear, hear) in pursuance of the old principles. We must firmly take our stand upon the ancient foundations (hear, hear) and look round the examples of our sires and imitate them.

And what are the Hindu custom and Hindu rights? Are they not the customs and rights which are imposed upon us by the wisdom of the age in which they were framed and formed? Has not the law of evolution been in force since then? Have we not progressed? Have we not advanced? Are we not always moving, whether forwards or backwards, whatever it may be? Is not motion a law of human nature and the law of laws? If so the custom of the past must be modified to suit the altered circumstances and environments, (hear, hear) of the present situation. Our fathers appreciated that principle thoroughly. When they were confronted with the militant forces of Budhism, what did they do? They cajoled, they fraternised with the Budhist, they took the principle from Budha; they installed Lord Budha as God Jagannath and in that way the extinction of Budhism was brought about. (Hear, hear) There was the principle of adaptation, and if you wish to preserve the ancient system which has come to us as a heritage, I think that you must follow the principle of adaptation. (Hear, hear). Gentlemen, it seems to me that it is because I am in entire accord with the teachings and principles of Mr. Justice Ranade (Hear, hear) that I desire to be thoroughly associated with this resolution of today. He called himself a Hindu. He was a Hindu of Hindus and yet a foremost reformer of his time and of his age. (Hear, hear) Pandit Ishwar Chandra Vidyasagar and Mr. Justice Ranade (Hear, hear) were Hindus and yet reformers.

Both were examples of the firmness of their conviction and that we must follow the principles of adaptation and that we must not discard the ancient system of our fathers. We must broaden the basis of Hinduism, we must elevate, we must educate ourselves in our social and domestic life. I am glad you have proposed to move this proposition. I trust that having placed this resolution on record and having accepted it you will allow it to be a dead letter. So many resolutions have been framed for the purposes of commemorating the good and the great men, and what has become of those resolutions? Where are the funds, where are the memorials, where are the mementos, where are the remembrances of those great and distinguished men? Bear this in mind that today by the acceptance of this resolution you pledge yourselves to certain proceedings (hear, hear) and I hope and trust that you will feel the solemnity of the vow you take, and that you will do what lies in your power to give it force. I hope and trust that this memorial will be an accomplished fact and that before we meet next year (hear, hear.) You will have raised a suitable memorial to that great and distinguished man, great as he was in the field of social Reform and greater by far in exemplification of those social and domestic virtues which ought to be the heritage of our race for ages that have to come.

Swadeshism

[The following speech on " Swadeshism " was delivered in December, 1906.]

Gentlemen,

Notwithstanding the encomium which has been bestowed upon me by my friend who sits to my left (Mr. *Tilak)* who has just told you that I possess a motor voice— *(laughter)*—I almost despair—notwithstanding this gift — of making myself heard by this vast gathering. Nothing was more gratifying to me than the shouts of "Bande Mataram" *(loud cries of " Bande Mataram")* with which you welcomed me on my arrival here. It is our national cry *(hear, hear), (loud cries of " Bande Mataram")*—not our battle cry *(laughter)* but the cry of peace, goodwill and harmony among the different Indian races. *(Hear, hear).* It is not a militant appeal to the Goddess Kali to lead us to victory against the English *(laughter)*—but a soft, generous and fervent patriotic effusion reminding us of our great duty to our Motherland. *(Hear, hear).*

Gentlemen, this meeting has been convened under the auspices of the "Swadeshi Bastu Pracharini Sabha" which flourished under the distinguished auspices of my patriotic friend who sits to my right *(Dr. Deshmukh).* So great has been the stimulus which the preachings this Sabha have imparted to the Swadeshi cause that I understand it is under contemplation to open an " Indian Store" with a capital of three lakhs of rupees, and it is proposed that India's Grand Old Man, Mr. Naoroji—*(loud applause),* should be accorded the honour of opening the Store when he comes here to preside *(hear, hear)* 'over the deliberation of the Congress. I further understand from the brief conversation I have had with my friend when I was coming here that it is the young men who form the pillars and the support of the "Swadeshi Bastu Pracharini Sabha." So it must always be. In the early years of the dawn the voices of children heard the loudest; so in the dawn of nation's birth, the voices of young are heard high above the jarring notes of strife and discord. *(Hear, hear).* In Bengal it is the young who have held aloft the banner of the Swadeshi Movement. *(Hear, hear).* It is the young men who were in the forefront and who have been our martyrs in the Swadeshi cause. *(Hear, hear).* Let me here repeat an incident which went straight to my heart. Three months ago as I was sitting in the *Bengali* office, 'attending to my duties, there came a lad as high as that *(pointing with his hand to the height of the boy by holding him at a certain distance from the ground).* He was about 16 or 17 years old; I said: " Who are you"?—for I have always had the tenderest feelings for our boys. *(Hear, hear).* I asked him: " Who are you, what brings you here; what is your work; how may I help you in that work"? I am Rajendralal Shaha." *(Tremendous applause).* Rajendralal Shaha was a name that was familiar to me, it was the name of a young martyr. *(Hear, hear).* I asked him what had brought him to Calcutta. He said that his appeal case had been heard at the High Court, that the case had been decided against him, and that he was going back to jail to, serve out his time.

He said that with more calmness and freedom, from fervour than what I am displaying at this, moment (Hear, hear). I said:

" Are you sorry?" He said " No, I rejoice that it has been permitted to me to serve my country." (Hear, *hear and cries of Bande Mataram).* That was the man who was cordially received by the inhabitants of Mymensingh the other day when they turned out in their hundreds near the precincts of the jail. But they were beaten and belaboured by a cowardly Police. *(Loud cries of "Shame").* I say " cowardly " deliberately with the full sense of my responsibility— " cowardly " in the sense that the police knew perfectly well that the mandate of the leaders was that they were to suffer in silence and never, under any circumstances, to commit any breaches of the Law. *(Hear, hear).* The police knew perfectly well that the boys would not return blow for blow. It was relying upon this sense of security that they attacked these young men. Don't you call that " cowardly" when you attack a man in the full consciousness that he will not return blow for blow? Well, then young men as you are, be ready to serve your motherland in this great movement and support it with all the fervour and enthusiasm that you are capable of. Don't for one moment accept the principle which is sought to be enforced in these days that students ought to have no concern whatever with Swadeshism. *(Shame).* Dismiss it as a delusion and as a myth which is manufactured to mislead you. There is no nobler school of apprenticeship for the young than the school of Swadeshism. *(Hear, hear).* Therefore gather round this movement in your hundreds, in your thousands, and in your tens of thousands. Above all, strive to prove your Mahratta courage, pluck, heroism and self-sacrifice. Nay more, carry with you in this onward progressive march other communities now linked together with you by an inseparable destiny. Let Gujratis, Mohammedans, Mahrattas, Bhatias,—all sections of the community, no matter what your political differences may be—gather together under the all-embracing banner of Swadeshism. *(Hear, hear).*

I wish to address a word of appeal, perhaps a word of remonstrance to the piece-goods merchants of Bombay. *(Laughter).* Bombay has a great destiny before her in' connection with the Swadeshi Movement, *(Hear, hear).* The inspiration may have come from Bengal, but the consummation and the accomplishment of the movement-lies with you, the people of Bombay. *(Hear, hear).* You can make or mar the fortunes of this movement. You have your great Mills here—in Bombay, Ahmednagar, Sholapur,

Ahmedabad and other places too numerous to be mentioned. *(Cheers).* You are manufacturers of large quantities of piece-goods which you place on the market. My earnest advice to you is—and will you excuse the impertinence of a layman in giving advice to the mercantile community—*(laughter)*—my earnest advice to you is to capture the markets of India by moderating your prices. I may tell you a case which occurs to me at the present moment Many years ago we had the Tudor Ice Company in Calcutta. They were monopolists. Another Company was started. Then what did the Tudor Company do'? It immediately lowered its prices and kept them at a low figure until the financial resources of the rival Company were exhausted, and then it had again the ancient monopoly. *(Laughter).*

I ask you not exactly to imitate their conduct but to recognise the principle that underlies it. In connection with the Swadeshi Movement the economic aspect of the question can never be overlooked. Cheapness must in the long run assert itself. If there is any disparity in respect of prices between your piece goods and the piece-goods of foreign countries and if that disparity is to your prejudice, then the effect of it would be to scare away purchasers, and you to that extent interfere with the expansion of the Swadeshi Movement. It was made a matter of complaint the year before last, during the Pujas of 1905, that the Bombay mill-owners had enormously raised their prices, and when I wrote back here to make enquiries I found that the statement was true. I think it was a great pity—I won't use a harsher word—unpatriotic was the word which had come to my lips—*(Hear, hear and laughter)*—that they should have raised their prices amid the exigencies of a national crisis. That is the first word of advice that I have to address to the merchants of Bombay. In the next place, I would ask you to expand the sphere of the Swadeshi Movement and open Swadeshi Stores in various parts of the country. I understand that there are places where there is only one Swadeshi shop as against half-a-dôzen videshi shops. *(Laughter and cries of Shame).* Why should the number not be transposed? *(Hear, hear.)* Have half-a-dozen Swadeshi shops as against one videshi shop, *(Hear, hear).* In our part of the country there are Marwary merchants. *(Laughter).* I have great respect for them. *(Hear, hear).* Do you know how we tackle them? We approach them in the spirit of compromise. Compromise is the law of the universe. Nature-makes her compromises and why should not man do likewise? We tell the Marwaries: " You Have got half-a-dozen bideshi shops; will you kindly reduce them by one-half? Let there be three bideshi shops and three Swadeshi shops. We shall see that your Swadeshi shops prosper and flourish, and the local leaders help you." *(Hear, hear).* The Swadeshi tide has set in; it is irresistible; it is not in the power of any one to set it back. No, that is impossible. Let our merchants flow with the tide and it is then alone that they will retain that position of affluence and influence which they possess at present. (Hear, *hear).* That is my earnest advice to them.

I have heard our movement described " the so-called Swadeshi movement." I have heard it thus described by high officials—one of the highest—not Lord Minto *(laughter)—for* His Excellency I have the highest possible respect. I have heard the Swadeshi movement described as " the so-called Swadeshi movement" by high officials and by the representatives of the Anglo-Indian press. *(Cries of Shame).* I have no quarrel with them. Personally I have none. On public grounds I may have. *(Hear, hear and laughter).* But when they commit mistakes we are bound to point out their errors. I confess I don't quite understand what is meant by the expression " the so-called Swadeshi movement." But I may make guess. What perhaps is implied is that ours is really a political movement masked under an economic guise. *(Laughter).* If I am right in this interpretation I will say this that the description is both inadequate and misleading. Swadeshism is, or more properly speaking, was, until its more recent developments a purely economic movement which, in the particular circumstances of our province, received an impetus from political considerations. Swadeshism came into being long before even Lord Curzon assumed the reins of office. *(Hear, hear).* Its existence was ignored amid the tumultuous distractions of our political controversies. While other and more ephemeral movements monopolised public attention, the infant Hercules was growing in strength and stature, laying for itself a rich reserve fund of energy which was to qualify it for its marvellous achievements in the future. *(Applause).* The infant Hercules has now grown into years of adolescence and his labours have just begun. *(Hear hear).* I have heard the Swadeshi movement described as being in the domain of economics what the Congress is in the domain of politics. I venture to think it is a good deal more than that. *(Laughter)*. It is not merely an economic or a social or a political movement, but it is an all-comprehensive movement—*(hear, hear)*—co-extensive with the entire circle of our national life, and in which are centred the many-sided activities of our growing community. *(Hear, hear).*

It seems to me as if some beneficent spirit had whispered into the ears of the genius of our motherland this *shibboleth* of our unity and industrial and political salvation. It is the rallying cry of all India, of her multitudinous races and peoples. It appeals to all—high and low rich and poor. It is understood by all. The Deccan peasant or the Bengali rustic may find some difficulty in understanding the merits of a system of representative Government. The subtleties of the question involved in the separation of judicial from executive functions, may elude the grasp of his untrained mind. But when you tell him that the wealth of the country that it is to his advantage that it should be so kept and that for this purpose he must purchase country-made articles in preference to foreign articles, he opens wide his eyes and ears and drinks in the lesson. A glow of intelligence illumines his features; hope for the moment chases away the settled melancholy of his countenance, and he recognises that herein lies the solution of what to him is the problem of problems, the removal of the poverty of himself and of his class. He stands by you and salutes you as his deliverer. *(Hear, hear).*

Gentlemen, fifteen months ago my late lamented, friend, Mr. A. M. Bose—(Hear, *hear)* whose memory you respect and whose name I revere and adore, had a conversation in connection with the partition question with, a high official of the Government. That official said to my friend: " Mr. Bose, if the masses were to interest themselves in public affairs, the Government of this country would have to be conducted upon totally different principles." We are resolved to bring the masses and the classes together *(hear, hear)* and to associate them with us in our political agitations. We are resolved to liberalise this great Government and broad-base it upon the foundations of the willing loyalty and the devoted allegiance of the people. (Hear, *hear)*. That represents the goal of our aspirations. I desire the Anglo-Indian community to note the fact that the tide of union between the classes and the masses which has set in with such force is a decree from the hands of Almighty Providence. (*Hear, hear*). None can resist it. The Congress has brought the educated community throughout the country upon the same platform: Swadeshism will bring the classes and the masses upon the same platform. *(Hear, hear)*. Swadeshism is of Divine origin. *(Cheers)*. The Swadeshi leaders are humble instruments in the hands of Divine Providence walking under the illumination of His Holy spirit. *(Hear, hear)*. Call it superstition, call it fanaticism, reckon us as being among the deluded maniacs of mankind, but you have read the lesson of History in vain if you do not recognise the fact that men working under such a conviction and fortified by such a belief will dare all and do all. *(Hear, hear)*. That is the spirit which animates us. *(Cheers)*.

Being of Divine origin, Swadeshism is based upon the love of country and not the hatred of the foreigner. (*Hear, hear*). I know the statement will at once be challenged. *(Laughter)*. It will be said Swadeshism has accentuated the acerbities of racial antagonism. If it has done so, we are guiltless. *(Hear, hear)*. We are in no way responsible for it. *(Hear, hear)*. We have been the persecuted rather than the persecutors. We have suffered, but we have not retaliated. I fail to see wherein the element of racial hatred comes in at all. If you don't choose to purchase an article manufactured by me, does it follow that you hate me! *(A voice,* No').

With similar consistency you may say that because you don't choose to eat food cooked by me, therefore you hate me. *(Hear, hear and laughter)*. Absolutely no sort of racial antagonism or strife is involved in Swadeshism. *(Hear, hear)*. Further in the domain of the emotions, the possession of particular quality involves the negation of its opposite. Love of justice involves the hatred of injustice. Love of truth involves the hatred' of falsehood. Love of the goods of one's own country necessarily involves a dislike—I will not say hatred—of the goods of a foreign country. *(Hear, hear)*. If there is an element of dislike, are we responsible for it? *(Laughter)*. It is inherent in the very nature of things. Your appeal must be to the Great Creator of this Universe against the necessary and natural order of things. Therefore once again I say that Swadeshism is based upon the love of country. (Hear, *hear*). Our object is to popularise the use of indigenous articles, to foster the growth and development of indigenous arts and industries and to safeguard the country against the growing evils of impoverishment. *(Cheers).*

Ours is one of the poorest countries in the world—so poor that there is none to do her obeisance. She is no longer the country which once excited the cupidity of foreign conquerors—a country whose pristine splendour brought down upon her fertile plains the marauding hordes from the arid steppes of Central Asia. Her days of prosperity are gone—I hope not for ever. *(Hear, hear).* Our poverty is accentuated by the drains— the official drain and the commercial drain. The official drain consists of the Home Charges. I may say that until there is a further expansion of the Legislative Councils and we have a potent voice over the public expenditure, the official drain will continue unchecked and undiminished. The commercial drain is a factor which we can grapple with at once. *(Hear, hear).* We spend about 50 crores of Rupees every year in purchasing foreign articles. In Bengal, gentlemen, we spend about 16 crores every year upon the purchase of foreign-manufactured piece-goods. Our population is 8 crores; therefore, independently of the taxes which we pay to the British Government we pay a poll-tax of Rs. 2 per head. *(Laughter).* We are resolved to put an end to this poll-tax. *(Hear, hear).* And I ask you to help us to do so. *(Hear, hear).*

Gentlemen, I feel I have already exhausted your patience. *(Cries, from all sides, of " No, no, go on").* If I have not exhausted your patience—*(laughter)*—at any rate, I am approaching the time when the cock crows—*(laughter)*—and it will be necessary for me to bid you farewell. *(Laughter).*

Swadeshism, as I have observed, is an all-comprehensive movement. In Bengal it has revolutionised our ideals and conceptions. The air is surcharged with the industrial spirit. The craze for service has received a check. The spirit of self-reliance is abroad. We are making an earnest and organised effort to place education, general and technical, under national control and conduct it in accordance with national ideals and aspirations. All this represents the trend of things in Bengal. The Bengal of today—Bengal after the partition is a very different place from Bengal before the partition. *(Hear, hear).* As I have referred to the partition I may perhaps for a moment be permitted to allude to that which fills the heart of every patriotic Bengali. Mr. Morley has told us that the partition is a settled fact.' *(Laughter).* We decline to accept what is a wrong, a grievous wrong, an outrage upon public sentiment as among the varieties of life and administration. The wrong must be undone. All nature cries out against it." The order of the universe is arrayed against it. It is a lie and we must all combine to undo it. You are assembled here in your thousands. My earnest appeal to you all is to sympathise and to cooperate with us in undoing that which is the most grievous injury that we have suffered in the whole course of our connection with England. I pray you to give a mandate to the delegates that you are sending to the National Congress that this shall be the first and the foremost question to-be considered. *(Hear, hear.)* Make it an all-India, question. *(Hear, hear).* It is not a question affecting a mere territorial redistribution. The issues are much graver than that. The question is whether the public-opinion of a' great province is to be flouted and treated with undisguised contempt in a matter which vitally affects the interests of that province. It is in another form and in a different garb the old question of the assertion of popular opinion, the vindication of the principle of self-government. (Hear, *hear).*

I will not detain you much longer.' If I have not exhausted your patience I certainly have exhausted-mine. (*Cries from all sides " Go on").* In conclusion, I would make an earnest appeal to you once again on behalf of Swadeshism. Gather round the Swadeshi movement and uplift its banner. (*Hear, hear).* Carry it from village to village, from town to town and from district to district—spread the glad tidings of great joy' throughout the length and breadth of this great Presidency. Swadeshism will save us from famine and pestilence and the nameless horrors which follow in the train of poverty. *(Hear, hear).* Take the Swadeshi vow and you will have laid broad and deep the foundations of your industrial and political emancipation. *(Hear, hear.)* Be Swadeshi in all things, in your thoughts and actions, in your ideals and aspirations. Bring back the ancient days of purity and self-sacrifice. Restore the Aryavarta of olden times when the Rishis sang the praises of God and did good to men. *(Cheers).* All Asia is astir with the pulsations of a new life. The sun has risen in the East Japan has saluted the rising sun. That sun in its meridian splendour will pass through our country. *(Hear, hear).* Oh, prepare yourselves for the advent of that glorious day. *(Hear, hear).* Dedicate yourselves with absolute self-denial to the service of your motherland. Let us consecrate ourselves to the service of this great and ancient land. Let all differences be buried, all strifes and animosities allayed, and let the jarring notes of party dissensions be hushed in the presence of the prostrate form of our motherland. Swadeshism does not exclude foreign ideals or foreign learning or foreign arts and industries, but insists that they shall be assimilated into the national system, be moulded after the national pattern and be incorporated into the life of the nation. Such is my conception of Swadeshism. Once again, in the name of Swadeshism, I ask you to take the Swadeshi vow that from this day forward you will devote yourselves life and soul to the service of your motherland. *(Hear, hear).* Live and die for her— *(hear, hear)*—and may God and your Country be glorified. " Bande Mataram." *(Loud applause).*

Dacca Conference

[In Moving the Resolution on Plague Measures. Babu Surendranath Banerjee said:]

Mr. President, brother-delegates, ladies and gentlemen;

My first duty is, as one of the oldest of the delegates, to tender our acknowledgments to the citizens of Dacca for the cordial reception and the princely hospitality of which we have been the recipients for the last few days. Great were the misgivings when it was announced that the Conference would be held at Dacca. Considerable disappoinment has been felt in all quarters that Dacca has not asserted its own in the public movements which mark the life of this generation. All these doubts and misgivings must now be dissipated in the light of accomplished facts. Dacca has poured forth her soul in one great act of princely hospitality. She is ablaze with patriotic fervour and devotion. The Conference has been a great success. I desire to congratulate the people of Dacca on their magnificent achievement. I desire to congratulate them on the awakened public spirit, of which this success is the symbol and the index. God grant that this spirit may grow and deepen to the lasting honour of the citizens of Dacca and the permanent benefit of the people of East Bengal.

Turning now to the Resolution before us, we are reminded of the words of the great Puritan bard—when stricken down by blindness and persecuted by his enemies—the last "relic of a great age—the sole survivor of a race of heroes—he exclaimed amid the passionate agonies of his great soul, " we are fallen upon evil times and upon evil tongues and by darkness and danger compassed round." It seems—such is our situation—as if the powers of nature had entered into an unholy combination against man and the interests of man— as if the primitive struggle between man and the elemental forces—a struggle which is coexistent with the history of the human race—was about to enter upon a new and a more acute phase—when man having vanquished his ancient enemies must now renew the contest with a foe, more insidious and more deadly than any which has hitherto taxed his energies or called forth his illimitable resources. Perplexed and bewildered by these reflections, lost in the contemplation of the awful solemnity of the situation, we involuntarily turn our eyes away from mundane affairs and raise them heavenward for such light and guidance as may be vouchsafed to us from on high, so that we may be in a position to meet the crisis in a manner befitting the citizens of the greatest Empire in the world and avert a calamity which bids fair to settle upon our fortunes with the depending shadows of everlasting night.

The Resolution speaks of the gratitude we feel to the Government of Bengal—especially to the Honoured head of that Government—for the sympathetic policy which the Government has adopted in dealing with the plague. Is this a mere empty phrase—or does it represent a deliberate conviction on our part—does it find a counterpart in our feelings? There is too great a tendency in these days to show our gratitude to high officers of Government, sometimes for no service, and sometimes even for positive disservice done. Why, Sir, only the other day, a great Association, possessed of venerated traditions, with a brilliant record of distinguished services connected with the honoured names of Ram Gopal Ghose, Hurrish Chander Mookerjee and Kristo Das Pal, so far forgot its traditions as to present a farewell address to a retiring Lieutenant-Governor, whose only claims to our gratitude lay—firstly in his use of offensive language in relation to some of our most cherished institutions, secondly in the enactment of a law which deprived the tenants in the Government Khas Mahals of a valued right, and lastly in the introduction into the local Council of a measure which if passed into law would deal a heavy and irreparable blow at the institution of Local Self-Government in the capital of the Indian Empire. Personally I have great respect for the gentlemen who took part in this ceremony—some of them are my personal friends—but I am bound to say that they prostituted their functions, debased the traditions of a great public body, by singing the praises of a ruler who deserved blame rather than praise. There is indeed too great a tendency in these days to bend the knee and burn the incense of adulation at the alter of greatness.

The worship of greatness, I do not deprecate. Greatness, be it intellectual, moral or spiritual, is worthy of the homage and reverence of man. Greatness such as is exemplified in the personality of the representative of our august Sovereign is entitled to our loyalty as dutiful subjects of the Crown. But whether the representative of the Sovereign shall, in addition to the allegiance to which he is entitled by virtue of his office, have i claim upon our love and gratitude must depend upon him and his measures. It is love, sympathy, good works that bind the hearts of the ruled to the rulers as if with a triple chain of gold.

It is these qualities, I am happy to be able to say, which distinguish the policy of Sir John Woodburn in dealing with the plague. He has enthroned himself in the hearts of the people—and I will say this on your behalf as well as on my own behalf that if these qualities distinguish his administration in regard to all other questions, he will take his place amongst the most sympathetic and therefore among the wisest of Indian rulers. Sir John Woodburn was instrumental in averting a great calamity which would have been inevitable, if Sir Alexander Mackenzie was Lieutenant-Governor. In June 1897 Sir Alexander Mackenzie addressed a communication to the Government of India, forwarding a report made by Dr. Lowson, an expert from, Hongkong. In this letter, the late Lieutenant-Governor suggested that the rules relating to segregation should be made more rigorous and that home-segregation which had been allowed by the Government of Sir Anthony MacDonald should be disallowed. Sir Alexander Mackenzie received a rebuff, the like of which in the whole course of my experience I had never seen administered to the head of a Provincial Government. He was told in reply that Dr. Lowson was in no sense the exponent of the views of the Government of India and that he was not authorised to speak in the name of that Government—that further the question of segregation was one which had to be determined not merely by reference to sanitary conditions but by reasons of a political and administrative character; and above all, considerations of humanity were to have a predominant place in the councils of the Government. The letter went on to say that having regard to the fatal character of the disease, it was inhuman to separate the husband from the wife and the wife from the husband.

Sir John Woodburn was then Home Member, guiding and controlling the domestic policy, of the Government of India. Are we not therefore justified in holding that it was he who inspired this letter? If so, we are equally justified in concluding that between the Government of Bengal and the Government of India, there is no difference of opinion whatsoever in regard to plague matters and the rumours to which certain newspapers gave credence as to the intended resignation of Sir John Woodburn, were absolutely without any foundation. In judging of the policy of the Government of Bengal in regard to the plague we must turn, to the provisions of the Venice Convention. This was an agreement which was arrived at in March 1897 between eighteen European Powers who signed the Convention. It was agreed among them that they should notify to each other the existence of the plague within their respective jurisdictions and the measures taken to prevent the spread of the infection. Among the measures insisted upon were disinfection, isolation and segregation. Now mark the contrast between the policy of the Government of Bengal and that of the Government of Bombay in regard to the measures for notification. Here in Bengal the notification is done by horn? By the members of the ward Committees —the representatives of the people. In Bombay, the Police and the Military were associated with the search-parties— and I regret to have to say that in Poona, the summer capital of the Western Presidency, Europeans soldiers were employed on this duty. No graver mistake could have been committed by the Government of Lord Sandhurst. Lord Sandhurst may do his best to white-wash his policy in this respect and obtain certificates of good conduct for these European soldiers from high authority; but all the prestige and the splendour of his great position will not avail to avert the merited sentence of condemnation which history will pronounce upon this part of his policy. In Bengal our search-parties consist of the representatives of the people. They are not armed with instruments for breaking open the neighbours' houses.

The hospitable doors of their neighbours are flung wide open for their reception. Moral persuasion and not military force is their weapon for the performance of their duties; and it has been found to be amply sufficient. The President referred yesterday in eloquent terms to the forces of repression which were abroad, and he alluded to the Calcutta Municipal Bill in support of his statement. Now one of the grounds upon which it was sought to justify the Bill is that the Constitution of the Municipality is unequal to the strain of a grave and sudden emergency. I ask— could there be a graver crisis—a more sudden emergency than what has been caused by the plague, or at any rate the apprehension of the plague? But in dealing with the plague the Government has entrusted the representatives of the people with a duty, as delicate and as difficult as any that can be thought of—viz. the duty of helping the Government to perform one of the most responsible functions, imposed upon the signatory powers by the terms of the Venice Convention. What then becomes of the plea that the representatives of the people charged with the work of a popular municipal Constitution are unequal to the exigencies of a grave and sudden emergency? I have heard it said that cases are liable to be concealed under such a system of voluntary agency. I dispute the proposition. I say there as no concealment of cases—there can be no concealment, if the Ward Committees do their work honestly. You and I are likely to know more about our neighbours' affairs than any set of officials, however able and experienced. Has the honesty of Ward Committees or their desire to help the Government in this matter been ever doubted? Trust begets trust, and speaking as a member of a Ward Committee, I will say this—that we are anxious to reciprocate the confidence which has been reposed in us by the Government, and we are resolved by every means in our power to show ourselves worthy of it. This is the feeling which animates the Ward Committees throughout Calcutta. Again unlike what they had in Bombay, home-segregation and segregation in gardens have been allowed here, subject to the sites being approved by the medical authorities.

In the rules effecting the mofussil published in February last, home-segregation is not allowed. But my Moffusil friends may be quite sure that any concession which is made to the people of Calcutta is bound in the nature of things to be extended to them. Further I have a piece of good news to communicate to you. I have the best reasons for believing that all plague rules and the measures taken in hand in connection with the moffusil have been suspended. There is no occasion for alarm or panic. Nothing will be done in haste—nothing in defiance of popular usage and customs. But let me ask—how many will be affected by the concession of home-segregation?

It will benefit the few but not the many. The poorest of the poor, the resident of our huts—they have no terraces or gardens which they may set apart for hospitals. The concession will not benefit them, and yet they are the people who are most likely to be attacked by the disease, for the plague is essentially the poor man's disease—it is born in poverty and bred in the filth which poverty creates in our large cities. This Conference is the Conference of the rich and the poor alike—much more is it the Conference of the poor than of the rich. We are here to ventilate their grievances and to give voice to the voiceless, and on behalf of the humblest and of the poorest section of our countrymen, we appeal to our rulers to dispense with segregation in their case, or at any rate to enforce it under conditions which would be in accordance with national usages and customs. It is not for one moment to be imagined that we are unfamiliar with segregation or isolation in connection with infectious diseases. The sentiment upon which the practice is based is as old as the hills and is graven deep on the instincts of our race. Smallpox is a virulently infectious disease, almost as infectious as the plague. (Babu Ananda Chander Roy—more infectious.) Perhaps so. Now what do we do on the occurrence of a case of smallpox in any of our families? Why, we isolate the patient and segregate the rest of the inmates of the house. We keep the patient in a separate room to which all access is refused to the other members of the family. The barber and the washer-man do not come to the house. No alms are given; no visits are paid. No invitations are issued or received. For all practical purposes the family is completely segregated. Now if we have to isolate or segregate, is it not wise and statesmanlike to enlist on its side the authority of immemorial usage and the habits of thought and the prejudices which immemorial usage has created? And after all is segregation practicable in an oriental city? Dr. Cook, the Health Officer of Calcutta, and Dr. Weir, the Health Officer of Bombay, are doubtful as to its expediency. Dr. Cook has observed in an official communication that it is unsuited to the requirements of an oriental city, that it has failed in Bombay and that it is bound to fail in Calcutta. In a conversation I had with him he said " It is all very well to segregate men and women. But what about the rodents which carry the infection from street to street and from house to house? No human ingenuity has yet contrived any agency to control them."

The Resolution appeals to the Government to declare Calcutta a non-infected area. We take our stand upon the terms of the Venice Convention quoted in the Resolution which say that no locality is to be deemed infected merely on account of the importation into it of a few cases of plague which have led to no diffusion of the malady. This description is exactly applicable to Calcutta. The cases are few in number and show no tendency to cause widespread infection. In more than six weeks' time there have been only about seventy seizures with about fifty-five deaths among a population of at least six hundred thousand souls, making allowance for the recent exodus. Further the cases are imported. We have the highest authority in support of this view of the matter. The Hon'ble Mr. Risley, in reply to question asked by my colleagues and myself made a statement in the Bengal Council which bears out the view which I have ventured to put forward. The statement is important, and I will read an extract from it:

> "As I have already stated, no connection can be traced between the persons affected, all of whom are residents of Calcutta, and any travellers who have arrived from the areas now infected in the Bombay Presidency and the Punjab. All such travellers are most carefully inspected at Chausa and at Chakradharpur. Their Railway tickets are punched with a peculiar mark before they leave the infected area, and persons holding such tickets are kept under observation throughout the journey and for ten days after their arrival in Calcutta. No suspicious cases have been discovered among the person from Bombay and the Punjab who are now under observation here, and the Health Officer, after making special enquiry into the point, has been unable to trace any connection between the local cases and the arrival from infected areas. Rats, however, have been found dead in considerable numbers in the press-room of the East Indian Railway and in the godowns connected with the coasting trade with Bombay, and it is possible that the infection has been imported by these animals."

Thus, in the opinion of the President of the plague commission, "it is possible that the infection has been imported by these animals" (rats). The cases being few, they being imported in the opinion of the highest authority in these matters, we have a right to appeal to the Government, taking our stand upon the terms of the Venice Convention, to declare the metropolis a non-infected area.

We base the appeal likewise on the highest considerations of expediency. Calcutta is in a panic. Panic succeeds panic, apparently in an endless series. Today it is the inoculation scare—tomorrow it is the quarantine scare—the day after, it is the house-to-house inspection scare. Each scare adds an impetus to the exodus movement. The business of the town has come to a standstill, and if this state of things continues for any length of time, Calcutta will have received a shock to her trade and commerce and her growing prosperity such as she has never felt during the whole course of her existence as the capital of the Indian Empire, and from which it will take long to recover. (Mr. Kemp— "Calcutta will never recover from the shock")

But after all have we got the plague? I have no desire to go behind the opinions of experts. I have no right to do so. You would not support me were I to do so. We are bound in a matter like this to defer to the judgement of experts, conversant with the technicalities of their art But it is quite possible to hold that the experts were right and yet there is no plague in Calcutta. In our present state of knowledge the bacteriological test is the best and the safest,—it is in-feed the only test that we possess. The only case that was subjected to this test was the Kapalitolla case. Since then in no instance has the blood of a patient been subjected to microscopical examination. The cases are only suspected cases of plague. They may or may not be cases of the true bubonic type. At least in one instance a case which had been entered as a case of suspected plague turned out upon enquiry to be merely a case of tonsillitis. That happened in my ward and I am personally cognizant of the facts. In the returns, I think it was on the 14th May last, I found that a case of suspected plague was entered against my ward, (ward no. XIV) I obtained the particulars from the Municipal Office, and sent one of the Secretaries to the parents of the child (a Eurasian girl, named Mildred Andrews) to make enquiries. The Secretary reported that according to the testimony of the girl's mother it was a case of simple fever. I placed myself in communication with the Health Officer and obtained through him the official report of the Medical College Hospital to which the patient had been admitted. And what do you think were the terms of the report? The doctor in attendance said it was a case of follicular tonsillitis ! In the plague returns it had been entered as a case of suspected plague. There may be other cases of the kind. The whole thing is unsatisfactory, without the only crucial test that we have in these cases—the bacteriological test.

Assuming, however, for argument's sake that we have the plague in our midst, what a fierce and glaring sidelight it throws upon the internal situation of the country ! Our rulers are never tired of congratulation themselves on the growing prosperity and the increasing wealth of the country under British rule. But what becomes of this boast when viewed in the light of this terrible visitation which is peculiarly the scourge of poverty-stricken countries ! The plague used to decimate Europe in the middle ages. Since 1660, London has been free from the plague, chiefly because the material condition of the people has so immensely improved.

The internal condition of the people, their prosperity or otherwise has an intimate bearing upon the existence of the disease. This is what Dr. Whyte of the Indian Medical Service wrote in an official report on the prevalence of the plague in Karachi in 1820:

> "All of the countries above-named agree in one general circumstance; and that is, that the inhabitants enjoy a less degree of that internal comfort, contentment, prosperity, peace of mind, which constitute the sum of human happiness (speaking generally) than of those of the countries which are exempted from the ravages of this disease (Plague). England probably is indebted to her improved condition, in the general diet and manners of the people, for its long exemption, and the other countries will be equally safe, when their internal situation shall be improved."

But plague or no plague, we owe a solemn duty to ourselves in the present juncture. It is a crisis that tests the manhood of a community. To me no spectacle has been more disappointing than the panic-stricken condition of some of our educated countrymen. I have seen them running away from Calcutta at the height of the scare, to come back, only to run away again. I have seen them accepting the wildest rumours and the most baseless stories without the slightest examination or scrutiny. What is more our women have exhibited greater courage, firmness and judgement than the educated representatives of the sterner sex. I blame no one. Their education is partly responsible. The Government is still more responsible. If the Government had afforded them ampler opportunities for familiarising themselves with public affairs, such knowledge and experience would have bred in them habits of thought such as would have been useful to the State at such a crisis. Even in matters of Government is it true that what is morally right is politically sound, and in this world of God's Providence the scriptural text that righteousness exalteth a nation is even commercially remunerative. However, that may be, let us realise the fact that we have a solemn duty which the situation imposes upon us, viz., to confront the crisis manfully and teach others to confront it manfully. God grant that we may be spared this terrible visitation ! God grant that if the plague should unhappily break out here, it may not rage with the epidemic virulence with which it decimated the towns of Western India. But if the worst comes to the worst, let us meet the crisis with courage and resolution, and if need be, let us die like men in the effort. Here, at any rate, there is no antagonism of interest as between race and race, between class and class, between the rulers and the ruled — here, no matter whether we are Hindus or Mahomedans, Christians or Sikhs or Parsis—no matter what may be our religious convictions or our social usages or our political creed — we are all united by a sense of common danger, resolved to do battle against a common enemy which if it once obtains a foot-hold in our country will dislocate our trade, disorganise our industries, shut up our schools and colleges and spread ruin and desolation over the fair face of our ancient land — the land of our birth, the home of our sires, the destined home of our children's children, associated in our minds with a thousand dear, tender, and affectionate remembrances.

Partition of Bengal

[Babu Surendranath Banerjee rose amidst deafening cheers and shouts of Bande Mataram which were kept up for nearly five minutes. He then addressed the Congress as follows on the resolution relating to the Partition of Bengal which was in these words:]

> "That this Congress records its emphatic protest against the Partition of Bengal in the face of the strongest opposition on the part of the people of the Province.
>
> "That having regard to the intense dissatisfaction felt by the entire Bengali community at the dismemberment of their Province and their manifest disinclination not to accept the partition as an accomplished fact, this Congress appeals to the Government of India and to the Secretary of State to reverse or modify the arrangements made in such a

> manner as to conciliate public opinion and allay the excitement and unrest manifest among large masses of the people.
>
> "That this Congress recommends the adoption of some arrangement which would be consistent with administrative efficiency, and would place the entire Bengali Community under one undivided administration either by the appointment, of a Governor and Council or by the adoption of some other administrative arrangement that may be thought desirable."

Brother-delegates, ladies and gentlemen, after the inspiriting strains of *Bande Mataram* it is meet and proper that this resolution should be placed before this house, the subject matter being one which has convulsed the whole of Bengal (A Voice: the Whole of India.) I rejoice to learn that our griefs, our sorrows, our disappointments and our trials are sympathised with by brother-delegates throughout the rest of the country (cheers). Encouraged by your moral support which we need as much as you can give, we are prepared to fight undaunted the battles of Bengal and the battles of India (cheers . I think, Sir, I am not guilty of the slightest exaggeration when I say that no question has, within the life of this generation, so profoundly stirred the hearts of our countrymen or has given rise to such wide spread and intense dissatisfaction, irritation and indignation as the Partition of our Province—our beautiful Motherland. In our Province this question is the talk of the marketplace; it is the gossip of the family circle; it is the burden of popular song; it is the theme of the inspiring eloquence of popular oratory (cheers). I never knew until now that my language, the language of my mother, the language she spoke to me and I spoke to her, was capable of such marvellous use for the purpose of explanation, of argument and inspiration (cheers). Sir, the year 1905 is one of the darkest and saddest in our annals, relieved by the reflection that it witnessed an upheaval of national life and an awakening of national consciousness without parallel in our history (loud cheers). Lord Curzon has divided our Province (shame); he has sought to bring about the disintegration of our race (shame), and to destroy the solidarity of our popular opinion.

Has he succeeded in this novel endeavour? (no, no) He has built better than he knew; he has laid broad and deep the foundations of our national life (cheers); he has stimulated those forces which contribute to the up-building of nations (cheers); he has made us a nation (hear, hear); and the most reactionary of the Indian Viceroys will go down to posterity as the Architect of the Indian National life (hear, hear). That will be the authoritative, final judgement of history and posterity on the work of Lord Curzon's Government and administration. Sir, the year 1905 opens, so far as this Partition question is concerned, with a great public meeting held at the Town Hall of Calcutta. It was presided over by Sir Henry Cotton (loud and prolonged cheers), a name honoured in Bengal as well as in India (cheers). Great as our obligations are to Sir Henry Cotton, they have been accentuated and enhanced by his strenuous efforts to avert the Partition of Bengal, and now that it has been accomplished, by still more arduous labours to undo it, he will be reckoned for all times to come, amongst the greatest benefactors of the Bengali people and race (three cheers to Sir Henry Cotton).

Sir, at that meeting held at the Town Hall we confessed to a sense of relief at no decision having been arrived at in connection with the Partition question, and we expressed the hope that if there was any modification of the scheme it would be submitted for public consideration. We were living in a fool's paradise, for, at the time when we held this public meeting and were felicitating ourselves upon our good luck, the judgement of Lord Curzon had been pronounced upon the Partition question though we knew nothing at all about it; for on the 4th of July Mr. Brodrick, replying to a question in the House of Commons said that he had already given his sanction to the Partition proposals of the Government of India which had been received by him on the 18th February last It, therefore, stands to reason that these proposals must have been submitted and sent to England towards the end of January. On the 12th January, Sir Henry Cotton forwarded his proposals to the Government of India. We received an acknowledgment in three weeks' time; that was about the beginning of February. The Government of India had our resolutions before them they were dealing with those resolutions; they knew that we had confessed to a sense of relief at the Government not having arrived at any pronouncement with regard to the Partition question. They knew that we were under a false impression. It was their duty to have removed that impression. They did nothing of the kind (shame). They lent countenance to the false impression which prevailed in the public mind. They became a conscious party to that false impression. Now, Sir, if a private person had dealt by me in that fashion I should have called him a dishonest fellow. Are we to understand that the code of morality which governs the proceedings of the Government of India is meaner and baser than the code which governs the relations of private life (laughter)? And if that be so then what are we to think of those lofty principles of morality which were enforced with such consummate eloquence by the Chancellor of the Calcutta University on the Convocation day (ironical cheers.)

Sir, in the early days of the controversy some deference was shown to public opinion. The proposals of the Government were published in the newspapers; conferences were held in Belvedere; my friend was one of the shining lights of this Conference. I do not know that much came out of them, but they used to be held at Belvedere and Lord Curzon went down to the Eastern districts to ascertain public opinion by personal conference and examination. Sir, if the truth has to be told Lord Curzon went to the Eastern districts not to learn but to teach, not to ascertain what the public felt but to compel the public to adopt his views and sentiment. He failed. The people of the Eastern districts are a manly and stubborn race, possessed of much grit. They are prosperous and they exhibited the independence which prosperity brings in its train. I see before me the representatives of those districts. Brothers from East Bengal, from North Bengal, we had been parted by that fiat of an autocratic power, but the stroke of autocracy has brought our hearts nearer to you (cheers). We are, and shall always remain, of one mind, of one soul, animated by kindred hopes and aspirations, marching side by side towards the accomplishment of our common destinies (cheers). Who can sunder those who are tied by the bonds of Nature? The omnipotence of Government quails before the Majesty of Heaven and ties of Nature (cheers).

Well, Sir, Lord Curzon failed, and when he failed to compel the people of the Eastern districts to adopt his views, the tactics of the Government underwent a great change. Then were held those secret conferences, those private deliberations of which the public knew nothing; they were not allowed to know anything. We knew nothing about the decision of the Government till the 4th of July last; I knew nothing about the particulars of the scheme till the Proclamation of the 20th of July. We begged, we prayed, we protested, but all in vain. No one would listen to us. Ours was a voice crying in the wilderness (shame). And then, in utter desperation, as a last resort, we were driven to the adoption of the boycott (cheers)—the policy of passive resistance which represents a memorable departure in our political programme (hear, hear). It was a protest, nothing more than a protest, against the indifference of the British public in regard to Indian affairs, and the consequent contemptuous treatment of Indian public opinion by the Government of India.

The protest went home! It was marvellously effective. What we could not achieve in 500 meetings extending over 2 years' time we secured by a boycott lasting for a period of three months (cheers) Those who came to scoff remained to pray. The members of the Manchester Chamber of Commerce, which felt a grandfatherly interest in our concerns (laughter), sent a gratuitous piece of advice to us to give up the boycott, but at the same time they exerted all their influence upon the Secretary of State to cancel the Partition of Bengal (hear, hear). I have the best reasons for believing, I have said so publicly, I said it to the Viceroy of India, I said so publicly, that a wire was sent by Mr. Brodrick to Lord Curzon on or about the 12th of October asking him if possible to postpone the Partition till the meeting of the Parliament (cheers). Lord Curzon declined to accept the suggestion (shame).

With that exuberant love for the Bengalis and for the Indians he would not conciliate them. He added that the agitation was childish, and that it was about to subside. That was said on the 12th of October, today it is the 29th of December: the agitation: has not subsided (no, no and cheers) the agitation will not subside until the Partition is cancelled. Today an immense meeting is being held in Calcutta to attract the Prince's attention to the consequences of the Partition (cheers). The agitation will not subside: it shows no signs of abatement until that perennial source of irritation—the Partition—has been modified or withdrawn (cheers).

Well, gentlemen, the boycott is a political instrument in our hands. We resolved to use it when necessary, subject, of course, to the safeguard that it is only to be used in extreme cases when there is a sufficiently powerful body of public opinion to justify its use and to ensure its success. It is a perfectly legitimate and constitutional weapon (hear, hear). If our rulers will not listen to us, if they will treat Indian public opinion with contumely and disrespect, and if they will trample under foot the constitutional usages which constitute the guarantee of the British power and have given us so much contentment and happiness, they must make up their minds to part with some portion of their trade with India, and they must not be surprised if we decline to fill their pockets with gold.

Well Sir, the Partition was carried out on the 16th October last despite the pledge which Mr. Brodrick had given to the House of Commons to the effect that he would lay the papers on the table of the House, a pledge which involved the undertaking that the Partition would be postponed pending the final pronouncement of Parliament. The 16th October is a memorable day in our annals, I trust it will be a memorable day in the annals of India (hear, hear). It was a day of universal mourning, of universal fasting and universal fraternising; Hindus and Mohammedans embracing each other in public streets (cheers), or in private places, vowing the vow of eternal love and concord (cheers and loud 'applause). The shops were closed, the domestic hearth was not lit, food was not cooked, Calcutta presented the aspect of the City of the Dead. A spirit of desolation seemed to hover over the scene. The genius of the Motherland was incarnate amidst this bewildering scene of grief and sorrow. Thousands, tens of thousands, hundreds of thousand of pious Hindus, and Hindus who were not pious, rushed to the waters of the Bhagirathi in order to purity themselves for the sins of their rulers (cheers).

Thousands, tens of thousands, hundreds of thousands of people walked through the streets of Calcutta bare-footed, clad in the garb of woe. Amidst the wild scene of excitement, the National Fund was started; amidst this wild scene of excitement the foundation stone of the Federation Hall was laid (cheers) by one who was our President and occupied that place which you, now, Sir, adorn. Prostrate on the bed of illness, scarcely capable of moving, my illustrious friend, Mr. Ananda Mohan Bose (cheers), came in a litter attended by Dr. Nilratan Sarcar, to lay the foundation stone, perhaps the last function which he will be privileged on this side of the grave to perform, and thus conferred another obligation upon his countrymen.

Well, gentlemen, while public excitement was so great, what was the Government doing? Forging instruments of repression, laying the foundations for the inauguration of a reign of terror (shame). Yes, it is a matter of inexpressible shame. Within eight days of the 16th of October, Mr. Carlyle issued his famous Circular (shame). Under the terms of that Circular, students are prohibited from taking part in public demonstrations (shame); and if they did what then? They were not to be punished, but the institutions to which they belong were to be disaffiliated, grants-in-aid were to be withdrawn from them and their teachers were to be exalted to the dignity of Special Constables ! (shame). A more outrageous scheme of vicarious punishment never entered the imagination of the greatest autocrat of the middle ages.

But it was in the new Province that the reign of terror was inaugurated after the latest and most approved Russian pattern. In the new Province public meetings in public place have been prohibited; Sankeertan parties are not permitted to march through public streets; the singing of the *Bande Mataram* (shouts of, *Bande Mataram* a voice once: more jointly *Bande Mataram* was sung by a large section of the audience rising to their feet) the singing of the *Bande Mataram* which you have just sung with so much zest and devotion is punished as a crime and offence (shame). Respectable people have been degraded by being enrolled as special constables (shame). Not long ago a veritable reign of terror was established at Sirajgang and Barisal, and the Police were let loose in the streets, indiscriminately assaulted the people, selecting the leaders of the Anti-Partition movement as objects for special vengeance. When an aggrieved complained to the Sub-Divisional Officer of Sirajgang the courts were closed against him. Magistrates would not receive the complaint. At Rajshahi the other Hay a public meeting was disbursed at the point of the bayonet. I use the words "at the point of the bayonet," advisedly. In a place, in a private place, fifty policemen armed with rifles and bayonets commanded by a posse of inspectors and sub-inspectors marched down to the place of meeting, ordered the leaders of the meeting to disperse. My friend, Mr. Abul Kasim, I do not see him here (A Voice, he is here) he was addressing the meeting and a gun was pointed at him (shame) (Voice: let us see him, let him come on the platform). My friend asked the inspector to produce his authority, and the inspector said that he has received confidential orders from the Magistrate which he declined to produce. Very properly then he ordered the meeting to dissolve.

Since the news of the incident arrived in Calcutta, Mr. J. Chaudhuri and six others, every one of them resolved to go to jail if necessary (loud and prolonged cheers), went down to Rajshahi in order to test the authority of the police and to vindicate the right of public meetings (hear, hear). They held a meeting, the largest ever held at Rajshahi, but the police would not submit to the test, the brave fellows that they were (ironical cheers). They were conspicuous by their absence, and since then we have been holding a meeting every day at Rajshahi (cheers).

Our boys are being prosecuted, and some of them even sent to jail (shame). I heard the other day touching incident regarding the pluck and heroism of young men—the pillars of popular movements—whom I always regard with a sense of affectionate and paternal interest (cheers). About half a dozen of them were locked up in jail in one of the towns of the Eastern districts. As soon as they found themselves inside the lock-up they made the walls resound with the echoes of their patriotic songs (shouts of *Bande Mataram*). The jailors were touched. They brought them food which they declined to accept (cries of *Bande Mataram*). If our rulers think that they will repress us in this way, kill the Anti-Partition movement by having recourse to despotic Russian methods they are greatly mistaken. Repression will not daunt us (hear, hear); rather it will stiffen us in our opposition to the Partition and our support of the Swadeshi Movement (cheers). The blood of the martyrs is the cement of the church (cheers); and our cause will be consecrated by the sufferings of our young martyrs. We regard that cause to be of divine origin. Rightly or wrongly we believe ourselves to be humble instruments in the hands of the Almighty Providence (cheers), walking under the illumination of His Holy Spirit. Call it delusion; call it superstition; call it fanaticism; reckon us as being among the deluded maniacs of mankind. You have read lessons of history in vain if you do not realise the fact that men fortified by such belief and working under such conviction are irresistible and invincible; there is no danger which they are not ready to brave, no difficulty which they are not prepared to surmount.

The Partition is now an accomplished fact; it has been carried out, but we at any rate do not regard it as a accomplished fact The resolution says that the Bengalis have exhibited considerable disinclination to regard it as an accomplished fact, and the resolution says truly. And, gentlemen, if you read the resolution you will find that the essence of our prayer is that we want the entire Bengali community to be placed under the same common administration. We do not want to be separated from our kith and kin. Is that not an aspiration which is reasonable and righteous, and is there any one who will not respond sympathetically to an aspiration of that kind? May we not, therefore, appeal to Lord Minto and Mr. John Morley, the new Secretary of the State, to reverse the decree which has been passed upon us by Lord Curzon? May we not be permitted to indulge the hope that Lord Minto's mission in India is to conciliate, to throw oil upon the troubled waters, to undo the mischief wrought by his predecessor? His illustrious ancestor who ruled over us about (100) hundred years ago gave us peace amidst war.

May we not appeal to him to emulate the example of his illustrious ancestor and spread the blessings of peace, contentment and happiness throughout the length and breadth of the country? As regards Mr. John Morley, we are all more or less his disciples. We have sat at his feet; our intellectual and moral natures have been fed, stimulated and ennobled by the great lessons which he enforced with such consummate eloquence. He has taught us in his life of Edmund Burke that Asiatics have rights and Europeans have their obligations in India. He has taught us the paramountcy of moral laws in the Government of human affairs. May we not ask him to apply his own principles to the solution of the Partition problem and the solution of other Indian problems? Above all, we must learn to depend upon ourselves. To native strength and native devotion and native courage dominated by the spirit of constitutionalism, we must look forward for our eventual emancipation. You know for the moment we have lost: for the moment we have been defeated; but let us not despond. The Irish have been fighting for Home Rule far over 100 years and they have not yet got it, but they are within a measurable distance of success. Let us emulate the courage, the enthusiasm and heroic self-sacrifice of the children of the Emerald Isle. Bear in mind that we are living through critical and great times.

The sun has risen in the East Japan has hedged the rising Sun but that Sun of Asia will pass in its meridian course over this hapless land and shed upon us its brilliance and lustre. Even now we feel the first flutterings of an awakened national consciousness. Oh ! let us strengthen them and invigorate them, ennoble them for the glorification of our Motherland, for the lasting credit of the great race to which we belong and for the permanence upon broad national lines of that great administration which in the past was fired with lofty ideals of duty towards India, but which, in the present moment, we are anxious to rescue from the reproach of reaction and retrogation (loud prolonged cheers). I thank you, gentlemen, once more, I have nothing to add to this resolution.

9

Lectures on Education

Universities' Commission

Brother-delegates, it is useless to disguise from ourselves the fact that the question which of all others looms largely on the view, which has more or less thrown into the shade all other considerations and before which even the attractions of the Delhi Durbar seem to fade from view— is the question of University Education. The report of the Universities Commission was till lately the one all-absorbing topic of discussion. It excited a measure of interest such as no other public question within living memory has done. I am old enough to remember the controversies of the last quarter of a century. I have in my own humble way been associated with them. My contributions to them were indeed insignificant, but my interest in them was deep and abiding; and this I will say that I do not remember any proposal, emanating from responsible authority, which has more profoundly stirred the hearts of the Indian community, or has caused deeper alarm, or evoked more strenuous opposition than the report of the Universities Commission.

The opposition to the Vernacular Press Act, to the Calcutta Municipal Bill, the Bombay Land Revenue Bill or even the Sedition Bill pales before the agitation which the Report of the Universities

Commission gave rise to, There was a sense of alarm, deep, genuine, all-pervading, felt by all sections of the educated community throughout India, by Hindus and Musalmans alike. Retired servants of Government, whom the Government delighted to honour, whom they have loaded with titles and distinctions and who have led their quiet lives, away from the storm and stress of political agitation, felt themselves constrained under a sense of overwhelming duty and in response to the general feeling of their community, to emerge from the seclusion of their quiet lives and place themselves in a line with those who condemned the Report. Old men, bent down with the weight of years, the representatives of an older school of thought and culture, the products of our pre-University system, came tottering to the Town Hall meeting to place on record their protest against the recommendations of the Commission. Professional men who had never before spoken at a public meeting and who had never identified themselves with any movement of any kind, but had earned their laurels in the quiet and undisturbed pursuit of their own professions, which were far too remunerative to permit them to think of anything else, for the moment forgot their professions and their profits and joined the general community in the universal protest against the recommendations of the Commission.

The Mohammedan community, unhappily for themselves, unhappily for us, have been somewhat backward in our public movements. They have been most forward in condemning the Report. They have promptly disavowed the representative character of the only Mohammedan member of the Commission and denounced him for signing a Report which they rightly believed would be fatal to the educational interests of their community. And if out of evil cometh good, it may truly be said that the Report of the Commission has furthered in an unforeseen and unexpected fashion the general interests of the community, by bringing Hindus and Mohammedans upon the same platform and linking them together by association in a common cause.

It has thus helped to promote that solidarity between the two communities which it has ever been the steadfast aim of the Congress to secure and upon which the interests of both the communities and the prospects of Indian advancement so largely depend. The feeling of alarm was genuine, widespread and universal, and well might it be; for the noblest gift which British rule has conferred upon India is the boon of high education. It lies at the root of our progress. It is the mainspring, the motive power, the germinal source of all those forces which make for progress. The three great boons which we have received from the British Government are High Education, the gift of a Free Press and Local Self-Government, supplemented by the reform and expansion of the Councils. But high education is the most prized, the most dearly cherished of them all.

It is high education which has made Local Self-Government the success that it is admitted to be. It is again high education which has elevated the tone of the Indian Press, has made it a power and has rendered it possible for us to look forward to the time when in the words of Lord Ripon it will become, as in Europe it is, "the irresistible and the unresisted master of the Government.' It is English education which has produced a splendid galaxy of distinguished men who have done incalculable service to morals and manners, who have ennobled the literature of their country and have made it a rich vehicle for the expression of the noblest sentiments, of the most abstruse reasonings in philosophy and science and of the varied and complicated requirements of modern life. It is English education which has overcome the barriers of race, religion and language, has dissipated the prejudices and misunderstandings of ages and has created those unifying influences which find a living expression in this vast, this stupendous, this majestic organisation of the National Congress. Could the educated community submit to the curtailment of this boon—to the restriction of its beneficent area? They are naturally anxious that nothing should be done to check the spread of that system of education which has produced such splendid results in the past and which is fraught with infinite possibilities of progress for future generations.

English education is a precious boon which has come down to us as a heritage from the past. If we cannot extend and broaden it, it ought at any rate to be our most sacred concern to safeguard it against encroachment and limitation, and so transmit it, with its beneficent area undiminished, to those who coming after us will bear our names. These are the feelings which inspired the agitation, intensified its volume and impressed upon it its distinctive tone and character. In our anxiety we appealed to Lord Curzon. It was united India which preferred its appeal to the Viceroy. Every Province took part in it. Every section of the educated community was represented in it. Whatever differences of opinion may exist with regard to the merits of Lord Curzons administration—and the time has not yet come for the final judgement— all will agree, even those who sec nothing good in it, that His Excellency is keenly responsive to the intimations of public opinion, and we felt convinced that His Excellency would not ignore the public opinion, of educated India, expressed with singular unanimity and unequalled emphasis and upon a question which to them was a question of life and death. In this hope we have not been disappointed.'! His-Excellency has recognised the truth, in the letter of Government to which I shall presently call attention, that no reform can be successful without the sympathetic cooperation of the community concerned, and that any reform forced upon an unwilling community, no matter how promising it might be, no matter how influentially supported it might be, is doomed, foredoomed to failure.

We desire to offer our congratulations to His Excellency, upon his circular letter upon the Report of the Universities Commission. We may not be able to agree with all the suggestions of the Viceroy, but it is a frank and straightforward recognition of public opinion—it is a praiseworthy attempt at compromise and conciliation; and effective compromise which ensures steady progress along the line of least resistance and which conciliates and enlists the social forces on behalf of Government, is, to my mind, the highest function of statesmanship. His Excellency has always felt a personal interest in the educational problem. Himself a distinguished University man, His Excellency has told us that the instinct of the educationist is deep down in his nature. The educational problem is one of his twelve chosen problems, and His Excellency has applied himself with characteristic ardour to its solution. So far back as the summer of 1901 a conference was held at Simla to which some European educational experts were invited. The proceedings of that Conference have not been published. I fail to understand why they should be withheld from publication. If there is one class of considerations more than another in regard to which the public should be taken into confidence, it is those which relate to the problem of Education. Here if anywhere, popular sympathy and cooperation is necessary. No useful purpose is served by investing educational problems with a quasi-political character and raising them to the dignity of State-secrets. A suspicious public, barred out of the confidence of the authorities, naturally interpret their proceedings in their own way and ascribe to them a sense and a significance which they perhaps will not bear, and thus between them and the Government there arises a misunderstanding when their mutual sympathy and cooperation is needed for the satisfactory solution of the educational problem. I can quote no higher authority against this policy of concealment in educational matters than that of His Excellency the Viceroy. Thus, did His Excellency denounce the policy of secrecy, in educational matters at the Conference whose proceedings have been withheld from publication:—"Concealment has been no part of my policy since I have been in India and the education of the people is assuredly the last subject to which I should think of applying any such canon."

Constitution of the Universities Commission

The conference was followed by the appointment in January 1902 of the Universities Commission. The Corn-mission was appointed "to enquire into the condition and prospects of the Universities established in British India; to consider and report upon any proposals which have been or may be, made for improving their Constitution and working, and to recommend to the Governor-General in Council such measures as may tend to elevate the standard of University teaching, and to promote the advancement of learning." The report of the Commission has long been before the public; and the views of the Government thereon have recently been published. His Excellency the Viceroy, while according a general support to the Report of the Commission, has not been able to accept all its conclusions. If there is one quality more than another which distinguishes the Viceroy, it is that he is the keeper of his own conscience, that he does not surrender his judgement or his convictions to the authority of names, however distinguished. I am bound to say that the Constitution of the Commission' was such, its method of procedure was such, that it was impossible that its recommendations could command the general approval of the public or the unqualified assent of the Government.

The Commission originally consisted of six members, with the Hon'ble Mr. Raleigh, Vice-Chancellor of the Calcutta University, as president. Not a single representative of the great Hindu community who had the largest stake in the educational problems under consideration was included among the Commissioners as originally nominated. Let us however thankfully note that when attention was called to this omission in the columns of the public prints, His Excellency was graciously pleased to geminate the Hon'ble Mr. Justice Guru Das Banerjee as a vital member of the Commission. The appointment of Mr. Justice Banerjee was received with universal approbation. One of the most brilliant graduates of the Calcutta University, he has long been honourably associated with the work of the University. He was twice appointed Vice-Chancellor of the University, and he was among the most distinguished of our Vice-Chancellors, regarding his office not as an ornamental adjunct to the high position which he held, but a new field of activity and usefulness, and setting an example of unflinching devotion to duty and of statesman-like concern in the interests of the University, of which he was so fine a product. Who will say that the Calcutta University has been a failure or has not fulfilled the high ends of its existence when it has produced men like Mr. Justice Guru Das Banerjee? The Commission, as now constituted, consisted of seven members, of whom five were officials, the sixth was a missionary gentleman, and the last but not the least was the Mohammedan member of the Viceroy's Council, whose experience of educational matters is confined to the Nizam's Dominions. His representative character has been disavowed by his community, and he has been described by my friend the Hon'ble Mr. Mehta and his colleagues of the Bombay Presidency Association in their memorial to the Viceroy as being disqualified to represent the views and feelings of the educated community, by reason of the avowedly hostile attitude he has taken towards them in his public writings and speeches.

On the Universities Bill

[Babu Surendranath Bannerjee in moving the resolution on the Universities Bill, said]

Mr. President, Brother Delegates and Gentlemen,—Last year when Congress assembled we recorded a protest against the Report of the Universities Commission. In that protest/we carried with us the sympathies and, I may add, the convictions of the entire educated community throughout India, irrespective of considerations of race or religion. Those who did not worship with us in the same temple—who did not profess the same political creed, but were separated from us by the widest of human barriers, viz., those of thought and feeling readily joined us in this universal protest. We then made it clear, abundantly clear, to the rulers of India and all else whom it might concern that next to religion, education was our most cherished interest, that into that domain we could permit no trespass, none of the arts of poaching, and that we were resolved by all the constitutional means at our disposal to safeguard our educational interests and to transmit our educational legacy, untarnished and undiminished, to those who, coining after us, would bear our names and inherit our privileges as well as our obligations.

The Government of Lord Curzon, whatever may be its demerits, and I, for one, have never been partial to them, has always been keenly responsive to the intimations of public opinion, and His Excellency recognising the situation, issued a circular-letter which went far to allay the agitation and to reassure the public rind. None the less we recorded a resolution formulating our objections to the main features of the Report of the Commission, for we felt that the controversy was not yet over and that the authoritative protest of educated India, voiced through our great organ of the National Congress, would have a value and a significance all its own. We were wise in making that protest, for the danger is not yet over, and today we stand face to face with a Bill (the Universities Bill) which, if embodied in the law of the land would officialise our Universities and reduce them to so many departments of the Government.

During the last thirty years no movement has been stronger. None has evoked in a more unstinted measure the approbation of public opinion than the movement of decentralisation, the steady but gradual delegation of centralised authority to subordinate bodies, vested with full responsibility and working under the general supervision of the central power. The movement began with Lord Mayo. It received a new impetus from the statesmanlike measures of Lord Ripon's Government, and in actual operation it has been attended with results with justify an expansion rather than a curtailment of the beneficent policy which it embodies. And the movement has gone on expanding, affording infinite relief to the Central Government and scattering broadcast in its train the investable blessing of the enlargement of popular authority. But, all this is now to be changed. The civic freedom of our corporations is to be curtailed by the intervention of Government—and you, the citizens of Madras, have a foretaste of the rich blessing that is in store for you, in the Madras Municipal Bill—and our Universities are to be subjected to the persistent pressure of official control.

The Government has made no secret of its intentions in this respect. Sir Denzil Ibbetson, speaking in support of Mr. Raleigh's Bill; with a candour and directness of purpose which I greatly admire, for it is so rare in these days, when duplicity and diplomacy have become interchangeable terms observed that the Government must now assume control over the system of higher education. I should have thought that imperialism—the new fangled imperialism which has darkened the prospects of human freedom in all parts of the world—would have rejoiced in a sort of general supervision over the repositories of delegated authority, and like the great orb of day would permit the subordinate planetary bodies to move in their respective spheres, content only to guide, to restrain and to control. But that is not to be. Imperialism must meddle—and shall I say muddle? For the officialisation of at least one great corporation has been attended with results which have assumed the proportions of a grave public scandal and have shocked the conscience of the citizens of Calcutta, of at least that portion which have yet any conscience left to them. What then is the justification for this new departure, and the policy of the departure which is embodied in this Bill. Have our Universities been tried and friend wanting? I will say no to this question, and I will ask you to say no when you have heard me. It is incumbent upon the framers of the Bill to make out their case. Have they discharged their responsibility—have they seriously attempted to discharge it? It will not do for them to point to a defect here—a failure there—and a break down elsewhere —or to urge that our University system does not come up to the requirements of an ideally perfect standard. They must carry their evidence much further than that. They must show that our system has so hopelessly broken down that no partial reform will avail, but that a complete and fundamental change is required to meet the exigencies of the situation—that the entire superstructure must be taken down and the ground cleared for the erection of an altogether new edifice. So far from there being any evidence in support of this view, whatever evidence there is points to a distinctly opposite conclusion. Our universities have a brilliant record associated with illustrious names of enduring fame. Mahadeo Gobind Ranade Kashinath Trimbuck Telang, Perozeshaw Merwanji Mehta, Guru Das Banerjee are honoured names (a voice—Surendranath Banerjee) whose labours have shed a lustre upon the universities with which they have been connected.

With the life of our Universities is associated the development of that progressive movement which has changed the moral aspect of the country and finds expression in every phase of our national life. It is no exaggeration to say that our Universities are the seed-plots upon which and around which have grown up the National Congress, the Social Conference, indeed every movement, social, moral, and political which has marked the activities of the present generation. It is our Universities and the beneficent influences which they have scattered broadcast, that have elevated the tone of the Indian Press and have made it a power for good.

It is our Universities that have produced a distinguished galaxy of eminent men who have adorned morals and manners, have ennobled the literature of their country and have made it a rich vehicle for the expression of the highest purposes and the varied requirements of modern life. It is again our Universities which have supplied a body of distinguished public servants whose ability and integrity have been the theme of Universal admiration and have vindicated the capacity of our countrymen for high offices in the State. All these achievements have been accomplished by the Universities under their old Constitution which it is now proposed to supersede. Lord Curzon stands forth as the champion of this Bill. I regret, all India regrets to see His Excellency in this position, for his culture, his genius, his fine imagination, the brilliancy of his rhetoric are all calculated to place him in the foremost rank of statesmen. I am sorry that His Excellency's name should go down to posterity indissolubly linked with a reactionary and retrograde measure which has been condemned by the unanimous opinion of educated India.

Those who will be most deeply affected by the measure have a right to be heard and have a right to urge that their views will be carefully considered and, so far as practicable, embodied, in the law of the land. Lord Curzon observes that the Government of India is overburdened with work and that it is most anxious to decentralise authority, but that it feels itself compelled to come to the, rescue of the Universities which, says His Excellency, are falling to pieces. With the utmost deference for His Excellency—and I can have no other feeling for the august representative of my sovereign — I ask where is the evidence in support of this view of the matter? I am free to admit that our Universities are capable of improvement What human institution is there that is not? But I again ask where is the evidence to show that our Universities have developed a condition of chronic inefficiency which alone would justify the drastic and revolutionary Bill which has been introduced into the Supreme Council? I can find none. But the vision of the discontented B. A.'s who with an exaggerated notion of their own abilities infest the avenues to our public offices, disturbs the equanimity of the Hon'ble member in charge of the Bill.

It is a serious nuisance, says he, and it must be suppressed. With all respect to Mr. Raleigh I venture to submit that the problem which he set has before himself is an administrative rather than educational one—and that no reconstitution of the Senates and no improvement in the method of teaching or of the examinations will allay,, this discontent, but that the Government must set about the task in an altogether different fashion. Our B. A's find that after a successful academical career all the avenues of honourable employments are closed against them, that with the exception of certain specified departments they are excluded from the Indian Civil Services and from the higher appointments in the Minor Civil Services and that they are entitled only to the crumbs that fall from the rich man's table to the subordinate appointments which the European does not care to accept or which the Government does not care to bestow upon him. It is not in human nature to repress the ambitions which culture and enlightenment have roused in the human breast. Remove these barriers, give the

B. A. full scope for the exercise of his talents and energies, and above all do not degrade him by branding him with the humiliating badge of racial inferiority and then the race of discontented B.A's will become as extinct as the Dodo. Further the discontented B.A. has read Sir William Lee Warner's book which the Government has been at so much pains to patronise. In that book he has read the Queen's proclamation, the terms of which he has inwardly digested.

He has learnt from the gracious message that race is no qualification or disqualification for office in India, and he has been assured by more than one distinguished Viceroy that the proclamation has been the golden rule of their conduct. But when he finds the very widest divergence between profession and practice, between exalted principles and their actual application to the measures of Government the situation is such as is not calculated to add to the serenity of his temper.

I look in vain for a satisfactory statement of reasons for this Bill in the speech of the Hon'ble member who introduced it. What I find is not so much a vindication as a statement of the circumstances which led to the framing of the measure. Mr. Raleigh has told us that a body of distinguished educational experts met in Simla somewhere about 1901 that they were of opinion that there were serious defects in our University system which called for wisely considered schemes of reform and they further agreed that the Senate must be reconstituted. We are not told what these serious defects were. We have a right to know the materials upon which their judgement was based, and we have a right to our own judgement upon these materials. We must know what their proceedings are before we are in a position to judge of them. But the Conference met in secret, deliberated in secret, resolved in secret and I presume dispersed in secret The only ray of light that has been vouchsafed upon the situation is that which has been afforded by the preliminary speech of His Excellency the Viceroy, now supplemented by the observations of the Hon'ble Mr. Raleigh.

But if the authority of the educational conference is invoked in support of the Bill, we may on the otherside invoke with at least equal confidence the counter authority of the Senates of the Indian Universities who have condemned the provisions, which now find a place in the Bill, with unparalleled unanimity and emphasis. But it be said that the Senates were interested bodies and that dominated by the instinct of self-preservation they could not be expected to pronounce an impartial verdict upon issues which affected their very existence. The argument would be convincing enough, if it were not the case that in this matter the Senates re-echoed the public voice and were supported by the unanimous testimony of public opinion.

The public cannot be expected to look at a consideration like this except from the standpoint of the public weal. A wisely-considered scheme of reform moving along the line of least resistance, harmonising the spirit of progress, the public would cordially approve of. Reforms they would welcome. Revolutions they abhor. And what could be more revolutionary than that the Senates, should be thoroughly reconstituted by the Government, and that the bulk of their members should be relegated to the cold shade of neglect by being made Honorary Fellows who are to hibernate during the greater part of their Senatorial lives, to emerge only into a sort of flickering existence on the eve of an election for a member of Council and then like the fast-vanishing ghost of Hamlet's father to sink back into their doomed non-entity even before the crowing of the cock. Sir, if I remember rightly, the agitation for reform of the University system was largely prompted by the desire to expand the Universities and invest them with the function of teaching.

Provision has been made for the creation of University chairs, the appointment of lecturers and the inspection and supervision of affiliated colleges. I hope the teaching function of the Universities will be largely availed of, and that before long an advanced school of learning will be founded under University auspices at the capital of each Province. But the question is one of ways and means and not of constitutional reform; and I confess that I fail to see how the reconstitution of the senates will promote University teaching. The Government has indeed promised a sum of five lakhs of Rupees for the next four or five years but this money will be devoted to the granting of subsidies to such colleges as are not able to conform to the requirements of the new standard of efficiency.

You rightly observe in the Resolution that the effect of this Bill will be to officialise our Universities and reduce them to the status of so many departments of the Government. These views of the matter His Excellency the Viceroy has protested against with all the eloquence and fervour of which he is capable. But facts are facts, and they cannot be challenged by authority, however distinguished. Let us for a moment look at the facts and note the inference which they irresistibly suggest. The Government will appoint So per cent, and may appoint 90 per cent, of the members of the Senate. The Government will affiliate or disaffiliate. The Government will sanction, modify, add to and even make regulations in case of delay on behalf of senates. If this is not officialising the Senates, will the official sponsors of the Kill deign to explain what it means? One of the professed objects of the Bill—by far the most important which the framers of the measure have in view—is the enlargement of the powers of the Senates and their consequent reconstitution, for says the Government, the present Senates are unfit for these wider powers and ampler functions. But the Government really takes away with the one hand what it confers with the other. For all these powers are to be exercised subject to the approval of the Government. The Senates are to be merely so many conduit pipes—subordinate bodies who are to enquire, to report and submit their opinions, the final decision being reserved to the Government. Thus, under the plea of expanding the power of the Senates, the Government monopolises all authority; and yet we are told that one of the objects of the Bill is to bestow larger powers upon the Senates for the more important and responsible functions which are now to be entrusted to them.

If language was given to men to conceal their thoughts in, have we not here notable illustration of it? Again it is said that one of the objects of the Bill is to place the Universities under the Government of experts. But who are to be these experts? The bulk of them will be Government educational officers wedded to the policy and the traditions of the Government. Thus, in placing the universities under the direction of experts, the screw of official control will have been all the more highly-fastened. Look again at that other provision of the Bill which discloses its drift, viz, to exalt official authority and to make it a predominant factor in the Government of the Universities. The fellowships are to be terminable, to be renewed at the option of the Government. To make the fellowships terminable in a body bulk of whose members are to be appointed by the Government, is to deal a deathblow at their independence; for the members will be only too ready to please the authorities; in order to obtain a renewal of their term of office. Mr. Raleigh is fully alive to this objection, but he tells in reply that in all the deliberative assemblies of the British Empire, the memberships are terminable. So they are, but he omits to notice a very important fact. These assemblies are entirely or in the main elective in their Constitution. Even if fifty per cent, of the members were elected there would be little or no objection to terminable fellowships.

This brings me to the question of the elective element in the Constitution of the Senates. We are thankful to the Government for the definite statutory recognition of the elective principle in the Constitution of our Universities. But the concession represents a very small instalment of reform— almost a homoeopathic dose— and its graciousness is very much minimised by the other provisions of the Bill. Our Universities are modelled upon that of London. The London University consists of 55 members, of whom only four are nominated by the King, the rest consisting of Fellows elected by different bodies. To say that our college professors with a leaven of our graduates are unfit to exercise the franchise to the extent I have suggested is to utter a calumny. Such a proposition would be in entire conflict with the spirit of the Bill, for if our College professors are fit to be our governors surely they are fit to elect half of those who are to govern the Universities.

I have tried to show that there is justification for this Bill. But this is a negative sort of argument which will not satisfy every body. I would go a step further and content that there are provisions in the Bill which, if accepted, would be positively mischievous and would be fatal to the interests of high education—you will remember that the Universities Commission had recommended the abolition of the second-grade colleges and the consequent restriction of the educational area. Now I have no hesitation in saying that the same object is sought to be attained by the Bill, though in somewhat roundabout way. The direct frontal attack has been given up I presume, in deference to modern tactics in favour of a dexterous flank movement which is all the more dangerous because it is insidious and unperceived. There are provisions in the Bill which will prevent the further growth of educational institutions under indigenous agency; there are provisions in the Bill which will wipe out of existence the colleges now managed and controlled by our countrymen. Let me ask you to consider the provisions of Section 21 of the Bill which lay down the conditions of affiliation.

The applicant among other things, must satisfy the University authorities that suitable provision will be made for the residence of students and of the professors in or near the college, and further he must give financial guarantees so as to ensure the permanence of the College. Now I have hesitation in saying that in Bengal at any rate, private enterprise launched under the most favourable conditions will not be in a position to comply with these requirements. The Government have a sort of idea that the private Colleges are very flourishing commercial concerns. I wish the Government would run some of them and discover for themselves how much money they are able to put into their pockets. They will find that instead of a balance, they will have a yearly-recurring deficit. I know something of the unaided colleges in Bengal. I have been connected with one of them which is now nearly of 25 years' standing. I have grown grey in the service of that College which, I venture to think, has been of some little help to the educational interests of my province, and I will say this, speaking from close familiarity and intimate knowledge, that we have enormous difficulties to face and overcome, that these difficulties are of yearly recurrence that our finances are our weakest point and that the provisions to which I have called attention will be the last straw on the camel's back.

But then it will be said that if there is to be no further expansion of high educational institutions under private agency, there is the Government and there are the Missionary bodies which will come to the rescue of menaced interests of high education. If the past is any guide for the future, I fear we cannot expect much help from the Government or the Missionary bodies. For the last thirty years there has been no addition in Bengal to the Missionary Colleges although no patriotic Indian can forget the debt immense of endless gratitude which we owe to Missionary effort fur the impetus which it gave to the cause of education and the magnificent Colleges which are now maintained by Missionary bodies.

What is true of the Missionary agency is true of the Government. There are 77 colleges affiliated to the Calcutta University of which only 11 are Government Colleges. Since 1878 no Government College has been founded or affiliated, save and except the Bethune College which is College for Hindu ladies and affiliated in 1888. Thus, if the policy of the past is to be maintained by the Government of the Missionary bodies, and we have seen no signs of any inclination to depart from it, the necessary effect of the provision for affiliation will be to prevent the further expansion of the educational area. Nay more, I fear its contraction will be inevitable—these provisions will bring about the abolition of most of the unaided Colleges in Bengal. By a subsequent section these provisions are made up applicable to all existing Colleges and the unaided Colleges, I fear, will collapse under their operation. Thus, Sir, I think, I have conclusively shown that the effect of these provisions will be to prevent the further growth of institutions for high education, to restrict the educational area, to subvert the educational policy of the Government, to tear up the Education Despatch of 1854, and to scatter to the winds the recommendations of the Education Commission of 1882. If this is not revolution — if this is not a reactionary measure of the most pronounced type, I know not what these terms mean.

It is against this policy that we desire to record our most emphatic protest. It is for the abandonment of this policy that we would appeal to His Excellency the Viceroy. It is a policy which is inconsistent with the highest traditions of British rule—those traditions which have founded, built up and consolidated this vast imperial fabric. "We are not here" said one of the greatest of Englishmen, to whom we are indebted for the liberation of the Press—"We are not here," said Sir Charles Metcalfe, in reply to the deputation that waited upon him on the emancipation of the Press, "merely to keep the peace, to collect the taxes and to make good the deficit. We are here for a higher and nobler purpose, viz., to pour into the East the knowledge, the culture and civilization of the West." Nobly has England fulfilled her mission—herself imposed, her heaven-appointed mission. Nobly has she earned her reward in the awakened public spirit and the affectionate gratitude of a loyal and contented people. The dry bone in the open valley have become instinct with life and all India is astir with the pulsations of new born impulse. I ask—is it seriously proposed to recall the past, to ignore the lessons of the past and to roll back the tide of progress which has set in with such an irresistible rush? I can promise no hopes of success to those who would fain embark upon so desperate an undertaking. Time and her beneficent influences are arrayed against them.

The writing on the wall—the inexorable decree of fate written with the pencil of Providence in the scrolls of light—is against them. Progress is the order of nature, the dispensation of divine Providence. Reaction is the exception which whets into renewed activity the sleeping forces of progress. It is the darkness of midnight which precedes the bursting of the new dawn when the gathering forces of progress sweep away the last relics of reaction in their onward and triumphant career. I desire to warn the rulers of India that they stand before the bar of history where all the pomp and the glitter and the circumstances of their proud position will avail them not, where their words will be critically examined and their measures as carefully judged—and that History will pronounce upon them her awful censure, viz., that being charged by the most enlightened of modern nations with a mission of progress and philanthropy they became reactionaries in the field of practical statesmanship and that they sought to temper with the interests of high education and to restrict the scope of those beneficent influence which it has always been the assiduous endeavour of Anglo-Indian statesmanship to foster and to promote. I know not what answer they will give. They know their duty, and we know ours, which is to do all that lies in our power to safeguard the precious boon of high education.

All our possibilities of progress are bound up with it. All our public movements derive from it their vital breath, their animating spirit, their sustaining influence. High education is the great heart, the mighty moving impulse of all our public activities. It affects and benefits even those whom it does not touch, elevating the general tone of society generating a purer atmosphere of lofty ideals and high aspirations. Such a boon we cannot part with. Such a boon we cannot allow to be tampered with. Such a boon we cling to with fond devotion, promoted by a spirit akin to that of filial reverence. Next to religion, education is our most sacred interest. The feelings prompted by religion deepen our affectionate devotion to our educational concerns. The hymns of the Bhagavat Gita which delight, instruct and inspire derive and added inspiration when addressed to minds strung to the music of the higher emotions by the combined culture of the East and the West.

Therefore, let there go forth a great protest from this congress,—protest which I hope and trust will be emphasised by similar protests from other parts of the country. Today we stand face to face with one of the gravest crises in our history. . Are we to succumb to it, or play the part of men? If you sleep over the situation and indulge in cowardly inaction or if you weakly hesitate or falter then the heritage of the past will be undone, the interests of the present will be compromised, and as to the future you will have forfeited your claim to that precious boon of constitutional liberty for which you have, for the last twenty years, maintained so arduous a struggle and which under the blessings of Almighty Providence and the fostering care of British statesmanship of the future, if not of the present, you are bound to win and which when won will glorify the name of England in India and will consecrate a new bond of union between the two countries that shall be proof against the machinations of European powers and the fleeting vicissitudes of Eastern politics.

Students' Union

[In the meeting at the City College Hall, September 8, 1905. The proceedings opened with an address by Babu Surendranath Banerjee in course of which he said:]

I am very glad that so many of you are assembled here for the purpose of organising the Students' Union. Here are so many of you that if you have three such meetings you will have still three such gatherings. All this testifies to the intense enthusiasm, the bitter sense of indignation, which the Partition of Bengal has evoked. The students have been found fault with by their Anglo-Indian critics for rowdysm, for aggressive conduct, for breaches of the peace and for acts of violence. I am certain that everyone of you will do your best to maintain and uphold the law and the Constitution, and you will not allow it to be said of you that you have broken the law or that you have done anything irregular, unlawful or unconstitutional. I ask you to bear this fact in mind that the success of the movement depends very largely upon the constitutional proceedings which you will adopt in this connection and that the breaches of the law are highly prejudicial to the best interests of the great cause which you have so much at heart. Therefore I ask you to exercise self-restraint and self-control and not to break the law on any account.

Let it not be levelled as a charge against you that you have broken the law, that you have acted unconstitutionally—let it not be said that you have exposed yourselves to the punishment of the law. You are law-abiding and peaceful citizens and you think of no means except those of constitutional agitation and those lawful means will give the political emancipation of your country. I ask you to stand by the Swadeshi Movement and to take care that you do not purchase, during the Pujahs, any articles that are not Indian. Let it be a fundamental principle of your doctrine. I am glad to find that you are going to form yourselves into a great organisation. The rules of that organisation have been laid down. I will read to you the first two sentences of that Constitution. (The speaker hear read the rules). That Union would be the platform of common meeting-ground for the interchange of their ideas. The object is economical. The object is national, the object is patriotic, and as such it ought to appeal to your innermost and deepest feeling. I ask you to follow up the high patriotic idea and then you will grow up as wealthy citizens. That is the hope, the aspiration which the Union aims. The students are to make a common cause and you will triumph in all directions; your industries will grow and political emancipation will follow. The eyes of Calcutta, of Bengal, of the Anglo-Indian community, of the rulers, are fixed upon you at present You are the cynosure of all eyes and all attention is centred upon you. Your ways are carefully watched, I ask you to conduct yourselves in such a way that you may come out of the ordeal unscathed and to pursue steadily the programme of the Swadeshi Movement, at the same time restrain yourselves within the boundary of law. This is my appeal and I make it in your best interests and I am confident all of you will have a hearty response to it.

10

Golden Words of S.N. Banerjee

- Every nation must be the arbiter of its own destinies — such as the omnipotent fact inscribed by nature with her own hands and in her own eternal book.
- If power were vested in us to legislate, to control the finance and to carry on the administration through and by our own men, in accordance with principles laid down by our own representatives, we should have self-government in the truest sense, and possess the simplest facilities for developing our powers and faculties and taking our legitimate place among the nations of the earth.
- I desire to place the moral consideration in the forefront: that which is morally indefensible cannot be politically expedient. Politics divorced from morality is no politics at all. It is political jugglery of the worst description.
- For the first time under the British rule, India with its varied races and religions had been brought upon the same platform for a common and unified effort. Thus, was it demonstrated ... that whatever might be our differences in respect of race and language or social and religious institutions, the people of India could combine and unite.

- Swadeshism will save us from famine and pestilence and the nameless horrors which follow in the train of poverty. Take the Swadeshi vow and you will have laid broad and deep the foundations of your industrial and political emancipation. Be Swadeshi in ail things, in your thoughts and actions, in your ideals and aspirations. Bring back the ancient days of purity and self sacrifice. Restore the Aryavarta of olden times when the Rishis sang the praises of God and did good to men... Swadeshi does not exclude foreign ideals or foreign learning or foreign arts and industries, but insists that they shall be assimilated into the national systems, be moulded after the national pattern and be incorporated into the life of a nation. Such is my conception of Swadeshism...

- I am glad to find that the Salvation Army have had their attention prominently called to the poverty-stricken condition of our masses. With an all-comprehensive philanthropy which does honour to their Christianity, they have not forgotten the Indian poor. Their scheme for the reclamation of the submerged tenth will include our submerged fifth. Their scheme for Indian peasant-settlements is well worth consideration; and, whatever we may think of its details, our sympathies must go forth on behalf of a project, so noble, so generous, so full of the spirit of true Christian charity.

- Ours is a political organisation (congress), but we cannot overlook considerations which affect the development of our industries and our manufactures. The economic condition of a people has an intimate bearing upon their political advancement.

- We claim to be admitted to all Competitive Examinations for the Indian Services, no matter to what particular Department of the Public Service they may refer. We claim to be admitted to the Competitive Examinations for the Police Service held in India as well as in England. We claim to be admitted to the Examinations for recruitment to the higher offices in the Forest Department. We are excluded from these Examinations, and we are excluded because we are natives of India. Our disqualification is our race. The crime of colour is alleged against up. We are supposed not to possess the qualities required for these services, by reason of our being members of the race to which it is our misfortune to belong.

- We should be unworthy of ourselves and of our preceptors—we should, indeed, be something less than human—if, with our souls stirred to their inmost depths, our warm Oriental sensibilities roused to an unwonted pitch of enthusiasm by the contemplation of these great ideals of public duty.

- In the constitutional struggle in which we are engaged, we need the cooperation of Englishmen and the sympathies of civilized mankind. It is England which has created in us those political aspirations, the fruition of which we now claim. Our minds are steeped in the literature of the West. Our souls have been stirred by the great models of public virtue which the pages of English history so freely present. Where shall we find the like of them? Their sobriety, their moderation, their lofty enthusiasm for the public good, their scrupulous regard for constitutional principles, even amid the fervour and heat of revolutionary agitation, place them in the front-rank of political leaders for all times and all countries. Englishmen must accept the consequences of their own policy—they must cheerfully face the results which are the outcome of their own beneficent administration. They must gratify the ambitions which they have roused and adopt their administration to the altered conditions which are of their own creation.

11

Great Life at a Glance

1848, Nov. 10: Surendranath Banerjee was born November 10, 1848, at Jaltola in Calcutta, in the province of Bengal, to a Brahmin Hindu family.

1868: After receiving early education at a village school, he graduated from Dovetone College, Calcutta.

1869: He sailed to England for higher education and joined University College, there.

1871: He succeeded in ICS examination.

— On return to India, he was appointed as Asstt. Magistrate at Sylhet. But was soon dismissed, due to caste discrimination.

1874: He went to England again and studied literature, there.

1875: He was appointed as Professor of English.

1876: He founded the Indian Association (Bharat Sabha), his mission was to make people aware of socio-political issues and help them become responsible citizens. The idea of a political organisation, representing different shades of opinion in the country originated with Surendranath Banerjee. He inaugurated the India Association, "to represent the views of the educated middle community and inspire them with a living".

— Became member of Calcutta Municipal Corporation.

1879: Brought out Bengali; a newspaper.

1883: He became the first Indian journalist to be imprisoned. In an angry editorial in "The Bengali" Banerjee had criticised a judge of Calcutta High Court for being insensitive to the religious sentiments.

1885: On the advice of Hume, the Indian National Congress was established. Its first meeting was held the same year in Bombay, under the presidency of W.C. Bannerjee, a Calcutta barrister. Most of its members were high-caste Hindu and Parsi intellectuals, lawyers and businessman. For about twenty years it was dominated by the moderates.

1895: He was elected Congress President at Poona.

1902: He was again elected Congress President at Ahmedabad.

1904: He vehemently opposed the partition of Bengal.

1905, Aug. 7: Surendranath Banerjee led the agitation against the partition of Bengal.

1908, Jan. 16: Surendranath Banerjee, presiding at a meeting, described Lajpat Rai's deportation, as an insult to the whole country.

1919: Surendranath Banerjee, Vithalbhai Patel and Sarojini Naidu were on a pro-freedom propaganda spree visiting, New Castle, Glasgow, Edinburgh, Belfast, Liverpool, Manchester, Halsend, Bedford, London, etc.

1921: Elected a member of Bengal Legislative Council.

1923: Surendranath Banerjee, the then minister of local self-government, piloted the Calcutta Municipal Act to set up an autonomous Corporation, to use his words, "as the realisation of the dreams of (his) life". He added, "We hear a great deal about Swaraj (self-government) in these days, but, here in the control of the municipal affairs of Calcutta as constituted under the new Act, we have veritable Swaraj in the government of the second city in the Empire".

1924: He lost election and quit politics.

1925, Aug. 6: Surendranath Banerjee passed away.

Bibliography

Abani Lahiri: *The Peasant and India's Freedom Movement*, Manak, 2001.

Anil Kumar Jana: *Quit India Movement in Bengal: A Study of Contai Subdivision*, Indian Pub, 2004.

Ashton, S. R.: *Indian independence, Living through history*, Batsford Academic and Educational, London, 1985.

Bakshi, S. R.: *Pherozeshah Mehta: Socio-Political Ideology*, Indian Freedom Fighters, Hardcover, 1991.

Banerjea, Surendranath, and Jadu Nath Kanjilal: A*n explanatory analysis of the Law of criminal procedure in India (Act V of 1898); intended for students for various law examinations and prepared under special instructions of Dr. Jadu Nath Kanjilal*, Olympian Press, Calcutta, 1918.

Banerjee, Bani: *Surendranath Banerjea and history of modern India, 1848-1925*, Metropolitan, New Delhi, 1979.

Bhattacharya, B. K.: *India's Freedom Movement: Legacy of Bipin Chandra Pal*, Deep and Deep, 2007.

Chandra, Bipan: *India's Struggle For Independence*, Penguin Books India (P) Ltd., New Delhi, 1989.

Diraviam, Leila: *Diraviam -Our Treasure*, Asian Printers, Chennai, 1999.

Erwin Neumayer and Christine Schelberger: *Bharat Mata: India's Freedom Movement in Popular Art*, Oxford University Press, 2008.

Gandhi, Rajmohan: *Rajaji, A Life,* Penguin Books India (P) Ltd., New Delhi, 1997.

Goyal, P. K.: *Battle of India's Freedom Movement,* Vista International, 2005.

Hari Hara Das: *The History of Freedom Movement in India (1857-1947),* National, 1998.

Indu Dave: *Indian Personality in Its Developmental Background,* Himanshu, 1991.

Iyengar, A. S.: *Role of Press and Indian Freedom Struggle: All through the Gandhian Era,* APH, 2001.

Jag Mohan, and M. Chalapathi Rau: *Twenty-five years of Indian independence,* Vikas Publishing House, Delhi, 1973.

Kailash Khanna: *History of Indian Freedom Struggle,* Commonwealth Pub, 2004.

Kamat, Jyostna: *The Pioneers: Kamaladevi Chattopadhyaya,* Kamat's, 2003.

Kapoor, A. N. Gupta, V. P. and Mohini Gupta: *An Encyclopaedic Dictionary of Freedom Movement 1757-1947,* Radha, 2004.

Kaushik, A. S.: *Great Freedom Fighters of India,* Indian Pub, 2007.

Khairul Anam, Md.: *Indian Freedom Movement and Murshidabad District 1905-1947,* Bagchi, K. P., 2008.

Krishan Mohan: *Encyclopaedic History of Indian Freedom Movement (4 Vols-Set),* Book Enclave, 1999.

Krishna, B.: *Indian Freedom Struggle: The Pathfinders From Surendranath Banerjea to Gandhi,* Manohar, 2002.

Lion Agrawal, M. G.: *Freedom Fighters of India (4 Vols-Set),* Isha Books, 2008.

Majumdar, R. C.: *History of the Freedom Movement in India (3 Vols-Set),* Firma KLM, 1997.

Manju Verma: *The Role of Women in the Freedom Movement in Punjab (1919-1947),* Abhijeet, 2003.

Maulana Syed Mohammad Mian: *The Prisoners of Malta (Asira'n-E-Malta): The Heart-Rending Tale of Muslim Freedom Fighters in British Period,* Manak, 2005.

Mazhar Kibriya: *Gandhi and Indian Freedom Struggle*, APH, 1999.

McLeod, John: *The history of India*, Greenwood histories of the modern nations, Greenwood Press, Westport, CT, 2002.

Muthaiah, S.: *Women Freedom Fighters*, The Hindu, 2004.

Nanda, S. P.: *Freedom Movement and Constitutional Development in India*, Dominant, 2004.

Om Prakash: *Encyclopaedic History of Indian Freedom Movement (12 to 21 Vols)*, Anmol, 2003.

Omesh Saigal: *Shaheed Bhagat Singh: Unique Martyr in Freedom Movement*, Gyan Pub, 2002.

Parmanand Parashar: *Kashmir and the Freedom Movement*, Sarup, 2004.

Pradhan, K. B.: *Freedom Movement in India*, Arise Pub, 2007.

Prafulla Kumar Pattanaik: *The First Indian War of Independence: Freedom Movement in Orissa, 1804-1825*, APH, 2005.

Rafiya Nisar: *Shaikh-Ul-Hind Maulana Mahmud Hasan and Indian Freedom Movement*, Manak Pub, 2008.

Raj Kumar: *Essays on Indian Freedom Movement*, History and Culture Series, Discovery, 2003.

Ram Sharma, S.: *Education of Women and Freedom Movement*, Discovery, 1996.

Ram, S. and Kumar, R.: *Quit India Movement: 1942-1945*, Commonwealth Pub, 2008.

Ramanathan, K. V.: *The Satyamurti Letters, Vol. II: The Indian Freedom Struggle Through the Eyes of a Parliamentarian*, Dorling Kindersley for Pearson Longman an Imprint of Pearson Education, 2008.

Ramu, P. S.: *Azad Hind Fauj (I.N.A.) and The Freedom Movement*, Freedom Movement Memorial Comm, 1998.

Ratna Ghosh: *Netaji Subhas Chandra Bose and Indian Freedom Struggle (2 Vols-Set)*, Deep and Deep, 2006.

Ravindra Kumar: *Champaran to Quit India Movement*, Mittal, 2002.

Romesh Chunder Dutt: *The Literature of Bengal*, T. Spink & co., Punthi Pustak, Calcutta, 1962.

Shachi Chakravarty: *Quit India Movement: A Study,* New Century Publication, 2002.

Shailesh Chandra: *90 Years of India's Struggle for Independence: 1857-1947,* Alfa Pub, 2008.

Shantinath Gupta: *Great Freedom Fighters of India,* Anmol, 2006.

Sharma, K. K.: *Encyclopaedia of Great Personalities of India (4 Vols-Set),* Book Enclave, 2007.

Sharma, S. K.: *Eminent Indian Freedom Fighters (2 Vols-Set),* Anmol, 2004.

Sirisa Kumar Shadangi: *The Prisons of South Orissa and the Freedom Fighters in Incarceration, 1900 - 1947,* Punthi Pustak, 2005.

Sumiti Malhotra: *Thoughts of Great Personalities in 20 Century,* Raj Publishing, 2003.

Sundaram, V.: *Great Crusader for Women's Emancipation,* News Today, 2005.

Sundararaja, Saroja: *March to Freedom in Madras Presidency, 1916-1947,* Lalitha Publication, Chennai, 1989.

Surinder Singh: *The Political Memoirs of an Indian Revolutionary: Naina Singh Dhoot (1904-1989),* Manohar, 2005.

Taneja, Anup: *Gandhi, Women and the National Movement, 1920-47,* Har-Anand Publications, Delhi, 2005.

Thapar-Bjorkert, Suruchi: *Women in the Indian Nationalist Movement,* Sage Publication India (P) Ltd., New Delhi, 2006.

Verma B. R. and Unnikrishnan K.: *Encyclopaedic Biography of Indian Freedom Fighters,* Commonwealth, 2004.

Vishnoo Bhagwan: *Indian Freedom Movement and Constitutional Acts,* Atma Ram, 1999.

Warrier, Shoba: *Quit India Movement: 60 Years,* Dr. Sarojini Varadappan, 2002.

Index

F

G

H

I

P

R

S

U

V

W

Z

❑❑❑